D1629673

THE GROVE DIARIES

THE GROVE DIARIES

*The Rise and Fall
of an English Family*
1809-1925

Edited and annotated with an Introduction by
DESMOND HAWKINS

THE DOVECOTE PRESS &
THE UNIVERSITY OF DELAWARE PRESS

First published in the United States of America by
The Associated University Presses, Inc.
440 Forsgate Drive, Cranbury, New Jersey 08512

Copyright © Desmond Hawkins 1995

Desmond Hawkins has asserted his rights
under the Copyright, Designs and Patents Act, 1988
to be identified as the author of this work

British ISBN 1 874336 30 X
US ISBN 0-87413-600-8

*A CIP catalogue record for this book
is available from the British Library*

Library of Congress Cataloging-in-Publication Data

The Grove Diaries: the rise and fall of an English family, 1809-1925
edited and annotated with an introduction by Desmond Hawkins.
p.   cm.
Includes bibliographical references (p.   ) and index.
ISBN 0 87413 600 8 (alk. paper)
1. Wiltshire (England) -- History -- Sources, 2. Family -- England -- History --
19th century -- Sources. 3. Family -- England -- History -- 20th century -- Sources.
4. Grove, Thomas, Sir, 1821-1897 -- Diaries. 5. Grove, Agnes Geraldine, Lady -- Diaries.
6. Grove, Charlotte, 1783-1860 -- Diaries. 7. Grove, Harriet, 1791-1867 -- Diaries.
8. Dorset (England) -- history -- Sources. 9. Wiltshire (England) -- Genealogy.
10. Dorset (England) -- Genealogy. 11. Grove family -- Diaries.
12. English diaries. I. Hawkins, Desmond, 1908- .
DA670.W7G76 1995
942.3'1 -- dc20   95-34694
CIP

The American publication of this volume has been aided by a grant
from the Carl and Lily Pforzheimer Foundation, Inc.

Designed by Humphrey Stone
Typeset in Sabon by The Typesetting Bureau, Wimborne Dorset
Printed and bound in Great Britain by
Biddles Ltd, Guildford and King's Lynn

Contents

The Illustrations   6

Foreword   9

Acknowledgements   10

Method of Presentation   13

PART ONE
The Diaries of Harriet & Charlotte Grove
1809 - 1858

The Principal Characters   17

The Diaries of Harriet Grove, 1809 - 1810   33

The Diaries of Charlotte Grove, 1811 - 1860   97

PART TWO
The Diaries of Sir Thomas Grove &
Agnes Geraldine, Lady Grove
1855 - 1925

The Principal Characters   207

The Diaries of Sir Thomas Grove, 1855 - 1897   227

The Diaries of Agnes, Lady Grove, 1882 - 1925   267

Select Bibliography   356

Index   358

List of Subscribers   373

The Illustrations

Harriet Grove (1791-1867) (*frontispiece*)

(*Between pages 96 & 97*)

Thomas Grove (1758-1847)
Mrs Elizabeth Chafin Grove (1756-1833)
'Uncle John' Pilfold (1768-1834)
Ferne House, 1850
Percy Bysshe Shelley (1792-1822)
Field Place
Shelley's diary, 15th January 1810
Harriet's diary, 5 March 1810
Lincoln's Inn Fields, 1810
Cwm Elan
The first house in Bournemouth, c. 1811
Ashcombe House
Coker Court
Wardour Castle

(*Between pages 240 & 241*)

Dr. John Grove (1784-1858)
Berwick St. John rectory
The sign of The Glove Inn
Pythouse
Rev. Charles Henry Grove (1794-1878)
Major William Chafyn Grove of Zeals (1786-1859)
Lady de Hoghton (1852-1919)
Thomas Fraser Grove (1821-1897)
Mrs Thomas Fraser Grove (died 1879)
The Ferne Lawn Tennis Club 1879

Ferne House
The Hall at Ferne House
Sir Thomas Fraser Grove MP
A political rally at Ferne, September 1890
Lord Rivers: Horace Pitt (1814-1880)
Rushmore

(Between pages 320 & 321)

General Augustus Pitt-Rivers (1827-1900)
Agnes Grove (1863-1926)
Walter Grove (1852-1932) on Harboro'
Agnes Grove
Sedgehill Manor
Sedgehill Manor, the Hall
Kate Grove (1861-1945)
Sir Thomas Grove with Olivia
Walter Grove, Charlotte Grove, Alex Pitt-Rivers,
    Sir Thomas Grove
Agnes Grove & Oenone
Honor Grove (1883-1944)
The Larmer Tree Grounds, Tollard Royal
A proof page of *The Social Fetich*
Agnes Grove in 1906
Thomas Hardy (1840-1928)
Lady Lubbock (1862-1947)
Mrs Thurber
'Sybil Q', Sybil, Marchioness of Queensberry
    (died 1935)
On Tom Grove's ranch, Matajanal
Ensenada, Mexico

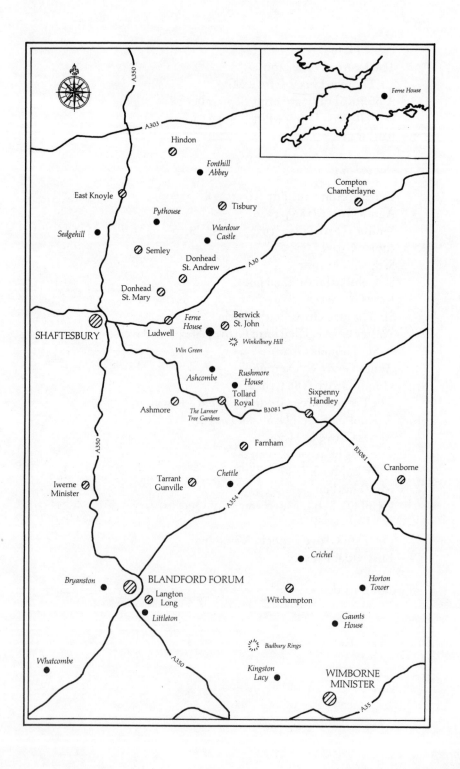

Foreword

It was in the course of my research into the friendship between Thomas Hardy and Agnes, Lady Grove, that – in 1973 – I first became aware of the Grove family's habit of writing diaries and preserving them among the land-deeds and marriage settlements in their muniment room at Ferne House, Donhead St. Andrew, and subsequently at Sedgehill Manor. By the kindness of the family's solicitors, and in the absence of a surviving head of the family, I was permitted to study over a hundred diaries, ranging from 1811 to 1925, and to facilitate their progress to the Wiltshire Record Office where they will be preserved.

My immediate attention was confined to the diaries of Agnes Grove and specifically to the references they contain to Thomas Hardy, but I gradually became addicted to the larger record of these county grandees and their children. That addiction was further stimulated when I learnt of the existence of two more Grove diaries, written in 1809 and 1810 by Harriet Grove at a time when she was in love with her cousin, the poet Percy Bysshe Shelley. To find this link between her 'dear Bysshe' and Agnes's Mr Hardy was indeed a surprise. Harriet's diaries are now part of the Pforzheimer Collection in New York Public Library, and I suppose it was inevitable that sooner or later I should be drawn to New York to study them and seek to bring them into the narrative sequence of the family history.

I have been reading these diaries, then, thinking about them, annotating them, trying to deepen my understanding of them, in a desultory way as a growing obsession over the past twenty years. They have become one of the pleasures of life that I want others to share. A friend, Jo Gittings, who read some of the earlier extracts described them as 'like a Jane Austen novel, but for real.' I can think of no better recommendation. Here is country life in southern England from the Regency to the aftermath of the Great War, told in plain terms with its faults and its merits, always aware of London and the greater world of fashion and politics but close to the soil and the life of cottage and field.

Acknowledgements

The editor of a book of this complexity, which has been more than twenty years in the making, must owe a debt of gratitude to many friends, colleagues and institutions for the wealth of background information that is needed. To recall the start of the enterprise I must look back to March 1973 when I wrote to the Grove family's solicitors in my search for any surviving letter from Thomas Hardy to Agnes Grove. Mr Michael Carey's reply gave me access to a miscellany of family papers, now deposited in the Wiltshire Record Office, among which I found Agnes's diaries, letters from her distinguished circle of friends, and many more diaries from earlier members of the Grove family. Since that day Michael Carey, with a noble patience and magnanimity, has allowed me to regard him as an honorary associate in this embalming of his vanished and unprofitable clients.

From the Wiltshire Record Office and the county's Local Studies Library I have had whole-hearted support, far beyond the call of duty. Throughout the whole period Andrew Crookston has guided me through the archives and met every request. The County Archivist, Ken Rogers and his successor Stephen Hobbs have breathed goodwill and helped with their expertise, as have John Chandler and Michael Marshman in local history generally; and if Wiltshire has borne the main burden of my enquiries I must acknowledge also the comparable assistance of Dorset's County Library and its Record Office. How would provincial historians fare without these institutions?

A second source of invaluable material has been the family papers and photographs held privately by collateral descendants, particularly through the line of Sir Thomas Grove's daughter, Kathleen Mansel-Pleydell, and grand-daughter Vivien Pleydell-Railstone. The latter gave me the greatest freedom to study her wide range of Grove material, and this happy relationship continued with her daughter, the late Patricia Chichester and her husband, Desmond Chichester. Their contribution to the second part of this book is greater than the reader could recognise or they themselves would claim. I am grateful also to a lineal descendant of Harriet Grove, Timothy Heneage, who allowed me to photograph the only known portrait of Harriet – the pencil sketch that I attribute to the hand of Elizabeth Shelley.

With the Thomas Hardy element in Agnes's diaries I was in less need of assistance as I had a measure of self-reliance, but for details of the Pitt-Rivers family I was fortunate in being able to consult Michael Pitt-Rivers of Tollard Royal and Anthony Pitt-Rivers of Hinton St Mary; and to become familiar with the Larmer Tree Gardens and Rushmore Park.

Quite a different matter was the Shelley element in the diaries of the two sisters, Harriet and Charlotte, for I had no claim to be regarded as a Shelley scholar in the sense that I might be considered a Hardy scholar. I searched the biographical literature for every account of the Shelley-Grove relationship and made contact, by good fortune, with one of America's foremost Shelley scholars, Dr. Donald H. Reiman, current editor of *Shelley and his Circle*, an ongoing project which had already published Harriet Grove's two diaries in 1961. It was Dr. Reiman's encouragement and editorial advice which inspired my wish to re-edit Harriet's diaries in the light of the unpublished testimony of Charlotte's diaries and my own knowledge of the local historical background of the villages east of Shaftesbury and so close to my home. I hope this new edition of the years 1809 and 1810 will be regarded by Shelley scholars as definitive.

For the reproduction of a page from Harriet's diary and a related one from Shelley's 1810 diary I acknowledge the Carl H. Pforzheimer Shelley and his Circle Collection, the New York Public Library Astor, Lenox and Tilden Foundations, offering my thanks to the curator, Stephen Wagner, for his valuable assistance; and to Doucet Fischer and her colleagues in the *Shelley and his Circle* office for their support during my working days in the Library.

Of the five portraits painted by Romney of individual Groves I have given pride of place to 'Aunt Chafin', who embodies the link between the two main branches of the family: born a Grove of Ferne she married William Chafin Grove of Zeals, which is why Romney painted two portraits of her – one to hang in each of the great mansions. Her Ferne portrait is reproduced as the book's jacket, courtesy of the Leger Galleries Ltd, London; that of Zeals, with the permission of its owner.

The Romney portrait of her brother, Thomas Grove – father of the
first two diarists – is kindly made available by the Detroit Institute of
Arts. I am grateful also to the Guildhall Library, London, for the print
of Lincoln's Inn Fields in 1810; the National Portrait Gallery for prints
of Shelley by Amelia Curran and Thomas Hardy by William Strange;
and the Salisbury and South Wiltshire Museum for the print of Ashcombe House. The reproduction of the proof-page of Agnes Grove's
The Social Fetich was given to me by its owner, the late R. L. Purdy.
Other illustrations are from private sources or the Dovecote Press collection. For help in locating and identifying illustrations I am indebted
to Jonathan Franklin, archivist of the National Portrait Gallery; and
Richard J. Smith.

There remain to be mentioned the many friends and associates who,
over the years, have given me some unexpected pieces of information
or productive clue in the slow accumulation of my knowledge of the
Groves and their world. To name them all would be an invidious task.
I trust they will accept this general expression of my thanks. I must,
however, pay a personal tribute to Malvina Tribe whose preparation
of successive drafts of my text has been a challenge even to her high
standard of excellence.

Method of Presentation

Many individual names of people and places mentioned in the diaries will be unfamiliar to readers who are not acquainted with south Wiltshire and north-east Dorset. To avoid overloading the pages of the text with notes the most prominent and frequently used names are set out in a biographical dictionary in alphabetical order, concentrating on [A] the Groves and their relations, [B] their friends and neighbours, [C] clergymen, servants and other minor worthies, and [D] buildings, landmarks and landscape features. The first mention of any of these will carry the appropriate letter – A, B, C or D – as an invitation to consult the biographical section, if the reader desires additional identification. A Christian name without a surname in the diaries refers to a close relative (brother or sister, nephew or niece) or domestic servant unless otherwise indicated. To glance through the biographical sections before starting to read the diaries would probably be helpful. Minor identifications are provided in dated footnotes to the text as it progresses. In the editorial narrative footnotes are indicated by an asterisk.

The raised letter ^N in the text refers to the notes at the end of each year, where fuller background information is given.

The two years of Harriet Grove's writing are a special case in one respect. Her sometimes total, sometimes partial deletions of references to Shelley are of particular importance to Shelley scholars and I have therefore adapted the technique employed to record these deletions in the 1961 edition of her diaries in Volume Two of *Shelley and his Circle*. For the same reason her text is given in full, with no abridgement or selection, whereas Charlotte's diaries – covering 35 years – are of necessity presented as a representative selection, as are the diaries that follow hers.

In the matter of spelling I have respected the preferences and occasional idiosyncrasies of the diarists. Harriet chooses 'pleasent' rather than 'pleasant'. Charlotte usually favours 'neices'. Frequently their spelling had to reflect words heard rather than words read. The name of their home has altered from generation to generation between Fern and Ferne. The latter was the original and is now the accepted form.

PART ONE

♥

The Diaries of
Harriet & Charlotte Grove
1809 - 1858

The Principal Characters

GROVE. Thomas senior (1758-1847) son of John Grove and Philippa, d. of Walter Long of Preshaw & Salisbury Close, m. 1782 Charlotte (died 1828) daughter of Charles Pilfold. Thomas was a magistrate, a Captain, later Major, in the Wiltshire Yeomanry Cavalry, a Master of Foxhounds for 20 years and Sheriff of Radnorshire in 1795, 1803 and 1805. He entered University College Oxford in 1776 and was admitted Lincoln's Inn 1780. He had two sisters, Philippa and Elizabeth:

Philippa (1757-1840) known as 'Aunt Grove' did not marry. She lived at Netherhampton near Salisbury with her widowed mother, who died in 1805.

Elizabeth (1756-1833) was known as 'Aunt Chafin' because of her marriage in 1776 to her kinsman William Chafin Grove MP (1731-1793) of Zeals. She had no children.

The children of Thomas and Charlotte were as follows:

1. Charlotte (1783-1860) in 1827 married Rev. Richard Downes (1777-1855) rector of Berwick St. John. They had no children.

2. Thomas junior (1783-1845) heir to Ferne but predeceased his father. In 1806 married Henrietta (died childless 1821) daughter of James Farquharson of Langton. In 1824 he married Elizabeth (died 1883) daughter of C. Hill of Gloucester, and by her had two daughters, one of whom, Charlotte, died in infancy; the other, Mary, married in 1849 Captain Cospatrick Baillie Hamilton R.N. and bore two daughters.

3. John M.D. (1784-1858) in 1818 married Jean Helen (died 1869), daughter of Sir William Fraser, Bart, and Betty Farquharson, who bore six children (a) Henrietta (1819-1893) married James Hussey of Salisbury; (b) Thomas Fraser (1821-1897) created baronet 1874, married in 1847 Katharine Grace daughter of Waller O'Grady,

third Lord Massy & son of Viscount Guillamore. She died in 1879. In 1882 Sir Thomas married Frances Hinton Best. (c) John of Mudeford (1823-1859) in 1851 married Clara Burrow (1832-1857): (d) Louisa Jean (1827-) in 1851 married Frederick Leopold Selwyn (died in 1881). (e) Helen Sophia (1835-) in 1865 married Major John Ross (died 1896); and (f) Emma Philippa (1837-1925) who did not marry.

4. Emma Philippa (1788-1819) m. 1805 John Horsey Waddington (1783-) of Little Park, near Gosport. Their six children include Caroline, Emma, Charles and John.

5. William (1790-1855) Lieutenant RN, later Commander (retired) married in 1828 his cousin Fanny (Frances Harriett) daughter of Dr. Charles Grove of Salisbury, and had no children. They inherited Netherhampton from 'Aunt Grove'.

6. Harriet (1791-1867) married November 1811 William Helyar of Sedgehill and Coker Court (1778-1841). She bore 14 children of whom seven survived to be named in their father's will in 1841.

7. Marianne (1792-1806), died from burns when her dress caught fire.

8. George (1793-1838) merchant-seaman married in 1834 Charlotte Louisa Eyre (died 1882) third daughter of the late Mrs Eyre of Newhouse, near Salisbury; after which he farmed at Sedgehill. They had no children.

9. Charles Henry (1794-1878) ordained 1817, rector of Sedgehill 1826. He married in 1820 Elizabeth Harriet Hopkins and by her had six daughters.

10. Louisa (1796-1810).

For later generations see page 203.

CHAFIN GROVE of Zeals (a junior branch of Grove of Ferne). The Chafin Groves stem from the marriage in 1686 of Mary Chafin, the heiress of Zeals near Mere, S. Wilts, with John Grove a great-grandson of the William Grove who purchased Ferne in 1563. The marriage of their grandson, William Chafin Grove, to his kinswoman, Elizabeth of Ferne ('Aunt Chafin') was childless so the succession passed to his nephews, Chafin and William Chafin. Those mentioned in the diaries include

1. Chafin (1781-1851) and his wife.

2. William Chafin (1786-1859) served with the 20th Foot in the Peninsular campaign.

3. Charles (1792-1868) rector of Odstock, near Salisbury.

4. Frances, married William Grove R.N. of Ferne, q.v.
5. Elizabeth (*née* Acland) widow of Dr Charles Grove of Salisbury and mother of Chafin, Charles and William Chafin (above).
6. Harry Thomas born 1803.
7. Jane, m. 1793 rev. John Auber.
8. Mary Anne, m. 1828 Lewis George St. Lo.
   For later generations see p.205

JACKSON. Rev. Richard was rector of Donhead St. Mary from 1747 until his death in 1796. He was succeeded by his nephew:

Very Rev. Gilbert, A.M. Magdalen Oxford, who in 1790 married Bathia Pilfold (1773-1847) of Donhead St. Andrew at Donhead St. Mary church. Bathia was presumably living at Ferne where her support would have been helpful to her sister, Charlotte Grove, with her brood of young children. In 1793 Gilbert became rector of Melbury Abbas, on the death there of Rev. Hugh Grove, resigning a year later to resume his studies (and make way conveniently for Hugh Grove's son, Rev. William Frederick, to become rector). In 1796 Gilbert became D.D. and was appointed by Thomas Grove as rector of Donhead St. Mary, in succession to Rev. Richard (above). He died in 1816, the father of eight children:

1. Major William Henry (1804-1843) died in action in India.
2. Captain Frederick (1811-1845) died in the East Indies.
3. Frances ('Fanny') (1797-1854).
4. Maria Jane (1809-1864).
5. Arabella married a Mr Walsh in 1821.
6. Rev. Charles, m. Arabella Knightley.
7. Thomas.
8. John.

The Jacksons may have had an earlier link with the Groves. In his will John Grove in 1740 made a residual bequest to 'my cousin Ann Jackson, single woman', a daughter of Joseph Jackson.

LONG. A numerous and influential Wiltshire family over many generations. Listed here are those whose associations with the Groves are reflected in the diaries. Philippa (1730-1805), eldest daughter of Walter Long of Preshaw near Winchester and of Close Gate, Salisbury, in 1755 married John Grove of Ferne & bore three children, Elizabeth, Philippa and Thomas senior qv above.

Walter, her brother (1733-1807) a Senior judge in the Sheriff's court of the City of London. Flaxman memorial in Salisbury Cathedral.

William, another brother (1748-1818) of Marwell Park, Hants: Master of the Royal College of Surgeons and a practising surgeon at Bart's for 33 years. He had a house in Lincoln's Inn Fields. His widow, Alice, died in 1840.

Walter of Corhampton (Preshaw House) (-1871) in 1810 married Lady Mary Carnegie who bore three children. He was High Sheriff of Hampshire 1824.

Richard Godolphin (1761-1835) of Rood Ashton, near Trowbridge, MP for Wiltshire 1806-1818. Founder of the Wiltshire Yeomanry. His children include his heir, Walter, Ann, Dionysia and Flora.

Samuel, of High Street, Salisbury, died c.1812. His widow, Eleanor, died 1824.

MEDWIN. Thomas, senior, married a niece of Charles Pilfold and cousin therefore of Shelley's mother. He was a lawyer and the Duke of Norfolk's steward.

Thomas, junior (1788-1869) close schoolfellow and teenage companion of his second cousin, Shelley, with whom he collaborated in early authorship. Published the first biography of Shelley, in 1847.

PILFOLD. Children of Charles Pilfold of Effingham, Surrey and Bathia White of Horsham.

Elizabeth married Timothy Shelley qv (below)

Charlotte married Thomas Grove senior qv (above)

John (1768-1834) Captain R.N. in 1803 married a daughter of Thomas South of Donhead. They lived at Cuckfield, near Horsham. She died September 1832. They had 2d, Emma and Helen.

James (1771-18--) of Effingham, Surrey, known as 'Uncle Jem'. In 1796 he married Ann Stanford: they had a daughter Elizabeth (1800-1821)

Bathia (1773-1847) in 1790 married Rev. Dr. Gilbert Jackson qv (above)

RUDGE. Philippa Long's younger sister Elizabeth in 1759 married Edward Rudge (1717-1790) of Salisbury and Bath. She bore two sons and a daughter, and died in 1820.

SHELLEY. Timothy (1753-1844) of Field Place, near Horsham, Sussex son and heir of Sir Bysshe Shelley (1731-1815, created baronet 1806) married Elizabeth (1763-1846) daughter of Charles Pilfold of Effingham, Surrey and by her had six children:

1. Percy Bysshe (1792-1822) in 1811 married Harriet Westbrook (1795-1816) and secondly Mary Wollstonecroft Godwin (1797-1851). As he predeceased his father their son Percy Florence (1819-1889 dsp) inherited the baronetcy.
2. Elizabeth (1794-1831) did not marry.
3. Mary (1797-1884) in 1819 married Daniel Franco Haynes of Ashtead, Surrey. After divorce she married James O'Hara Trevor, with whom she had eloped.
4 & 5. Hellen (1799-1885) and Margaret (1801-1887) did not marry.
6. John (1806-1866) m. Elizabeth eldest daughter of Charles Bowen and had issue, including Edward (1827-1890 dsp) the fourth baronet.

WADDINGTON, John Horsey (1783-) of Little Park near Gosport, Hants and later of Clay Hall, Herts, m. Emma Philippa Grove (1788-1819) q.v.

B. *Friends and Neighbours*

ARUNDELL, James Everard (1763-1817) became the ninth baron by marrying Mary-Christina, daughter and co-heir of his cousin Henry, the eighth baron Arundell (1740-1808). Their children included Catharine (born 1795, married 1827), Laura (born 1789, married 1827) and Juliana (born 1791, married 1815). Traditionally the Arundells were the overlords of the Donheads and neighbouring villages. Mr & Mrs Raymond Arundell lived at Ashcombe before they let it in 1811. Mary Wyndham Arundell (died October 1809) previously lived at Ashcombe.

The 10th Baron, also named James Everard (1785-1834) was succeeded by Henry Benedict Arundell (1804-1862) as 11th Baron Arundell. Wardour Castle was the ancestral seat.

BECKFORD, Peter (1740-1811) of Iwerne Stepleton near Blandford married Louisa Pitt, sister of Lord Rivers, in 1773. Their second son William Horace (1777-1831) succeeded his uncle as third Baron Rivers and Lord of Cranborne Chase.

Peter published his *Thoughts on Hunting* in 1782 and lived in Italy 1783-1799. His cousin William, author of *Vathek*, resided at Fonthill Abbey, near Tisbury.

BENETT. The families of two Benett brothers occur in the diaries. Thomas Benett (1729-1797) inherited Pythouse from his father, originally of Norton Bavant, and was succeeded by his son John (1773-1852) MP Wilts 1819 and 1829. Thomas's other children were Thomas, who died aged 17, William, Anna Maria who married a son of Sir Henry Fane, and Etheldred (1776-1845) a pioneer authority on Wiltshire fossils. John married Lucy Lambert in 1801. She died in 1827 leaving four daughters and two sons. The eldest daughter, Lucy, married Anna Maria's son, Rev. Arthur Fane, and the son of these cousins, Vere Fane (1840-1894), adopted the family name when he inherited Pythouse in 1856 as Vere Fane Benett.

The other brother, John Benett LLD (1730-1808) was rector of Donhead St. Andrew. His wife died in 1795 leaving five sons and four daughters. One of the sons, Captain Charles Cowper Benett RN married Sarah Burlton in 1810 and lived at Sedgehill; the other sons were Frederick, George, William Wake and Henry Cowper. Of the daughters, Frances, Catherine, Arabella and Amelia ('Emily') Frances m. Gregory Doyle of Shaftesbury and Co. Carlow in 1814 and Catherine m. Stanford Carroll of Dublin.

BOWLES. A Shaftesbury family with strong clerical traditions in south Wiltshire, represented in the diaries by two brothers and their three sisters.

1. William Lisle Bowles (1762-1850) vicar of Bremhill and canon of Salisbury Cathedral m. Magdalen d. Dr Charles Wake, rector of Knoyle. A distinguished poet Bowles was hailed by some as 'the father of modern poetry' on account of his early sonnets. Coleridge visited Donhead to pay tribute to Bowles, who was then a curate at Donhead St. Andrew. Until 1804 or 1805 Bowles lived in a house later known as Burltons in consequence of its occupation by Bowles's widowed sister, Sarah Burlton, q.v. Bowles's friendship with Thomas Grove was expressed in the poem 'Coombe Ellen' published in 1798, following a stay at the Groves' Welsh estate, Cwm Elan.

2. Charles Bowles (1766-1837) recorder of Shaftesbury, Lord Grosvenor's land agent and local historian, author of *The Hundred of*

Chalke 1830. He resided at Higher Coombe, west of Donhead St. Mary, was married and had children.

3. Amy (1769-) married (i) Rev. Peregrine Bingham, rector of Berwick St. John who died in 1826; and (ii) Sir Richard Williams KCB who died in 1839. She had two sons, Peregrine and Edward, and a daughter by her first marriage.

4. Margaret Charlotte Elizabeth – 'Eliza' (1761-1807) m. Rev. Christopher Erle (died 1817).

5. Sarah: see Burlton.

BURLTON, Mrs, *née* Sarah Bowles (1772-1843) widow of William Burlton or Burleton of Wyken Hall, Leicestershire, lived for over thirty years at Donhead St. Mary in the house reputed to have been previously occupied by her brother William and still known to this day as 'Burltons'. She had five children, three of whom survived her and erected a plaque in her honour in Donhead St. Mary Church. Her son William also erected a memorial to two of his sons massacred in the Indian Mutiny. Her second son, Philip Bowles, lieutenant in the Bengal Artillery, was massacred by natives in Assam in 1829, and her third son, Charles was ordained but died at an early age in Rome. Her daughter Sarah married Charles Benett q.v. Her younger daughter, Marianne, was expected in 1824 to marry Lord Grosvenor's land steward, Mr. Jones. A memorial to Mrs. Burlton in East Knoyle church probably reflects the fact that in her final years she also resided with her daughter, Sarah Benett, at Sedgehill.

CHAFIN, Rev. William (1733-1818) of Chettle. Eccentric sporting parson and magistrate. Author of *Anecdotes and History of Cranborne Chase* (1818 & 1991)

COOKE, Captain John RN of Donhead Lodge, killed in action at Trafalgar in command of HMS *Bellerophon*. Memorials in St. Paul's Cathedral and Donhead St. Andrew church, and a poetic elegy from his friend William Lisle Bowles. His widow and daughter Louisa were very hospitable to the younger Groves.

DU BOULAY family: lived in Donhead St Mary at Charlton 1831-35 and by 1857 at Donhead Hall, succeeding Charles Wyndham's widow there, until John Du Boulay's death in 1896.

EYRE of Newhouse, Redlynch, Salisbury: a family with a distin-
guished record in the legal profession and political life. Susannah
Harriet Eyre (1755-1833) sole heiress to Newhouse married William
Purvis (1757-1810) who adopted the name of Eyre. Of their four
daughters the eldest Harriet m. William George Matcham, nephew of
Earl Nelson. Another, Charlotte Louisa Purvis Eyre (1796-1882) m.
George Grove, q.v. Susannah Harriet's younger sister m. Alexander
Popham, q.v.

FARQUHARSON, James John (1784-1871) was eleven when his father
died. He lived with his mother (1753-1837) at Littleton, Blandford St.
Mary, subsequently building his permanent home at Langton Long,
near Blandford. He married twice, his first wife dying in 1834, and
leaving four sons, James John, Robert, Frederick and Henry. Known
as 'the Squire' he hunted as MFH, at his own expense, for 52 years. His
sister Henrietta Ann (1783-1821) married Thomas Grove junior q.v.
His half-sister Betty married Sir William Fraser q.v.

FRASER, Sir William, baronet of Inverness-shire and London, in 1786
m. Elizabeth (Betty) Farquharson q.v. and died 1818, father of three
sons – William, James John and Keith – and eleven daughters, of
whom Jean Helen in 1818 married John Grove of Ferne q.v.

GLYN, Richard Carr (1755-1838) created Baronet 1830. Mary his wife,
née Plumtre. George, their 4th son, later 1st Baron Wolverton.

GORDON, John (1774-1834) of Wincombe Park, Donhead St. Mary
and Jamaica m. (1) Sybella Partridge (died 1822) and (2) Maria
(1778-1853) widow of Richard Oliver of Antigua. By his first wife he
had two sons, John Robert (1795-1826 dsp) of the 7th Hussars who
fought at Waterloo, and Thomas W., Royal Horseguards (1798-1830).
He had two brothers William (1776-1831 unmarried) and George
(1776-1832) whose only son Charles William (1819-1897) inherited
Wincombe, married twice and had a dozen children, five of them by
his second wife Alice (married 1868) a daughter of Charles Grove, q.v.
    At Wincombe John Gordon built a 'cottage-villa' for himself where
he resided until about 1815, letting it in 1820 to John Waddington and
in 1824 to Thomas Grove junior whose second wife, 'Bessy', was a
niece of Gordon's. However his own second marriage in 1825 brought
Gordon back to Wincombe eventually. There are memorials to his

second wife and to his sons in Donhead St. Mary church.

HELYAR, William of Coker Court, near Yeovil (1745-1820) in 1777 married Elizabeth Hawker. He owned land in Sedgehill where in 1781 he built Sedgehill House, the residence in 1809 of his son and heir William junior (1778-1841) who in 1811 married Harriet Grove q.v. Other children of William senior included Henry, George, Hugh, Charles John, Elizabeth and Caroline.

The younger brother of William senior, Rev. John Helyar (-1823) was rector of Tollard Royal 1798-1823. In 1810 he and his wife resided at Tollard Farnham while his rectory probably accommodated the Grove family during the rebuilding of Ferne.

KNELLER, Godfrey-John (Jacky) of Donhead Hall (1791-) married in 1812 'a very pretty elegant woman'. His father John (1751-1811) m. Sophia Hayne of Totnes. She subsequently married Col. De Burgh. The Knellers left Donhead Hall in 1821 and sold it in 1825 to Charles Wyndham for £9,000-10,000.

PARKER, Sir William Parker in 1808 m. Elizabeth Still of East Knoyle. An aunt of his was Mrs. Bowles. c.1811 Sir Hyde Parker bought Chicklade House, north of East Knoyle.

PENRUDDOCKE of Compton Chamberlayne. The Groves liked to visit the Penruddockes in their journeys along the turnpike to and from Netherhampton and Salisbury. John Hungerford Penruddocke (-1841) Sheriff of Wilts 1817, M.P. 1825, m. 1792 Maria Pearce (obit 1831). In 1837 he married (2) a Pearce cousin of his first wife.

His younger brother Charles died 1799 leaving a son, also Charles, born 1798. There were three other brothers, Thomas, George and Edward, of whom Thomas (died Sept 8, 1832) had a son, also Thomas, born Feb 1804 and apparently living at Fovant in 1833.

PHELIPS of Montacute, near Yeovil. Connected by marriage with Farquharsons and Helyars. See page 221.

PITT-RIVERS, George Pitt, 2nd baron Rivers (1751-1828) did not marry. Having sold his principal seat, Stratfieldsaye (then presented by the nation to the Duke of Wellington) he developed what had been his hunting headquarters at Rushmore Lodge in Cranborne Chase, the lordship of which he had inherited. He was succeeded by his sister Louisa's son, William Horace Beckford. The barony became extinct in 1880 and the estate passed to General Augustus Henry Lane Fox who adopted the name Pitt-Rivers: his daughter Agnes Geraldine in 1882 married Sir Walter Grove of Ferne (q.v.)

PLEYDELL, Edmund Morton (1756-1835) of Whatcombe House, near Blandford, m. Elizabeth Margaretta. Their daughters include Ann, Cornelia (died 1844) Mary-Sophia (died 1827) Louisa (died 1863) Margaretta still living 1864 at Whatcombe, the surviving representative there of the family. Emma-Septima, also living 1864, was widow of Sir George Bingham, who died 1833.

POPHAM, Laetitia Harriet (1781-1856) d. of Alexander Popham of Bagborough, Somerset, by his second wife Charlotte Louisa, d. of Sam Eyre of Newhouse, married 1776. She was a godchild of Aunt Philippa Grove.

PORTMAN, Edward Berkeley (1771-1823) in 1798 married Lucy Whitby. She died 1812, leaving four sons and three daughters. In 1816 he married (2) Mary, eldest daughter of Sir Edward Hulse of Breamore. Edward's eldest son Edward Berkeley Portman born 1799 married Lady Emma Lascelles, third daughter of the Earl of Harewood. He became Baron Portman in 1837. The family seat, Bryanston House, was rebuilt in 1778. It is on the outskirts of Blandford.

RIVERS, Lord: see Pitt-Rivers (above)

SERGISON, Colonel Warden, of Butlers Green House married Mary Ann Ker (1767-1804) and inherited Cuckfield Place, near Horsham, Sussex two years after her death. In 1810 his friend Captain John Pilfold hoped that Charlotte Grove, his niece, might become the second Mrs. Sergison. Sergison died in July 1811.

STILL, James (1720-1803) of Clouds, East Knoyle, had three sons – (a) Peter (1750-1832) of Lincoln's Inn (b) James Charles (1753-1828) of East Knoyle, m. Charlotte, d. of Charles Wake, rector of Knoyle. They had a son Robert (1808-1875) of Lincoln's Inn; and (c) John of Berwick House, born at Clouds 1761, became rector of Fonthill Gifford.

Probably to be identified as daughters of James Charles Still are

Elizabeth who in 1808 m. Sir William Parker RN, and Fanny mentioned in 1812-13. Robert Still, in 1812, might be a fourth son, with a 4 year old namesake nephew.

TREGONWELL, Lewis-Dimoke-Grosvenor (1758-1832) m. (1) Katherine, sole heiress of St. Barbe Sydenham. Their children St. Barbe (1782-1859) dsp and Helen (1783-1866) m. Captain (later Rear-Admiral) John Duff Markland R.N. (1788-1848). Mr. Grove drew up their marriage-settlement and was a trustee. Helen and Charlotte Grove were at boarding-school together and lifelong friends. Mr. Tregonwell m. (2) Henrietta Portman of Brianston and had issue (a) Henrietta Lewina (1802-) m. Hector Monro of Edmondsham; and (b) John (1811-) of Cranborne Lodge and Bournemouth, married and had issue.

WHINDHAM: see Wyndham

WYNDHAM: a prominent family in south Wiltshire since 1658 when Sir Wadham Wyndham bought Norrington in Alvediston, previously held by the Gawens since 1379. The following occur in the Grove diaries:

Charles (1783-1846) bought Donhead Hall in 1825 and lived there until his death, younger brother of William of Dinton.

Henry Penruddocke (1736-1819) MP Wilts 1795-1812. First son of Henry Wyndham of the Close, Salisbury, by Arundel, d. of Thomas Penruddocke. He married 1768 Caroline d. & h. of Edward Hearst of the Close, 5s. 2d. Mayor of Salisbury 1770, Sheriff Wilts 1772-3. His uncle Charles Penruddocke had previously held the seat as MP 1770-78. Henry was an infrequent attendant with little interest in public affairs – he is not known to have spoken in any debate. He wished to promote a history of the county of Wiltshire and published Bubb Dodington's Diary in 1784. His residence was St Edmund's College, Salisbury.

Wadham (1773-1843) MP Salisbury 1818-33, 1835-43. First surviving son of Henry Penruddocke Wyndham. His political career, like his father's, was undistinguished.

William (1769-1841) of Dinton and Norrington. Sheriff of Wilts 1814.

His sons William junior (1796-1862) MP 1857; and Alex (1799-1869).

c. *Minor Gentry, Servants and Others*

Baker, (?Sir) Edward. Married, two daughters. Donhead landowner.

Bingham, rev. Peregrine, rector of Berwick St. John from 1817 to 1826, m. Amy Bowles, 2 sons – Peregrine, became Recorder of Southampton, and Edward, a naval officer, murdered in Peru.

Blackmore, rev. Richard, rector of Donhead St. Mary, 3 daughters Ann, Eliz and Sarah.

Boys, rev. P. rector of Berwick St. John 1792 to 1817, died 1823.

Bromley, Mr of Bishopstone, rural dean, his wife a sister of Admiral Heath.

Bury, Lucy, a friend of Louisa Grove.

Butler, rev. William (Billy), vicar of Frampton, Dorset 1800. Died 1843. Celebrated sporting parson.

Daniel: see Lampard.

Dansey, rev. William (1792-1856) born Blandford, son of John Dansey, became rector of Donhead St. Andrew 1820-1856. Canon of Salisbury, m. 1849 Sarah, youngest d. Rev. Richard Blackmore, rector of Donhead St. Mary.

Dimmer, Mary, family nurse at Ferne.

Eason or Easton, rev., deputising minister; a midshipman son, William, and 2 daughters.

Edwards, William, butler at Ferne, subsequently kept the Lamb Inn at Hindon and later The Grosvenor Arms, Shaftesbury.

Fletcher, rev. William, rector of Donhead St. Andrew, died 1809: succeeded by rev. Nathaniel Fletcher.

Habbersham, Mrs., presumed widow, object of lighthearted ridicule among young Shelleys and Groves. Later married a Mr. Merrick.

Hamilton, James (1748-1829) Weymouth architect, designed George III statue and St. Mary's church there. Rebuilt Ferne House 1809-11.

Lampard, Daniel, a servant at Ferne and later, with his wife Jane, at East Hayes for George Grove.

Merrick: see Habbersham.

Methuen M.P., Paul of Ashcombe House q.v. and later of Corsham Court, near Chippenham, Wilts.

Ogle, rev. John Savile, rector of East Knoyle 1797-1820.

Partridge, Emma, niece of John Gordon, q.v., of Wincombe, whose first wife was Sybella Partridge.

Peachey, Col. (later Major-General) William, friend and executor of Dr. Gilbert Jackson q.v.

Shere, Thomas, possibly farm bailiff at Ferne, and in 1832 tenant of a Grove farm in Berwick St. John.

Snow, George (1744-1822) of Langton Lodge, Blandford. Had his own coach and four. His son Capt. Thomas (1782-1875) died at Ostend. Rev. Thomas of Langton Lodge had a daughter Harriet m. Robert Farquharson (1809-) who became rector of Langton Long 1855.

South family of Charlton, Donhead St. Mary: various associations with the Groves since before 1750. George served them as land agent or lawyer. A South daughter married Mrs Grove's brother, Capt John Pilfold, in 1803.

Stockwell, Marian of Netherhampton, close friend and long-stay visitor of Charlotte Downes.

Susan, a lady's maid at Ferne.

Vashti, Aunt Philippa Grove's personal maid.

Wake, rev. Henry (1770-1851): a curate closely associated with Sedgehill and later vicar of Mere and rector of Over Wallop, m. 1813 Camilla Wallop, who died 1815.

Wilsonn, Mrs. Headmistress of a boarding school at Bath.

D. Family Seats, and other Places of Interest

Ashcombe: an Arundell property between Ferne and Tollard Royal, sold to Thomas Grove junior in 1815 for £8,700. Previously let to Paul Methuen MP.

Berry Court: the earliest seat of the Groves. The house, of fifteenth century origin, stands on the boundary separating the two Donhead parishes: known today as Lower Berry Court, in distinction from Higher Berry Court Farm which was originally the estate's barn.

Bryanston: the seat of the Portman family, on the NW outskirts of Blandford Forum. Is now Bryanston School.

Chettle: the seat of the Chafin family, about five miles north-east of Blandford.

Clouds: the seat of the Still family of East Knoyle from 1672 to 1828. From 1877 to 1936 it belonged to Hon. Percy Scawen Wyndham and his descendants, including Rt. Hon. George Wyndham.

Close Gate: the reference is to Salisbury cathedral close.

Coker Court: family seat near Yeovil of the Helyars, adjoining East Coker church.

Compton Chamberlayne: seat of the Penruddocke family on the

Shaftesbury-Salisbury turnpike about five miles west of Wilton.

Cranborne Chase: an extensive hunting-ground in the border ter-
ritories of Dorset, Wiltshire and Hampshire where the franchise to
preserve deer was enforced by the lord of the Chase under forest
law. Its origins are associated with King John. The franchise was
held by the monarch or a close relative until James I gave it to
Robert Cecil, whom he created Viscount Cranborne (later Earl of
Salisbury). The franchise was enforced until 1830 – the last such in
England except the New Forest, which was still held by the Crown
and disfranchised by Queen Victoria in 1851.

The outer bounds of the Chase were defined mainly by the rivers
Stour, Nadder, Avon, Crane and Allen, with Shaftesbury, Salisbury
and Wimborne as the principal entry-points. The inner or lesser
bounds concentrated particularly on the wooded downland of the
Dorset-Wiltshire border from Ashcombe and Pimperne to Sixpenny
Handley and the Chalke villages. The last and longest reigning of
the non-regal Lords of the Chase were the Pitt family of Rushmore.

Crichel: various spellings include Critchill. The seat of the Sturt
family, later Lords Alington: about six miles east of Blandford.

Cwm Elan: estate in Wales near Rhayader, bought by Thomas Grove
senior in 1792 as summer residence. Subject of poems by William
Lisle Bowles and Shelley who were guests there at various times.
Given to Tom Grove after his marriage to Henrietta and sold by
him in 1815. The house was later submerged beneath the waters of a
reservoir.

Dinton: seat of William Wyndham, between Wilton and Tisbury.

Donhead Hall: seat of the Kneller family in Donhead St. Mary until
1825 when Charles Wyndham bought it. After his death in 1846 it
passed to the Du Boulays.

Donhead Lodge: the home of Captain John Cooke R.N., killed at the
battle of Trafalgar in command of HMS *Bellerophon*. His wife and
daughter remained in residence until 1813, after which the house
changed hands several times in the following decades.

Eastbury: see Tarrant Gunville.

East Hayes: a Grove property in Sedgehill given by Thomas Grove
senior to his son George when the latter gave up his seafaring life to
marry and become a farmer.

Farnham: see Tollard Farnham.

Field Place: the seat in Sussex, near Horsham, of the Shelley family.

Fonthill Abbey: spectacular residence of William Beckford between

East Knoyle and Tisbury.

Gaunts House: the seat of the Glyn family, about 3 miles north of Wimborne.

Glove Inn, The: on the Shaftesbury-Salisbury road at the foot of Whitesheet Hill in Donhead. Now a farmhouse.

Gunville: see Tarrant Gunville.

Hanley: familiar abbreviation of Sixpenny Handley village, about 4 miles east of Tollard Royal.

Hordell [Hordle] Cliff: overlooking Christchurch Bay, close to Milford-on-Sea, Hants.

Horton Tower: a seven-storey observatory between Wimborne and Cranborne built in mid-eighteenth century by Humphrey Sturt; still a prominent landmark.

King John's House or Palace: ancient building in Tollard Royal, subject of monograph by Lt-Gen. A. Pitt-Rivers (1890).

Langton House: at Langton Long Blandford, east of Blandford Forum, the residence built for himself by 'Squire' Farquharson.

Littleton (or Lyttleton) House, Blandford St. Mary: Farquharson family seat until Langton House replaced it. Henrietta Farquharson and her husband Thomas Grove junior moved from Gunville to Littleton in 1810 and spent part of each year there until 1815.

Lower Donhead, Nether Donhead: local names for Donhead St. Andrew.

Lyttleton: see Littleton above.

Marwell Hall: about 10 miles SSE of Winchester, seat of William Long qv.

Montacute House: near Yeovil, Somerset, seat of the Phelips family.

Muddiford (modern Mudeford) coastal village east of Christchurch harbour.

Netherhampton House, near Salisbury: seat of Philippa 'Aunt' Grove until her death, and subsequently of her nephew William Grove.

Newhouse, Redlynch, near Salisbury: seat of the Eyre family.

Norrington Manor: earlier seat of the Wyndham family, near Berwick St. John.

Preshaw House: about 12 miles ESE of Winchester, seat of Walter Long I, II and III qv.

Pythouse: usually as one word. Three miles north of Donhead, the seat of John Benett MP (1773-1852) passing subsequently to his grandson Vere Fane who adopted the family name, adding later his wife's surname also to become Vere Fane Benett-Stanford.

Rood Ashton: seat of Richard Godolphin Long, near Trowbridge, Wilts.

Rushmore: the country seat much enlarged 1842 at Tollard Royal of the Pitt family, the Barons Rivers, and subsequently of General Augustus Lane Fox Pitt-Rivers and his descendants. Now Sandroyd School.

Shaston: abbreviated form of Shaftesbury.

Sedgehill House: about 5 miles north of Shaftesbury, built in 1798 by William Helyar senior of Coker Court near Yeovil, occupied by his eldest son and other members of the family. Harriet Grove's early married life was spent here. Now known as Hays House.

Tarrant Gunville: a village about 5 miles NE of Blandford, dominated by Eastbury House which Vanbrugh created for Bubb Dodington. Much of it was destroyed in the 1780s. What survived was acquired in 1807 by J.J. Farquharson. As his sister Henrietta and her husband Thomas Grove junior lived for a time at 'Gunville' (1807?-April 1810) it seems probable that they occupied Eastbury House in its reduced state.

Tollard Farnham: lies to the south of Tollard Royal from which it is separated by the Wilts-Dorset county boundary and little else.

Tollard Royal: between Ashmore and Sixpenny Handley, a village about 3 miles south of Ferne (Tollard is the shortened form).

Upper Donhead: local form of Donhead St. Mary.

Vespasian's Camp: the Iron Age hill-fort on Winkelbury Hill, south of Berwick St. John.

Wardour Castle: ancestral seat between Donhead and Tisbury of the Arundell family. Left in ruins after the Civil War and replaced on a fresh site in 1770.

Whitesheet Hill: 'Whiteschut' in 1392, the steep ascent from Donhead to the pre-turnpike track along the downland crest to Wilton and Salisbury. The milestone at the top of Whitesheet indicates Salisbury 14 miles, Hyde Park Corner 97, and the date 1796.

Wilton: the seat of the Earls of Pembroke.

Wincombe Park: the seat of John Gordon, between Donhead St. Mary and Shaftesbury.

Win[d] Green: just short of an altitude of 1000 feet, it is the highest point in Cranborne Chase, between Donhead and Tollard Royal. A National Trust property.

Woodyates Inn: a posting inn midway between Salisbury and Blandford.

Zeals House, near Mere: the family seat of the Chafyn Groves.

I

The Diaries of Harriet Grove
1809 - 1810

INTRODUCTION

Ferne, the seat of the Grove family, is an estate in Donhead St. Andrew, one of two parishes – Donhead St. Mary is the other – which together form a large, diffuse village on the Dorset-Wiltshire border in the vicinity of Shaftesbury. The recorded history of the manor of Ferne dates back certainly to 1236 when Amice, abbess of Shaftesbury, granted 'common of pasture' in Donhead to nine men described as the convent's free men of Donhead – one of whom was 'Philip de Ferne'. The nuns of Shaftesbury traced their extensive ownership of land in Donhead back to a grant by King Alfred in the ninth century of 40 hides of land in Donhead and Compton 'as they stand with their produce and their men'.

Philip de Ferne held Ferne from Walter of Middlemarsh who in 1256 granted Philip a life-lease, which passed on to his descendants, until the end of the fifteenth century saw Ferne in the possession of the Brockway family, one of whom became mayor of Shaftesbury in 1497. It is at this point that the first records occur of the Groves' association with Shaftesbury.* In 1498 Robert Grove was signing documents as an administrator acting for the abbess of Shaftesbury. In 1521 Thomas Grove was employed as an attorney by David Brockway of Ferne in the preparation of the marriage settlement for Brockway's wedding with Anne Benger, a cousin of the abbess of Shaftesbury, Dame Elizabeth Shalford. Brockway was to provide an annual income for his wife of £10. In return the Abbey promised a dowry of £40 and 'new apparell lyke a gentillwoman'.

---

* The arms granted in 1560 by the College of Heralds to Robert Grove imply a connection (as yet unsubstantiated) with the earlier Groves of Buckinghamshire. A critique of the Grove of Ferne pedigree is in preparation.

The residence of the Groves at this time – the first to be identified with them – was Berry Court, an abbey property in Donhead, still held by the family in the nineteenth century.

Where they came from is by no means clear. Their legal training and administrative skill equipped them to prosper in the rapidly changing society of Tudor England. In the scramble for land and positions of power which followed the dissolution of the monasteries Robert Grove attached himself to Sir Thomas Arundell of Wardour, becoming his steward and surveyor of his lands. It was by Arundell's influence that in 1545 Robert Grove became M.P. for Shaftesbury.

The political downfall and execution of Arundell in 1552 was a severe check for Grove but his merits were soon recognised by the Earl of Pembroke who employed him, in partnership with Charles Vaughan, to make a detailed survey of the Pembroke estates. In 1561 Grove was appointed feodary for Wiltshire and in 1571 he was again elected to Parliament. Pembroke gave him a house set in its own deer park at Stoke Trister near Wincanton, Somerset which was held by his descendants until 1860. The Wiltshire Visitation of 1565 confirmed his right to 'bear arms' – the status symbol of the new Elizabethan gentry. From obscure origins Robert Grove had become a pillar of the establishment and the founder of his family's fortunes, when he died in 1579-80.

Ferne was never his, however. It was bought by his son William, of New College Oxford and Gray's Inn, who was well placed to consolidate his father's achievements. When David Brockway died childless at Ferne the property passed to his next of kin who sold it in 1563 to William Grove on the understanding that the widowed Anne should remain in occupation for life. The purchase was evidently made as an investment as William leased Ferne after Anne's death, in the same way as he did with his purchase of the manor of Sedgehill in 1573 and various other properties listed in his personal accounts for the three years 1578-80. Ferne was 'letten for £40 by the yeare and 52 bushells of barley, val at £6/13/4'. As the impressive list unfolds there are repeated interjections of 'Laus deo' (Praise be to God). With a net income annually of about £350-370 he had a substantial reason to feel grateful.

Continuing to reside at Berry Court, and inheriting Stoke Trister on his father's death, William had no need to occupy Ferne. His only brother, Matthew, seems to have gone his own way. After William's death, however, his widow had four young sons to deal with while she herself lived on until 1622 at Berry Court. John, the eldest, took Ferne. Robert, the third son, eventually occupied Stoke Trister and coveted Sedgehill. The youngest, Hugh, migrated to Chissenbury, perhaps to join his uncle Matthew who had married a daughter of Leonard Maton of Chissenbury. The second son, William, married the heiress daughter of John Boden, a prominent citizen of Shaftesbury, and was established in a 'fine house' next to Lord Arundell's in Bimport, Shaftesbury – the only two residences identified on a map of 1615. William was there described as 'a very worthy gentleman'. John of Ferne remains a shadowy figure. From Magdalen Hall Oxford he passed on to the Middle Temple in 1582, the year his father died. He did not marry and may not have taken much interest in Ferne as he also had a house in Shaftesbury next to brother William's, according to a map of 1620. Additionally as the eldest son he kept a legal connection with Berry Court. The Recusant Roll of 34 Elizabeth (1592-93) names him as 'of Burry Courte in Dunhedd Sancti Andrei' and imposes fines for his recusancy amounting to £35/11/1. He thereupon went to live in Ireland for about seven years. When he returned in August 1599 he was interrogated at Bristol by the Recorder of Bristol. He claimed to have been impoverished by disinheritance and to have gone to Ireland because he did not like the religion used in England. He now proposed to obey the statute but still refused to go to church or take communion. He also refused to say whether he would take the oath of supremacy but asserted that if the Spaniards or any army from the Pope should invade England he would fight for the defence of Her Majesty and the realm. Incidentally the mention of disinheritance must have been a tactical lie to deceive his interrogator. His father did not disinherit him. His father's trustees may have put some constraint on him if his controversial beliefs looked financially dangerous, but there is no evidence for that.

It is William Grove III, John's younger brother, who followed most closely in their father's footsteps. His marriage to Jane or Joan Boden (or Boddon) brought him into a close association with one of the most powerful men in Shaftesbury. John Boden was elected MP in 1601 and 1603. In 1604 he became Shaftesbury's first Recorder, to be succeeded in that office after his death in 1615 by William Grove. In land purchase and speculation they had acted together in partnership. As an index of the affluence William derived from his marriage an almshouse inscription records a bequest he made jointly with his wife of £26 annually for ever. He became indeed so closely identified with

Shaftesbury as one of its leading citizens that, unlike his brothers, he changed his county allegiance and in the 1623 Visitation of Dorset is William Grove of Shaftesbury.

His son and heir John was expected to inherit Ferne in due course from his childless uncle but death intervened and the succession passed to Thomas Grove, son of William's younger brother, Robert. Born in 1610 Thomas was eighteen when he inherited Ferne and with it an obligation to marry the widow of his suddenly deceased cousin, whom he was replacing. It is he who finally established Ferne as the recognised seat of the Grove family.

Living to be over 80 Thomas Grove of Ferne saw the full span of the Stuart monarchy and the intervening Civil War. A staunch protestant he was appointed a member of the Westminster Assembly in 1643 and represented Shaftesbury in the Long Parliament. In the religious and political turmoil of the Commonwealth his course was very different from that of his cousin Hugh Grove of Chissenbury, an impetuous royalist who joined forces with John Penruddock of Compton Chamberlaine in raising the standard of revolt in 1655 in Salisbury market-place and demanding the restoration of the Stuart monarchy. The rebellion was quickly suppressed by Cromwell who ordered the beheading of the two leaders at Exeter – an event commemorated in a broadsheet ballad of many verses with the refrain,

> Grove and Penruddock did rebell,
> But now they bid the world farewell.

The record of Shaftesbury's parliamentary elections is lost for the years 1641-68 but Thomas Grove was certainly the sitting member in 1661, in the new atmosphere of the Restoration. The nation was now at peace with itself in a military sense but the religious divisions were unabated and even harsher in some respects. Thomas's allegiance had been to the Independents among the puritan forerunners of nonconformity. In 1662 the Act of Uniformity, designed to impose a rigid orthodoxy on the Anglican church, drove about a fifth of the English clergy from their parishes. It was a savage backlash of vengeance for the earlier ejections during the Civil War.

The history of Donhead St. Mary is typical. In 1645 its elderly minister, George Pope, was ejected because of his royalist sympathies, after serving the parish for nearly 50 years. He was replaced by an Independent, Peter Ince, who in turn was ejected in 1660 and imprisoned for a time in Dorchester. Grove befriended Ince and gave him sanctuary, with other ejected clergy, at Ferne. After the Conventicle Act of 1664 Ferne became a centre of nonconformist resistance. By 1669 the pressure on Thomas Grove had increased to the point where he had to leave Ferne and go into exile. The eminent nonconformist divine, Richard Baxter, wrote this account of events:

'This year [1669] Salisbury Diocese was more fiercely driven on to conformity by Dr. Seth Ward, their Bishop, than any place else. Many hundreds were prosecuted by him with great industry. And among others, that learned, humble holy Gentleman, Mr. Thomas Grove, an Ancient Parliament-Man, of as great Sincerity and Integrity, as almost any Man I ever knew. He stood it out for a while in a lawsuit, but was overthrown, and fain to forsake his Country.'

In 1671 Thomas Grove returned to Ferne. A less hostile dispensation now began to make it possible for nonconformists to have a private house licensed for their meetings. 13 May 1672 Ferne was licensed in this way, described as the house of Robert Grove, Thomas's son. This was shortly after a licence on the first of May to the house in Donhead of Thomas Grove esquire, which suggests that Berry Court also may have been legalised for meetings described as 'Presbyterian'.

At the age of 78 Thomas had the satisfaction of having survived to witness the 'Glorious Revolution' of 1688 and the ultimate triumph of the protestant cause for which he had suffered. 1688 was memorable in a more personal way also with the birth of a great-grandson. There were now four generations of Grove living at Ferne: the elderly widower Thomas, his son Robert whose wife died during 1688, their son Thomas and the wife, Elizabeth Hooke, whom he had married in 1686, and the newly born Thomas.

The senior Thomas lived for three more years and Ferne then settled down to a domestic life in which Thomas and Elizabeth cared for the widowed Robert and their little son. Within a year, however, Robert took a second wife, Tryphena Lloyd, widow of a citizen of London and daughter of Lady Alice Lisle of Moyle's Court, whose brutal execution after Monmouth's Rebellion in 1685 preserves her remembrance in the infamous record of the Bloody Assize.

The introduction of a stepmother evidently disturbed the household. In 1695 Robert provided an annuity for his son Thomas so that they might keep 'distinct and separate houses' for their 'better conveniency of living'. Robert and Tryphena now had Ferne to themselves, but only briefly; Robert died within the year. As his widow,

Tryphena remained in occupation until her death in January 1725/26.

The 'distinct and separate' house to which Thomas moved in 1695 was not another of the existing Grove properties, which were already occupied under lease, but an unidentified residence in the village of Martin, north of Cranborne and on the eastern side of the great earthwork known as Bokerly Dyke. His younger brother John may have joined him there in an interlude lasting over thirty years which remains one of the most obscure periods in Grove history. Very little documentary evidence has survived, and an element of confusion is added by the presence of established Grove families in Martin who also used the familiar christian names of Thomas and John, but yield no positive link of kindred. The earliest Grove record in Martin refers to David Grove in 1576. From 1595 onwards a Thomas Grove was fathering children and giving them names which suggest no kinship with the Ferne pedigree – Nicholas, Edmund, Alice, Patience. He himself was described as husbandman, not as gentleman. Among later Groves at Martin a Thomas or a John may appear but has no claim to a kinship with Ferne. A striking example is a John Grove named in an agreement with Thomas of Ferne but who seals his signature with a seal displaying a coat of arms or a badge which is not the Ferne family seal. The presence of Thomas and Elizabeth Grove at Martin after 1695 is well attested. Their younger son, John, was born at Ferne but baptised at Martin in November 1696. In 1697 Thomas is described as 'Thomas Grove of Martin' in an indenture concerning property at Donhead St. Andrew, with the inference that there was no head of the family at Ferne at that time. Other references in 1700 and 1713 show him as continuing at Martin. When his wife died, in 1726, she was buried at Berwick St. John (adjacent to Ferne) and in the same year Tryphena died. The two deaths evidently prompted Thomas to return to Ferne. In 1730 he made his will as Thomas Grove of Ferne and was so described when he died in 1738. Like his grandfather he represented Shaftesbury in Parliament (elected 1713) and in 1727 he was appointed as a Deputy Lieutenant of Wiltshire.

Martin is not mentioned in his will. His younger son, John, evidently remained at Martin when Thomas returned to Ferne. In a will made by John, in 1740, the trustees are men of social prominence in Martin.

It is an odd fact that throughout the first half of the eighteenth century Ferne was occupied by a partnerless head. The widow Tryphena was followed by her widower stepson, succeeded in turn by his elder son

(Thomas again) who did not marry. When this Thomas died, in 1750, Ferne passed to his younger brother John, aged 54 and presumably living at Martin. He too was unmarried but he evidently came to Ferne with the intention of renewing the male line. His first wife died in childbirth. Within a year he found a second bride who was more fortunate, bearing two daughters and – at the third attempt – a son, given inevitably the name appropriate to a first-born son and heir, Thomas. Having met his family obligation, John died in 1769 leaving his eleven-year-old heir in the care of his mother and with two sisters for companions.

It is with this latest Thomas Grove that we reach the year 1809 when the sequence of diaries commences: he is the father of two diarists – his daughters, Harriet (aged 17) and Charlotte (aged 26). Thanks to them he appears in more detailed and personal terms than any of his predecessors. Correspondence has also survived which discloses that his mother sent him to an unusually progressive boarding school where the headmaster, Dr. Samuel Glasse FRS, declared as his policy that 'we use not the Rod at this place' – contrary to the accepted view at the time that flogging was an indispensable aid to teaching.* When the time came for Tom to end his schooldays and pass on to university Dr. Glasse, himself an Oxonian, offered to accompany Tom to Oxford and see him settled there. Following three years at University College he was admitted to Lincoln's Inn in January 1780. In due course he became a magistrate and a major in the Wiltshire Yeomanry Cavalry.

In 1782 he married Charlotte Pilfold of a Horsham family, whose sister Elizabeth nine years later married Timothy Shelley and became the mother of the poet, Percy Bysshe Shelley. This connection of the Grove and Shelley families was maintained by visits and correspondence over three generations throughout the nineteenth century. One of the first consequences of their relationship appears to arise from the fact that Timothy Shelley's father, Sir Bysshe Shelley, was High Sheriff of Radnorshire in 1784 and may therefore have aroused Grove's interest in investing in land there, which he did in 1792 – purchasing what a contemporary described as '10,000 almost worthless acres, which he is converting into a paradise'. This was the Cwm Elan estate near Rhayader.** In 1795 Grove became the county's High Sheriff, was

* For a fuller account of Dr Glasse see 'Sparing the Rod' *Country Life* 2 April 1981, pp 891-2.
** See 'The Groves of Cwm Elan' in *The Radnorshire Society Transactions* 1985, pp45-49.

again appointed in 1803 and 1805, and in 1812 saw his eldest son, Thomas junior, hold the office.

There were five sons in all and five daughters, two of whom died in their teens. In the social life of Regency England the Groves were a 'county' family of power and influence. Thomas Grove's 'overlord' by tradition was Lord Arundell of Wardour Castle and his most powerful neighbour was Lord Rivers of Rushmore who had inherited the lordship of Cranborne Chase [D]. Wardour and Rushmore figure repeatedly in the diaries.

Thomas himself was a man of firmly held conventional principles who performed his duties in the ways he had been taught and then turned for his pleasures to the hunting field. As soon as he had command of his inheritance he started his own pack of foxhounds and was its Master for twenty years. He is probably the unnamed friend to whom Peter Beckford addressed his classic *Thoughts on Hunting* in 1781. His son, Thomas junior, married a daughter of another celebrated figure in the history of westcountry foxhunting, 'Squire' Farquharson of Dorset. The Farquharsons feature prominently in the diaries.

It was Thomas Grove's custom to treat Christmas Day as a primarily religious occasion and to look to the dawning of the new year as the occasion for the fullest possible family gathering and the giving of presents. By 1808 the house was no longer full of children: two were married, three sons were probably away at sea and a fourth – John – lived in London and was visiting the home of the Shelleys, Field Place, in the first week of 1809. The family circle at Ferne therefore in the last week of 1808 consisted of three daughters, Charlotte, Harriet and the youngest, Louisa, with their parents. On Friday December 30, 1808 they drove to Blandford to stay with the Portman family at Bryanston and to attend the annual New Year Ball at Blandford, which was one of their customary engagements. Harriet was aware that another ball, which she would have preferred to attend, was being held the same evening at Field Place, given by Aunt Shelley. This Harriet knew from the correspondence she was having with her cousin and sweetheart, Bysshe.

What may have been their first meeting took place in 1804 when Shelley – not yet twelve years old – was invited to spend a school vacation at Ferne. Harriet probably visited the Shelley's home Field Place in 1808, during which year she and cousin Bysshe were engaged in what became a voluminous correspondence during 1809 and 1810 –

the years for which her diaries have survived. They evidently regarded themselves as lovers and were so considered by their parents. There was an expectation that at a suitable later stage – presumably when Shelley had graduated from Oxford – they might contemplate marriage. Meanwhile Shelley wrote poems to Harriet and she recorded in her diaries her longing to go again to Field Place.

The manner in which their love-affair faltered is complex and obscure* but there are signs of a rupture in the autumn of 1810 and the unmistakable termination followed Shelley's elopement in 1811 with a school-girl friend of his sisters. It was probably this event which provoked Harriet to go through her diaries striking out many of the references to 'dear Bysshe', though fortunately enough of them escaped to give testimony to a keenly felt teenage romance.

The two diaries of Harriet's which have survived, for 1809 and 1810, were sold at public auction in 1930 and are now part of the Pforzheimer Collection in New York Public Library. They were first transcribed and edited in 1932 by Roger Ingpen in a private edition of twelve copies printed in London. In 1961 the texts became generally available as part of *Shelley and his Circle 1773-1822* (Cambridge, Masssachusetts) extensively annotated by F.L. Jones under the general editorship of Kenneth Neill Cameron. They have not been republished since 1961.

In their red leather binding with a wrap-over tongue the two pocket-books closely resemble the one used by sister Charlotte in 1811 and subsequently, but Charlotte's is roughly half as big again – 7 x 5 inches as against Harriet's 4½ x approx. 3 inches. After some preliminary printed matter the diary is ruled to accommodate one week of personal entries to a page, with the facing page carrying cash rulings for financial items. In such limited space Harriet's diary sometimes spread across the accounts page or was crammed awkwardly into the centre binding. As a practical economy she often reduced lengthy familiar names to bare initials or abbreviations: her brother Tom's wife, Henrietta, for instance, invites the shortening of her name, and a dear friend – Helen Tregonwell – saves valuable space as H.T. Where it seems helpful to restore a name in full the missing letters are added in square brackets. The minor vagaries of Harriet's spelling are retained.

The 1961 edition substantially accepted Ingpen's 1932 transcription

* It is discussed in detail in my *Shelley's First Love* 1992 (London, Kyle Cathie Ltd. and Hamden, Conn. USA., Archon Books)

with only minor amendments. To represent the scale of Harriet's deletions Dr. Jones used dashes between brackets to indicate a deletion
of less than a manuscript line (which usually contains three to five
words). Where the deletion exceeds one line a note at the foot of the
page gives the number of lines deleted, adding the word 'plus' if the
final line is incomplete. This method is retained in the present edition. In those cases where legible words escaped an attempted deletion
they are here printed normally but in italics. Elsewhere, in editorial
passages, italics assume their normal uses – for book titles, to add
emphasis etc. A dash not in brackets is simply what it appears to be – a
dash used by Harriet at the end of a sentence, instead of a full-stop.
Where a fresh scrutiny of the diaries undertaken in 1993 justifies a
revision of the text it is noted.

All the subsequent diaries, 1811 to 1925, are published here for the
first time.

1809

The 1809 diary is inscribed on the flyleaf 'Harriet Grove, given by her Dear Mother as a New Year's Gift Jan 2 1809'. As January 1st was a Sunday it appears at the foot of an otherwise blank page, giving Harriet an opportunity to add some preliminary material as follows:

We went to Mr Portmans[B] on Friday & went to a pleasent Ball at Blandford in the Evening came home Saturday 31st of Decr 1808 *Bysshe tells me in his Letter that* < --- > –

The long dash in brackets before her own final dash represents the deletion of two lines, following a failure to delete the still legible start of her sentence which is therefore in italics.

In this preliminary space some minor cash transactions are noted. The diary proper then commences.

JANUARY

Sunday 1   < ------ > Col^n *staid* Peachy[C] dined here with my Uncle & Aunt Jackson[A] & Mr Wake[C]

Mon 2   My Aunt Jackson & the rest of the party left us –

Tues 3   < ------ >

Wed 4   Wrote to my Aunt Shelley[A] & Charles – Mr & Mrs [J.] Bennett[B] & M^r J: Evans came here–

Thurs 5   *I heard from my dear Bysshe* & Louisa heard from Mary Shelley[A]–

Fri 6   The Bennetts left us & Mr Evans staid to go to the Gordons[B] with us

Sat 7   We had a very pleasent Dance at Mr Gordons I have written to *Bysshe* & heard from Dear Charles, a very long letter from him M^r E left us

Sun 8   Wrote to my Dear Charles the first thing to day – Louisa has written to Mary Shelley   Charlotte wrote to Dear Jack we did not go to Church as it was to Wet. My Father read Prayers.

1 Jan. Three lines cancelled; 'staid' not certain, probably a cancelled mistake
3 Jan. Three lines cancelled
8 Jan. Jack is her brother, John

Mon 9 *Bysshe will get my letter to day* Packed up in readiness for tomorrow–

Tues 10 Left Fern for Little Park[D] & arrived here quite safe & found them all well *Heard from Bysshe two letters from him*

Wed 11 Wrote to Charles & John the latter is at Field Place[D] My Nephew [John Waddington[A]] is a fine Child he has been innoculated to day for the Small Pox–

Thurs 12 a Mr George Waddington came here – Played with my little niece [Emma]–

Fri 13 Went to Portsmouth George returned with us Dear Boy this is the last time we shall see him

Sat 14 George went away early *Heard from Bysshe* & Louisa heard from Mary–

Sun 15 Wrote to *Bysshe* & Charles Snow on the ground Packed up as we go tomorrow if the snow does not prevent us–

Mon 16 Left Little Park & got home quite safe tho' the snow was very deep – Charlotte Louisa & Susan[C] nearly overturned in Clay lane by the snow

Tues 17 Nothing particularly happened Miss Popham[B] did not come

Wed 18 We have not heard or seen her to day – Louisa is in a great hurry to hear from Mary Shelley as she expects a present from her but has not heard from her to day

Thurs 19 had a letter from *Bysshe* & began an answer to it & wrote to my Aunt Shelley

Fri 20 Finished my letter to *B* & wrote to George–

Sat 21 I heard from Johnny he is coming here Tuesday–

Sun 22 Good gracious a deep snow Mr Wake is here I am quite afraid he will be snowed in here.

Mon 23 I hope John will be able to get here tomorrow <u>as I long to see him</u>

Tues 24 Dear fellow he is come to our great surprise & pleasure *Heard from dear Bysshe* Mr Wake went away

Wed 25 John talked a great deal about the Shelleys he has been spending a week there <u>at that delightful place.</u> *I wrote to Bysshe -*

Thurs 26 Sent my Letter to day Mrs Bennett called here yesterday & invited us to a Ball ^for Friday Week – heard that F & A Jackson[A] are going to School – next Tuesday

Fri 27 Practiced Music before breakfast – <u>quite a wonder</u> – Louisa & I walked out

Sat 28 Miss Popham came here The Fox hunters breakfasted here

Louisa & I took such an immense <u>long</u> walk–

Sun 29 Heard from *Bysshe* & Louisa heard from Mary

Mon 30 Overturned in our way to Gunville[D] on the Top of Wind green[D]–

Tues 31 < ------ > < -/-/-/- > we are none of us hurt in consequence of our overturn

FEBRUARY

Wednesday 1 at Gunville – received a letter from George & Charles–

Thurs 2 Came home quite safe walked down Wind green–

Fri 3 Wrote to Aunt S[helle]y & George & Charles – C[harlotte] my Father & Mother & John have gone to a Ball at Pitt house[D]

Sat 4 Mrs Bennetts Youngest Child is very ill *I heard from Bysshe* they returned home–

Sun 5 < ------ > Mrs Bennetts Child is very ill indeed–

Mon 6 Mrs Bennetts Child is dead–

Tues 7 had a great many Letters–

Wed 8 Went to Church a Fast day < ------ > –

Thurs 9 < ------ > *Bysshe* < ------ > Miss Tregonwell[B] came here

Fri 10 Charlotte's Birthday 26 – I am very much dissappointed at not hearing from my Aunt Shelley–

Sat 11 Emma & Waddington & their children came here – My mother heard from Aunt Shelley–

Sun 12 Thomas left us

Mon 13 Emma calls her Grandmama a Ninny–

Tues 14 John had a letter from Bysshe with a Valentine enclosed for Mrs Habbersham[C]

Wed 15 *I heard from Bysshe*

Thurs 16 < ------ > Bysshe < ------ > & Aunt Grove[A] came here – < ------ >

Fri 17 < ------ > wrote to my Dearest Aunt Shelley

Sat 18 <u>Dear</u> <u>Dear</u> <u>Louisa</u> is gone back to School [at Bath] I miss her so much–

Sun 19 Heard from Dear Charles

Mon 20 My Father Mr Waddington & John returned from Bath

---

31 Jan. < -/-/-/- > The pen went through the paper.

5 Feb. One plus lines cancelled.

8 Feb. Two half lines cancelled.

16 Feb. One line cancelled.

17 Feb. One plus lines cancelled.

Tues 21 Heard from *Bysshe* & we shall <u>certainly</u> see *him* in London <u>I</u>
<u>am so glad of it</u>–

Wed 22 Took a long walk to Berry-Court,[D] the <u>Old</u> Family
Mansion. The Old woman that lives there is mad–

Thurs 23 *Wrote to Bysshe*

Fri 24 Wrote to Louisa & Henrietta–

Sat 25 ----

Sun 26 < ------ > *Bysshe* –

Mon 27 < ------ > –

Tues 28 Sent my letter to < ------ > Henrietta[A] has sent to invite us
to Gunville[D] after the Assizes–

MARCH

Wednesday 1 Dear John left us – Received an immense long letter
from < ------ > – and wrote to Louisa

Thurs 2 Heard from My Dear Louisa *& wrote to Bysshe*

Fri 3 Louisa's Birthday 13 – A large party to Dinner – Wrote to Aunt
Shelley heard from *Bysshe* & Charles

Sat 4 Miss Popham left us–

Sun 5 Wrote to Dear Charles   Heard from Dear Louisa

Mon 6 Wrote to Louisa under cover to Mrs Wilsonn[C]–

Tues 7 < ------ > *Bysshe* < ------ > My Mother heard from Dear Aunt
Shelley

Wed 8 The Waddingtons left us – *Heard from Bysshe*

Thurs 9 Charlotte & Miss Tre[gonwe]ll[B] went out a walking over
hedges & Ditches–

Fri 10 I heard from John   Mrs Bennett called here

Sat 11 *Wrote to dear Bysshe* Dear Hellen [Tregonwell] left us – Heard
from My Dearest Aunt Shelley–

Sun 12 Wrote to Aunt Shelley to day & went to S[alisbur]y to Col:
Breretons–

Mon 13 Very pleasant, went to the Assize Ball (but did not dance)
owing to my foot

Tues 14 Went to the play of Paul & Virginia ^Liked it^ pretty well
< ------ >

Wed 15 Returned home after having spent a very pleasent time at
Salisbury

26 Feb. One line cancelled.
27 Feb. One line cancelled.
14 March. One or possibly two lines cancelled.

Thurs 16 Went to Gunville; < ------ > Heard from < ------ > C-s &
   L-a   Got safe to Gunville

Fri 17 Staid in doors all day Aunt Grove is here–

Sat 18 Aunt Grove went away wrote to John & C-s–

Sun 19 Emma's Birthday 21 – wrote to Louisa Mrs Farquharson[B]
   called here–

Mon 20 Came home from G[unvill]e came down Wind green in the
   carriage The Wad[dington]s returned home with us–

Tues 21 < ------ > (Henrietta came here)

Wed 22 Walked out for the 1st time since my foot was bad–

Thurs 23 < ------ > began a letter to George to send to St. Helena–

Fri 24 Heard from John & answered his letter

Sat 25 Practised that <u>beautiful</u> thing Fitz-Eustace – M^r F[arquharson]s
   ho^unds came here

Sun 26 Went to Church My Mother heard from Hellen Tregonwell–

Mon 27 The Waddingtons & Thos & Henrietta left us   we miss the
   Dear Children very much indeed

Tues 28 Charlotte & myself walked up White Sheet Hill[D] where
   frightened by two Horses running in the Park < ------ >

Wed 29 < ------ > Charlotte heard from Miss Popham & Aunt
   C[hafin] Grove[A]

Thurs 30 heard from Louisa

Fri 31 wrote to Tit & Helen–

APRIL

Saturday 1 Dyed My Gown. We heard from John who thinks we shall
   see Aunt Shelley in Town which I am very glad of – *heard from
   Bysshe* I hope this Month I shall be more fortunate <u>in seeing the
   person I wish</u> than I was at Xmas – I think I Shall–

Sun 2 Went to Church & received the Sacrament–

Mon 3 The Weather is rather warmer took a long walk–

16 Mar. First cancellation one line. C[harle]s & L[ouis]a
21 Mar. Two lines cancelled 23 Mar. one line cancelled. St Helena was the recognised
port of call in the south Atlantic for the collection of mail.
25 Mar. Jones read this as 'The EF-s ho^unds'. Ingpen's version was 'The F[o]x
hounds'. Visits by Mr. Farquharson's hounds to Ferne were a familiar event.
29 Mar. One line cancelled.
31 Mar. Tit – a pet-name for Louisa.
 1 Apr. 'I hope ... I think I Shall' is on the Account of Cash page under date April 1. 'I
Shall' is written in thick large letters.

Tues 4 *Wrote letter to Bysshe* The Miss Benetts[B] & Aunt Grove[A] came here–

Wed 5 Miss Popham has sent Charlotte & me a silver Clasp for our belts

Thurs 6 The Miss Benetts of Lower Donhead[D] dined here–

Fri 7 Miss Catherine Benett Dined & slept here Met Miss F[rances] Bennett going to Wardour[D]–

Sat 8 our party Left us Wrote to Louisa – never heard so much talking as I have since the Miss Benetts have been here as my Aunt Grove & Miss Benett are the greatest talkers in the World–

Sun 9 *Went to Church saw the Miss Benetts – Heard from Bysshe*

Mon 10 Packed up, < ------ >

Tues 11 Left Fern & got to Halford Bridge–

Wed 12 Got to London like Johns House – *received a long letter from Bysshe*

Thurs 13 Had another letter from *B-e* who is at Col: Sergisons[B] at Cuckfield M[r] Bromley[C] called here – *I wrote* < ------ >

Fri 14 Went Shopping & saw M[rs] Cook & M[rs] Ainsley

Sat 15 *Heard from Bysshe* < ------ > & my Mother heard from George–

Sun 16 *Dear* Bysshe & M[r] Shelley arrived here the former I am very glad to see – I think M[r] Shelley appears cross < ------ > for what reason I know not–

Mon 17 We went to the Play of Richard the third the farce of Mother Goose

Tues 18 Bysshe went about Town with us to Miss Fernwoods Exhibition of Worsted & then to the Panorama of Grand Cairo–

Wed 19 < ------ > went to Clapham[N] & saw my cousin Shelleys[A] who I think the Nicest Girls I ever saw went to the Play of the Cabinet & the farce of Love in a Tub & the virgin unmasked.

Thurs 20 *Dear* Bysshe *has* left us < ------ > wrote to my Dear Aunt Shelley *& Bysshe*

---

10 Apr. Three plus lines cancelled.

11 Apr. Halford was Harriet's incorrect version of Hartford Bridge, near Basingstoke.

12 Apr. John's house was 49 Lincoln's Inn Fields.

13 Apr. B[yssh]e; one line cancelled.

15 Apr. One plus lines cancelled.

18 Apr. Ingpen has 'Fenwood'.

19 Apr. One line cancelled.

20 Apr. One line cancelled.

Fri 21 *I wrote Bysshe a good letter* Mr Shelley called here – he & M^r W[illiam] Benett[B] dined with us yesterday

Sat 22 < ------ > went morning visiting & shopping–

Sun 23 Received from Bysshe the songs   M^r W: Benett & Mr Vincent dined here

Mon 24 Charlotte has made me a present of the Pink Dress *dear Bysshe chose for us* for which I am very much obliged to them

Tues 25 I heard from Dear Aunt Shelley yesterday < ------ > *Bysshe* Mrs Cooke[B] & Miss C[atherine] Benett drank tea here

Wed 26 < ------ > Dined at M^{rs} P Stills[B] went with Lady Fraser[B] to a Rout at Lady Glins[B]

Thurs 27 < ------ > Charlotte went to Mrs Goslins rout with Mrs Long Mr Shelley dined with us

Fri 28 Wrote to my Dearest Aunt went to the play of Grievinges of folly & the Devil to pay Waddington went with us–

Sat 29 had an immense long letter from *B*   Dined at M^{rs} [William] Longs–

Sun 30 Rode in hide Park & went to the Foundling Chapel heard an excellent sermon

MAY

Monday 1 < ------ > Heard from my Dear Aunt S[helley] & went to the Opera liked it very much–

Tues 2 Dined at Mr Knellers[B] & were much entertained by the odd creatures I saw there

Wed 3 < ------ > The Stills[B] dined here rather a stupid Party Charlotte flirted as usual with W: Long[A]

Thurs 4 Mr Shelley came with Col: Sergison, the former gave me a frank *for B* went to a Rout at Mrs Devons with Mrs Long–

Fri 5 Dined at home – John & Papa Dined with W. Long heard from Dear Aunt Shelley

Sat 6 Wrote to Aunt S: Dined at Mr Rudges[A] *Letter from Bysshe*

22 Apr. Two plus lines cancelled.
24 Apr. Ingpen has 'chose for me', but 'for us' is correct. The pretence that the sisters were to share the gift was a concession to etiquette.
25 Apr. One line cancelled.
26 Apr. One line cancelled.
27 Apr. Two lines cancelled.
 3 May. One plus lines cancelled.

Sun 7 Mr Shelley & a party dined here, Waddington & Lord Hinton called in the morning–

Mon 8 < ------ > heard from Mary Shelley Mr J. Wad. Lord Hinton & Coll: Sergison D^r M^{rs} & Miss Jackson[A] Dined here

Tues 9 Went to the Exhibition liked it pretty well & to Astleys in the Evening–

Wed 10 Went to the Tower < ------ > & St Pauls Miss Kilderbee went with us & a Party–

Thurs 11 < ------ > Dined at Sir W: Frasers[B]–

Fri 12 Went shopping in the morning – the two Mr Benetts & Mr Barnes dined here

Sat 13 Dined at Mr Greens & went to the Opera with Mrs Grey & the Kilderbee's–

Sun 14 Walked in Kensington Gardens with Mrs Grey & the Kilderbees

Mon 15 Heard from *Bysshe &* ^{Aunt} Shelley Mrs Hamilton & Children called here the Knellers dined here – < ------ >

Tues 16 Went to Westminster Abbey with the Miss Frasers – & the Rudges[A] dined here rather stupid

Wed 17 < ------ > The Bromleys[B] came to spend the day with us went to the Play of the Honey Moon & saw Elliston

Thurs 18 < ------ > *Bysshe* the Bromleys left us, This is our last day we have to spend with Dear John

Fri 19 < ------ > Mr Kilderbee called upon us   left Town & reached Halford Bridge – where Mr Benett met us

Sat 20 Reached Salisbury & dined with Thomas at Mrs Gushers [?] Lodgings

Sun 21 Unpacked < ------ > so happy to be at Dear Fern Had Letters from Dear John < ------ >

Mon 22 Dear William has made 2000£ Prize Money My Mother rode on her Horse & ^{we} took a long walk with Walter Long to Wardour–

10 May. One line cancelled.

11 May. One plus lines cancelled.

17 May. Two lines cancelled. *The Honey Moon*, a comedy by John Tobin. Robert William Elliston (1774-1831) was one of the leading actor-managers of his day. In 1809 he was manager of the Surrey Theatre.

18 May. One line cancelled

19 May. Halford Bridge: see April 11 note.

20 May. Gushers: Ingpen and Jones thus interpret this inscrutable name, but the first letter is not G. 'Lushes' seems more plausible; it is a familiar local name.

Tues 23 < ------ > Walked to Farringdon   quite tired by W. Longs
nonsensical conversation

Wed 24 < ------ > went to Salisbury. went to the Play there.

Thurs 25 Walked about the Town paying morning visits & gossiping
went to the Ball–

Fri 26 took a long walk in the morning, went to Mrs Whindhams[B]
rout

Sat 27 Went to the play we are so gay here more so than in Town

Sun 28 Went to the Cathedral Morning & Evening the Militia were
there in the morning & the Yeomanry in ^{the} eveng

Mon 29 Staid at home this Evening Mrs Gordon Dined with us

Tues 30 Went to the Play bespoke by the officers of the Yeomanry

Wed 31 Mrs Benett & Mrs Gordon[B] dined with us   called on M^{rs}
Harris – < ------ >

JUNE

Thursday 1 Went to a Dance at Mrs Whindhams very pleasent M^{r}
Colley was so very entertaining Heard from Aunt Shelley

Fri 2 Mrs Harris came with her 5 Children went to a Dance at Col:
Breretons Mr Colley again the life of the party Danced till 4 O-clock

Sat 3 this morning we are returned to Fern again   I am not sorry

Sun 4 did not rise this morning till ten to recruit after all this raking,
Wrote to my Aunt Shelley

Mon 5 Walked by myself in the wood & garden & wrote to John–

Tues 6 < ------ > M^{r} & M^{rs} W: Long[A] & Aunt Grove came here–

Wed 7 My Father & Mr Long have found out that Old Fern will
tumble down as the front is cracked all the way down^{N} I am very
sorry for it

Thurs 8 Heard from Dear Louisa I have not heard from her a long
time before–

Fri 9 M^{r} & Mrs Long & Aunt Grove left us

Sat 10 Walked out & have been reading a novel called Novice of St
Dominick like it very well–

Sun 11 Went to Upper Donhead[D] Church & saw all our neighbours
there–

23 May. One plus lines cancelled.
26 May. Whindham[B]; Harriet's usual spelling for Wyndham.
27 May. 'In Town': that is, in London.
31 May. One plus lines cancelled.
 6 June. One line cancelled.

Mon 12 Mr Hamilton [c] came here & drew a plan for altering old
 Fern–

Tues 13 < ------ > Walked to the Glove[D] I fear we shall not walk
 there many times more this year–

Wed 14 Wrote *to B--- and* Charles, We Dined at the Gordons who are
 very sorry to hear we are to leave Fern

Thurs 15 My Father went to Bath to fetch Louisa home. Charlotte &
 myself got up to make his breakfast–

Fri 16 The two Miss Benetts [Catherine and Frances] called here &
 Louisa came home for her Holidays

Sat 17 Went rumaging over an old Bureau & walked out with Tit.
 some of our neighbours dined here–

Sun 18 Went to Lower Donhead Church & looked at the Parsonage
 house which we have some idea of inhabiting whilst Fern is
 rebuilding

Mon 19 Saw the plan which Mr Hamilton has drawn for altering Fern
 & we all like it very much–

Tues 20 < ------ > & Louisa < ------ >

Wed 21 Heard from John & heard we are to go to the Parsonage to
 remain whilst the house is done

Thurs 22 < ------ > *from Bysshe* < ------ > –

Fri 23 Packed up as we are to leave Dear Old Fern on Monday
 Walked to Lower Donhead went through Mad Grove & Drank tea
 with Aunt J[ackson]

Sat 24 < ------ > *letter* < ------ >

Sun 25 *Wrote to* < ------ > & went to Berwick Church M^r & M^{rs}
 Boys[c] & Miss Croom Drank tea here This is our last day

Mon 26 My birthday 18 years old Such a bustle left Dear Old Fern
 Mama & Louisa went in the Pheaton with two family pictures
 before them & Charlotte & myself walked to the Parsonage Lower
 Donhead & very very busy unpacking

Tues 27 *Had letter from Bysshe* equally as busy unpacking as we
 were yesterday

Wed 28 Walked out in the Evening to Upper Donhead & saw a little
 boy who was afraid to pass the Parsonage because he heard such a
 Hammering

13 June. One plus lines cancelled. Ingpen wrongly transcribed 'Glove' as 'Grove'.
20 June. One and one plus lines cancelled.
22 June. First cancellation two plus lines
24 June. Second cancellation three lines

Thurs 29 *Heard & wrote to B-* Walked half way to Fern but
  C[harlotte] & L[ouisa] were afraid of a Thunder Storm – M[r]
  Eason[C] dined here

Fri 30 Walked to Fern & were much surprised to see how much they
  have pulled down, it looks now in a very deplorable state

JULY

Saturday 1 Went to Drink tea with M[rs] Burlton[B] but as she was not
  at home we walked in Bury wood M[rs] & Miss Cooke[B] came &
  called upon us in the Evening–

Sun 2 Went to Church twice made a long morning visit on M[rs] Cooke
  what I dislike very much that tiresome M[r] Wake dines here–

Mon 3 It rained all day M[rs] Cooke came here to gossip in the
  Evening–

Tues 4 My Mother received a letter from Aunt S[helley] that was
  written 24th June in which she says even if we had stayed at Fern we
  should not have seen her

Wed 5 My Mother & Louisa called on M[rs] & Miss Cooke if it is fine
  we are to drink tea with my Aunt Jackson–

Thurs 6 *Heard from & wrote to B.* M[rs] & Miss Cooke Dined here a
  very stupid evening was the result–

Fri 7 Very wet & therefore did not go out–

Sat 8 *Received a letter from B* & walked to Fern in the morning–

Sun 9 *Wrote to B-* a great many morning visitors D[r] Jackson &
  Arabella dined with us; walked

Mon 10 Walked round M[rs] Cooke's Garden with her–

Tues 11 *Heard & wrote to B* also heard from Dear Charles – wrote to
  Aunt Shelley & Henrietta & John

Wed 12 My Mother heard from Aunt S[helley], Elizabeth has written
  a letter to John to invite him to Field Place

Thurs 13 < ------ > *letter from Aunt Shelley – heard from B* Made a
  bet with Louisa that Fern will be finished in 2 years & a half – L says
  it <u>won't</u> our bet is a Shilling–

Fri 14 *Received* < -/-/-/- > *letter* we went to Fern yesterday to fix
  where the New House is to stand – Louisa heard from Mary

---

1 July. Harriet writes Mrs Burlton's name awkwardly. Ingpen & Jones transcribed it
as 'Buttson'

14 July. < -/-/-/- >; Harriet's pen went through the paper; one word is lost.

Sat 15 Poor Marrianne[A]'s Birthday she would have been 17 – Heard
from *B* & Dear George his letter dated 19th March,

Sun 16 *Heard from Bysshe & wrote to him* Charlotte & Mama went
to call on M[rs] Benett in the morning

Mon 17 Aunt Grove came here & we all took a very pleasent walk in
the Evening–

Tues 18 M[rs] & Miss Cooke dined here & we went in the Evening to
Fern to fix where the New House is to stand but we did not fix

Wed 19 D[r] & Aunt Jackson dined here–

Thurs 20 Walked up upon Barkers Hill with Aunt Grove & Louisa,
Drank tea with M[rs] Cooke – In our walk met an Old Woman who
amused Tit by pulling up her Petticoats to shew us her bad leg
Aunt G- was much shocked

Fri 21 Went to Fern as M[r] Hamilton came to measure out the plan for
the New House, we went to choose the Spot

Sat 22 Heard *& wrote to B-* Aunt Grove left us Dined at D[r] Jackson's

Sun 23 Walked to Upper Donhead[D] very hot, Charlotte & I took a
most delightful walk in the Evening–

Mon 24 Louisa & I walked together in the garden & had a most
interesting conversation–

Tues 25 Heard from Henrietta I am happy to hear they are quite well
at Cwm Elen[D] Louisa & I went in M[rs] Cookes Car intending to go
to Pitt House but M[rs] C- fancied there would be Thunder–

Wed 26 walked upon the pavement

Thurs 27 *Heard & wrote to B-*. I think we have a chance of going to
Field Place   it makes me very happy.

Fri 28 This is Louisa's last day she has to stay with us, I wrote to John
& sent it to Field Place where he is now–

Sat 29 Louisa went to school miss her very much indeed–

Sun 30 Went to Netherhampton[D] staid there all night, M[r] S & M[rs] E
Long[A] dined here

Mon 31 < ------ > We got to Little Park[D] < ------ > *from B*. Dear
Emma knows us very well   Came from Netherhampton by Romsey
here, the Country is very beautiful.

20 July. 'Barkers Hill', still a well-known name locally, wrongly transcribed by Ingpen
& Jones as 'Barton Hill'

31 July. First cancellation one plus lines.

AUGUST

Tuesday 1　What a pleasent month this was last year – Dear little Emma talks & is very entertaining – Little John is grown a fine little fellow　a Mr Minchin Dined here he is a great talker

Wed 2　*Wrote to Bysshe* – Charlotte & myself walked out & took a very long walk told little Emma to call her Aunt C- Dolly Rump

Thurs 3　Wrote to Helen [Tregonwell] & Louisa　a man came with a Bear to the Gate & made it dance which amused little Emma very much

Fri 4　*Heard & wrote to Eliz Shelley* I am afraid Mr Shelley wont ask us to Field Place this Summer–

Sat 5　a very wet day our new Barouche is come, I played with dear little Emma I am still a great favorite of hers

Sun 6　*Heard from B-* went to Church at Wickham & then payed morning visits but fortunately they were none of them at home except Mr Garnier

Mon 7　Walked with my Mother & talked to her upon a subject that always interests me–

Tues 8　< ------ > heard from Mrs Wilsonn[c] & Miss Tregonwell–

Wed 9　*Heard from B* dined at the Garniers very very stupid　they laid the first stone at Fern today

Thurs 10　Went home felt sorry to leave Emma & the Dear Children – *received a letter from B- before I left Little Park* a most tremendous Thunder storm in the evening

Fri 11　< ------ > – My Mother C[harlotte] & myself went to Fern in the Pheaton

Sat 12　the Jacksons dined here upon a haunch of venison–

Sun 13　heard the good news that Mrs Benett of Pitt [House] has a son and heir Wrote to Louisa

Mon 14　very wet so staid in all day–

Tues 15　*Heard from* < ------ > We have gained a victory over the French by Sir A W[ellesle]y in the battle of Talavera de la Reyna –

Wed 16　Went to Fern in the morning they are got on a great deal with the Foundation, *heard from* < ------ >.

Thurs 17　Wrote to Aunt Shelley called on the Ansleys at Mrs Cookes[B] Lord & Lady Arundell[B] called here, Drank Tea at Mrs Cookes, my Dear Father returned home–

1 Aug. Mr Minchin of Botley Grange, near Wickham
6 Aug. G. Garnier of Wickham Corner, Wickham, adjacent to Little Park.

Fri 18 My Father has made me a present of a Lottery Ticket which I am very much obliged to him for

Sat 19 *Wrote to* < ------ > *& heard from him* < ------ > the Annesleys & Gordons Dined here—

Sun 20 Wrote to Louisa we have heard M[r] Fletcher[C] the Rector of this place is dead I fear we shall not reside here much longer[N] – as that is the case –

Mon 21 M[r] Wake[C] went away this morning

Tues 22 C[harles] Jackson & J[ohn] Gordon came here this morning to hunt with my Father we dined at the Gordons – met M[r] Benett there & M[r] Wake who played upon his Fiddle—

Wed 23 Nothing particularly happened today—

Thurs 24 *Heard from & wrote to Bysshe* < ------ > heard from Emma – My Mother & Father are gone to Knoyle[D] to pay morning visits

Fri 25 < ------ > The Parkers[B] are at Field Place

Sat 26 M[rs] Cooke & her Brother M[r] Cooke dined here—

Sun 27 *Heard from my Dear Bysshe* took a very pretty walk—

Mon 28 M[rs] & Miss Burlton[B] M[r] & M[rs] Boys & Miss Croome dined here on a Haunch of Venison Mama & Charlotte went in the morning to call on Lady A[rundel]l at Ashcombe[D]—

Tues 29 *Wrote to Bysshe,* received a letter from *him &* John Elizabeth has sent me my Picture – called on the Jacksons Miss Burlton came in so smartly dressed in Lavender Coloured Satin dress & a muslin Turband with white beads—

Wed 30 < ------ > Lord & Lady Arundell & Miss L[aura] A[rundell][B] Dined here

Thurs 31 < ------ > Heard from John who will be here Tomorrow—

SEPTEMBER

Friday 1 Dear John came Charlotte & myself drank tea [with] M[rs] C[ooke] last night & M[r] Douglas & M[r] Butler came Mary Dimmer[C] saw them go into the Church this morning to look at M[rs] Cooke's Door & called them the two Bishops

25 Aug. Three lines cancelled.

29 Aug. 'Miss Burlton' transcribed by Ingpen and Jones as 'Miss Button'. See July 1 above.

30 Aug. Two lines cancelled.

31 Aug. One plus lines cancelled.

1 Sept. 'the Church' – Donhead St. Andrew.

Sat 2 received a letter from Emma Dined at Mrs Cookes walked to
    Wardour[D] Woods
Sun 3 *Heard from Bysshe* walked to Upper Donhead with John
Mon 4 < ------ > M^r W[illiam] Benett dined here
Tues 5 *Heard from Bysshe* Got a quiz from Elizabeth Went to see
    Tollard[D] we all like it pretty well^N–
Wed 6 John dines at M^r W- Hilyars[B] today he then goes to Norton
    & does not return here till Saturday   I heard from Dearest Louisa
Thurs 7 < ------ > Mr Hamilton came here–
Fri 8 We went to Fern Mrs Cooke went with us in her Car, it rained all
    the time we were there–
Sat 9 < ------ > I long for Mama to hear from Aunt Shelley–
Sun 10 < ------ > Catherine Benett L[ouisa] Cooke Mr Wake & M^r W:
    Hilyar dined here–
Mon 11 *This is a very pleasent thing to* < ------ >
Tues 12 < ------ >
Wed 13 M^rs & Miss Cooke called here before they set off for
    Weymouth   I heard from dear George yesterday·
Thurs 14 < ------ > (Aunt Jackson was brought to bed of a little girl
    last Tuesday 12th)
Fri 15 My Father & John dined at Pytt House
Sat 16 M^r C[harles] Benett[B] breakfasted here Charlotte & myself
    intended to have walked to Fern but were prevented by the rain–
Sun 17 My Mother heard from Dear Aunt Shelley who says she shall
    always be glad to hear from me, John went to Netherhampton to
    day
Mon 18 John has hired an Old Woman for his Housekeeper he says
    she is not quite so ugly as his last–
Tues 19 Wrote to Dear Aunt S-y & to Mrs Wilsonn & Louisa & heard
    from Elizabeth who has written me a most affec^t letter, < ------ >
Wed 20 Answered Elizabeth Shelleys letter, dined & slept at Pytt

---

4 Sept. Seven plus lines cancelled
6 Sept. 'Norton' – probably Norton Bavant, a residence of the Benett family.
7 Sept. Two plus lines cancelled.
10 Sept. Five lines cancelled. 'Hilyar': Ingpen and Jones have 'Helyar' but the dotted i is
plain to see. Harriet was still mis-spelling her future married name as in 6 Sept. above.
11 Sept. Three lines cancelled.
12 Sept. Nine lines cancelled.
14 Sept. Three plus lines cancelled.
19 Sept. Four lines cancelled.

House Met Sir W: & Lady Parker[B] there the latter is looking beautiful–

Thurs 21   We returned home after spending our time at Pyt house pleasently, We met at Dinner there M[r] J Kneller[B] & his friend M[r] Jarvis both great quizes We called upon Aunt J[ackson] after our return home & I saw my Goddaughter that is to be–

Fri 22   M[r] Eason[C] Dined here on a Haunch of Venison wrote to Louisa, was much amused by the quantity of venison M[r] E – eat–

Sat 23   Went to Compton[D] John went to Langton[D] – met M[r] & M[rs] [Richard] Long the Member & Miss Flora Long[A] there   M[rs] P[enruddocke][B] is quite recovered

Sun 24   Went to Church & John came a M[r] Powell dined with [us] I think Miss F Long is a pleasent Girl–

Mon 25   Came home, the Water was so high that we thought we should have been drowned–

Tues 26   Dear John left us   the Farmers dined here – had a droll letter from Louisa & one from M[rs] Wilsonn <u>Joy Joy Joy</u> William Dear Dear William's come home such an unexpected pleasure

Wed 27   Wrote a great many letters to tell the Joyfull event of Williams arrival   heard from Eliz[th] Shelley – < ------ > William is so altered I should not have known him any where

Thurs 28   M[r] Fletcher came with D[r] Jackson & M[r] Brotherton [and] was inducted into the Church   walked to Fern William went out a hunting M[rs] Cooke Drank tea here We began sending some of the things to Tollard–

Fri 29   Went with Dear William to see Aunt Jackson   Tom was here when we came back – he wanted William to go to Gunville but we could not part with him

Sat 30   My Father & W[illiam] went out hunting The Miss Hilyars[B] called here   Mama had a droll letter from John–

OCTOBER

Sunday 1   Received the Sacrament Wrote to Eliz[th] Shelley – M[r] Wake as usual dined here, Mary Dimmer went to Fern – M[rs] Cooke went into Church through the large Door by which means she has gained a victory over M[r] Brotherton

Mon 2   Walked to Fern with Dear William   sent almost all the things to Tollard

27 Sept. One plus lines cancelled.
28 Sept. Nathaniel Fletcher was the new rector of Donhead St. Andrew.

Tues 3 Left Donhead & got to Tollard called on Mrs Cooke to wish
    her well. We are in as great a Bustle as when we left Fern—

Wed 4 I like this House better than Lower Donhead – heard from
    Dear Louisa & Aunt Shelley Williams room is so close to mine that
    I hear every thing he says, Tom & a Mr Fraser[B] called here

Thurs 5 Tom & Mr Fraser breakfasted here, & went out hunting with
    my Father – Henrietta M^{rs} F[arquharson] & two Miss Frasers[B]
    called here—

Fri 6 Wrote to Aunt Shelley & Louisa We went in the Pheaton to
    Sedgehill saw there Mrs Ogle[C] & M^r & Mrs John Still[B]—

Sat 7 Mr John Helyer[B] called whilst we were at breakfast wrote in
    William's name to Emma I wonder if she will find it out—

Sun 8 Went to Church M^r J: Helyar I think is a good preacher. went to
    Gunville after Church & found Fanny & Arabella Jackson there.

Mon 9 My Mother & I returned to Tollard to get some more Cloaths
    & then went to Gunville again Danced in the Evening – John came
    here—

Tues 10 We have heard poor Miss W: Arundell[B] is dead   stayed at
    Gunville Mr Snow[C] & his two sons dined here – danced again this
    Evening

Wed 11 Went home, & then to Fern to meet Miss Helyar who was not
    there – Saw Old Mary Dimmer

Thurs 12 We went to Farnham[D] to call on M^r J: Helyar. I did not
    take much fancy to her she can make herself pleasent

Fri 13 John & William went to Gunville – M^r Wm: Helyar & Miss
    C[atherine] Benett called here   heard from E[lizabeth] S[helley] she
    has sent me some verses of Bysshe's – *which I think very good*

Sat 14 Wrote to Eliz:th C[harlotte] & myself were going Post haste to
    walk to Fern but Mama prevented us   John & Wm. came home. M^r
    & Mrs J. Helyar & Tom & Mr Fraser dined here

Sun 15 Received the Sacrament Mr Helyar gave us a most beautiful
    Sermon C & myself walked to Fern, John & W^m went to Langton—

Mon 16 Mrs Brereton & Henrietta have both sent us an invitation to a
    Ball on the 25th when there is to be a Jubilee, We are obliged to
    refuse both because we are engaged to go to Preshaw[D] for which
    we are all <u>very</u> sorry—

Tues 17 Charlotte had a most shocking cross letter from Aunt Grove
    John & Wm. are gone there Mr Bingham[C] called here John does
    not return here again

16 Oct. The Jubilee of October 25, 1809, was in celebration of the beginning of the
fiftieth year of George III's reign.

Wed 18 Took a very pretty walk to a Cottage near Ashcombe
    Charlotte & I have made a bargain that if either of us have a prize in
    the lottery we are to share it between us–

Thurs 19 William says Miss Wilsonn is very ugly – The Miss Frasers
    & their Brother came here I played at Commerce won 15 owing to
    Mr W. Frasers cheating for me–

Fri 20 This is the day the Lottery is drawn – My Mother & the Miss
    Frasers went to Fern Charlotte & myself walked to Ashcombe–

Sat 21 Walked to Ashcombe Miss J: Fraser rode on our Poney M^r
    Markland Brother of Capt. M.[B] called here M^r Wm. Fraser went
    away

Sun 22 Mr W. Fraser returned went to Church, afterwards walked
    out with the Miss Frasers, Charlotte could not go to Church as she
    has got a swelled face – I fear my Ticket is come up a blank indeed I
    believe we are none of us fortunes favorite

Mon 23 Left the Miss F[raser]s at Tollard as we set off for Preshaw
    Tom is to fetch them to Gunville We arrived at Preshaw W- Long is
    here who is going to be married to Lady Mary Carnigie

Tues 24 My Mother Charlotte & myself walked out William says he
    shall go to Little Park

Wed 25 Went to Church at Mr Ferrers heard a most excellent Sermon
    on The Kings accession on the throne We dined at Lord Northesks
    on Turtle met a very pleasent party & we danced in the Evening

Thurs 26 Emma came here with little Emma they took W[illiam] back
    with them We went with the Northesks to a Winchester ball & saw
    Lady Mildmay

Fri 27 The Waddingtons dined here & M^r & Miss Ferrers & her
    Lover Mr Courtney The Northesks came in the Evening & we had
    a very pleasent Dance

Sat 28 Left Preshaw & reached my Aunt Groves called at Close
    Gate[D] in our way were I received a letter from E[lizabeth]
    S[helley]

Sun 29 Heard of our Lottery Tickets they are all Blanks but
    C[harlotte]s who has a prize of 30 Miss Packington is here who
    sang to us yesterday Evening–

Mon 30 Left Netherhampton & in our way home stopped at Fern
    which we were surprised to see they had got on so much with–

23 Oct. Lady Mary Carnegie, the daughter of William Carnegie, Lord Northesk,
married Walter Long on February 12, 1810. (Burke's Landed Gentry, 1898)
29 Oct. 'A prize of 30' – the 3 is definite, the 0 doubtful. 3£ is a plausible conjecture.

Tues 31 To our great surprise Miss Tregonwell & her Brother paid us
a morning visit, Tom & H[enrietta] & Mr Fraser also called here.
William returned from Little Park

NOVEMBER
Wednesday 1 Wrote to E- S- Mr Farquharson has sent to invite us to
Langton on Friday–
Thurs 2 Been very busy all day mending old Clothes – Received a
letter from my Dear Aunt Shelley
Fri 3 Wrote to John went to Dinner to Langton The Miss Frasers &
their Brother are here–
Sat 4 Walked to Blandford with the Miss Frasers My Mother & M^{rs}
Farquharson called on Mr Portman,[B] & in their way home went to
St. Mary's for Fanny & Arabella Jackson, in the Evening played at
Commerce M^r W- Fraser caused me to win the Pool–
Sun 5 Went to Langton Church afterwards walked to the Farm & we
all exercised our lungs whilst doing so   a Mr Riddon came by which
caused a good laugh Henrietta Tom & Miss Tregonwell came here
& a M^r & Mrs Ocden & their little Girl–
Mon 6 Left Langton & returned to Tollard I think Mrs Okden
without exception the most affected woman I ever met with
Tues 7 Answered my Aunt Shelleys letter & told her William would
be with her on the 22nd Mr Hamilton dined & slept here–
Wed 8 Went in the Pheaton to Fern & to Mrs Cookes – & my Aunt
Jacksons with my Mother, Charlotte & Wm – walked to Fern, my
Mother & I both agree in thinking Mr Wm Fraser a very pleasent
young man–
Thurs 9 Charlotte & myself walked through the Parish & were
frightened by the Silly man wanting to shake hands with us M^{rs} &
Miss Cooke came here–
Fri 10 M^{rs} & Miss Cooke remained here I think Miss C- more
troublesome than ever–
Sat 11 M^{rs} & Miss C- left us walked intending to call on M^{rs} R
Arundel[B] at Ashcombe but rain came on & prevented us
Sun 12 M^r J Helyar came from Sedgehill & preached here heard
from my dearest Aunt Shelley – Tom called here H[elen]
Tregonwell came to stay
Mon 13 We all went to Fern Dear William left us & went to Gunville
he goes tomorrow to Little Park with Tom & Henrietta

5 Nov. The David Okedens of Turnworth, near Blandford, and their daughter
Catherine Jane.

Tues 14 Helen talked to me about her dear Duffy as she calls Capt
    Markland   wrote to Aunt Shelley – & Louisa–

Wed 15 Mama & Charlotte went to call upon M^r & Mrs Fletcher the
    new Rector of Lower Donhead Miss Tre[gonwe]ll & myself walked
    to Ashcombe–

Thurs 16 a very hard frost the Building at Fern must now stop for the
    Winter   wrote to William–

Fri 17 Took a walk with Charlotte through the village it was so dirty
    that we were near being stuck–

Sat 18 went out walking directly after breakfast. Shewed King Johns
    House[D] to Helen   W^m is to leave Little Park to day – heard &
    wrote to Dear William & wrote to Henrietta–

Sun 19 Wm did not leave Little P[ark] till to day – last night We
    fancied the House was on fire so Charlotte Helen & myself went
    down stairs in our night shifts to see if it was & found it was a Tea
    Kettle on the fire boiling–

Mon 20 Wrote to Dear Charles whom we have not heard from for a
    long time & also wrote to W^m took a very pretty walk–

Tues 21 received some Baskets that dear W^m has sent us from Little
    Park – M^r & Mrs Tregonwell came here–

Wed 22 The Tregonwells left us & we went to M^r J: Stills at Berwick
    & met Miss Helyar there who I like excessively   M^{rs} J Stills
    children are the prettiest I ever saw

Thurs 23 Much entertained in the morning by Miss Helyar the Stills
    Lady Parker &c.   & Mrs John Helyar & M^r W^m H[elyar] Dined
    here & they took Miss Helyar back with them at night

Fri 24 Returned to Tollard & heard that Dear W^m is going out to sea
    again immediately   a letter from Charles to say he is arrived at
    Yarmouth & still dislikes his Profession, it is both very bad news,
    for I am very sorry Dear W^m is going away again

Sat 25 Wrote a great many letters & walked out

Sun 26 Heard from dear W^m which was written at Field Place M^r
    Helyar gave us a most excellent sermon which he generally does–

Mon 27 Miss Catherine Benett came here yesterday & left us to day
    which I am glad of–

Tues 28 My Father went out hunting   a very unpleasant day for
    Walking–

Wed 29 Dear W^m returned before Breakfast Dear Fellow he leaves us
    again tomorrow for which we are all very sorry We all dined at M^r
    J: H[elyar] met the young Helyars there, Dear W^m enjoyed himself
    very much he tried to open a Piano forte but could not succeed–

Thurs 30 *My Dear* < ------ > *left us* < ------ > *to day* < ------ >

DECEMBER

Friday 1 The Helyars dined here all but Mrs John who was ill with a
   cold We had a pleasent little Dance

Sat 2 Walked out before the House My Father hunted with M^{r}
   Chafins[B] Hounds Mr Wm Helyar returned here with ^{him} & sat
   some time with us–

Sun 3 Heard a <u>most</u> beautiful sermon from M^{r} J: H- Miss C. H- M^{r}
   Wm & M^{r} J: H. & Miss Camplin came here after Church–

Mon 4 Mr William Helyar breakfasted here & went hunting with my
   Father who had a very pretty run at first close to the House, they
   went afterwards to Fern–

Tues 5 Heard almost from everyone of our friends Emma is to be
   confined again either in Feb^{r} or March

Wed 6 This day seven years ago it was Dear William went to the East
   Indies. *How glad he now is returned safe* I am glad he returned from
   thence safe but most sorry he is gone again We heard from him
   today Dear fellow he arrived safe on board the Orestes on Friday he
   says the Officers on board are very pleasing he has not seen his Capt
   yet–

Thurs 7 Wrote to my Aunt Shelley Charlotte heard from H[ellen]
   S[helley] < ------ >

Fri 8 Went to Mr Boy's[C] at Berwick Wrote to H: S: met Dr Jackson
   & Col: Peachy[C] at Berwick the latter talks more than ever altho'
   he has lost his Wife so lately

Sat 9 left Berwick & called on my Aunt Jackson in our way home Saw
   & heard that tiresome Col: again heard from Dear George

Sun 10 Heard & wrote to Dear W^{m} the Orestes is sailed on a short
   cruize, a Mr Napper preached here as Mr John Helyar I am sorry to
   say has a bad cold, M^{r} N- dined here he appears a sensible young
   man

Mon 11 Wrote to Charles M^{r} & Mrs Boys dined & slept here
   laughed a good deal at M^{r} B- calling his Wife my Bess–

Tues 12 The Boy's went away walked out for an hour–

Wed 13 Dear Tom came here Charles has written word he has left

30 Nov. Whole entry of four lines cancelled.
   3 Dec. H[elyar] in each case.
   6 Dec. The Orestes was a small 16-gun craft which had been captured from the
French. (The Court and City Register for 1807, p.141.)
   7 Dec. three lines cancelled.
   10 Dec. 'Mr Napper': Rev John Tregonwell Napier (1785-1819) later rector of Chettle

the Bellerophon & is coming home

Thurs 14 Mr Harry Helyar called here as we thought to invite us to
Sedgehill but no such thing, the rest of the [Helyar] family are not
returned from Bath

Fri 15 Tom & Henrietta came here I am afraid they won't go to the
Shaftesbury Ball with us–

Sat 16 Heard from W: & Emma – Tom & my Father went out
Hunting–

Sun 17 Louisa & Charles came here the latter has left the Navy & is
to be a – Phisician which we all like very much–

Mon 18 Charles began studying Greek we are a very happy party–

Tues 19 Wrote to Eliz:th Shelley. M^r J: Helyar, & M^{rs} & Miss
Fletcher called here < ------ >

Wed 20 Tom & Henrietta went away which we are sorry for – Heard
from Eliz:th Shelley she writes very drole Letters–

Thurs 21 Louisa heard from M[ary] Shelley who has heard that I am
going to be married, – Put Beads upon our Gowns

Fri 22 Went to the Shaftesbury ball Had a most excellent Ball more
than 20 Couple   Danced thro' two with M^r W^m H[elyar]

Sat 23 Returned home & in our way called on Mary D[immer] who is
looking very well

Sun 24 Heard M^r J: Helyar I am so glad he is well again he came in &
we had a very agreable conversation

Mon 25 Heard a most excellent sermon from M^r J[ohn] H[elyar] it
being Xmas Day We all then received the Sacrament Charles for the
1st time

Tues 26 Wrote to Eliz:th & W^m My Father met M^r J: H- going to
Sedgehill–

Wed 27 Walked from hence to Gunville Waddington came from Little
Park

Thurs 28 M^r W: Helyar came here Tom was in a very drole humour
& made us laugh

Fri 29 Got up early as the Gentlemen went out hunting–

Sat 30 Mrs Portman & a party called here & Mrs Farquharson with
< >

13 Dec. The *Bellerophon*, a 74-gun warship, had recently seen action (off the Swedish
coast on June 19). In 1815 the *Bellerophon* achieved fame as the ship on board which
Napoleon surrendered.

19 Dec. One line cancelled.

30 Dec. < > A one-inch strip is torn from the bottom of the page, taking with it half
the entry for December 30, and all for December 31. The next leaf is also missing. The
remaining stub indicates that there was writing on both sides of it.

NOTES TO 1809

April 19 *The journey to Clapham was made to visit Shelley's younger sisters at their boarding-school, Mrs Fenning's. Hellen Shelley, who was nine and a half years old at the time, recalled many years later her impression of her brother's 'early love', commenting 'How fresh and pretty she looked!'*

June 7 *The discovery of a structural fault, threatening the imminent collapse of Ferne House, brought a radical upheaval of family life over the next two years while the house was demolished and rebuilt. It had been able to accommodate ten children, a numerous house-staff and frequent visitors, so the finding of an alternative at short notice was not easy. A vacant parsonage was the immediate answer. The design and construction of the new house was entrusted to James Hamilton [C]*

August 1 *Harriet's inconsequential remark – 'What a pleasent month this was last year', followed by her entry three days later 'I am afraid Mr Shelley wont ask us to Field Place this year' suggests strongly that in August 1808 she had stayed at Field Place and enjoyed moonlight walks with Bysshe. Their romantic relationship was certainly well established before she began to write her 1809 diary.*

Aug 20 *'I fear we shall not reside here much longer'*

Sept 5 *'Went to see Tollard we all like it pretty well' The arrival of a new rector wishing to occupy Donhead St Andrew rectory meant that the Groves must search again for temporary accommodation. They looked to the south of Ferne, beyond Win Green and Ashcombe to Tollard Royal. Neither Harriet nor Charlotte identifies the house they occupied, but everything points to its being again a rectory. Rev John Helyar was the rector, married and childless. He resided with his wife at Dove's Mansion House in Tollard Farnham, so his rectory at Tollard Royal was presumably available. A close friendship with the John Helyars sprang up as soon as the Groves settled in Tollard and must have helped to bring Harriet in touch with John Helyar's nephew, her future husband.*

1810

This diary is very similar in format and lay-out to the previous year's, though from a different publisher. 'The New Ladies' Memorandum Book for 1809' had been published in London by Baldwin. Harriet's 1810 diary is written in 'Silvester's Housekeeper's Pocket Book and Ladies' Daily Journal for 1810' published at Newport, Shropshire. It is inscribed 'Harriet Grove given her by her Mother Jany 1st 1810'. A note on the flyleaf to the effect that Harriet has 'got a great deal to tell my dear Louisa when she comes home next Monday' lacks a date, which might have given it significance.

After a spell of severe cold and heavy snowfalls in February Harriet's naturally buoyant spirits were raised by two packages from Shelley which arrived during March. His literary ambitions were now taking shape. The first package contained a poem of some length on which he was working, the second was a copy of his first published book, a novel in the Gothic manner which appealed to them both at that time. The hope that this year Harriet might achieve what had eluded her last year – a visit to Field Place – gained increasing strength. Surprisingly her mother developed a mysterious reluctance, possibly because she wished to visit her brother John Pilfold at Cuckfield and was aware that relations were strained between Cuckfield and Field Place. However the visit did take place, though only briefly, and it was again as in the previous year that in London, at Lincoln's Inn Fields, Harriet and Shelley had the longest time in each other's company.

The troubles of the following autumn and the fading of the romance are veiled in a maidenly restraint in the diary, although some clues are plain enough. The loss of the 1811 diary that Harriet bought and presumably used leaves her own account unfinished. Fortunately the pen of her sister, Charlotte, in *her* 1811 diary has at last replaced surmise with fact.

But first, January 1810 – the first six days of which are missing from the diary.

JANUARY

Sunday 7 Went to Gunville to fetch Charlotte home told her the Col: had thoughts of making proposals to a Miss Carter of Horsham *the daughter of* < ------ >

Mon 8 Wrote a long letter to Elizth Shelley, walked with my Mother, received my allowance from my Father–

Tues 9 Heard from < -/-/-/- > ar John who has been at Field Place & been very gay there & liked his visit very much Waddington left us to day–

Wed 10 Heard from Dear Aunt Shelley & Elizth Mrs Portman has invited C[harlotte] & me to a Ball Tomorrow, we are going – Poor Thos Shere[c] fell off a ladder to day & is very much hurt–

Thurs 11 Went to B[ryanston][D] Had a most pleasent Ball at Blandford it was made up of the Portman & Langton Parties < ------ > Old Mr Snow the life of the Ball Room

Fri 12 M^{rs} P[ortman] sent us as far as Thorny Down in her chaise & four, we then went on in the Barouche to Cranbourne Poor Helen very unwell

Sat 13 The Portmans and Wares came Poor Helen ^{still} very unwell laughed at Mrs J. for having taken off her Under Petticoat at the ball the other night–

Sun 14 Left Cranbourne & got to <u>Dear</u> Tollard the Weather <u>very</u> cold

Mon 15 My Mother gave me a letter from Dear W^m which I ought to have had before–

Tues 16 The Miss Frasers were to have come here but sent excuses as they had colds Louisa Charles & myself took a nice long walk & got over Hedges to avoid cows heard from E. S: & the Col: has not made proposals to Miss Carter nor do I think from what I hear he ever intended it

Wed 17 Louisa bought some Poor peoples Coloured Linen for her Pinbefores

---

1-6. Jan The page with the entries for January 1-6 has been torn out. Some words which flowed over on the opposite "House Expences" page survive. Belonging probably to the January 1 entry is the phrase 'at Gunville' – To the January 3 entry a passage of eight cancelled lines probably belongs; of these only the following words can be read: < > 'very which' < > 'to be only a bit of red silk. I am happy to say C is better.' To the entry for January 4 probably belong three other cancelled words.

7 Jan. Two lines cancelled. The 'Col' is Colonel Sergison.

9 Jan. < -/-/-/- > accidental ink blot on the first part of 'dear'.

11 Jan. Two lines cancelled.

12 Jan. Thorney Down: a meeting-point on the Blandford/Salisbury road.

Thurs 18 Walked out towards the Chase with my two Dear Sisters

Fri 19 Old Mr Snow called here & told us M^r & M^rs J: Helyar were going to live at Bath Charles took a nice long walk with us–

Sat 20 We all went to pay a morning visit on Mr J. H- They were both at Home & we staid an hour with them the time went so pleasently that it appeared much shorter Mr Snow made a mistake about there going to Bath as they are not going to live there which I am glad of

Sun 21 Heard from Dear Wm Mr Napper Tregonwell preached here he dined with us with a friend of his a Mr Skinner – they are neither very Gentlemanlike

Mon 22 Charlotte heard from Miss Fraser who will be here Wednesday She certainly was not the Authoress of the verses Charlotte received the other day

Tues 23 tryed to Play with a Shuttle Cock Daniel[c] made, but could not succeed The Snow going away–

Wed 24 Miss Frasers came, We Played all sorts of Xmas Caroles in the Evening & laughed amazingly–

Thurs 25 Walked out, then Charlotte Read the Beggar Girl to us She Acted in the Evening to the great Entertainment of the Miss Frasers

Fri 26 Read the Beggar girl The Miss Frasers are got very interested in it

Sat 27 Tom came here, Did not make up for the interruption he made in the Beggar girl as he did nothing but talk of his grievances

Sun 28 We all went to Church & then took a pleasent walk, read the Beggar Girl in the Evening–

Mon 29 So Sorry the Miss Frasers left us, My Father & Charles walked to Fern, Wrote to Eliz:^th Shelley–

Tues 30 We heard from Dear John who says Mr Shelley & Bysshe dined with him on Saturday, heard from Dear Aunt Shelley–

Wed 31 Louisa & myself took our Drawing into the Parlour were we spent a pleasent morning together

FEBRUARY

Thursday 1 Went a most Dirty walk to the shop met M^r J: Helyar, coming home met some Cows which frightened us, Louisa we lost

18 Jan. 'The Chase': Cranborne Chase.
21 Jan. 'Mr Napper Tregonwell'. See 10 December above.
24 Jan. 'Caroles' is conjectural. Ingpen has 'gambols'. The word is difficult to decipher but certainly ends in 'es' and could mean a ring-dance with song (OED).
25 Jan. Elizabeth Bennett, *The Beggar Girl and Her Benefactors* (7 vols.).

owing to it for some time which frightened us even more than the
Cows–

Fri 2 Louisa & I as usual sat together in the Drawing room, it was a
wet day so Charles could not go out & he came annoying us–

Sat 3 M^{rs} J: Helyar called here Louisa & I were both in the Drawing
room, hearing the Door bell we both ran up stairs with our Drawing
apparatus

Sun 4 Tom & Mr Fraser called here, in the Evening Charles Louisa &
myself sat in our Room talking leaving the rest of the party reading
down stairs

Mon 5 Dearest Louisa went to School I miss her very much Charles
went into the world Saw Aunt Jackson who has got all her children
ill in the measles

Tues 6 Susan[C] returned from Bath & brought me a letter from Dear
Louisa She saw M^{rs} C[hafin] Grove[A] who was dressed very smart
for a Rout

Wed 7 Wrote to my Dear Louisa Charlotte heard from Wm who says
he thinks I shall never be married that I do not care whether I ever
do or not, He says he thinks I never liked any one so much as
< ------ > that is a thing no one will ever know but myself/

Thurs 8 My Father went out Hunting, So wet we none of us stirred
out–

Fri 9 quite stupified by staying in Doors   Miss Dear Louisa more than
ever

Sat 10 a Beautiful Day Mr Benett sent to invite us to Pytt House on
Wednesday   took a long walk with Charles, I do not quite like his
sentiments he thinks too much of appearances–

Sun 11 So wet could not go to Church Tom called here, heard from &
wrote to E: S: Dear W^m I heard from who is sailed for a three weeks
cruize–

Mon 12 My Aunt Grove came told us all the Gossip of Salisbury
Charles went to Gunville he says there was a letter for Mr Fraser –
with an express put on it

Tues 13 Walked out heard from Mrs Wilsonne[C] Aunt Grove talked
incessantly

Wed 14 Aunt Grove Charlotte & myself went to Fern in the Pheaton

5 Feb. 'Charles went into the world' is Jones's version. Ingpen has 'into the woods'.
Harriet's writing is virtually illegible here.
14 Feb. Mr Grove sat as a magistrate on the bench at Hindon.

Charles Rode   met Miss C[atherine] Benett coming here in our way
Poor Old Mary [Dimmer] looks very ill which I was very sorry to
see. My Father Rode to Hindon is to sleep at Pytt House
Thurs 15 A Deep snow My Father returned from Pytt house he heard
there the last Shaston[D] Ball was very bad
Fri 16 Walked out Aunt Grove talks incessantly heard from Elizabeth
Sat 17 very cold snow as Deep as ever, wrote a long letter to Elizabeth.
Aunt Grove cannot go owing to the Snow, My Father read a Play to
us in the Evening the Merchant of Venice–
Sun 18 My Mother heard of the Death of Old Mr Hethfield who
owing to his not signing his will wherin he left – considerably to my
Mother & her Brothers & Sisters, but they get nothing as he did not
sign it
Mon 19 Aunt Grove cannot go away, nor Miss Tregonwell come
here, as the weather is as bad–
Tues 20 Had a very droll Letter from Dear John, the weather as bad
Wed 21 Did the same as usual walked for an hour up & down on the
Road, & employed myself within doors as usual
Thurs 22 The frost still remains My Aunt gave Charles a sort of a
Lecture, he did not swallow it very quietly–
Fri 23 Tom hunted with my Father as the thaw is at last come, heard
from Elizth who has sent a part of Bs Poem
Sat 24 Aunt Grove left us Miss Tregonwell came The Box of Novels
came in the Evening & we all began reading them, Charles thinks
Aunt Grove a very pleasent Woman–
Sun 25 As to Louisa I shall give her a good scolding when she comes
home for not writing We took a walk after Church & talked of this
time last year when H.T. was at Fern with us & used to walk out &
get over Hedges Little did we think then where we should be Now
& that Poor Old Fern would be no more
Mon 26 Such a sight for this place the Green was filled with men who
came to buy M^r J: H[elyar's] cows which were sold by Auction
Tues 27 M^r J: H: called here, we took a very pleasent walk in the Park–
Wed 28 A fast Day, Dear W^m is returned to us again We are all so
happy W^m returned in a small prize the Orestes recaptured from the
French, he remains with us till Tuesday when he must join the
Orestes when it comes in to Plymouth–

15 Feb. 'Shaston' – a local name for Shaftesbury.
18 Feb. Hethfield; see May 26, May 29 entries

MARCH

Thursday 1   Dear W^m is in his usual Spirits, he Cut Charles Hair,
C[harlotte] H.T. & myself walked to Fern & saw Mary Dimmer

Fri 2   Charles & W^m rode to Gunville the latter flirted as usual with his
lovely Miss J: Fraser–

Sat 3   We Played at Commerce as usual Dear good tempered Willy made
us laugh by his great earnestness

Sun 4   W^m walked with us to Rushmore[D] We all got very Dirty
particularly H: T- W^m & Charles dined at Gunville

Mon 5   Most agreably surprised by receiving a Parcel & letter from my
Greatest Friend < ------ >

Tues 6   Wrote to E: S: Tom & H: came here – H.T. slept with me
Dear W^m in such spirits said Charlotte was in love with a Capt
Moustard–

Wed 7   Dear W^m is gone. I hope only for a short time, heard the
delightful news that Dear Emma is safe & has got a fine Boy
Henrietta & Tom went back to G[unville] Charlotte has received
another anonymous letter with a bit of the Gentlemans Hair, fine
doings indeed

Thurs 8   Shewed the Poem < ------ > They < ------ > think it nonsense
< ------ >

Fri 9   We heard yesterday that Emma [Waddington] is doing well & the
Child is to be named Geo: Grove   it will please his Uncle G: G: when
he returns fr China

Sat 10   Catherine Benett came here, sent B[ysshe's] Poem away Walked
with H: Tre, talked on various subjects

Sun 11   Mr Napier brought his love Miss Skinner with him She is pretty,
but no diffidence, Heard from Dear W^m who is safe arrived at
Plymouth I hope we shall see him again soon

Mon 12   Miss Tre. left us, My Father & Mother talk of going to Field
P[lace] in our way to Town, How Happy I am for that

Tues 13   Did as usual in the morning & Played at Chess with Charles in
the Evening–

Wed 14   Charles Benett[B] called here C- & I were walking up & down
with Books in our hands on seeing him ran in Doors. He is building a

5 Mar. Seven lines cancelled, six on "House Expences" page. It can hardly be doubted
that the 'Greatest Friend' was Shelley. Four days earlier he had written in his diary
'Parcel to Harriet'.

8 Mar. Two lines cancelled; then two words; third cancellation twelve lines, which
take up the lower half of the "House Expences" page.

House at Sedgehill   Miss B[urlton] & him are to be married in the
course of the Summer

Thurs 15   Mr Bingham[C] called here heard from Mrs Wilsonn Wrote to
Dear Louisa, took a most Blowing walk on the Down with Charlotte-

Fri 16   Walked out in the village the fool came & took hold of my hand
& frightened me, My Father read aloud in the Evening one of
Walkers lectures-

Sat 17   Tom called here I do not think he looks quite so fat as he did-

Sun 18   My Father & Charles rode over to Gunville where we are to
dine next Thursday walked after Church

Mon 19   Took a most delightful walk to Ashcombe My Father went to
Fern to receive his rents – Charles was in a most shocking gloomy
humour-

Tues 20   Went to Dear Fern with C- & my Father & Mother they are
got on a good deal with the Building since I was last here-

Wed 21   Walked to Gunville with Charlotte a most delightful day M^r
Wm Helyar called at Tollard before we left it – I have sent E: S: a
letter which I hope may be the means of our going to Dear Field Place
in our way to Town

Thurs 22   The Miss Frasers & Mr Far[quharson] came here in the
morning Charlotte & myself took a most pleasent walk in
Eastbury[D] park-

Fri 23   C- & I walked home from G[unville] Received on my return a
letter from E[lizabeth] just such a one as I wished for   Tom & H-
came here to day after first going to Fern-

Sat 24   Tom & his Wife left us C[atherine] Benett came she seems to
look rather grumpy-

Sun 25   The Shelleys have sent us word they shall be most happy to see
us, but I fear owing to some fancy my Mother has in her head we
shall not go for which I feel the greatest sorrow as I had made up my
mind for the pleasure of spending a few days at Dear Field-Place
heard from dear W^m who is comfortably settled on board the Scipion
– walked after Church with C. Benett & Charlotte & were caught in
the Rain-

Mon 26   Miss C. Benett took leave of us & returned home but to our
surprise returned again to Dinner, as her Sister was not at home to
receive her

22 Mar. Eastbury Park was at Gunville.
25 Mar. The *Scipion* was a large warship with 74 guns. (The Court and City Register
for 1807, p.136.)

Tues 27 < ------ > at last they say they will go to Field- Place for one
day. I have written to tell E- of it, for it makes me so happy

Wed 28 Thank goodness C[atherine] B[enett] has at last taken her
departure. Bysshe has sent C- & me Zastrozzi as it is come out

Thurs 29 Went to Aunt Jacksons & Fern, Charles does nothing but
abuse B[ysshe's] Romance. I believe he does it the more because he
thinks it makes him appear a great man, but I think it makes him
appear very illnatured to critisise it so very much

Fri 30 Mrs Penruddocke,[B] Hen:^ta & Miss Fraser called here from
Gunville M^rs P is more romantic than ever – Mr Hamilton Dined &
slept here

Sat 31 Packed up   they have given Charlotte & me such a little bit of a
Trunk

APRIL

Sunday 1 Tom called here & he told us he has given up Gunville, M^r
Napier dined here & made us laugh by telling us the Prince of Wales
asked him to come & see him & called him his little Fox hunting
friend

Mon 2 Left Tollard for my Aunt Grove's called at Compton[D] in our
way M^rs P[enruddocke] did not talk quite so much about Napoleon

Tues 3 Stayed at Netherhampton Charlotte read a little of Raymond
& Agnes to me which I like very much indeed–

Wed 4 left Aunt Groves & got to Mr Bromleys[B] at Southampton
they both look very well & glad to see us, Mr Lowdon dined here he
looks very ill –

Thurs 5 We all walked upon the Key   afterwards Charles & myself
walked in the Town Waddington came here & Mr Lowdon went
away–

Fri 6 A Mr Hughs & Mr Skifington Dined here the latter was very

27 Mar. One line cancelled
28 Mar. *Zastrozzi* was a short Gothic novel, the first of Shelley's published prose
works. It was published in London by G. Wilkie and J. Robinson, 57 Paternoster
Row. In his diary Shelley wrote on 15 January – '30 copies of Zastrozzi to come – not
to forget Harriet'
1 Apr. The Prince of Wales had set up his own hunting establishment locally, at
Crichel House, so that he could hunt in Cranborne Chase
3 Apr. *Raymond & Agnes* was a melodrama by Matthew G. Lewis.
4 Apr. The first day of travel to Netherhampton from Tollard was about sixteen miles;
the second to Southampton about seventeen miles; the third to Little Park about ten
miles; the fourth to Field Place was fifty-odd miles – a total of almost a hundred miles.

entertaining, the former fancied he had been my Fathers Tutor at Oxford

Sat 7 Left Southampton & got to Little Park, found them all well Little G:G: a fine little fellow, Dear little Emma is very much improved –

Sun 8 Played with Dear little Emma & John [Waddington] walked out with Charlotte & so got through the Day–

Mon 9 Wrote to my Dearest Louisa Played with Emma, very wet & were obliged to amuse ourselves as we could

Tues 10 Another wet day I seldom go near Matty for which she told me to day she supposed *had affronted me* she had affronted me

Wed 11 It being fine we walked out & talked of the pleasures of Tollard   afterwards Charlotte read Joseph Andrews to me –

Thurs 12 Went in the Chaise with [sister] Emma & my Niece afterwards walked with C – Mr Stanhope called here played with the dear Children, played at whist &c as usual

Fri 13 Heard the first thing in the morning that Dear W^m was here it makes me so happy to see him again I am afraid he cant go to F[ield] P[lace] with us

Sat 14 A large party dined here Dear W^m says he shall go to F-P- with us which I am glad of, How happy I feel at the idea of going there < ------ >

Sun 15 Went to Wickham Church   afterwards called on Mrs Rusham She has two of the prettiest little girls I ever saw–

Mon 16 left L.P. very early got to Dear F.P. < ------ > *they* are all very glad to see us. I can not tell what to make of it very strange

Tues 17 Still more odd, Walked to Horsham saw the Old House St Irvyne had a long conversation but more perplexed than ever walked in the evening to Strood by moonlight

---

7 Apr. Little G[eorge] G[rove] Waddington, who was only a month old.

10 Apr. Matty may be the Madeline Waddington mentioned in the entry for July 23 below. She was probably the sister of John Waddington, Emma's husband.

14 Apr. One plus lines cancelled.

16 Apr. One plus lines cancelled.

17 Apr. 'St. Irvyne' was Hill Place, a reputedly Elizabethan house belonging to Lady Irwin or Irvine, currently in ruins and being acquired by the Duke of Norfolk. It lay south-east of Field Place. Strood was an estate in the opposite direction. Both places had romantic associations for Bysshe and Harriet, deriving from moonlight walks at some previous time. The title of Shelley's second novel was *St. Irvyne*.

Harriet's perplexity is not explained. Her happiness in Shelley's company is not in doubt. Her brother Charles, who had not seen Shelley since their early schooldays, commented later that 'Bysshe was at that time [April 1810] more attached to my sister Harriet than I can express'.

Wed 18 This morning we went before we left the pleasentest party in
the world for the most unpleasent to Horsham that is E[lizabeth]
B[ysshe] & my Brothers & self   I still know not what is meant We
reached Cuckfield to Dinner What a disagreable place after the one
we have just left

Thurs 19 Walked in Col. S[ergison's] Park very pretty I daresay but
my thoughts wont let me think about it

Fri 20 Went to Church heard a most excellent Sermon saw the Col: he
dined here was very entertaining. Charlotte is half in love with him
I think he drinks too much

Sat 21 left that tiresome M^{rs} P[ilfold] & got to Johns found him & his
cat perfectly well & very happy to see us as we are to see him, My
faculties are all whirling round as they always are in this disagreable
Place—

Sun 22 Charles took a walk with Charlotte & me into High Holborn
we soon found that was not a fit place for us, Mr Wm Fraser called
here   called on the Longs & they called on us—

Mon 23 Lady Fraser called here, we went & Paid Morning visits to
Mrs Long Mrs Lee & Mrs Green, after Dinner Charlotte John
Charles & myself walked in the Fields—

Tues 24 Charlotte & myself walked out & had a long Chat We then
went out in the Chaise & made purchases I am sorry to say my
Mother was very unwell all the time We are pleased with our
Bargains we have bought

Wed 25 We made morning visits on Miss Packington & Dear M^{rs}
Portman. Dear Aunt Shelley & my Cousins came Mr Wm Fraser
dined with us & we spent a most pleasent day—

Thurs 26 Walked in the Fields *with dear Bysshe* then went shopping
& had great fun left Aunt & Mama at Mrs Bartons & they came
home in a Hackney Coach a shocking dirty one   Aunt S- says she
shall send for a Chain & Chain us to her – Went to the Play M^r W^m
Fraser with us

Fri 27 Walked out < ------ > *Percy* then went shopping went to the
Play   C. my Father & Mother came home directly as the Play was
over   P, Mama & myself sat up till the rest of the party came home

18 Apr. At Cuckfield they were the guests of Harriet's uncle, Captain John Pilfold R.N.
19 Apr. Colonel Warden Sergison inherited Cuckfield Place in 1806
21 Apr. Her brother John's London residence was 49 Lincoln's Inn Fields.
25 Apr. Harriet's cousins were Elizabeth and Percy Bysshe Shelley.
27 Apr. It will be noted that from this time on Harriet calls Shelley Percy instead of
Bysshe.

& had a most delightful conversation

Sat 28 Went shopping with the Shelleys in a Hackney Coach < ------ >
We staid at home Elizabeth as noisy as ever

Sun 29 Went to St Pauls in time to meet every body coming out Two
Jack Tars said I was painted so Aunt S- said – Went afterwards in
Ken[sington] Gardens & saw the Persian Ambassador there   hurt
my foot, a dinner party

Mon 30 Staid at home all day on account of my Foot the rest of the
party went to the Play all but Mama & Percy

MAY

Tuesday 1 *Percy &* I staid in doors the rest went out We all staid at
home in the evening I played & they all danced Eliz[th] talks & is in
as great spirits as ever

Wed 2 < ------ > I staid at home < ------ > my foot still being bad,
however I went to the Play in the Evening & liked it well enough–

Thurs 3 All the Party went out but me *& Dearest P.* Tom Medwin[A]
dined here   went to the Opera I hate it more than ever, *so does P–*

Fri 4 Staid in again < ------ > , Dined at M[r] [William] Longs a most
stupid ES has told me something that kills me with laughing but
which hinders her from coming to Tollard I am sorry to say–

Sat 5 < ------ > The Shelleys left us   very sorry

Sun 6 Went out to pay visits walked in the square staid at home in the
evening < ------ >

Mon 7 Graham came here & gave me my lesson in Music, much
surprised by the arrival of my two Uncle Pilfolds. Uncle Jem[A] sang
to us after supper–

Tues 8 Wrote walked in the Fields M[r] Long[A] M.P. & Wife &
daughters dined here   like Miss Flora very much she suits me

Wed 9 Went & called at Mrs Greys < ------ > came there yesterday

28 Apr. Two lines cancelled.

2 May. Second cancellation one line.

4 May. Two lines cancelled.

5 May. Seven lines cancelled.

7 May. Edward Fergus Graham, a youthful musician and protégé of Shelley's
parents. He sometimes executed commissions from Shelley to purchase and despatch
books. The "two Uncle Pilfolds" were Captain John and James Pilfold.

8 May. Ingpen and Jones both mis-read M.P. (Member of Parliament) as 'Mr P.' The
wife and daughters belonged not to this fictitious Mr. P but to Richard Godolphin
Long (1761-1835) of Rood Ashton, Trowbridge, Wilts, MP for Wilts 1806-1818. Harriet refers to him elsewhere as 'the Member'. Miss Flora was one of his daughters.

9 May. Two words illegible and 'Greys' is doubtful.

My Mother ill with a cold   went shopping dined at M^r
Whindhams[B] saw there Capt. Heathcote who is going to take the
Persian Ambassador home in the Lion   My Uncles went into the
City My Mother too unwell to go out at all

Thurs 10   Went out shopping as usual very stupid *heard from P* they
all went to see Plays in the evening but my Mother & me our colds
prevented us–

Fri 11   We went to the water coloured Exhibition some figures by
McFee & landscapes by Glover very well done indeed   stayed at
home practiced a difficult piece of music for Graham

Sat 12   I staid at home writing   Charlotte & Uncle [John] Pilfold
walked together   My Mother & Aunt Grove went together to the
Exhibition Staid at home this evening John Charles & Uncle went
to the play at half price–

Sun 13   Staid in all the morning < ------ > in the Evening Mr Shelley
came here he looks very unwell < ------ > Uncle & him shook hands
& were friends during the time he staid–

Mon 14   Walked to Bond street with Uncle Papa &c, a party to dinner
Breretons & Mr Helyar Aunt Grove & Mr Shelley the latter so
pleasent, I am quite happy to see him so   he gave me a letter from
Elizth –

Tues 15   Went in the carriage   Graham came & we stayed at home in
the evening

Wed 16 Went in the evening to Mr Longs Mr Wm Helyar there heard very
good singing by Lady Bayers & Miss Williamson

Thurs 17   M^r & Mrs Green Aunt Grove Miss Cluse &c dined here
Charlotte John Charles & myself went to a Mrs Jenkins Ball
Danced & found it very pleasent

Fri 18   Graham came   Mrs Hamilton & Children & Mr Shelley the
latter in great spirits. Graham made me try to sing, he says I have a
voice but I do not believe it–

Sat 19   We left London Friday   Oh how sorry am I to leave Dear John

---

11 May. John Glover (1767-1849), landscape painter, president of the Water-colour
Society in 1815.

13 May. This entry shows that Shelley's father and Captain Pilfold had recently quar-
relled.

19 May. One plus lines cancelled. The remainder of this long entry, beginning with the
date, is on the "House Expences" page facing the entries for May 20-26 four plus lines
cancelled.

Charlotte spent almost three months with her uncle at Cuckfield. It was hoped that
Colonel Sergison, a widower, might propose marriage to her. The "Local" means the
Local Militia.

Charlotte & Capt P[ilfold] set off together to Cuckfield I am sorry
she is gone but hope she will like her visit – Saturday 19th We slept
at Overton & got to Tollard to day < ------ > we dined at Salisbury
with Tom & Henrietta who are at Mr Frenche's Lodging's, T: being
out with the Local – The last Evening we spent in Town which was
Friday Mr Shelley dined with us < ------ > (see footnote on page 77)

Sun 20 Went to Church heard M^r J Helyars delightful Preaching he came
here after Church, I am sorry to say they are going to reside at Bath

Mon 21 Went to Fern with my Mother in the Pheaton she begins to
croak again about the building Mary Dimmer pretty well Charles &
I walked out for a little while the only happiness I have here

Tues 22 Charles read to me in the morning Milton. We walked together
after Dinner, after tea we sat in my room & he read Romeo & Juliet
to me –

Wed 23 My Father & Mother went to Farnham Charles rode to
Donhead I stayed at home alone after dinner walked with Charles,
< ------ >

Thurs 24 My Mother & I went in the Pheaton to Pytt house Mr Benett
is looking better than we expected to see him, the Miss B & M^r W^m
Benett there Saw the Children M^{rs} B gone to Bath Mr Wake we met
there who came back with us a great bore

Fri 25 Called at Wardour & Mrs Cookes the last time I fear of seeing
Lady A[rundell][B] My Aunt Jackson went to Wardour with us Miss
Laura & Miss Julia[B] were there & were glad to see us

Sat 26 < ------ > Charles dined at Aunt Jacksons I walked with my
Father & Mother to Ashcombe Miss C Benett called here in the
morning – saw in the newspaper the Death of Mrs Heathfield,

Sun 27 Went to Church heard a most excellent sermon M^r J: Helyar
came here after the service & told us M^{rs} H: had got a rash I think he
has learnt to Prose, walked with Charles on the green in the evening
read one of Stern's Sermons < ------ >

Mon 28 Went to Fern to meet my Aunt Jackson & Arabella, during the
time we were there a fire broke out at the Glove owing to the timely
assistance most of the Poor mans goods were saved, My Dear Father
with his usual goodness went & did every thing he could & saved the
Stables & outer Buildings but the Inn was entirely burnt down – but
fortunately being in the day time no one was burnt I am very glad to

23 May one plus lines cancelled.
26 May three plus lines cancelled.
27 May three lines cancelled. Laurence Sterne, *Sermons* (7 vols., 1760-1769).

hear poor Mr Westeridge will not lose much by it, tho Lord Arundell will which I am sorry for –

Tues 29 employed myself as usual in the morning Charles dined at Aunt J[ackson's] Mrs Heathfield is dead & left it all to my Uncles

Wed 30 Went to Fern very hot read sentimental Journey there   on our return found C[atherine] Benett she stayed & walked in the evening

Thurs 31 Miss C B stayed here My Mother heard from M^{rs} H to say Dear L[ouisa] had the Hooping Cough & is very unwell   I am in such a fright for her—

JUNE

Friday 1 My Father & Mother went to Bath for Dearest L[ouisa] Miss C B went home & Charles dined at Donhead, quite alone had a letter from Dear Louisa she is better thank Goodness I am so glad for that comfort

Sat 2 Tom called here & stayed some time Charles went to Gunville with him & so I dined alone again, & walked as I did yesterday from 5 till 8 by myself

Sun 3 Charles & I went to Church Mr J. Helyar walked to the House with us & then went away. after dinner walked out made C[harles] write to Percy

Mon 4 Expected my Father Mother & Dearest Louisa home but they did not come, Tom dined with us, he has taken Littleton[D] Charles would walk out without his Hat, all I could say to him.

Tues 5 My Dearest Louisa is come home & looks better than I expected to see her   took a solitary walk as usual *by myself* after dinner

Wed 6 Dear Louisa I think is very weak but change of air will do her good My Father & Charles drank tea at Gunville Tom & Hen^t go to Cwm Elen[D] tomorrow

Thurs 7 Dear Louisa & I dined together in the drawing room Mr Wilkins has been here & rather frightened us about her he says she must not eat meat

Fri 8 Dear Louisa was kept in bed all day but is much better as her fever is gone My Father with his troop went to Devizes to quel a

---

30 May. Laurence Sterne, *A Sentimental Journey* (2 vols., 1768).

31 May. Louisa was at the school at Bath. Jones's identification of 'Mrs H' as Mrs Helyar is surprising as, four days earlier, she was reported to be at home unwell and therefore unlikely to travel to Bath and visit Louisa's school. In a letter in April to brother John, Louisa had mentioned a 'Mrs H' as a member of the school community.

mutiny[N] there amongst the local Militia we are anxious for him to
return safe—

Sat 9 Dear Louisa we think better, Mrs Gordon drank tea here,
Charles & myself walked till it was almost dark – Dear Louisa told
me she liked me to be with her

Sun 10 Dear Louisa is still very unwell & M[r] W[ilkins] bled her which
rather frightened her, My Father returned safe from Devizes

Mon 11 M[r] W- has been here & pronounces Louisa much better but
thought it necessary to bleed her again, I am so glad to hear the
Dear little thing is better I long for her to be quite well again – She is
quiet

Tues 12 Dear Louisa's fever as high as ever they sent for D[r] Bearwood
who bled her as M[r] W has three times before   I sat up with my
Dearest Sister tonight

Wed 13 Dearest Louisa is better to day & we have the greatest hopes
She was bled for the fourth time to day My dear Father quite cryed
with joy to think Dear Louisa was nearly out of danger

Thurs 14 Dear Louisa still continues better which makes us all so
happy, M[r] W[m] Benett called here in the morning & they asked him
to dine he told us John Gordons arm was wasted away almost to
nothing & that they were going to send him to Town for the best
advice

Fri 15 Much the same as usual Louisa is better thank God—

Sat 16 Dear Louisa had a slight return of fever which frightened us but
it went away very soon, M[r] Hamilton came & dined & went away

Sun 17 Went to Church Dear Louisa was worse again & M[r] Wilkins
bled her again, I sat up with her all night – *I hope & pray that my
Dearest Sister during her illness at least—*

Mon 18 We still have hopes of the recovery of my Dear little Sister

Tues 19 In the morning great hope but at four oclock the Dear little
Angel was released from her Pain What a lesson of Fortitude &
resignation has she left us all   I hope it may please God that I never
may forget it as long as I live

Wed 20 My Aunt Grove & Aunt Jackson came the former stays with
us till after the Dear remains are gone

Thurs 21 My Aunt Grove is so good & at times my Dear Mother is in
Spirits Aunt Jackson dined here

Fri 22 My Dearest Louisa was put into her coffin where I hope she will
  < ------ >

22 June. Two lines partly blotted out and cancelled.

Sat 23 how *solemn* & holy we feel yet it is a happiness to know Dear
   Louisa < ------ >
Sun 24 The last day My Poor little Sisters remains will be above
   ground–
Mon 25 She was buried to day & my Dear Father went as chief
   Mourner My Aunt Grove is very kind & does every thing in her
   power to comfort us & I am happy to say she in some degree has
   made us all bear our loss better   Dear Charlotte how I long to see
   you
Tues 26 Heard from my Dear Sister C & H Tre[ll] I am sorry to hear
   Dear Tom too is ill
Wed 27 Went to Fern in our way to Netherhampton Saw Mary
   [Dimmer] who is looking dreadfully ill Poor Old Soul
Thurs 28 Went to Wilton[D] with Mama & Aunt Grove & walked in
   the Park – My Father came to look for us but we did not meet them
Fri 29 M[r] & M[rs] Sam[l] Long[A] dined here – they look both very well–
Sat 30 I went with Aunt Grove to Salisbury to buy some things for my
   Mother–

JULY

Sunday 1 Wet & a thunder storm could not get to Church & my
   Father read Prayers & a Sermon in the Evening
Mon 2 My Father & Charles went to Fern & saw Aunt Jackson & all
   the family there–
Tues 3 left Netherhampton for Muddiford[D] as we went through
   Ringwood I thought on Poor dear Louisa, as that is where her friend
   Mary Jessup lives   I cannot say much for the beauty of this Place
   [i.e. Muddiford]
Wed 4 We all walked on the Sands the Tregonwells are here & very
   kind to us We went after dinner to see a Place M[r] T has bought &
   talks of building on called bourn it is very barren but a pretty sea
   view
Thurs 5 I bathed this morning   Yesterday we were much surprised as
   Dear W[m] arrived
Fri 6 Walked before breakfast   M[rs] & Miss Tre[ll] dined with us &
   then drank tea with their friends the Hobsons   afterwards we all
   walked on the Sands–
Sat 7 Bathed Dear Helen went with me We went to Hordell Cliff[D]

23 June. One line cancelled.
   4 July. Mr Tregonwell's initiative founded the town of Bournemouth.

before Dinner in the Carriage with the Tregonwell[s] Aunt Grove
&c, a most beautiful view from it–

Sun 8 Waked at seven by a tremendous Thunder storm, We went after
Dinner to the Lookout with the Tre[ll] & ourselves

Mon 9 The Tregonwells left us, which we are very sorry Walked with
Helen & my brothers on the sands before she went

Tues 10 Went with my Father & Brothers to choose a Lodging for the
Waddingtons who I am happy to say are coming here, Dear W[m] left
us–

Wed 11 It rained so could not walk out, Charles & my Aunt had a
little squabble on the subject of M[r] W[m] long a very tender [subject] one
always with my Aunt–

Thurs 12 Wrote to my Aunt Shelley went in the Carriage on the
Sands, we have taken a Hous belonging to Lady Stewart- for the
Waddingtons

Fri 13 It blew so hard we could not walk went after Dinner to
XChurch & bought Toys for Emma & John

Sat 14 Wrote to B & Eliz[th] Shelley Called on M[rs] Pen Whyndham[B]
who I like very much she told us a melancholy story of the Bank at
Salisbury being broke in consequence of which many are ruined–

Sun 15 My Dear Father & Mother went with Charles to my Aunt
Jacksons. Left alone with Aunt Grove, Went to Church twice with
M[rs] Pen Whyndham

Mon 16 My Dear Father & Mother & the Waddingtons came the
Children are much grown My Mother is better for her Jaunt–

Tues 17 The Waddingtons spent the day with us, talk to Emma of our
late sad loss–

Wed 18 Walked on the sands & helped to pick up shells for Emma
who was delighted Received a letter from Miss Bury[C] a friend of
my dear sister L[ouisa]

Thurs 19 Went to bathe. Dear little Emma accompanied me & was a
little alarmed   the gentlemen went to the Isle of Wight–

Fri 20 Walked on the Sands a little Boy gave Emma some Shells & she
made him a fine Curtesey–

12 July. Lady Stuart was the widow of Sir Charles Stuart KB; their son Lord Stuart de
Rothesay built Highcliffe Castle, adjacent to Mudeford.

14 July. The Henry Penruddocke Wyndhams lived at Salisbury. The failure of the
bank of Brickwood, Raine and Co. in London "produced considerable loss and incon-
venience" in Salisbury. The local firm of Bowles, Ogden and Co. which was "in
intimate connection" with this bank had to suspend payments, and so, too, "Mr.
Burrough's" bank. (Hoare, Wiltshire, VI, 558.)

18 July. This Emma was sister Emma's small daughter.

Sat 21 Walked on the Sands, bathed &c as usual–

Sun 22 My Aunt Grove Mama & myself went to Church at Xt
Church   afterwards walked round it & found it very well worth
seeing

Mon 23 My Dear Father very unwell in his bowels *left Xt Church*
Madeline Waddington returned to Tollard with us Emma & the
Children went to Little Park–

Tues 24 Mr Wilkins came to see my Dear Father who is much better
we all went to see Fern which is much got on   My Father is over
tired by going to Fern

Wed 25 Charles & Waddington went to the Salisbury Races & slept
at Netherhampton we were to have gone to Fern after dinner but the
rain prevented us–

Thurs 26 Charles returned & was much pleased with the Races. My
F.M. & myself went to Fern in the evening found Poor old Mary
[Dimmer] very unwell I fear she will not live over the year

Fri 27 My Mother does all she can to keep up her ^spirits but finds it
very difficult sometimes

Sat 28 Rained so we could not go to Fern we ^are all reading Saint
Sebastian which my Father bought at Muddiford

Sun 29 Went to Church in the morning – Charles Jackson dined &
slept here   heard from Charlotte who I believe we shall not see [for]
some time She is very happy where she is she says

Mon 30 Mr Hamilton came here, in the Evening wrote to dear
Charlotte.

Tues 31 Went to Fern in the morning, found Mary Dimmer better,
much disappointed the letter bag did not come as we expected to
have heard from Dear George–

AUGUST

Wednesday 1 Went to Fern in our way to Netherhampton & received
letters from Dear Geo: who is quite well–

Thurs 2 Got to Little Park & found them all well we dined at
Southampton

Fri 3 Walked in the Garden played with Emma & John &c as usual
here

Sat 4 Wet so could not walk did much the same as usual–

Sun 5 Emma & the Gentlemen went to Church My Mother & I staid
at home not being quite well–

23 July. Madeline was probably John Waddington's sister. See entry for April 10

Mon 6 The Gentlemen went to Portsmouth & went on Board the Donegal to see W[m] M[r] Cook the Clergyman called here

Tues 7 Wrote letters & walked with my Mother & Emma &cc–

Wed 8 < ------ > called on Lady Mary Long to day they have improved Preshaw[D] by new furnishing it very well

Thurs 9 Lady Mary told us yesterday of the death of Poor Lady Mildmay, which I was sorry to hear altho' I know so little of her & pity her friends very much

Fri 10 Packed up & played with Emma & John–

Sat 11 Left L:P: & reached Aunt Grove's to Dinner had a very wet drive in the Pheaton from Little Park–

Sun 12 Staid at Netherhampton & walked to the Race Course & went to Church–

Mon 13 Much rejoiced at the return of Dear Charlotte & George the latter is much improved, we went to Fern in our way to Tollard & found the House with the Roof putting on, & Tho[s] Shere[C] has been married since we left home

Tues 14 Charlotte & myself very busy in the morning unpacking. M[r] Hamilton dined here George made us all laugh he is so droll

Wed 15 So Wet we could not go to Fern George went to Weymouth to see William–

Thurs 16 George returned from Weymouth but without seeing W[m] as his ship was sailed Charlotte & my Mother went to Fern–

Fri 17 We all went to Fern & in our way met M[rs] Gordon M[rs] Benett & Miss Partridge[C] coming to call here they all returned to Fern with us & we shewed them the House &cc

Sat 18 My Mother & myself called on M[rs] J Helyar but not being at home we proceeded on to Fern – Aunt Grove came – George as noisy as ever

Sun 19 Went to Church M[r] & M[rs] J Helyar dined here & were very pleasent–

Mon 20 Went to Fern with Aunt Grove in her way home Charlotte & myself walked with my Father round the Plantation Mary Dimmer moved from the Kitchen to the room over the Dairy

Tues 21 Went with my Mother to M[rs] Cooke & Fern when we came back found Helen Tregonwell here & her brother. George & Charles dined at Aunt Jacksons

Wed 22 Charlotte & I walked to the Shop H.T. & my Mother went to Fern M[r] Eason & M[rs] J. Helyar dined here–

8 Aug. Two plus lines cancelled.

Thurs 23 Mrs Farquharson dined here   walked in the Evening, George very rude–

Fri 24 Charlotte Helen & myself walked by ourselves

Sat 25 Helen left us   in the Evening Charlotte & myself took a pleasent walk with my Brothers–

Sun 26 Went to Church   afterwards went to Fern with my brothers < ------ > –

Mon 27 My Father & Mother went to Langton the rest of the Party staid at home & were very merry dancing & singing

Tues 28 My Father & Mother returned from Langton were they saw only Mrs Farquharson–

Wed 29 Went to Fern walked with Charlotte up White Sheet Hill[D] where Fern House looked very well   the Miss Benetts drank tea here & Mr Hamilton came in the Evening

Thurs 30 Wrote to Lucy Bury[C] *Percy* &c My Mother & Susan went to Fern–

Fri 31 Went to Fern Charlotte & myself walked round the Plantation & met with a snake, which frightened us

SEPTEMBER

Saturday 1 In our way to Fern met M^rs J Helyar. Aunt Jackson & Arabella met us at Fern, & stayed there all the time we did

Sun 2 Went to Langton to Dinner Mr Hamilton Capt Donalson M^r R Parker & Mr James Fraser there

Mon 3 Charles Poney very ill so he could not go to the Tollard Hunt we returned from Langton

Tues 4 Miss Hughes & Miss Cooke came George more noisy than ever – we danced after tea – Sir Arthur Paget called here   We Ladies did not see him which as he is so Handsome perhaps was fortunate

Wed 5 As Charlotte & I were walking in front of the House Lord Rivers[B] rode up I only could perceive that he had got Grey Locks C- took him for Mr Beckford[B] of Steepleton

Thurs 6 All went to Fern but Charlotte & me, heard that W^m is going to the East Indies again

Fri 7 Charlotte & I walked on the Down with Daniel[C] behind us Dear W^m is sailed for the East Indies

Sat 8 Took a long walk with my sister Daniel & Tommy behind us

26 Aug. One plus lines cancelled.

4 Sept. Sir Arthur Paget (1771-1840), diplomatist; brother of Sir Henry William Paget, 1st Marquis of Anglesey. From 1807 to 1809 he was ambassador to Turkey.

8 Sept. Tommy, apparently a small child, has not been identified.

Tommy fell down two or three times & we were rude enough to laugh at him

Sun 9 Walked after Church to the Top of Ashcombe Hill laughed at Geo: because he said this was Monday by the Nautical day & proved it so–

Mon 10 Miss Hughes & Miss Cooke left us, It rained which prevented us from going to Fern–

Tues 11 Wet &c &c &c &c

Wed 12 Went to Zeals.[D] Mrs Chaffin [Grove] [A] received us with her usual form

Thurs 13 Walked to Mere with my brothers & sister. George was nearly running over us being so riotous he nearly spoilt the Musical Clock

Fri 14 left Zeals & met Tom & his Wife & John at Fern. Miss C. Benett also met us there–

Sat 15 the Building at Fern completely covered in & the People supped in the House & enjoyed themselves very much–

Sun 16 Walked to the top of Ashcombe Hill with Charlotte < ------ >

Mon 17 Received the Poetry of Victor & Cazire,[N] Charlotte offended & with reason as I think they have done very wrong in publishing what they have of her

Tues 18 Mrs J. Helyar went to Fern with my Mother   My sister & I walked in the Chase escorted by Tommy

Wed 19 Dined at Farnham[D] Met M^r & Mrs Bingham & Son[C] M^{rs} J Helyar as entertaining as ever–

Thurs 20 Went to Mrs Cookes met the Miss Lipscombes & had a very pleasent day & a dance in the Evening

Fri 21 Returned from Donhead & Brought the Miss L- & Miss Cooke to Fern to shew them the House   M^{rs} J Helyar dined with us M^r J H. too unwell the former did nothing but make us laugh

Sat 22 Returned to Mrs Cookes dined with the Fletchers[C] & a dance in the Evening. Mrs F- made us laugh by telling us her Son had a swelling on his knee which was merely a puff & that she M^r & Miss F. had all had huff.

16 Sept. Two lines cancelled.

17 Sept. *Original Poetry* by Victor and Cazire was privately printed at Shelley's expense and distributed by a London publisher. 'Victor' was Shelley's pseudonym, 'Cazire' Elizabeth's. Shelley's love-poems to Harriet written during the summer were included, and there was a plagiarism which was detected and caused the book's withdrawal. What offended the Groves was a letter in verse addressed to Harriet by Elizabeth which referred to Charlotte's lengthy sojourn at Cuckfield in crude terms which implied husband-hunting.

Sun 23 After going to Church & hearing a most delightful Sermon from Mr Lipscom[be] returned home much pleased with our visit & very sorry the Miss Lip- have left the Country as we are all much pleased with them–

Mon 24 Went to Fern in the Pheaton with George & my Mother. Henrietta & Tom dined & slept here

Tues 25 Walked from Fern to call on the Miss Benetts at Berwick My Father had a letter from M^r S[helley] which I am sorry for, as it gives more trouble.

Wed 26 Went to Fern met Mrs Cooke & party there walked with Miss Lipscombe round the plantation

Thurs 27 as usual went to Fern walked round by the Glove & the White Cottage with my Sister, met M^r & M^{rs} R Arundell[B] in their Gig in our way home

Fri 28 Walked from Fern to Wardour with Charlotte–

Sat 29 Walked at Fern &c as usual   in the evening my Father & John entered into an argument

Sun 30 Walked in the Chase after Church with my Sister & Brothers, John went to Gunville–

OCTOBER

Monday 1 Charlotte & myself did not go to Fern which we were glad of, John returned from Gunville

Tues 2 Went to Fern Mr Hamilton there   my brothers returned so late from shooting that we began to be frightened Mr Eason dined here

Wed 3 called at the Cottage in our way to Fern the Shepherds daughter was in less pain

Thurs 4 Called on Lord & Lady Arundell at Wardour. We saw her pretty little girl & she shewed us her drawings   we met M^r & Mrs Benett there

Fri 5 Charlotte & myself stayed at home & laughed very much making a Comb Bonnet–

Sat 6 Went to Fern & my Mother very nearly left us behind there

Sun 7 After Church John & Charles left us We were all most sorry to part with them–

Mon 8 in our way to Fern met Lord & Lady Arundell coming here they returned & went to Fern with us

Tues 9 Went to Pyt house called in our way on Mrs Cooke, Mrs Burlton & M^r & Mrs Charles Benett[B] met us & Mr Bowles[B] who

27 Sept. The R. Arundells lived at Ashcombe.

was very entertaining.

Wed 10 Lady Parker[B] & Mrs Still &c called on us, Lord & Lady & Mr Arundell & the Gordons dined here, & we spent a very pleasent day

Thurs 11 Went to a fête Champetre at Mrs Peter Stills,[B] saw M^rs & Miss Dobson Lady Parker &c & her little Girl   thought M^rs D- a very pleasent woman, returned to Tollard by 5 Oclock

Fri 12 Went to Fern & were agreably surprised by seeing Miss Popham Mrs Warre & Mrs Whindham   Miss Popham returned with us to Tollard–

Sat 13 Went to Dinton[D] with my Sister & Miss Popham, on our arrival found only Mrs Warre there as Mrs Whindham was gone to London to her Father who was very ill   Spent a very pleasent day with Mrs Warre who I think very pleasent   Saw her three Children & all the little Whindhams who are very fine

Sun 14 Mrs Warre set off at 9 Oclock, My Sister & myself left Dinton at eleven, found M^r J: Helyar here on our arrival–

Mon 15 My Mother went to Fern & brought Miss Hughes & Miss Lipscomb here–

Tues 16 Charlotte & myself went as far as Ashcombe in our way to Fern & then returned as it rained which wetted us through before we got home

Wed 17 It rained the whole day so we were obliged to stay in doors all day   in the evening we went on with the Children of the Abbey–

Thurs 18 My Mother & Miss Hughes went to Fern My Sister Miss Lipscum & myself walked out between the showers–

Fri 19 Went to the Gordons in our way took Miss H- & Miss L. to Mrs Cookes – Aunt Jackson & Arabella dined at the Gordons

Sat 20 Rained all the morning read M^rs [Maria] Edgeworths Tales M^r & Mrs Benett came to dinner in the Evening. looked at some drawings in a sketch book–

Sun 21 Returned to Tollard My Mother heard from Aunt S. It rained very hard the whole way home–

Mon 22 Drew an Old woman   M^r J Helyar called here   went on in the Evening with the Children of the Abbey

Tues 23 Did not go to Fern as my Mother thought it would rain, went on in the evening with our Novel–

Wed 24 George went to Littleton & we went to Fern where we met M^rs C[harles] & the Miss Benetts   we shewed them the House & then walked to Berwick with them

9 Oct. Mrs Burlton. Ingpen and Jones have 'Burton' incorrectly.

Thurs 25 George returned from Littleton to hunt with my Father, we called on Mrs J. Helyar –

Fri 26 Rode one of my Fathers Horses to Fern, met Mrs Cooke & party there Geo: returned to Donhead with them

Sat 27 My Father & George went out hunting & met their friend Mr Adams, heard from John–

Sun 28 Very Wet & my Father read Prayers at home < ------ >

Mon 29 Tom & Henrietta came here both grown fat & looking very well

Tues 30 Henrietta & Mama went to Fern, Charlotte & I walked our hour–

Wed 31 My Mother & Hen^t went to Rushmore the latter delighted with that place–

NOVEMBER

Thursday 1 My Mother & Henrietta went to Hanley[D] to call on Mrs Adams & Mrs Mills who where neither of them at home   Lady Arundell sent us an invitation to come to Wardour

Fri 2 Mr Adams was to have dined here but sent word his wife had family pains–

Sat 3 staid in all day on account of the weather–

Sun 4 Went to Church Mr J.H so ill he could scarcely go through the service Mr Adams dined here

Mon 5 My Brother & Sister left us & George went with them

Tues 6 We went to Wardour where we met M^r & M^{rs} R Arundell M^r & Mrs Dotter & Miss Benson My Father & Mother slept in the State Bedroom Lady Arundell was kind enough to invite C[harlotte] & me to stay some time with her–

Wed 7 After Breakfast we left W[ardour] & went to Mr Longs [at] Rood Ashton & found the House more comfortable than Wardour

Thurs 8 Rained the whole day so C. read out a Novel to us which was a very stupid one

Fri 9 Came home which we are none of us sorry for, tho' we spent a very pleasent day at Mr Longs

Sat 10 a most shocking wet day read the Reformist in the Evening–

Sun 11 George returned from Littleton, M^r J Helyar preached & to our great surprise ^{is} as well as ever he was–

Mon 12 My Father & George went out hunting & in the Evening we read our Novel as usual

5 Nov. The brother and sister[in-law] were Tom and Henrietta.
10 Nov. Sarah Green, *The Reformist!!!* A Serio-Comic-Political Novel (2 vols., 1810).

Tues 13 Went to Fern to meet my Aunt & Miss Pakington   George
went to Mrs Cookes

Wed 14 Rained the whole day so my Father & Brother could not go
out hunting–

Thurs 15 Walked &c as usual

Fri 16 Went on with our stupid novel we are reading, called Edmund
of the forest–

Sat 17 Took a walk with my Sister & we fancied we heard a great
noise like the falling of armour–

Sun 18 M^r & M^{rs} J Helyar called here, & they told us the Helyars
were arrived at Sedghill–

Mon 19 Tom called here & gave us a long account of M^r
Farquharson's Lady who he has seen at Cadstock

Tues 20 Sent letters to W^m in India, M^r & Mrs Gordon came here
whom we are very glad to see–

Wed 21 Arabella [Jackson] Charlotte & I played Battledore &
Shuttlecock & in the Evening Chess–

Thurs 22 M^r & Mrs Gordon left us   George went to Mrs Cookes for
the last time as M^{rs} C goes to Town Tomorrow

Fri 23 Went to Fern Mary Dimmer was a little better, in the Evening
we read Sir Charles Grandison – George much amused by Charlotte
rapping out the d-m-n-s

Sat 24 Began to learn one of Shakespeares speeches & C & I took it in
our heads to Sing & fancy we have voices – Mr Easton breakfasted
here

Sun 25 M^r & M^{rs} J: Helyar dined here, & were very pleasent They
have invited us to come & see them when we go to Bath which we
shall certainly do–

Mon 26 Play at Chess with Ch < >. she beat me which I cannot but
say I was displeased at

Tues 27 We practised our singing & my Father was greatly pleased to
hear his Daughters sing so finely

Wed 28 My Fathers birth day I wish he may see many many happy

---

16 Nov. *Edmund of the Forest* (4 vols., 1797), no author discoverable.

19 Nov. Squire Farquharson had a second hunting establishment at Cattistock, north-
west of Dorchester, where a relative of his presumably was accompanied by his wife-
to-be (see below, October 29, 1811 for their marriage). This Mr Farquharson not
identified but possibly one of the sons of Capt Farqhuarson mentioned Feb 11, 1811.

23 Nov. Samuel Richardson, *Sir Charles Grandison* (7 vols., 1754).

26 Nov. Ch < >. possibly Ch[uck.] for Charlotte. The word is compressed and
contracted: the y of Play on the line above comes down into it.

returns of this day – George nearly killed us with laughing he was so droll

Thurs 29 Went to Littleton where I never was before think it a very nice House

Fri 30 Charlotte & I walked in the Fields going to Blandford Mrs Farquharson & M^r & Miss Marsh dined here, beat C[harlotte] at Chess

DECEMBER

Saturday 1 We were alone Charlotte beat me at Chess, we acted in the Evening Brutus & Cassius–

Sun 2 Went to Church at Langton & called on Mrs Kirby who was confined to her room with a Cold

Mon 3 M^r & M^{rs} J Basturd & Mr Snow dined here I think M^{rs} J: B: rather pretty beat C. at Chess

Tues 4 The Gentlemen went out Hunting with the Fox Hounds, We Ladies called on Mrs Portman & saw her & her beautiful Children – beat Geo: at Chess

Wed 5 We all went to the Convent at Spetsbury, the Revd Mother & Sister Placider the dirtiest Creatures I ever saw Sister Mary Barbara very clean & pretty & she sold us some work bags &c Mrs Farquharson made me a present of a work basket

Thurs 6 M^r & Mrs Pleydell[B] & there two daughters & M^r & Mrs Baker[B] dined here – L[ouisa] P[leydell] I think looks ill

Fri 7 We went [to] Langton where we met Mr Ford who dined here – He was at Cambridge with J: Waddington

Sat 8 Returned to Tollard to our great surprise Miss C. Benett came in just before dinner, she told us Old Mr Helyar was nearly blind,–

Sun 9 C. Benett Charlotte & myself took a walk I stumbled over a style to their great amusement but did not hurt myself

Mon 10 very Wet & Miss [Frances] Benett sent a Hack Chaise for her Sister, the Box came from Tom & we began Modern Philosophy

---

29 Nov. Her brother Thomas had moved to Littleton House in Blandford St. Mary in June.

 3 Dec. The Reverend J. Bastard lived at West Lodge, some four miles north of Blandford. (Cary's Roads, 1819, p.850. See also Hutchins, *Dorset*, I, 272, III, 523.)

 5 Dec. The convent was a short distance south of Blandford. According to Hutchins's *Dorset* (III, 519) a 'society of religious ladies of the order of St. Augustine' had been set up at Spetisbury House shortly before Harriet Grove's visit. There were thirty-three women in the community. The 'superior' was a 'Mrs Stoner, of Stoner in Oxfordshire.'

 8 Dec. 'Old Mr Helyar' was the father of William Helyar.

Tues 11 Heard from L[ucy] B[ury] Mr Easton[c] dined here & we
    entertained him with our Novel in the Evening–
Wed 12 We all played Battledore it being wet   Mr Easton made us all
    laugh
Thurs 13 M^r & Mrs Adams called here C. & I escaped seeing them by
    walking out – Geo: laughed a good deal at Miss Biddy Botherim
Fri 14 It rained as usual we played Battledore & read Miss Botherim
Sat 15 I am sorry to hear the King is not well & a Regency is
    determined on We finished our Novel, which we liked very much–
Sun 16 Heard a very good Sermon on the subject of receiving the
    Sacrement – Wrote a letter to Aunt Jackson–
Mon 17 Played at Battledore with my Mother & made her laugh–
Tues 18 Went to Whatcombe[D] met M^r & Mrs Hodges & two
    daughters   in the Evening we danced & began to learn a Cotillion
    & had a great deal of laughing
Wed 19 We walked out the two Miss Hodges & C[ornelia] &
    E[mma] Pleydell walked through some water the rest of the party
    more prudent We danced again this Evening–
Thurs 20 A very wet day & we made a great noise playing all sorts of
    games & danced the morning with our Cotillon to a famous band
    In the Evening Charlotte & I acted & did all sorts of things to make
    them laugh
Fri 21 Left Whatcombe for which we are all very sorry went to
    Littleton in our way home found Mr Hamilton here, who told us
    Fern was very much got on
Sat 22 Sat. Geo: learnt the Cotillon steps, & we read a novel–
Sun 23 Dear George left us for Little Park we miss him very much
    went to Church & did the same as usual–
Mon 24 Very Wet, read our Novel in the Evening as usual–
Tues 25 Went to Church being Xmas day, heard a most excellent
    Sermon, bought pocket Book for next year – Drank Toms health
    who is 27 to day
Wed 26 Betty told us the 1st thing to day that poor Old Mary Dimmer
    died yesterday morning, Poor Old Woman she is now happy for
    there never was a better woman – & we shall all regret her as long
    as we live–

13 Dec. *Miss Biddy Botherim* was a novel.
26 Dec. On the title page of the diary Harriet added this memorial tribute – Mary
Dimmer Born April 17th 1736: Taken from the Register at Lower Donhead - She died
Dec^{br} 25 1810 <u>sincerely regretted</u> by the Grove Family where she lived as Nurse for
more than 20 years.

Thurs 27 John Gordon breakfasted here, & told us there is to be a
   Shaftesbury Ball soon which we are very glad of–
Fri 28 My Brothers came joyful event, George more noisy than ever,
   Hen^{tta} sent us an invitation for the 1st of Jan^{ry} – 1811–
Sat 29 a most severe frost – John went out a shooting had three shots
   & killed every time, in the evening had a great deal of laughing
   teaching my Brothers the rigadoon step–
Sun 30 Went to Church & received the Sacrement. John Gordon came
   to dinner George more noisy than ever
Mon 31 I wish my Father would give us our allowance   John Gordon
   left us this morning I gave him some Country Dances for the Band
   at Shaftesbury. We danced in the Evening Daniel[c] played the
   Violin & W^m [c] the Tamborine to us. We are very much afraid the
   snow will prevent us from going to Littleton Tomorrow–

28 Dec. "My Brothers came": George, John and Charles. 31 Dec. The tamborine
player was William the groom.

The back fly-leaf itemises various expenditures etc, including the purchase of a pair of
clogs during her April visit to the Waddingtons at Little Park.

NOTES TO 1810

June 8 'My Father with his troop went to Devizes to quel[l] a mutiny there amongst the local Militia. We are anxious for him to return safe'. It was in response to an appeal from the Mayor of Devizes for a military force to support the civil power that the Yeomanry Cavalry mustered and rode out. The trouble had started with general discontent among the lower ranks of the Local Militia and took a serious turn when a sergeant became openly mutinous and was committed to the guard-room. Some of his sympathisers advanced on the guard-room with fixed bayonets and forced the release of the sergeant and also two privates who were under confinement. When the cavalry arrived there was a tense confrontation. Bloodshed was narrowly averted, the ring- leaders were court-martialed and sentenced to severe floggings and the other militiamen departed quietly to their homes as their term of duty had now ended. The episode was extensively reported in the Salisbury & Winchester Journal of the 11th June and The Examiner of the 17th.

Sept 17 'Received the Poetry of Victor & Cazire'. The angry outburst that follows – ' Charlotte offended with reason . . . they have done very wrong' – gains added force from its contrast with the uncommonly good-natured and rancour-free spirit of Harriet's writing throughout. Her distress at the emotional fall-out within the Grove household shows in occasional flashes. A letter from Shelley's father to Mr Grove 'gives more trouble'. Four days later there was a family row when her brother John 'entered into an argument' with their father. Despite the discretion which quickly takes charge of her pen it is plainly a loyalty to her sister rather than to her lover that governed her immediate response. Added to other uncertainties about Bysshe's increasingly radical views on what were politely termed 'speculative subjects' – meaning religion and the sacrament of marriage – the gratuitous humiliation of Charlotte in the offensive poem seems to mark a turning-point heralding the end of the long impassioned exchange of love-letters. In October Shelley went up to Oxford and found new interests.

The poem which provoked or emphasised the rupture is included, with a more detailed account of the surrounding circumstances, in Shelley's First Love by Desmond Hawkins (Kyle Cathie, London and Archon Books, Hamden, Conn. U.S.A. 1992).

At this point Harriet's personal account breaks off. The pocket book for 1811 that she bought on Christmas Day has not survived and it is her sister Charlotte's diary which takes up the narrative. From this we know that Shelley's elopement with Harriet Westbrook in August precipitated a general desire at Ferne to turn Harriet's thoughts towards an alternative suitor, William Helyar junior of Sedgehill. She married Helyar on November 14, 1811 and settled at Sedgehill to rear a large family, moving to Coker Court – the Helyar family seat – when her father-in-law died in 1820. Her dowry was £3000, ensuring an annuity of £500 p.a. if her husband predeceased her. He did so, dying in 1841 when seven of their twelve children survived him. As a widow she lived for a time at Montacute with her daughter Ellen, who married William Phelips of Montacute in 1845.

The habit of keeping a diary did not forsake her. In 1852 a cheap notebook* was used by her to record the passing days, including her sixty-first birthday. In mid-May she set off, accompanied by her maid, to visit sister Charlotte who was now Mrs Downes, wife of the rector of Berwick St. John. Their first evening together ended 'with prayers and a hymn, Mrs D playing the piano – servants and Mr D singing'. The firmness of Harriet's religious practice is notable. On Sunday she attended church twice and closed the day with prayer and a psalm. The visit lasted a fortnight, much occupied with family reunions at Ferne and with her Jackson cousins. In the following month she received a visit from her brother Charles Henry Grove, who was then at Torquay.

In 1867 Harriet may perhaps have had a last sight of Field Place on her way to Brighton, where she died on December 5.

* Now in Somerset Record Office, Ref. DD/PH 241.

Thomas Grove (1758-1847) father of the diarists, Harriet and Charlotte.
Portrait, 1788, by George Romney.

'Aunt Chafin': Elizabeth Grove of Ferne (1756-1833) who married in 1776 her kinsman William Chafin Grove (1731-1793) of Zeals. This portrait, one of two by Romney, hung at Zeals House: the other at Ferne.

'Uncle John' Pilfold RN (1768-1834).

Ferne House in 1850: the replacement, completed in 1811, of the much earlier house demolished as unsafe in 1809.

Percy Bysshe Shelley (1792-1822): an unfinished oil portrait c. 1822 by Amelia Curran.

Field Place, near Horsham, Sussex: the home of the Shelleys.

Shelley's diary, 15 January 1810:
'30 copies of Zastrozzi to come – not to forget Harriet'.

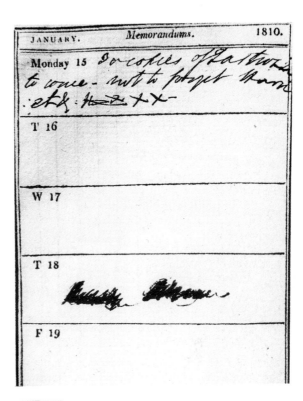

Harriet's diary 5 March 1810: 'Most agreeably surprised by receiving a Parcel & letter from my Greatest Friend'. Shelley's diary March 1 – 'Parcel to Harriet'.

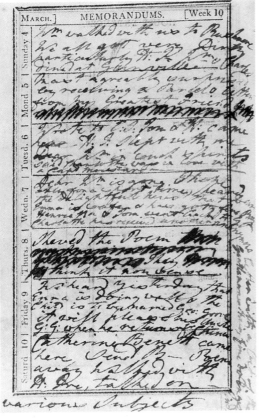

Lincoln's Inn Fields, 1810: a contemporary engraving of the view in front of John Grove's house, number 49, in the year when Shelley and Harriet stayed there.

Cwm Elan: Thomas Grove's Welsh estate near Rhayader, bought in 1792, where Shelley stayed in 1811 and again, with his first wife, in 1812. Painting by R. Eustace Tickell (*The Vale of Nantgwyllt*, 1894).

The first house in Bournemouth, c. 1811: built by Lewis Tregonwell. 'We went after dinner to see a place Mr T has bought and talks of building on called bourn' (Harriet's diary 4 July 1810).

Ashcombe House: an eighteenth century view from the south-east. Thomas Grove junior bought Ashcombe in 1815.

Coker Court: the family seat, near Yeovil in Somerset, of the Helyars: inherited in 1821 by Harriet Grove's husband, William Helyar.

Wardour Castle: family seat of the Arundells, near Tisbury, Wiltshire.

II

The Diaries of Charlotte Grove
(later Mrs Downes)
1811 - 1860

INTRODUCTION

The 1811 diary is a gentleman's and tradesman's Daily Journal similar in general style to Harriet's, bound in red leather with a wrap-over tongue. After five years she began to use a variety of books, ranging from a plain notebook to the nationally popular Letts diaries. Her daily entries were not always written exclusively for her own eyes. One or two of her most intimate circle were occasionally permitted to hear Charlotte read extracts from earlier years. This leads to moments of excessive discretion when an enticing thread of gossip is cut short. As compensation she uses fly-leaves and other blank spaces for less decorous matters such as bets with Harriet, news of their cousin Bysshe Shelley's expulsion from Oxford and the resemblance of Miss Rackett's eyes to billiard balls.

Proportionately more entries are selected from the earliest diaries for several reasons. The 1811 diary provides hitherto unknown information on the ending of her sister's romance with Shelley. Charlotte's unmarried status gives her a much wider variety of social visits within a large family group than she could enjoy later as the wife of a country parson. And it seems desirable to immerse the reader at the outset in the cumulative atmosphere of Charlotte's personal world.

Charlotte had an excessive fondness for initial capital letters, extending even to the indefinite article A. She was also liberal with underlinings in defiance of the law of diminishing returns. I have taken the liberty of curbing excesses in these respects but her text is otherwise as she wrote it. Editorial interpolations to clarify a word or a phrase are indicated by square brackets.

1811

The final words of Harriet's 1810 diary, expressing concern that snow might prevent the next day's visit to brother Tom at Lyttleton, is immediately answered by Charlotte's opening sentence 'We went to Lyttleton''. The chronicle of family life continues until the two sisters prepare for a visit to Bath with Aunt Chafin – a strategem concerted perhaps by the family elders to compensate for the previous year's disappointments in love. The death of Colonel Sergison in July closes one affair impassively. The arrival from London of brothers John and Charles at the end of August must have brought the first news of Shelley's elopement with Miss Westbrook, though Charlotte refrains from comment. The effect on the family, however, soon becomes plain in a growing intimacy between Harriet's brothers and William Helyar.

The first flyleaf is inscribed – 'Charlotte Grove, Tollard Royal, Jan 1. 1811. May this be a happy propitious year to all the Grove family however extensive their branches. I bought this at Salisbury'.

The inside cover deals with the temporary exile from Ferne. She has written here – 'from June 26th left old Fern. Three months at L. Donhead [Lower Donhead, sc. Donhead St. Andrew]. At Tollard two years, whilst building the new house at Fern'.

The inside back cover records a bet on this subject. 'Laid a penny with H[arriet] that we get into Fern next Sept'. The bet is not dated. Other items are titles of novels and addresses. The back flyleaf has writing on both sides as follows – 'The beginning of this year our good King being ill the Prince of Wales was appointed Regent – and as he <u>ought</u> kept in his Father's Ministers'. 'To write out sweet Richard for Mr. W. Long'. 'Laid 6d with Harriet that we shall meet thick head Somerset 1st time at Brianston'. 'I paid for H's stays 3-11-0'. 'April 2nd sorry to hear Bysshe was expelled Oxford for writing to the Bishops on Atheism'. 'April 30 Miss Caroline Russell married to Mr. Lloyd of Cardiganshire'.

Before the start of the diary proper there is a blank single page intended for memoranda. Charlotte started her diary on this page as follows:

1st We had a very pleasant dance at my brother's house; 5 Miss Pleydells, 2 Miss Williams's, Miss Tregonwell & Miss Bastard. Mr. Gibbs, Bryne, Bastard, Dansey[c] and Stewarts were the dancers. Miss T. was <u>dressed</u> like a <u>bride</u>. Harriet, George & myself danced a cotillon with the Miss Pleydells, dear charming friends of ours. Henrietta called a cousin of hers a goose.

5th Read Bysshe's new novel [St Irvyne]. <u>Great stuff</u>. John says Miss Racquet's eyes are like two billiard balls. Little Bonaparte King of Rome born in April.

The diary proper follows, in selected extracts.

Jan 1 We went to Lyttleton and left my Father & Mother at home. A Dutch concert the whole way. Henrietta greeted us most cordially.

Jan 2 Mr. Snow called at Lyttleton. Tom was angry that we could not stay with them longer. We came home and found a large pacquet from the Pleydells.

Jan 3 It snowed. Heard a most wonderful event, that Mrs. Habersham is going to be married. This news Aunt Chafin Grove told us.

Jan 4 Played Battledore in our bedroom. Susan made us some white crape aprons trimmed with black ribbon for second mourning for the Princess.

Jan 5 My brothers John, George & Charles walked to Aunt Jackson's & slept there. The former lost his hat on Wingreen & the good humoured noisy George tied a Hdf [handkerchief] over his head and lent John his hat.

Jan 6 Went into second mourning. Harriet & I went to the Evening Service (so cold). My brothers came home to dinner. The frost continued very hard indeed.

Jan 7 My sister and self walked to Ferne with my Father. A very disagreeable walk – the wind blew so I was stiff the whole evening. The new kitchen is a delightful room & I like the grand staircase. John, Charles and my father set out for London.

Jan 9 We went to Mrs. Gordon's & over Ashcombe Hill in a <u>cart</u> were fearful the bottom of it would come out. Mrs. Benett dined with us & accompanied us to the Shaston[D] Ball, not many people & very freezing cold.

Jan 10 George walked home in the rain. We staid at Mr. Gordon's enjoyed ourselves much & danced in the evening. The Gordons a delightful family.

Jan 11 Went to Pythouse. Met a large party. A ball. George Benett[B]

Jan 1. A Dutch concert – 'where each performer plays a different tune' (O.E.D.).

dressed up as <u>Miss Easton</u> & deceived us completely. The Helyars there. I am in hopes from circumstances of what I have long wished taking place.

Jan 12 We staid at Pythouse. Mr. Harry Helyar called. Played Dumb Crambo in the evening. Mr. Benett practised twice on me the rhyme of Miss. We played chess with him.

Jan 13 With regret left the dear Benetts and Gordons. Saw Mrs. Warren. Arrived at Tollard in safety. Found dear Helen Tregonwell here.

Jan 14 Harriet & I played Battledore thinking it too wet to walk out as Helen & my mother did. Taught Helen chess in the evening.

Jan 15 A ladys party. We laughed, talked and were very merry about Miss Kneller's song.

Jan 16 George came home. The little man ties his cravat so well since he has been to Town that he looks quite smart.

Jan 17 I made a parody on the song of the Maid of the Mill. I hope <u>he</u> will really make all the love that he can (propitious be my wishes).

Jan 18 We heard that Mrs. Habersham is <u>really</u> going to be married to Mr. Merrick[C] & that Mrs. Cooke has sold her house to young Mr. Arundell. Helen lent me some pretty flowers to copy. She is a dear creature.

Jan 19 Harriet & I rehearsed Lady Grace & Lady Townley's parts, whilst we were taking our usual walk. George flirted with Helen about a ring.

Jan 21 My dearest of brothers George left us to join his ship. We drank William's health, it being his birthday and he of age. This day success attend both George & him.

Jan 23 My father hunted at Cranbourne.

Jan 24 The King is better. I hope he will be well before the Regency takes place.

Jan 26 Harriet & I sent up the box of books to London. I stumbled in pattens, thought I had broke my leg, stuck in the mud. Helen hung in a hedge like a petticoat out to dry.

Jan 27 Went to morning church & staid an hour & half before Mr Ridout [the curate] came in. Walked afterwards with Miss Tregonwell & Harriet.

Jan 28 Miss T [Helen Tregonwell] Harriet & I walked to Ferne. Met Henrietta in the Cottage Lane. Saw 6 foxhunters at Fern. Mr Farquharson took us for witches. On our return found Mr. H. Helyar at Tollard. A disappointment – H[arriet] thought it was

<u>Billy</u>. He dined & slept here. We acted, sang etc. to him. He brought us a song of Handel's.

Jan 29 Mr. Henry Helyar left us. We are invited to Sedgehill as soon as the Waddingtons have left us. May our visit be productive of everything I wish & much pleasure.

Jan 30 I gave Helen a pocket book for the year. Helen, Harriet & I took a walk and built castles in the air. May they have a strong foundation before the summer. Tried Handell's songs – too fine for us.

Jan 31 Harriet & I acted Mrs. Prim & Mrs Lovely & made Daddy & Mummy laugh a lot.

Feb 1 Charles Jackson & Hugh Helyar called. The former has charming manners. The latter is very shy indeed.

Feb 2 Our dear friend Helen went home. She ran away with my young Roscius. We saw Mr. J. Helyar's servant at the cottage. Harriet knew the livery directly.

Feb 3 Susan related something of Ld & Lady Arundell. I hope it is not true.

Feb 4 My mother rode to Rushmore. Mr. William Helyar called on us. Joked me about my acting. We could not prevail on him to stay. The books came from Town.

Feb 6 Miss F. Benett came. We acted to her in the evening.

Feb 7 We shewed Miss Benett King John's Palace.[D] She admired it & wished to live there.

Feb 8 [Friday] The fair Catholick fasted. H & I took her blowing her nose for some of her devotions. H. thought she was whipping herself.

Feb 9 Miss F. Benett went home. My father hunted so late that we did not dine till 7 O'clock & it made us very sleepy.

Feb 10 My birthday – 28. We heard Mr. Popham[B] had behaved in a most noble manner to his sisters – given them £500 each out of the legacy given him by Master Popham. This has done Laetitia more good than her doctors by a great deal.

Feb 11 Moved out of our own bedroom in a fine bustle preparatory to the Waddingtons coming. So crowded in this room we can scarce move. Captain Donaldson called on us with one of Captain Farquharson's[B] sons: the third morning we have had some beaux call on us.

Feb 12 About 5 O'clock to our great joy the Waddingtons arrived with my dear little niece and two beautiful nephews. Little Emma so very entertaining.

Feb 14 [The Waddingtons' 6th wedding anniversary]. The servants drank punch on the occasion and were very merry. We heard that the Isle of France is taken.

Feb 15 Lottery drawn. May it be propitious to my mother who has a 9th of a ticket.

Feb 16 Walked with Harriet in the field on the hill. Talked of our schemes for Bath.

Feb 19 My mother had a quarter of a £25 prize. Mrs. Still is not at home, therefore we shall not go to Clouds[D] as intended next week.

Feb 20 Dyed our crape gowns & made a fine dirty room of it.

Feb 23 Waddington and my father called at Lyttleton & saw the portraits. W. says Mr. Gray does not flatter enough: a great fault.

Feb 25 The dear Waddingtons left us for Lyttleton. Very sorry to part with them. We all hope Waddington will get off his bargain & live at Woodcots [a hamlet approx. 3 miles east of Tollard].

Feb 28 Last day at Tollard before our Bath expedition. In a bustle, packing up. A great event to us rusticks.

March 1 Arrived at Bath just as it was dark. Passing Sedgehill saw two ladies in red cloaks walking, & some gentlemen came out of the house seeing our livery. Aunt Chafin received us à l'ordinaire.

March 2 We called at Capt. Wilsonn's [C] & Mrs. J. Helyar's – heard the sad news that the latter leave Bath on Monday for a fortnight as they have sold Farnham. We drank tea at Mrs. Freke's, met the Viletts, Mrs. Lear and daughter & Mrs. Gapper. Miss Longs called on us.

March 3 Too wet to go to church. Fine afterwards. Walked in the Crescent. Met Emma Wilsonn, I think her much improved. We walked with the Penruddocks. Mrs. Merrick [C] called.

March 4 We went to a party at Mrs. Thresher's, met Mrs. & Miss Longs – the old aunt quite lame. The servants ran up and down the rooms with her. She looked like a corpse.

March 5 Miss Bury and Miss Jessop called on us. We went to the play with Mrs. Knightley & daughters. The play was 'The Way to get Married'. Elfistone performed delightfully, Miss Jameson a good actress.

March 6 We met Miss Bury & Jessop & walked with them all the morning. Saw a Dr. & Mrs. Starky in the Pump Room. Capn.

Wilsonn there. Walked up Lansdown & called on Mr. & Mrs. Merrick. Delighted with Mr. M.

March 7 Mrs. Grove took us to the Rooms. Being wet, no chance of getting into a cotillon. Miss Walsh Porter very handsome, like a beloved friend of ours.

March 8 Wet day. Went to the Pump Room with my aunt. [She was their hostess in Bath].

March 9 We drank tea with Mrs. Penruddock. Heard Lady Mary Long has a daughter & Mrs. C. Benett a son about a fortnight ago.

March 10 Poor Miss Randolph died of a decline. We dined with Mrs. Rudge – the old lady in high spirits. Walked with our friend Miss Jessop all the morning. Saw Mrs. Starky in the Pump Room.

March 11 We went to the ball, but did not dance. Miss Jessop of our party. She delighted in quizzing.

March 12 We went with Mrs. Armswick to the play, 'The Foundling of the Forest'. A gentleman impertinently wished to get acquainted with me.

March 13 Read Marmion to Mrs. C. Grove. I intend it as a present to my father. Mrs. Parker called on us.

March 14 Practised cotillons in the morning. A Mr. Riman hid himself & we could not dance it. I danced in Miss Dalrymple's set. Harriet danced country dances. A Mr. Cratton rather struck with her.

March 16 Heard a curious story of Mrs. Merrick but do not believe it. Saw the play of 'Know your own mind' and 'The Farmer'. Miss Long is not a good neighbour at a play.

March 17 Sunday. Went to [? St.] Margarets, heard Mr. Bowen, a shocking preacher. Mrs. Merrick & her son drank tea with us.

March 18 In the evening to Mrs. Jekyll's rout – stupid enough. To the ball afterwards which we liked. I danced before tea with Mr. Willoughby, afterwards with a gentleman introduced by Mr. King & Mrs. Marsh, our chaperone.

March 19 Dined with the Wilsonns. Went to the ball at the Lower Rooms. Danced with Mr. Brock & a gentleman introduced by Mr. Cratton. Harriet danced with Mr. Cratton all the evening.

March 20 We heard Mr. & Mrs. J. Helyar were arrived.

March 21 Fagging about our cotillons in the morning. Disappointed in the evening. A stupid hot ball. Danced country dances with Mr. Roos.

March 22 Took leave of Miss Jessop. Met Mrs. J. Helyar, drove about in her carriage, laughed with her and enjoyed ourselves very much.

She is such a pleasant woman. Aunt very good humoured about it.

March 23 Walked out with Miss Marsh & Mr. Cratton. Saw Jagger's miniatures. A likeness of Mr. King so striking. Met a mad man & his attendant.

March 25 Went to the Upper Rooms. Mr. King introduced me to a Mr. Scott, a very gentlemanlike man with whom I danced country dances before tea. He is engaged as my partner for cotillons.

March 27 Went to the concert with Mrs. Helyar. The concert as usual stupid but our chaperone very pleasant.

March 28 Practised in the morning & danced cotillons in the evening – my partner, Mr. Scott. Many young ladies wished to be introduced to him.

March 29 Called on the Helyars. Mr. Harry Helyar there. We walked in Sydney Gardens & got into the swing. Mr. J. Helyar left us in the Labyrinth with his nephew.

March 30 Went out in the coach. Met Lord Northesk & Col. Peachy. We acted to my aunt in the evening.

March 31 [Making social calls]. Col. Peachy whom we met gave us a treble How d'ye do.

April 1 Went to the pleasantest rout at Mrs. Parker's, introduced to several beaux. Went to the ball, danced with a vulgar partner. Preferred the rout.

April 2 We went to the Lower Rooms. I am nearly tired of dancing. Mrs. Merrick nearly lamed me.

April 3 Mrs. Bowles & Helyar called on us. We walked home with the latter. Went to Dr. Hingworth's rout. I did not like it at all. The ice the best thing there. Mrs. Chafin played carols.

April 4 We tried to persuade Mr. H. Helyar to dance cotillons but he would not. However, we made up our set after tea.

April 5 Aunt Jackson has another son. Heard it the 1st of April.

April 6 Left Bath, sorry to part with my Aunt Chafin. We read Shakespeare in the carriage. Met Mr. Wm. Helyar & Mr.. Wake close to Sedgehill. Found our dear parents quite well on our return to Tollard & my dear friend Helen Tregonwell with them.

April 7 Mr Elwin called. Those naughty girls did not call me downstairs, choosing to have the agreeable man all to themselves. We had a very pleasant conversation after dinner about Atheism.

7 April. 'About Atheism' – prompted by the news of cousin Bysshe's expulsion from Oxford.

April 8 My Aunt Grove came & received us rather coolly. Mrs.
Burlton & Marianne[B] came over in the gig to dinner & return
home at night.

April 9 My mother & aunt went to Fern in the phaeton. Miss Tregonwell, Harriet and myself went a pleasant walk to Ashcombe. We
saw the house. Mr. Hamilton went to Fern & has promised to send
some plaisterers. Mr. & Mrs. Elwin called on us yesterday.

April 10 Aunt Grove went home. I told my aunt I would write to Sir
John to ask Miss P's direction. She said it would give him an
hysterick fit.

April 14 Easter Sunday. Went to church in the evening. Knelt too
devoutly in the wrong place. Helen & my mother laughed at me &
the little man looked as grave as a judge. Lost a nice walk, by our
laziness.

April 15 Harriet & myself staid at home purposely to receive Mr.
John Helyar and he did not call on us. My mother & Helen met the
impolite man on Ashcombe Hill & he was highly flattered by our
attention – proud enough, I make no doubt.

April 24 Walked again in the Chase & heard the cuckow. [Reading
Cumberland's last novel 'John de Lancaster'] Like de Lancaster
better. The old gentleman does not prose quite so much.

April 26 We walked to Ashgrove. Helen descried three villains lurking
behind a hedge which forced us to a hasty retreat in as quick a
manner as Wellington drove Messina from Portugal.

April 27 Miss Tregonwell left us, to our regret. My father dined at
Netherhampton. I began 'The Mysteries of Udolpho'.

April 29 Harriet & myself kept ourselves awake at night building
Welsh Castles. May they be realised this summer.

Sunday May 5 Entertained after dinner by watching the Dog & Cat
upon the Green. Quite an event at Tollard Royal.[D]

May 6 Amused ourselves in packing up the box of books & also in
some indescribable mischief known only to Harriet & myself.

May 7 We went to Mr. Still's at Clouds, surprized to meet Mrs.
Bowles there. Mr. Robert Still & Mr. Wake dined with us. The
latter accompanied me on the violin. Sir Wm. Parker in high spirits
with his aunt Bowles.

May 10 We went to Compton. The Penruddocks received us very
kindly. Mr. George Penruddock[B] came in the evening - a silly
young man.

May 12 Harriet & myself walked after dinner for the first time this spring. Bysshe Shelley is returned home.

May 13 Tom came over to see us with a budget of grievances.

May 14 I began reading Smollett's 'Peregrine Pickle'.

May 18 We walked out in the evening and played our flageolets to the cows whilst they were milked. My father saw us & laughed at us.

May 20 Received before breakfast a kind note & a present of a gown from Tom & Henrietta. The latter has invited Harriet & myself to go with her to Col. Pleydell's ball next Wednesday.

May 26 The weather intensely hot. We shall for the future walk after tea. Mrs. Warren & the plaisterer dined here. I hope it will induce the latter to keep sober.

May 27 Mrs. White the miller's wife at Critchell brought to bed of three girls. My father gave them a £1 note on the occasion.

May 29 We went to Cranbourne, met Mr. & Mrs. Pleydell, Margaretta & Louise. St. Barbe [Tregonwell] there. He is very good tempered & particularly civil to the ladies.

May 30 A party of pleasure to Bourne Cliff. Mr. Tregonwell's new house – dined on cold meat in the house. St. Barbe walked through a brook 8 times to help us over. Mrs. Portman & the Miss Williams met us at Bourne. The sea shore there beautiful.

June 1 We came home – St. Barbe gave us a beautiful nosegay. My father rode to Fern, the building has proceeded very fast this last week. A budget of distresses came from my aunt Grove to my father.

June 3 My father met Mr. Arundell who told him he had let Ashcombe to Mr. Paul Methuen.[c] They are to take possession in September.

June 5 Walter Long commanded the Hindon Troop at the Review. He drives Lady Mary 4 in hand [in his coach, drawn by 4 horses].

June 8 Walked with my father in the evening into the Chase & back by Tollard Green. We saw some deer.

June 17 A Mr Towsey came to cut the arms & could not do it. My father sent to Mr. Hyscock of Blandford.

June 22 [While staying at Netherhampton] Dined at Close Gate with our old uncle & aunt [Samuel Long] the former facetious. Went into the cathedral & saw my uncle [Walter] Long's monument by Flaxman – the most elegant one there.

June 17 'the arms' were presumably the heraldic arms of the Groves.

June 25 Harriet & myself walked in the hayfield. She <u>impudently</u> threw me on the haycocks.

June 26 Harriet's birthday – 20.

June 27 We called at Donhead Lodge. Miss Cooke sang to us.

June 28 Walked in the evening with my father & Harriet to Rushmore. The <u>little man</u> rather <u>frisky.</u> We were obliged to keep him in order.

June 29 John writes word that the Duchess of Rutland got him & Charles to see Carlton House.

July 1 Mr. Foot's son of the Barick [Berwick] Farm met with an accident. His left hand was blown off – particularly unfortunate as he is a lawyer.

July 2 A thunderstorm. My mother hid herself in the cellar.

July 3 My father went to the Hindon meeting & did not return home till after 11 O'clock at night. The Penruddocks have invited us to Compton at the Assizes.

July 4 We received a large pacquet from William. He is now a first lieutenant on board the 'Hecate' frigate. They are going to take the island of Java.

July 7 A dissertation after dinner upon steel busks & writing in pocket books – a sure sign, Daddy & Mummy say, of being an old maid (that is, writing in pocket books).

July 14 Read in the newspapers Col. Sergison's death who died at Northampton on the 9th.

July 18 Surprized by the arrival of my Aunt Grove. Edwards[c] bounced into the room & announced her.

July 20 It rained so hard my mother & aunt could not go to Fern. The latter has ordered us to attend the Salisbury Races. We read out 'Ennui' by Miss Edgeworth – the best of her fashionable tales.

July 24 We came to Netherhampton & then went upon the race-course, Aunt Grove with us.

July 25 Harriet & I went on the racecourse in aunt Grove's carriage. Enjoyed it much. Went to the ball – a very pleasant one. I danced with Mr. Locke & Mr. E. Penruddocke[b].

July 27 We went to Compton. Mr & Mrs Calley came – very pleasant people.

July 28 Mr. Long & Miss Flora Long came. Mr. Gordon dined with us. He is deafer than ever.

July 29 The gentlemen went to the Assizes & dined with the judge.

July 31 My father & mother commenced their journey. We came to Netherhampton.

August 2 Arrived at Zeals. My aunt Chafin received us most cordially & kissed both of us.

August 4 Went to church in the great lumbering coach. Called on Miss [Maria] Grove. We received a letter from my mother dated London.

August 12 Came back to Netherhampton. Aunt Chafin accompanied us. We saw Fern at a distance & met Mr. [William] Beckford's[B] dwarf.

August 21 We came to Cranbourne. Mrs. & the Miss Portmans there. Mr. Tregonwell & St. Barbe came home from Bourne in the evening.

August 22 Mr. P. Bingham[C] called in the morning, played an elevating game of chess with Harriet. Improves her beauty.

August 23 We hunted after gypsies to have our fortunes told. Miss W. Portman dressed up as a married lady likely to increase her family but unluckily we did not meet with them.

August 24 Cranbourne Fair. We went there in the evening. St. Barbe & myself led the way; coming home in the dark through the shrubbery we had some fun. Mrs. T[regonwell] gave H[arriet] & myself Fairings. So did HT & St. Barbe.

August 25 Sunday Mr. T. Napier did the duty & dined here as also Mr. & Mrs. Smart & Mr. Peregrine Bingham. The latter played & sang to us with great taste & expression.

August 29 The phaeton sent for us with a pair of new horses in it. On our return to Tollard found my father & mother quite well. A happy meeting to us all. [after a month's absence].

August 31 Walked to Fern with my Mother & Harriet. John & Charles met us there – rode their horses to Tollard & we returned home in the phaeton. <u>Placed our beds</u> to <u>our satisfaction</u>. We saw the Marble Chimney piece for the Drawing Room.

Sept. 3rd My father went into the garden & eat a great many nuts (naughty little man).

Sept 6 Met Mr. J & W. Helyar on our way to Fern. [Later] We saw the comet.

Aug. 25 Mr Smart was probably Robert Smart (1771-1840) 44 years a surgeon in Cranborne and father of T.W. Wake Smart, author of *A Chronicle of Cranborne* 1841.

Sept 8 My father, mother & brothers called at Langton, found Mr. & Mrs. Farquharson quite well.

Sept 9 Mr. Wm. Helyar dined here after shooting with John in the morning. We walked up the hill after tea to look at the Comet. Charles thinks there are two comets.

Sept 17 Waggons going off. Bustle & confusion sending our things to Fern.

Sept 18 A haunch of venison for dinner. Mr. Easton & John Gordon dined with us.

Sept 20 One of our waggons overturned going down Ashcombe Hill.

Sept 21 We got into the new house at Fern to our great joy. May the owners of this charming mansion enjoy years of happiness within these walls. My brothers dined at Donhead Hall & we made an excellent dinner upon roast beef.

Sept 22 Walked out with Harriet, attended by Sybil, to the Glove.

Sept 23 John met with an accident. The horse he rode hunting threw back his head & gave him a black eye, which made this Beau fear that he should not look as well at the races.

Sept 24 We went to Rood Ashton. The Long family we found quite well: introduced to Miss Ann & Dianntia Long. Played at 'Commerce' in the evening. Miss Flora Long won the immense pool of 3/6d.

Sept 25 We went to Chippenham, 1st day of the races. Very wet. Lady Arundell & Miss Jones accompanied us in the barouche. We laughed & talked the whole time. A pleasant ball. I danced with Cap. Longham R.N., Mr. Walter Long & Lord Arundell.

Sept 26 All the young party went together. John contrived well in taking some money from Miss F. Long. A concert & ball afterwards. Mr. Peach struck with Miss Flora Long as well as a friend of mine is.

Sept 27 Dined at Corsham – Mr. Methuen's – a fine house. In the morning we danced in the brewhouse of our lodgings.

Sept 28 Walked out with the Miss Longs. We had a little dance in the evening. Mr. Long & my father & mother joined the gay party.

Sept 29 John & Miss Flora jumped over the stiles very prettily together (Good luck attend JG in Cupid's court).

Sept. 9 Known as 'the Great Comet of 1811' it is fully reported in *The Gentleman's Magazine* of September 1811. Seen from the Earth its coma or head appeared larger than the sun.

Sept 27 Corsham Court near Chippenham, Wilts, the seat of the Methuen family.

Sept 30 Arrived at home. At Warminster met Mr. Cratton. Lady
Parker has a son & also Mrs. Tregonwell. A note to John gave me
some hopes of my former castle building.

Oct 1 John & Charles went to Sedgehill to shoot with Mr. Wm.
Helyar & staid there as Mr. Walker dined there. We talked of two
events that I sincerely hope will happen.
Oct 2 My dear brother & sister Thomas Grove came, as also Mr.
Wm. Helyar returned from Sedgehill with my two brothers. He
danced with Harriet in the evening & I have hopes that what I wish
may happen.
Oct 3 Our castles have a good foundation. Harriet check-mated by
WH. The Miss Benetts of Barick [Berwick St John] called on us. Mr.
H. drove Harriet out in his curricle. We danced in the evening.
Oct 5 Walked round the plantation alone. I like my future brother
better every day.
Oct 6 Sunday Mr. W. Helyar went to Coker. Harriet, Tom & I went
to Barick church. Mr. Easton preached & afterwards dined with us,
as also did Mr. Wake. The latter fished extremely to know about his
young squire of Sedgehill & made us all laugh at his ingenuity.
Oct 10 Mr. Wm. Helyar came home to a very late dinner. We sang in
the evening.
Oct 11 My mother & I called at Wardour. A large party there. We
were congratulated on the approaching happy event.
Oct 12 We went to Sedgehill to look at my sister's future residence.
Oct 19 Mr. Wm. Helyar and his uncle Mr. John Helyar came. We
spent a very pleasant evening.
Oct 21 We left Fern. Harriet & I read to Mr. Wm. Helyar all the way.
We dined and slept at Halford Bridge [Hartfordbridge, east of
Basingstoke]
Oct 22 At Hounslow met my father & brothers. Arrived in London,
my uncle came to us in the evening. He told us odd circumstances.[N]
Oct 24 Walked out with Mr. Wm Helyar & Harriet. He treated us
with ice. Went to Covent Garden. We saw 'The Cabinet' & 'Animal
Magnetism'. We were much entertained.
Oct 25 Walked out with Billy [Wm. Helyar], Harriet & Charles.
Oct 26 Lady Mary & Mrs. Long dined with us & accompanied us to
the play of Henry 8th – or He would be a Prince. Mrs. Siddons &
Kemble acted.
Oct 27 Walked out in Lincoln's Inn Fields with my sister, brother &

Mr. & Mrs. Helyar. Left Town about three O'clock. We slept at Halford Bridge [Hartfordbridge]. Heard of Mr. Kneller's death.

Oct 29 We heard of Mr. Farquharson's marriage. Mrs. Paul Methuen & her sister called. Mrs. Cooke & Louisa called. Mrs. C. thinks Catherine Benett will be a catholick. Miss Charlotte Kneller died.

Oct 31 Harriet measured for <u>Fatimas.</u> Wishes to have them large enough: provident certainly.

Nov 6 Old Mr. Kneller's funeral. My father & mother & Mr. Gordon attended. Mr. Wm. Helyar went to Sedgehill. Mr. & Mrs. Gordon, their son & Mrs. Bowles dined here. [Young] Mr. Kneller staid.

Nov 9 Harriet & I went to Mrs. Cooke's & Edwards cut our hair like Miss Cooke's.

Nov 10 A quartette in the gallery in the evening. <u>Billy rather rude</u> to Harriet & me.

Nov 14 Dr. Jackson & Fanny break-fasted here. We then proceeded to church where Harriet was married to Mr. Wm Helyar. Dr. Jackson performed the ceremony. Miss Tregonwell, Fanny, myself & little niece [Emma Waddington] bridesmaids.

Nov 21. Mr & Mrs Wm Helyar came. I was delighted to see my sister Harriet again.

Nov 24. My brother & sister Helyar left us.

Nov 27 The dear Waddingtons left us, to our regret. Mr. & Mrs. Boys[C] called on us. We read 'Humphrey Clinker' in the evening.

Dec 1 Helen [Tregonwell]'s birthday – 28.

Dec 2 Mr. Warren hung up two pictures over my chimney piece – 'Agnes de Grove' & 'Charity'. We finished 'Humphrey Clinker' & read some of Shakespeare's Winter's Tale.

Dec 13 Mr. & Mrs. Wyndham & their eldest son came. Helen & I played chess & the gentlemen pelted us with oyster shells to prevent our finishing our game.

Dec 17 My father received a letter from William with the bad news that he has undergone a court martial, instead of being promoted at the taking of Batavia & acquiring £3000 prize money as we hoped & expected[N].

Dec 19 Charles arrived & cheered us all in regard to William, entertained us with his account of Bysshe Shelley.

Oct. 29 Mr Farquharson's marriage: see footnote Nov 19, 1810.
Oct. 31 'Fatimas' not identified. The context suggests a maternity garment.

Dec 20 My dear brother William arrived.

Dec 26 It snowed. The singers sang all the day in the hall. In the evening went to the Glove[D] ball: We met a great many of our neighbours there. I danced every dance.

Dec 27 To Lyttleton. Went to the Blandford Ball.

Dec 28 The mummers came to Lyttleton in the evening.

Dec 30 [Back at Ferne] A dance in the evening. Daniel & William the groom played to us.

Dec 31 Charles accompanied Mr Long to a ball at Devizes.

NOTES TO 1811

October 22 'My uncle' was Captain John Pilfold who had travelled from Cuckfield to London with cousin Bysshe, the latter making a connection with the coach to York. The 'odd circumstances' were indeed odd. Following his marriage under Scottish law Bysshe had left his wife temporarily at York while he travelled to Horsham to attend to family matters at Field Place. He was denied admittance by order of his father who feared a violent assault and was talking of swearing-in Especial Constables to protect himself and his household. Bysshe had therefore stayed at Cuckfield with Uncle John, who thereupon received a letter from Timothy Shelley informing him of his determination not to admit his son and 'to place everything respecting him into the hands of Mr Whitton [a solicitor], that no other person may interfere'.

Dec 17 The court-martial of acting Lieutenant William Grove had been held in the East Indies on June 6, 1811, when he was accused of 'behaving in a cruel and oppressive manner to the company of HMS Hecate, contrary to the 33rd Article of War'. He was said to have punished three petty officers for an alleged crime of which they were innocent and to have stopped the liquor of the fourth mess for three or four days and afterwards mixed it with salt water for a further 17 days in punishment of a comparatively trivial offence.

William's defence was that he wished to establish a firm discipline early and so avoid recourse later to flogging and more severe punishment. He was acquitted of 'cruel manner' but convicted of 'oppressive manner' and sentenced to be dismissed, though with a rider mentioning mitigating circumstances. As he had joined the Royal Navy in 1799 shortly before his tenth birthday as a First-class Volunteer, had been in action almost immediately and continued wholly dedicated to the naval career, the dismissal was a crushing blow. Returning to England seven months later he went directly to his brother John in London and wrote an appeal to the Admiralty. His petition was refused but after further consideration and the intervention of Lord Pembroke he was reinstated with the rank of Lieutenant in HMS Primrose.

1812

The fly-leaves, front and back, have miscellaneous shopping and reading notes, lists of clothes and money taken on visits and in particular an inventory of clothes and jewellery taken to Bath.

With Harriet now established at Sedgehill Charlotte was the last of the ten Grove children to remain in the company of her parents in their newly rebuilt mansion. Her unmarried brothers came home from time to time but were more often pursuing careers elsewhere. To replace the companionship that Harriet had provided Charlotte looked now to particular friendships with Laetitia Popham and Helen Tregonwell locally and with Elizabeth Shelley on visits to Ferne and Bath.

By August Harriet's first pregnancy was sufficiently advanced to call for Charlotte to join her at Sedgehill. With her customary interest in the marital prospects of her brothers Charlotte watched closely George's courtship of Louisa Cooke and – at the year's end – renewed her hope of a suitable wife for John.

Jan 1 A thaw. New year's gifts & the compliments of the season passed at breakfast time.

Jan 2 Harriet came to Fern to fetch Helen & myself [to Sedgehill]. My mother rather low at our leaving her.

Jan 9 Surprised after breakfast by the arrival of my mother, brothers & Miss F. Benett in the barouche. Helen and myself much grieved as they took us home with them from the pleasantest visit I ever paid in my life.

Jan 10 We danced in the evening. The Fern Band played to us.

Jan 11 A letter from Mrs. Cooke to inform William he must appear before the Board of Admiralty. He was rather in the dumps but recovered his spirits afterwards.

Jan 20 I came to Lyttleton. Mr. Phelips[B] came into the drawing room whilst I was alone and that was our introduction to each other.

Jan 21 We called at Langton. Mr. Farquharson rather unwell. The old lady there. Mr. Eyton did not return till late from hunting with Mr. Chafin's hounds. We feared he was lost.

Feb 13 My father heard from my cousin Walter [Long] that Lady

Mary is safe in her bed with another daughter. Gave Laetitia
another lesson of chess.

Feb 14 I received a valentine from Abingdon.

Feb 15 William becoming very polite under the tuition of Laetitia
Popham.

Feb 16 I read out to Miss Popham my pocket books & it flattered me
as she appeared to listen to the recital with pleasure.

Feb 20 Laetitia & myself walked to Barrick. On our return found
Mr. Bingham & his son Edward[c] here. Mr. B. went home & Mr.
E.B. staid. The latter entertained us with an account of the Bath
ladies.

Feb 22 I received a letter from Harriet who has added Agnes to her
christian name.

March 2 I had my favourite medlar tree transplanted.

March 5 We walked to the Glove, heard an anecdote of my cousin E.
Rudge not much to his credit.

March 9 A letter from Lord Pembroke saying William is reinstated in
the Navy, but put at the bottom of the list of lieutenants.

March 11 Miss F. Benett & her brother George called upon us. The
Catholick would not eat my luncheon. Col. Peachy is married to a
Mrs. Henry.

March 13 We went to Sedgehill. Old Mr. & Mrs. Helyar there, the
former very odd & made fine speeches to Laetitia & me.

March 16 Miss Popham left us. Her departure is sincerely regretted by
us all.

March 19 Charles arrived, being the Oxford vacation.

March 23 My cousin Elizabeth Shelley arrived from Bath; entertained
us with her account of the 12 Apostles. She is in the highest spirits.

March 26 Elizabeth rode on horseback accompanied by my brother.
Tom & Henrietta came here. Charles & my cousin played a game
of cribbage.

March 29 [Easter Sunday] My father & brothers accompanied me to
Berwick Church where we received the sacrament. A wet day again.
Politicks our topic of conversation. Elizabeth as usual permitted her
tongue its full office.

April 9 Elizabeth not quite well before dinner. She had an hysterical
laugh.

April 10 Charles returned to Oxford.

April 20 Dear William left us to join the *Primrose* sloop off the

Downs. He gave me a cameo brooch. Fanny Jackson returned to us. We walked up White Sheet Hill & home by the Glove.

April 21 Elizabeth & I left Fern with very great regret. Went as far as Warminster in the phaeton. There we met Mrs. Parker's carriage & proceeded to Bath in it. I found my Aunt Chafin looking much better.

April 25 Went shopping with my aunt. Called on Elizabeth. We went to the play together in Mrs. Rudge's party. Saw Betty perform Orestes & extremely well he did it.

May 9 Called upon Elizabeth & proceeded together to Sydney Gardens. I met Mr. & Mrs. H. Hinxman. Caught in shower at the Gardens & obliged to return home in chairs.

May 15 I spent my morning with Elizabeth. Took leave of my dear cousin with the greatest regret. Remained at home with my aunt, being the last evening.

May 16 Left Bath about 10 o'clock & did not get home till 6 in the evening. My aunt Grove here but in a few minutes after my arrival set out for Netherhampton.

May 19 We called upon the bride & bridegroom, Mr. & Mrs. Kneller. I think that Jacky shows a good taste in his wife. She is a very pretty elegant brown woman.

May 20 George to our very great joy came in the morning. He immediately called upon Mrs. Cooke. Mr. & Mrs. Wm. Helyar came to dinner, Harriet looking <u>remarkably</u> well. Her husband has the hooping cough.

May 21 I received a letter from Elizabeth [Shelley]. They go to Town next month.

June 2 I assisted Harriet to pack up for Muddiford. After dinner I left my kind friends at Sedgehill with the greatest regret. Our new carriage arrived: no arms on it.

June 4 We met the shepherd's wife & daughter. They are going to live at Berry Court.[D] The cottage is to be pulled down.

June 6 After dinner we all went into the garden & hunted the snails off the fruit trees. After tea my father & I walked as far as his new road.

Apr. 25 The actor William Henry West Betty (1791-1874) known as 'the young Roscius'.

June 7 Helen has decided properly in regard to Captain Markland.

June 10 We went in the barouche to Blandford, called at Lyttleton & saw Mr. Kerley's drawing of Cwm Elan.[D]

June 18 A wet day. I read out <u>Sense & Sensibility</u> – one of the best novels.

June 23 In the evening I took a nice walk with Charles, <u>both of us in pattens.</u>

June 27 Charles accompanied me to Preshaw.[D] Walter's alterations there are very good. We saw little Ellen, Lady Mary's youngest child. The eldest too ill & unfortunate-looking to be seen.

July 2 [At Winchester Races] Went on the course with Lady Mary. Very wet & no sport. The Steward's ball an excellent one. Lady Rivers very pretty. We kept it up with spirit till 5 in the morning.

July 3 My brothers & self left Winchester about 2 o'clock & arrived at Fern by teatime. Had our dinner there. George in <u>high</u> spirits in again breathing his <u>native air</u>, he said.

July 4 My brother & sister Helyar & the Miss Helyars came. Miss Cooke & Miss Lypscombe drank tea here & we had a little dance afterwards.

July 7 I took a nice walk in the morning with my father. A shower prevented the hay being carried. My brothers drank tea & supped at Mrs. Cooke's.

July 11 In the evening walked with my brothers to Donhead Lodge. <u>Success attend George</u>. We supped there & did not return till past eleven o'clock.

July 23 George & Charles went both morning & evening to Mrs. Cooke's.

July 24 For a <u>wonder</u> my brothers staid an evening at <u>home</u>.

July 25 I walked over the farm & to Berricourt cottage with my Aunt Grove & my father. We saw a beautiful sample of winter barley. Mrs. & Miss Cooke, Mr. & Miss Lypscombe came in the evening & we had a dance. George very <u>alert</u> with <u>his</u> partner.

July 28 In the evening myself & brothers went to Donhead Lodge, where we met the Fletchers, Mr. and Mrs. Shakspear, 2 Miss Nevilles & Charles Burlton.[B] We danced till two in the morning.

July 29 My brothers as usual went to Mrs. Cooke's.

June 7 Helen Tregonwell became Mrs Markland.
July 2 Lady Rivers – mistaken identity: Lord Rivers did not marry.

July 30 Lady Arundell, her mother & another lady called here, her Ladyship dressed in a yellow pelisse & bonnett with pink roses & brown & yellow Columbine boots.

July 31 Mrs. Cooke, her daughter & Mr. & Miss Lypscombe drank tea here & danced afterwards. George in the highest glee.

August 1 Mrs. Benett rode here. George & Charles dined & spent the evening at Mrs. Cooke's. Mrs. B read Humphrey Clinker & was much pleased with it.

August 2 Mrs. Benett went to Down House to attend the Blandford Races. My mother & I went to Lyttleton. Old Mrs. Farquharson gave us a very kind reception.

August 3 My brothers came to Lyttleton. Mrs. J. Farquharson dined with us & we afterwards went upon the race-course in her barouche. Mr. Kneller's horse lost. A ball – we danced till two in the morning. Miss Banks is grown much handsomer.

August 4 In the morning we saw Moon the conjuror exhibit some very curious tricks. Went upon the race-course with Mrs. J. Farquharson. Saw Mr. W. Butler.[c] A ball – I danced till 6 o'clock. 18 couple ended with The Boulanger.

August 10 Mr. & Mrs. J. Helyar called in their way to Sedgehill. I went to Sedgehill tho' my Flirt Mr. Snow[c] was coming to Fern.

August 11 Mr. J. Helyar called at Pythouse & saw the little boy. Thinks the same as we do of a certain likeness. Mr. C. Bowles dined here. William & Harriet played me a fine Brush Trick. I owe them two.

August 13 Mr. J. Helyar intends making a spectatorial garden at Tollard.

August 15 Mr. Hugh Helyar, having but one coat, came down into the library, whilst it was brushed, in his night- gown. A ring at the bell – he thought it Lady Arundell & leaped out of the window over the flower pots etc. It proved to be Mr. J. Ogle.[c] We had a pleasant ladies party at home. Mr. H. Helyar has a design of making his aunt tipsey.

August 17 My father & brothers set off very early in the morning for Wales. Good news of Ld Wellington's victory.

August 24 At five o'clock in the morning Harriet was taken ill &

Aug. 17 Wellington's victory in the Peninsular War at Salamanca.

brought to bed of a fine boy a little after 8 o'clock. I saw the baby dressed & had him in my lap as soon as he was born.

August 25 Mr. Wake dined here, privately baptised the child by the name of William Hawker.

August 28 I accompanied Wm. to the wheat field. I assisted in putting up the sheaves. In the evening Wm & myself played chess. Harriet got up at 5 & staid up till bed-time.

August 29 About ten o'clock at night my father & brothers returned from Wales.

August 30 My father introduced to his little grandchild. Mr. Phelips & Mr. Wake dined here upon a haunch of venison. Mr. W. rather too bad with his jokes. George & Charles dined at Mrs. Cooke's.

Sept 2 George again went to Donhead. Charles dined here & went to Mrs. Cooke's in the evening.

Sept 3 Mrs. Peter Still[B] & Miss [Camilla] Wallop called. George & Charles dined with us – a conversation between them about Love which entertained us very much.

Sept 4 Wm. dined at Mr. Peter Still's & was entertained with Mr. Wake & Miss Wallop.

Sept 5 Mr. Wake dined & slept here. He does not think Cupid so beautiful divested of two livings & money. Mr. James Still has I think cured him of the Wallop flame.

Sept 7 Wm. went to Coker. Harriet came downstairs into the drawing-room. In the evening we went into her drawing-room above stairs.

Sept 9 [After a search for a wet-nurse] A woman & her love child came. Little Wm. after a little hesitation took the breast.

Sept 10 A bustle. James came to tell us the Helyars are coming at about five o'clock. Mr. & Mrs. Helyar arrived with a wet nurse & her child. We sent off the first wet nurse & kept this last one. Wm. very anxious about his little boy.

Sept 11 Mr. Helyar very odd. He drinks a great deal.

Sept 12 Mr. J. Helyar called. He has taken Mr. Ogle's house for two or three years. He is so fickle I dare say he will soon be tired of it.

Sept 13 Mr. Wake dined here. He went home early being Miss Wallop's last evening at Knoyle. I read aloud one of Blair's sermons.

Sept 15 My mother came in the phaeton & took me home with her. On my return happy to see dear John. George went Monday [14th] to his ship.

Sept 19 The pointers <u>ran away</u> with two or three <u>joints</u> from the breakfast table.

Oct 8 My father went to Mr. Long's of Rood Ashton to attend the county meeting & propose him as a Member.

Oct 13 Tom went into Wales. Being High Sheriff his presence was indispensable at the ensuing election.

Oct 20 George arrived. Mr. & Mrs. P. Methuen called. We went in the evening to a little dance at Mrs. Cooke's. Two of the Mr. Austins were there. Miss Goodspeed & Lucy Benett kept it up with spirit till one oclock.

Oct 21 My brother [Tom] & Henrietta came. We had a <u>large</u> party & danced in the evening. We supped about one oclock & then ended our gay ball.

Oct 25 Too wet to go to church. My father read prayers. George dined at Donhead Lodge.

Oct 26 Mrs. Miss Cooke & Miss Lypscombe dined here. Alas! the <u>last</u> day of the lovers being together before the voyage to China.

Nov 7 My father has given his harriers to old Mr. Helyar.

Nov 16 Mr. Butler[C] breakfasted with us & <u>enticed</u> the gentlemen out hunting though it was a very wet day. Afterwards Mr. Butler dined with us & entertained us <u>very much</u>.

Nov 21, 22 Mr. Woodridge of the Glove [Inn] died very suddenly, being thrown from his horse. Poor Mrs. Woodridge is left a distressed widow with seven children.

Nov 27 Elizabeth Shelley sent us a present of painted china & card racks.

Nov 29 We went to Berwick church. Mr. Boys shewed us a document in the parish register which ascertains my father's possession of the north chancel of Berwick church.

Dec 14 Charles arrived from Oxford having travelled all night in an open gig.

Dec 28 Mrs. the 4 Miss Eyres[B] & Miss F. Benett came.

Dec 29 The Miss Eyres, John & myself walked as far as the turnpike & a very dirty walk we had. We danced in the evening. Mrs. Eyre said what looks well in favor of <u>somebody</u>.

May what I particularly wish the end of this year come to pass.

Sept. 19 'The pointers': gun-dogs.
Oct. 26 'The lovers': Louisa Cooke and George Grove.

1813

The diary is inscribed 'Charlotte Grove the gift of her affectionate sister Harriet Helyar Jan 1st 1813'. The space before January 1 has this entry 'I hope to have a new sister-in-law before the end of this year'. Charlotte is expecting brother John to wed Miss Eyre of Newhouse.

Jan 1 The Miss Eyres & my brother accompanied me to Wardour[D] chapel. John received a New Year's gift from Miss Eyre.

Jan 2 Mrs. & Miss Eyres left us. We are invited to New House. Things put on a promising appearance.

Jan 9 My father went to Newhouse.

Jan 11 I & my brother went to Newhouse, called at Netherhampton for John on our way.

Jan 20 We went to Newhouse in our way called at Netherhampton. The old Eyre gave us a cool reception. Mr. Popham there.

Jan 21 A thunderbolt upon us all. John looked the picture of woe. Mr. Popham went home. The old lady went to bed with a headache.

Jan 22 We took a hasty flight from Newhouse. My mother & I had a conversation with Harriet. Went to Netherhampton, my aunts & us talked over the behaviour of a certain lady.

Jan 23 My father planned a nice scheme. Miss Kneller to be Cupid's messenger. We returned home & could talk but on one topick the whole evening.

Jan 24 I received a note which looks favorable. John went to Lyttleton.

Jan 26 John rode over to Salisbury but was disappointed in meeting with Miss Eyre. Miss Kneller is very strenuous in the cause. My father wrote to Mr. Popham on this subject.

Jan 27 John wrote a letter to Miss Eyre.

Jan 29 A letter from Mr. Popham. He has given my father's letter to Miss Eyre but he cannot interfere any further in this business.

Jan 31 [An entry beginning 'Miss Eyre' has been heavily scored out. All that remains is as follows] John called on Aunt Jackson. My

Jan. 26 Mr Popham, Laetitia's brother, was a nephew of Mrs Eyre.

brother, I hope, will soon get over it.

Feb 6 John gave me a pretty brooch set in pearls with his hair.

Feb 7 My brother John went to Sedgehill intending to go in the coach tomorrow to town.

Feb 10 My birthday – 30.

Feb 17 A satisfactory letter from John.

Feb 19 John wrote us word that there is a vacancy in St. Bartholomew's – I hope he will get it. I wrote to my friend Mr. Snow for his interest.

Feb 22 A bustle in the house in the evening, the library chimney being on fire. Edwards, Susan & one or two more sat up all night.

Feb 28 We went to Berwick church & met Mr. George Graeme at the end of the park coming to call on us. Helen as usual builds castles in the air. I bet with her half a crown. I wish I may lose it.

March 3rd Heard an anecdote relative to William that very much surprized me & all of us.

March 10 John made a speech before the Governors of St. Bartholomew's & was applauded.[N]

March 11 We went to Wyncombe, dined & slept there. Ld John Somerset of the party – a very gentlemanlike young man.

April 5 I received a letter from my dear friend Laetitia Popham who is quite well and at her brother's house at Clarendon Park.

April 14 Arrived in Town. William here. John grown quite fat & looking well.

April 16 William left us to join his ship. We left John's house & arrived at Clay Hall where we found Emma & Waddington with their four lovely children. I like the place very much.

May 2 [In London] We called upon Sir William & Lady Fraser.[B] We saw 9 of their daughters, two being at school.

June 5 [At Sedgehill] We were called up in the morning. Harriet being unexpectedly in labour & brought to bed of a 7 months child – a very little boy.

June 9 My little nephew's name is Carey, a family surname.

June 12 Mr. Wm. Helyar dined at Mr. J. Helyar's where he met the Mrs. Helyars of Bath.

Apr. 16 Clay Hall in Hertfordshire was now John Waddington's residence.

July 1 Mr. John Helyar called. Rather more fire than ice in his composition. He had quite a dispute with Mrs. Helyar.

August 15 [Sunday] We went to Berwick church. Afterwards drove to Pyt House. We went to the Lawns & had a fine view of Fonthill Abbey.[D]

Aug 23 Lady Mary, Mr Arundell, the Miss Arundells, Mr. & Mrs. Raymond Arundell & their two daughters came to us.

Aug 24 My mother accompanied Lady Mary & Mrs Arundell to Sedgehill. The Miss Arundells walked to Ashcombe. I & Miss Catherine strolled about, the air on the hill being too <u>keen</u> for her.

Aug 31 We all went to see Marwell,[D] the house my uncle Long is building.

Sept 5 We went to Berwick church. Mr. Easton dined with us. I wish some <u>rich</u> person would give him a <u>good</u> <u>living</u>.

Sept 13 Delightful weather for my father's harvest, & he has such a <u>quantity</u> of wheat this year one cannot be too thankful for it.

Sept 19 We dined at Donhead Hall, met the Jacksons. A fine set out of <u>Plate</u> at dinner time.

Sept 26 Mr. Rudge did the duty at Upper Donhead. My father recommended him a wife.

Sept 29 Miss Cooke & Miss C. Bennett dined & slept here. We danced in the evening. Mr. Rudge is certainly not one of Cupid's votaries.

[October 8-13, a great family visit to Coker – evidently Charlotte's first – where Harriet's two boys were christened. Montacute also was visited.]

Oct 21 I took the Miss Pleydells [Louisa & Emma] to see Wardour & we called upon the Miss Arundells. Miss Catherine shewed me hers & her sister's bed rooms.

Oct 30 Very happy & alone. My mother's application to the Duke of Richmond successful.

Dec 27 The singers came in the morning. In the evening we were entertained with the mummers.

Dec 31 I walked with my father to see the new road he is making up Ashcombe Hill.

Postscript This year ended with good news from our armies & the Allies. Buonaparte is rather on the <u>Decline</u> of his power I am in hopes.

NOTE TO 1813

*March 10. John Grove was one of four candidates for the post of Assistant
Surgeon at St. Bartholomew's Hospital. An apprentice of John Abernethy's,
William Lawrence, had applied previously in 1807 when he withdrew as
being the younger candidate. In 1811 he succeeded, John Grove and the two
other candidates withdrawing in his favour. (SBH Archives HAL/16 p.495.)*

1814

In general the entries are briefer, often limited to the weather & the usual
catalogue of social visits and games of chess won or lost. Her discretion has
become such that anything disturbing or questionable is concealed in cryptic
phrasing e.g. April 2 'Surprized at a circumstance that happened'.

She went to Bath, March 2 to April 1, stayed with Aunt Chafin Grove as
before & saw Aunt Rudge but, lacking the stimulating company of sister
Harriet or Elizabeth Shelley (as in previous years) she is less animated. There
are some parties, balls & theatregoing but also evenings alone with Aunt.

The flyleaves contain only trivia, & one bet: dated 7th Jan – 'with Miss
Fanny Still, who Mr. Strickland will marry. I say Miss Catherine Arundell,
she says Miss Laura Arundell'. The diary eventually introduces a Mrs. Strickland who appears to have Arundell connections but her christian name is not
mentioned. From June 29 two Fraser girls – Ann & Henrietta – stay at Ferne
& circulate in the neighbourhood. Their mother was a Farquharson so the
connections with Langton & Lyttleton are strengthened. Henrietta is much
involved (Aug 8-12 & Sept 2) with the illness of 'Little Frederick' & his
subsequent christening, but as his aunt: she remains childless.

Harriet had her third child in three years on October 26 – a daughter
Agnes Grove Helyar. Charlotte was her godmother. A cryptic reference to
Harriet follows on Dec 17 – 'A note from Harriet announcing some good
news that we have long wished for'. No indication of what it is.

A reference to Tom's 31st birthday on Christmas Day confirms that he was
born in the same year as Charlotte - 1783.

Jan 1 My dear sister Harriet & her two children began this year with
    us. We partook of some doe venison.
Jan 7 The two Miss Stills came & accompanied us to the Glove ball.
    It was a very pleasant meeting of the neighbours though we had
    only 8 couple of dancers.
Jan 11 It snowed very hard. Charles contrived to walk down to Mrs.
    Cooke's.

Jan 12 Charles <u>deterred</u> from dining with Mrs. Cooke by the <u>arrival</u>
of a lady whom he is <u>not</u> very fond of.

Jan 20 A very deep snow. The mail prevented from coming.

Jan 25 I walked with my father to the sheep fold. The icicles on the
hedge look like the most beautiful cut glass.

Feb 9 My father went in the morning to Cranbourne & settled some
business relative to the marriage of Capt. Markland with Miss
Tregonwell.

March 2 I came to Bath to see my Aunt C. Grove.

March 5 I went to the play with Miss E. Penruddock in Mrs. E.
Clark's private box. It was the Rivals & the wandering Boys. A very
indifferent set of actors.

March 25 A very pleasant private ball at Admiral Gardiner's. We had
a great deal of dancing & kept it up with great spirit till 6 o'clock in
the morning.

March 26 I did not <u>wake</u> till a quarter past 3 in the afternoon & got
up in time for my aunt's dinner hour.

April 1 Arrived at my own dear home just as the family were seated at
dinner.

April 26 Madame d'Arblay's novel <u>such stuff</u> that we cannot finish it.

May 6 Aunt Grove came. An <u>unexpected</u> visit from Mr. Chafin Grove
who dined with us. <u>Manoeuvring</u> <u>necessary</u> <u>sometimes</u>.

May 15 My mother & I paid a long visit at Upper Donhead
parsonage. Dr. Jackson looks ill. My aunt [Bathia Jackson] told us
some curious anecdotes.

May 16 In the garden-house Edwards showed us an effigy the
workpeople have made of Buonaparte.

June 11 A dinner on account of the peace given to our work-people.
The effigy of Buonaparte burnt upon Whitesheet Hill.

June 12 Saw the two new Alderney cows.

June 13 Miss F. Benett married today to Mr. Doyle.

June 21 After dinner I went out & met with two poor travellers &
their child, going to Penzance in Cornwall. I collected a subscription
for them & they slept at the Glove Inn.

June 26 Mrs. Boys says that her new neighbour Mr. Simpson <u>shoots</u>
with a <u>long bow</u>.

Feb. 9 Mr Grove prepared the marriage settlement and was a trustee.

June 27 Charles has arrived from Oxford for the long vacation. He has been to Portsmouth to see the Allied Sovereigns after their having visited Oxford.

July 7 Shakespeare our companion in the phaeton.

July 26 We went to Salisbury, called upon Mrs. Long & the Miss Wyndhams, where we saw their eldest brother the Sheriff, in his dressed coat & bag wig. My father dined with the Sheriff.

Aug 20 Mr. Douglas wanted to frighten me out of taking snuff.

Aug 22 I came home – found my dear brother George arrived.

Sept 10 We had in the evening the merry round game of Snip Snap Snorum.

Sept 20 John talked about living on a very spare diet denominated Love.

Sept 22 In the evening we danced, Daniel played on the violin & my mother on the tambourine.

Sept 27 All my brothers came home excepting my eldest brother. William received a letter from the Admiralty appointing him to the 'Hope' sloop.

Sept 29 Hyscock arrived with my brother's drawing-room furniture from Lincoln's Inn Fields.

Oct 4 My father, mother, John & myself went to Hall Place. Wm. joined his ship the Hope at Portsmouth.

Oct 6 We went to Marwell. The building is gothick & very much got on since I saw it last.

Oct 17 My mother took me to Sedgehill. Miss Caroline Helyar here. In the evening I practised waltzing.

Oct 20 A pleasant trio of ladies at home. I read Shakespeare's play of As You Like It to them.

Nov 3 A shocking elopement of Sir H. Mildmay with Lady Roseberry his sister-in-law.

Dec 13 I read Ld. Roseberry's divorce. Sir H. Mildmay is to pay £15,000.

Dec 20 Capt Donaldson has got George appointed to the prow East Indiaman.

July 26 William Wyndham of Dinton was Sheriff of Wiltshire 1814.
Oct. 4 Hall Place: probably Place Farm, Tisbury.

Dec 21 My dear brother George left us.
Dec 29 Mr. & Mrs. Benett dined here, the latter dressed like a
Colombine in <u>want</u> of a Hdf [handkerchief].

1815

A note on a back flyleaf records '29th July. Louisa Pleydell married to Col.
Mansell'. Other flyleaves list titles of novels, items of clothing taken to
Sedgehill and her individual victories & defeats at chess between April 14 &
May 30.

Jan 1 Mrs. Wake is dead [in childbirth].
Jan 3 Capt. Markland sent his poodle dog as a present to my father.
Jan 5 My father went to Pyt House. I hope his & Mr. Benett's plan
will answer for the sake of old England.
Jan 7 My father returned. They had a good meeting at Warminster
though the <u>officious</u> Mr. Hunt tried to make it as <u>disagreeable</u> as he
could.
Jan 8 Sir Bysshe Shelley is dead. My uncle succeeds to the baronetcy.
Jan 31 At dinner time poor Henrietta had a violent hysterical fit.

April 5 My father went to the Justices Meeting. Only Mr. Wyndham
there. The rest of the gentlemen out foxhunting.
April 8 A shocking circumstance happened at Donhead Hall. A
servant had secreted a child she had had ever since Christmas.
April 10 Mr. Kneller's maid servant that secreted the child is run
away.
April 25 We heard the good news that Tom has purchased Ashcombe.
April 27 The business relative to Ashcombe finally settled & <u>it is my
brother's.</u> (How happy this has made me)
April 29 Miss Cooke called upon us & played several songs. Her voice
not so good as it was.

May 2 Tom called upon us after having looked at his <u>delightful</u>
Ashcombe. The dining parlour the same length as ours.
May 4 Tom called upon us having received a letter from Mr. Davis
relative to the sale of Cwm Elan.

Jan. 7 Henry Hunt (1773-1835) radical activist known as Orator Hunt. He was a
Wiltshire farmer.

May 6 I walked to Ashcombe with Susan. My mother rode the Poney. My father also went with us. I went into <u>every room</u> in the house.

May 8 My father & Tom set out on their journey into Norfolk & Derbyshire [where there were Grove properties].

May 24 My Aunt Shelley & her three eldest daughters came to Fern.

May 31 I accompanied my Aunt Shelley & Fanny [Jackson] in a walk to Ludwell.

June 1 We walked out in the morning. A <u>joke</u> about a <u>watch- key</u>.

June 4 (Sunday) We all went to Berwick church. Something occurred I would <u>much rather</u> had not.

June 12 My Aunt Shelley & my cousins left us.

June 23 The glorious news that Wellington & Blucher have beat Buonoparte. Harriet & I walked to Knoyle to buy a cheese.

June 30 William left us. He is to join Lord Exmouth in the Mediterranean.

July 4 William returned home as his ship does not sail till the 14th.

July 6 My father finished his hay making having made 8 ricks.

July 10 We called at Bishopstone. Mrs. Bromley in low spirits having lost her brother Admiral Heath. Called upon Mrs. King. We heard the good news that Miss Julia Arundell[B] is going to be married to Sir John Talbot.

July 14 Mr. Wyndham called. He is engaged in a Chase cause[N] against Lord Rivers in which I sincerely hope he will be successful.

Aug 2 My father went to the Justice Meeting. Mr. Wyndham & his eldest son accompanied him home.

Aug 12 We dined at Mr. Gordon's – a sumptuous dinner of turtle & venison.

Aug 21 We went to Bourne to visit Mr. & Mrs. Tregonwell.

Aug 22 We walked on the sea shore. We saw Mrs. Grosvenor's cottage – the bedrooms <u>miserable</u>.

Sept 9 My brother's bailiff Mr. James & his family arrived from Wales. They dined here & went to Ashcombe afterwards.

Sept 11 I was waked about 3 in the morning by a summons from Tollard for my mother, Mrs. Markland being taken in labour.

Sept 12 I heard the joyful news that Mrs. Markland is brought to bed of a son. I went to Tollard in the phaeton to fetch my mother home & saw Helen & her little boy.

Sept 13 Mr. Wm. Easton[C] came for my father to sign his certificate to the Patriotick Fund. We dined at Wardour & saw Miss Julia's lover, Sir J. Talbot. A <u>silly</u> man he <u>appears</u> to be.

Sept 17 I took an excursion to Horton Tower[D] with Miss Plum-Tree & drove her in the donkey cart.

Sept 19 Capt. Markland called here. He is made Companion to the Bath as also is uncle [John] Pilfold.

Sept 30 Tom called here. My father accompanied him to Ashcombe where Henrietta was very busy unpacking.

Oct 14 My father heard from Mr. Methuen but not any thing in favor of William's promotion.

Oct 23 A very wet day. We walked up & down the corridor by way of Exercise.

Nov 1 The poachers were fined at the Justice meeting.

Nov 7 We heard from Charles. He has not got into All Souls.

Nov 8 My mother rather <u>witty</u> upon my father calling him a <u>hum drum</u> husband.

Nov 13 My mother & I walked to Eddys. My father has permitted Robert Lathy to make her husband a new wooden leg.

Nov 16 Capt. Benett & his troop came up here in compliment to my father who afterwards dined with them at the Glove inn.

Nov 22 We read Richardson's Sir Charles Grandison.

Nov 28 Aunt Grove has given me her harpsichord.

Nov 29 The harpsichord was put in the hall between the pillars & surrounded by the plants.

Nov 30 Mr. Parker came to tune the instruments.

Dec 1 My mother & I sung very finely to the harpsichord.

Dec 11 I walked as far as the house at Ashcombe by myself. I went up the hill by the green path.

Dec 15 Mrs. Markland has bought Mrs. Burlton's donkeys - a foolish purchase as they are very stubborn & never go the right way.

Dec 16 Tom called upon us. It did us good to see him – he is so cheerful. He has received the money from Cwm Elan.

Dec 22 Tom came here to meet Mr. Chitty on the Cwm Elan business.

Dec 26 The Berwick, Upper Donhead & Lower Donhead Singers came here as usual & the Bulls & Mummers in the evening.

Sept. 13 The Patriotick Fund provided compensation for wounds received on active service. Rev. Mr. Easton's son William had lost his left hand in a naval action. Juliana Arundell married Sir John Talbot of Rhodes Hill, Dorset 17 October 1815.

Dec 28 The gentlemen hunted. Mr. John Helyar paid us a long morning visit & was very pleasant. He read Cobbett's speech about Mr. Benett.

NOTE TO 1815

July 14 *Within the Inner Bounds of Cranborne Chase*[D] *the enforcement of Lord Rivers's right to preserve deer throughout the area was increasingly irksome to farmers whose crops were damaged by the deer. Mr Wyndham had become indirectly involved in this hotly disputed issue in consequence of a confrontation between one of his tenants, Thomas King of Alvediston, and the Chase keepers. Mr King rented Norrington farm from William Wyndham and appears to have contrived a test case at Norrington with Mr Wyndham's tacit support. A legal action between Lord Rivers and Thomas King was to be heard at the next assizes at Salisbury and was regarded as a direct challenge to the preservation franchise. It is a continuing topic through Charlotte's diary entries in 1816 (Feb 22, March 2, July 10 & 31, August 1, 2 & 4). For a full account of the campaign to disfranchise the Chase see* Cranborne Chase *by Desmond Hawkins (Dovecote Press 1993).*

1816

This volume is not a printed diary but a blank notebook adapted to the purpose. The first two sheets, which had contained writing, were cut out & the diary entries started from the other end.

Jan 3 We saw my father with his greyhounds coursing a hare.
Jan 6 Mr. Farquharson's hounds hunted at Wardour. Master Farquharson came with his beagles & went into the wood to look for rabbits but could not find any.
Jan 10 My mother received a letter from Jane Auber [*née* Grove of Zeals. (A)] (a friend desired to be <u>particularly</u> remembered to me).
Jan 16 Miss Popham & myself walked over to Ashcombe. A most dirty walk, nearly stuck <u>fast</u> in a ploughed field. I took a bundle of clean stockings & shoes with us.
Jan 20 Mr. Wm. Wyndham went out foxhunting with my brother

Dec. 28 In his attacks on John Benett's political attitude to rural wages William Cobbett nicknamed him 'Gallon Loaf Benett'.

William & afterwards he returned to Dinton. In the evening we read 'Mansfield Park' & I like it very much.

Jan 22 My father & William hunted with Mr. Wm. Grove.

Feb 9 My father & mother were very merry in the evening. Miss Burney's novel of Evelina entertained them so much.

Feb 14 My father much better today. I cannot bear to have anything the matter with him, dear little man.

Feb 22 Mr. Wyndham called. He is very earnest about his Chace cause against Lord Rivers.

Feb 23 My mother had some shrubs planted on the lawn before the house, a cedar of Lebanon opposite my window & one in front of the house. I had planted an acorn Laetitia gave me.

March 2 Mr. King breakfasted with us. The Chace cause is put off.

March 5 My mother heard from Lady Shelley – her and her daughters intend coming here Friday the 15th in their way into Sussex.

March 22 Lady Shelley & her four daughters with Charles arrived from Bath.

March 24 I accompanied Mary, Helen & Margaret [Shelley] to afternoon church at Berwick. My brothers went with us.

March 25 My Aunt Shelley & cousins left us. Charles rode as far as Salisbury with them.

March 26 We read Lara, Lord Byron's poem: the poetry beautiful but story confused.

April 24 I arrived at Sedgehill. My brother-in-law has the gout in his foot.

June 12 In the evening I walked out on the turnpike & met Edwards who had been to Warminster to reclaim a silver spoon that had been stolen from us by a gypsy last autumn.

June 28 Harriet was brought to bed of a little girl. Mr. Hodson named her Ellen Harriet.

July 1 Mr. Wm. Helyar began his haymaking. Batt & his two sons mowed the grass & worked very hard.

July 5 George is arrived in old England.

July 10 My father & brothers went into the Chace to meet Mr. Wyndham. The latter is very anxious about his Chace Cause.

Jan. 22 Mr William Chafin Grove (1786-1859) had served with the 20th Foot in Spain.

July 14 We went to Berwick church. Tom met us there & received the sacrament to intitle him to be a Justice.

July 22 Tom & Mr. Brown dined with us. Farmers Grove & Co. croaked exceedingly about the weather.

July 30 My father came home from the assizes. The Shelleys are gone to Brighton.

July 31 Charles went to Salisbury to hear Mr. Wyndham's Chace cause.

Aug 1 Charles returned from Salisbury. The Chace cause not finished. He gave us a very good account of it.

Aug 2 Mr. Wyndham has gained his Chace cause against Lord Rivers. I am delighted about it.

Aug 4 We went to Berwick church. Mr. Boys [the rector] did not rejoice so much as he ought upon the Chace cause being gained.

Aug 7 First day of Salisbury Races. We went to Netherhampton. Mr. & Mrs. Bromley met us. My mother went in their Landilet with Mrs. B. & I on the barouche box with Mr. B. I got rather wet. Good sport.

Aug 8 I went in the landilet with my mother. Mrs. B. accompanied my aunt in her carriage.

Aug 9 I went on the barouche box with Mr. Bromley. I betted every day with Mr. H. Hetley & won upon the whole.

Aug 15 First day of Blandford Races. I & my mother accompanied Mrs. Farquharson in her barouche. I went to the Ball & danced 4 dances.

Aug 16 I betted with Mr. Hetley & won. We danced after the races & had a large party. I danced every dance. The Miss Hodges danced the quadrille most beautifully.

Aug 17 Sir John Pollen very entertaining in the evening imitating a little partner of mine who made a proposition at the Ball.

Aug 22 We heard the melancholy news that my uncle Jackson is dead.

Aug 25 George is appointed second mate to the Rose, East Indiaman.

Aug 30 My brothers went to Zeals[D] to dine with Aunt Chafin upon a haunch of venison.

Sept 2 The Tollard Hunt. The gentlemen had rather a jovial party.

Oct 15 John brought us a letter. He is in high glee with the contents of it.

Oct. 15 John was now courting Jane Fraser and had received some encouragement.

Oct 16 John called to shew us a letter from Sir W.F[raser].

Oct 22 [Visiting Gaunts House][D] Lady Glynn shewed us several of her tricks. Mr. Sturt & Mr. George Bank[e]s dined with us. The latter is a very pleasant young man.

Nov 5 We were very much amused with the novel of Pride & Prejudice.

Nov 9 My father had a letter from Charles to say that he is not elected at All Souls & he came home just before dinner. We consoled him as well as we could.

Nov 18 Mr. Bedford & Charles rode to Summerleaze & hunted with Mr. Wm. Helyar's hounds.

Nov 27 We read aloud Shakespeare's play of Cymbeline.

Dec 16 My brothers George & Charles & Mr. Bedford rode to Salisbury to see the Indian jugglers.

Dec 31 George heard that the proprietor of the Rose [See Aug 25 above] is dead. He wrote to Captain Donaldson to know what he should do, who advised him to go to Town immediately.

1817

A Letts diary with a 6 day week layout: no space for Sundays, which Charlotte had to improvise. Flyleaves include detailed spending account during a visit to Weymouth with other minor memoranda & the following postscript to the events of January 1813 – '14th Feb – Miss Eyre of New House married to Mr. Matcham, nephew of Earl Nelson'.

Jan 1 George went to Town on business relative to his ship.

Jan 3 A great deal of snow on the ground. William went to Blandford to meet Mr. Bedford & Charles, & to accompany them to a Ball at the Crown Hotel.

Jan 8 Mr. Bedford & Charles called at Donhead Hall & saw Mrs. Kneller. I like my intended sister Jane Fraser better every day.

Jan 9 I acted in the evening the part of Mark Anthony: Mr. Bedford & Charles were the plebeians.

Jan 12 We had Church at home. Mr. Bedford read prayers & Charles preached.

Oct. 22 Mr Sturt was probably Humphry Sturt of Horton. George Bankes was of Kingston Lacy.

Jan 15 Tom & Mr. Wm. Butler called upon us. The latter is fond of telling droll stories & generally twice over.

Feb 7 My father wishes to make me a politician as he makes me read the speeches every day after dinner.

Feb 11 The old woman of my aunt's lodge at Zeals was robbed & came before my father who committed the man to Salisbury gaol.

Feb 12 John wrote to Sir Wm. Fraser, to be married in May. The baronet answered he could only give his daughter to Dr. Grove.

Feb 25 My mother received a very civil letter from Lady Mary Arundell in answer to an application she made to get one of my Jackson cousins into the Charter House.

March 11 [At Whatcombe] The gentlemen went out roebuck hunting & had very good sport.

March 14 A letter from John – like all the rest of my brothers he makes but a <u>desponding</u> lover.

April 11 William walked to Farnham to call upon Capt. & Mrs. Markland. Lady Mary [Arundell] has bought the Captain's donkeys.

April 15 My mother received two letters from John. He is very anxious about getting into the Infirmary at Salisbury.

April 19 John & George rode to Salisbury. They met Mr. Robert Still & were just in time to <u>put off</u> the election of the hospital till September.

April 28 I arrived at Langton before Mrs. Farquharson had crossed the Stour. A pretty sight, the procession with the palanquin.

May 3 Mrs. Farquharson went out in her palanquin. Mr. Farquharson & myself walked by her side. Old Mrs. Farquharson came. She dined & slept here.

May 27 Eleanora Fraser is such an <u>extraordinary</u> girl. [Two days later] She is a <u>very odd girl</u>.

June 3 I walked to Edie's cottage, saw her husband to whom I gave the subscription we had made for him that he may be able to put in three lives for the house he has built.

Apr. 28 Below Blandford the river Stour was fordable at a point known as Langton Shallows.

June 3 The lifetimes of three named individuals customarily provided the formula for the duration of land-tenure in the West Country.

July 14 Mr. Tom Gordon came here, played at cricket with the gentlemen.

Aug 7 [At Weymouth] An old woman with <u>large pockets</u> brought us some silks to look at. I bought a brown silk gown.

Aug 8 I heard from my mother Sir T[imothy], Lady Shelley & their four daughters have been at Fern.

Aug 30 Mr. George Glynn[B] came. Sir Richard Glynn,[B] my father & brothers went to Salisbury to vote for John & he was elected Physician of the Hospital & voted for (with great eclat).

Aug 31 We went to Berwick church. Dr. Boys preached his farewell sermon after having had the living 25 years. He has exchanged livings with Mr. Bingham.

Sept 2 [In Salisbury] We went to my brother Dr. Grove's house & were busily employed buying furniture etc for him.

Sept 5 We had a haunch of venison which my brother gave us from the Tollard Hunt. [She had noted the Tollard Hunt on Monday Sept. 1st.]

Sept 26 We went to the Cathedral [Salisbury] & heard a most excellent sermon. My aunt Grove had three beehives stolen during the night out of her garden. My mother & I attended the concert & ball.

Oct 16 [At Marwell][D] In the dining room is a fine picture of Romney's representing Lady Hamilton in the character of Circe.

Nov 4 In the evening my father, brothers & myself read aloud Hazlitt's essay on Shakespeare which I like very much.

Nov 6 Charles & myself read Lallah Rookh, my father too hoarse with his cold to read aloud.

Nov 17 Charles returned from Salisbury. He was ordained yesterday by the Bishop, as also was his friend Mr. Walter Earle.

Dec 1 A wet day. Charles amused himself in copying out from parchments trying to make out our pedigree. We read out 'Clarissa Harlowe' & my brother was much entertained with Miss Bella & the rest of the Harlowe family.

Dec 6 My brother Dr. Grove came to visit us. We talked a great deal about his intended wedding which is to take place in January.

Aug. 7 Large pockets were much favoured by smugglers and illicit traders.

Dec 7 Tom came & went to Berwick church where we heard Charles
    preach. My brothers think the same as I do about his reading.
Dec 11 I walked to the shop at Ludwell [a frequent event] & bought
    some muslin etc. My mother heard from Lady Shelley. They go
    to Bath next week, as their house in the Circus is now ready for
    them.
Dec 18 We heard from George. He is not able to get the second mate's
    berth in Capt. Drummond's ship.
Dec 23 Mr. Phelips & Charles busily employed in making out our
    pedigree. We read out in the evening Pride & Prejudice.
Dec 26 In the evening Mr. Phelips & I went into the Servants Hall to
    see the mummers & Bulls. We were much entertained with them.

1818

The continual round of social visiting continues – long morning visits and
tea-drinking in the afternoon with a move after two or three days from one
house-party to the next. When she is not at Ferne Charlotte is likely to be
found helping to cope with Harriet's children at Sedgehill or acting as
companion to Tom's invalid wife Henrietta at Weymouth. It is noticeable
that she no longer goes to the summer race meetings at Salisbury and
Blandford although 'the gentlemen' do. She finds contentment in the 'fireside
trio' of her parents & herself, and in the reading aloud of Jane Austen novels,
Shakespeare plays & whatever new books the library sends to Ferne.

Her brothers are settling down in their future roles – Charles looking for a
curacy, John referred to with some pride as 'Dr Grove' & about to become a
husband at last, and George giving up the sea to develop a Grove property at
Sedgehill.

Chess is increasingly Charlotte's ruling passion. The number & variety of
her opponents indicate the extent to which some proficiency at the game was
an expected social accomplishment.

Jan 2 Mr. Phelips has found out that this place formerly belonged to
    Philip de Ferne.
Jan 10 My father went out hunting with his four sons. Tom
    afterwards returned to Weymouth.
Jan 11 Edwards by accident locked George into the library where he
    spent the night.
Jan 13 George talked in high glee of the estate he is to have at
    Sedgehill.

Jan 14 Mr. C. Bowles breakfasted here & offered a curacy to my brother.

Jan 16 My father & George went to see the estate the latter is to have at Sedgehill. I have named it – East Hayes.

Jan 17 We drank the <u>two</u> brides' and bridegrooms' healths in Bedford Square.

Jan 19 We finished Northanger Abbey & like it very much. We waited dinner in expectation of the bride & bridegroom.

Jan 20 My brother & sister Dr. and Mrs. John Grove came. We spent rather a <u>dull evening</u>.

Jan 22 In the evening we read Persuasion & liked it <u>very</u> <u>much</u>. I played at chess with George & won a game of him.

Jan 23 John does not like novels. But his wife enjoys our reading very much.

Jan 27 Dr. Grove went to Salisbury to see his patients. Charles rode out with Mrs. John.

Feb 16 Our friends Mr. & Mrs. Penruddocke left us. The latter played us <u>all</u> a very <u>good trick</u> at breakfast time.

Feb 17 Sir Wm. Frazer is dead. He dropped down suddenly in an apoplectick fit.

Feb 23 Mr. Benett called here to canvass for my father's vote, wishing to stand for the county.

Feb 24 My mother received a letter from Mr. Bromley. Mr. B. has offered the curacy of Bighton to Charles & I <u>suppose</u> he will be <u>happy</u> to accept it.

Feb 26 Mr. Phillips was busy with the parchments all the evening.

March 3 We came to Sedgehill. Harriet wants me to stay with her till after her confinement.

March 17 I hope my mother will go next week to Bath without me. Lady Shelley has been giving a very gay Ball & supper.

March 19 Harriet was brought to bed of a son. He was baptised Albert, the same day.

April 1 I returned to Fern. My father seemed very glad to see me. He gave me 2 black gowns.

Jan. 17 Sir William Fraser's London residence was in Bedford Square. One of the bridegrooms was John Grove.

Feb. 24 Bighton is in Hampshire, near Alresford.

Feb. 26 The parchments were Grove family documents from which a family-tree could be derived.

April 5 Mr. Wm. Long [recently dead] has left a handsome legacy to
my Aunt Philippa & not to any other of the Grove family.

April 7 Charles has taken lodgings at Alresford as there was not any
to be had in Bighton.

April 10 The Lord Chancellor will not permit my brother to buy
Ashcombe & Tollard. [See Nov 30 below]

April 16 I & Fanny [Jackson] walked to Ashcombe. We met with
something extrordinary in one of the atticks.

April 21 A dissertation after tea upon the Gentlemens' fashionable
long coats.

April 23 I was busily employed preparing to go to Weymouth. George
set off at four in the morning for Downton Fair where he bought
some oxen.

April 28 [At Weymouth] I walked on the Esplanade by the side of
Henrietta's wheel chair.

April 29 I walked to Jordan Hill with my brother [Tom] where he
used to mount picquet guard when encamped at Weymouth.

May 4 Bysshe's novel of Prometheus came.[N]

May 15 Henrietta bathed in the sea & I hope it will do her a great deal
of good.

May 25 Henrietta & I rode in the sedan chair.

May 31 (At Sedgehill). Mr. Ames vaccinated little Albert [Helyar] the
third time.

June 12 Mr. Goodford, Mr. Wm. Helyar & George went to Mr.
Benett's dinner at Devizes, the latter being a candidate for the
county at the ensuing election & they did not return until early the
next morning.

June 18 [At Devizes Charlotte's father seconded Mr. Benett's
nomination]

June 23 My father went to Netherhampton to be in readiness to
attend the election tomorrow.

June 24 My father returned from the Election. He has proposed Mr.
Methuen.

July 1 Mr. Benett 381 below Mr. Wellesley. I fear he will lose his
Election.

July 2 Today Mr. Benett gave up his Election finding by the conduct of

July 1 For Mr Wellesley see Aug 21 footnote below.

his opponent & <u>mob</u> there was no chance of his succeeding. The gentlemen played at cricket.

July 5 Heard some girls of Amys school their Cathecism before church, to whom we gave ribbons.

July 14 My father went with Mr. George South[c] into Oxfordshire to see his estate.

July 31 We left Compton ... arrived at Corsham rather late. A fine house with several beautiful pictures. Little Paul Methuen is very like the miniature we had seen of him.

Aug 3 We left Corsham. We came home by Fonthill. A man opened a door & let us see a rear view of the Abbey.

Aug 17 George has begun digging the foundation of his house at East Hayes.

Aug 20 The Messiah at the Cathedral [Salisbury]. Two old men discomposed us by chattering during the singing. We went to the Concert & Ball. Finale God save the King beautifully sung. I danced with Mr. Charles Wyndham two quadrilles & two country dances.

Aug 21 We returned home [from Salisbury]. In our way we called at Compton. Mrs. Penruddock as usual talked of her friend Mr. Long Wellesley. He has given her a miniature of Lord Byron. We called on Mrs. Fitzgerald. My mother very <u>luckily</u> for <u>me</u> made a <u>mistake</u>. [The nature of this mistake is not specified].

Aug 22 I walked to Wingreen – met a smart barouche & four with several ladies & gentlemen in it.

Aug 24 [Monday] Bank Holiday. I walked to Hascals at Lower Donhead & bought some lace there. George went to Woodyates Inn[D] where he played a cricket match.

Sept 7 I walked to Berwick & saw Mr. J. Lushes house. They have begun covering it with reed.

Sept 30 I walked to Talbots [shop]. My cousin Charles Jackson dined & slept here. He has been visiting Mr. Kneller where he had turtle, venison & every luxury.

Oct 2 I saw them making cyder.

Oct 30 I walked to Berwick & afterwards to Vespasian's Camp[D] with Mrs. Bingham.

Aug. 21 Long-Wellesley, William Pole Tylney (1788-1857) nephew of the Duke of Wellington, was MP for Wiltshire 1818-1820; in 1845 he succeeded his father as 4th Earl of Mornington.

Nov 5   We began reading The Heart of Midlothian a new tale by
   Walter Scott.

Nov 6   A letter from Charles. He has not succeeded at All Souls.

Nov 16 George rode to East Hayes. He has had some depredations
   committed there & went to Justice Helyar about it.

Nov 21 I met Mrs. Bingham in Clay Lane. The Blandford bank has
   not stopped. We read Tom Jones in the evening.

Nov 27 George went out hunting with Mr. Wm. Grove & he shot the
   fox.

Nov 30 My father came home. They will purchase Ashcombe &
   Ashgrove if Lady Arundell will give up her jointure on that estate.

Dec 6   I heard something about my brother & sister Helyar that I hope
   is not true.

NOTE TO 1818

May 4 *The 'novel of Prometheus' may have been sent by Bysshe but he was
not the author. The book must have been* Frankenstein or a Modern
Prometheus, *published in 1818 anonymously and written by Bysshe's
second wife Mary Shelley. The author was at first suspected to be
Shelley.*

1819

A Letts diary. Back of front cover and flyleaf devoted to a day-by-day record
of the number of votes cast in a parliamentary election. Charlotte's ardent
support for candidate John Benett of Pythouse breaks through the statistical
listing momentarily with the single word "Hurrah". The rear flyleaves carry
various expenditure details, including 'Sacrament one shilling', and mention
her possession of £7 in England bank notes and £13 in Blandford notes.

   Apart from the excitement of the election the year was marked with the
death of Charlotte's eldest sister Emma Waddington. Emma's two little
daughters were brought back to Ferne with their governess, Miss Hutchins,
and cared for by Charlotte until Waddington could restore family life.

Jan 1   My mother gave us her usual gifts of pocket books, almanacs
   etc.

Jan 5   Mr. Fletcher I hear has parted with the Living of L[owe]r
   Donhead.

Jan 6   Bank Holiday. I was going to walk upon the hill but met my father who told me there was a troop of Merry Andrews etc coming down which induced me to turn back.

Jan 9 Dr. Grove returned to us. He has had Mrs. Charles Grove as a patient.

Jan 12 Mary Shelley is going to be well married.

Feb 10 My birthday – 36. I walked to Berwick, scolded some poor women for picking my father's hedge.

Feb 23 An invitation to dine at Donhead Hall. We declined it, there being no moon.

Feb 24 My mother heard from my sister Waddington. Their governess Miss Moxon is going to be married to their butler.

March 8 A gang of footpads have been found out by the police officers, & some of them taken at Blandford.

March 13 My father sent Alice Burden in a chaise to the Salisbury Infirmary.

March 14 Alice Burden could not be admitted into the Infirmary.

March 15 I walked to Berricourt to see Alice Burden. She is not at all the worse for her journey to Salisbury.

March 19 At dinner time we were alarmed by the library chimney being on fire, the 3rd time it has happened. It was swept with a holly bush immediately.

March 22 A letter from Henrietta to tell us Sir Wm. Fraser has got a cadetship for William Jackson.

April 5 My aunt Lady Shelley & her daughters arrived. We had a great deal of talking.

April 7 I talked a great deal with Mary [Shelley] about Mr. H[aynes].

April 8 Helen [Shelley] played to us in the evening & Charles Jackson played on the flute.

April 10 [Easter Saturday] Lady Shelley & her daughters left us.

April 15 Harriet miscarried of a stillborn female infant.

April 27 George & Thos. Shere came here for a search warrant as some persons have been stealing my father's hedges.

May 1 The children had a Maypole with flowers upon the Green, being May Day.

May 7 The kitchenmaid at Fern has produced a little one.

Jan. 9 The patient was the widow of Dr Charles Grove of Salisbury, of the Zeals branch of the family.

Apr. 7 Daniel Franco Haynes married Mary Shelley two months later.

May 14 The kitchen girl & her baby left Fern.

May 17 I called at Berricourt. The bride rather entertained me with her <u>reflections</u>. The shepherd is making a nice garden there.

May 29 A letter from Waddington saying Emma is dangerously ill. My mother & I immediately set out for Salisbury. John joined our party. We went to Stockbridge.

May 30 Left Stockbridge at 5 o'clock arrived at Clay Hall in the evening. Emma has had an inflammation of the windpipe.

May 31 I sat up at night with dear Emma. I sincerely pray she may recover, dear love.

June 1 I went to sleep for about two hours & when I waked was very near fainting away from my late fatigues. John left us. He had not been gone two hours when Emma had an abscess broke.

June 2 My sister continues very ill. My mother & I have completely made up our minds for the worst.

June 4 Emma was dangerously ill all day. We are in very great affliction about her, dear creature.

June 9 Dear Mary Shelley was married today. My dearest sister felt faint all day. Towards evening she grew worse & about 12 o'clock at night died without a struggle. Oh what a heartrending scene to us all.

June 18 We set out on our journey early in the morning. I accompanied Miss Hutchins [governess] in the back chaise. Tom & Waddington went in the former's barouchette. Dined at Windsor, went through part of the Forest.

July 2 There is a report that Mr. Methuen is going to resign being Member of the county.

July 14 Mr. Parker came in a Velosopied.

   July 15 A message from Mr. Benett to beg my father & brother to attend the Nomination.

July 16 My father & Tom accompanied Mr. Wm. Helyar to the Nomination at Devizes. A lawyer came with the papers relative to the purchase of Ashcombe etc.

July 19 George attended the hustings being the first day of the Election. State of the poll. Mr. Benett 302 Mr. Astley 199.

July 20 A sad riot at the Election. One of Mr. Benett's voters much wounded & sent to the hospital at Salisbury.

July 14 The velocipede was an early form of bicycle. In 1819 its name was a novelty and its spelling a challenge.

July 21 Thos. Shere went to the Election. The Freeholders voted in a malthouse at Salisbury, the hustings being pulled down by the mob.

July 22 Capt. Haines accompanied my father to Salisbury where they voted for Mr. Benett.

July 31 George rode to Salisbury. His vote could not be taken for Mr. Benett.

Aug 4 Mr. Benett has gained the Election.

Aug 18 To Sally Pinnocks. We found her in bed very ill with a sick headache. My mother sent her some sago & port wine.

Sept 2 Thursday, Bank Holiday. Dr. Grove came & dined with us on a haunch of venison, which Ld. Rivers sent.

Sept 4 I walked with Miss Hutchins & the girls to Ashcombe, brought some relicks from the house.

Oct 11 Mr. John Brine has eloped with Miss Bastard.

Oct 18 The carpenters are taking up the dining room floor at Ashcombe for Fern. Two pictures arrived from that house for me.

Oct 20 My mother mended my picture of the Carnival at Venice which Mr. Methuen had shot a hole in when he lived at Ashcombe. George returned from Salisbury. He saw a gnu at the Fair – like a bull.

Nov 4 Thursday, Bank Holiday. Fanny [Jackson] and I walked to Rushmore. We saw the house: a beautiful picture of Lady Ligonire, Ld. Rivers's sister. Met a strange old dame on the down, keeping sheep.

Nov 8 George dined with the Yeomanry at Hindon & got very tipsy.

Dec 13 I walked to Talbots to enquire about some clothes for poor people, my Aunt Grove having been so kind as to give 5£ for that purpose.

Nov. 4 Lady Ligonier was only 17 when, as Penelope Pitt, she married Viscount later Earl Ligonier in 1766. Neglected by him and divorced for adultery with Count Vittorio Alfieri she married Trooper Smith of the Blues in 1784. A full-length portrait of her is at Hinton St. Mary manor-house, the property of Anthony Pitt-Rivers Esq.

1820

A Letts diary. Flyleaves carry a few unremarkable notes of personal expenditure, addresses of tradespeople, a bet with Mr. Wyndham and a list of literary extracts under the heading 'Charlotte Grove repeats by heart.'

At times her daily entries are almost taken over by her nephew and nieces. To her regular support for Harriet's ever-increasing brood is added an urgent concern for the little Waddingtons following the death of Emma. In addition to the role of attentive aunt she increased the range of her succour to the village poor, with encouragement from her formidable Aunt Grove. Politically there was disenchantment with John Benett, and matrimonially her brother Charles Henry brought back a wife from his curacy at Bighton, near Alresford.

Jan 3 Mr. Wallinger & Charles arrived from Alresford. The latter has a wig which does not improve him.

Jan 4 I like the description of Miss Hopkins my intended sister-in-law.

Feb 2 Met Mr. Jones the Presbyterian preacher. He is a Whig & I am a Tory.

Feb 15 Betty Stretch called upon us. I gave her a piece of Charles's Bride-cake and took the rest to Sedgehill.

Feb 25 My brother Charles & his bride called here [Sedgehill] in their way from Bath to Fern. She is a very pretty young woman. Fanny & Harriet agree with me that Charles is amazingly disguised by his wig. Agnes [Helyar] put herself in a passion about having the leeches applied.

March 4 My father intends voting for Mr. Astley this contest instead of Mr. Benett.

March 7 We heard at Shaftesbury that Mr. Long Wellesley has resigned the contest for the county of Wilts.

March 8 Mr. George Helyar came in his way to Dorchester on the western circuit. He says the people hooted at Mr. Long Wellesley at the play, & he made a most excellent speech on the occasion & spoke remarkably well.

March 11 Mr. Wm. Helyar rode to his farm at Wincanton.

March 13 Mr. Kneller told my father that Waddington has taken Wyncombe.[D] I wish it may be true.

March 15 My father proposed Mr. Astley at the Election.

March 16 I read my <u>favorite</u> book, Sir Charles Grandison.

March 20 He [Mr. John Still] perfectly coincides with me in regard to Mr. Benett's conduct in the House of Commons.

March 23 Waddington has taken Wyncombe.

March 24 My sister [Harriet] brought to bed of a little girl. Mr. Hodson . . . named her Marian Elizabeth.

April 4 I walked to Ashcombe. It looks very melancholy, the trees being cut down & the house pulling down.

April 11 Charles has left off his wig & he looks much better without it.

April 14 The new married pair both very unwell. They sat in their dressing room all day. My father very facetious.

May 4 I lent Charles Henry my 8 vols of 'Clarissa Harlowe'.

May 8 Ashcombe is now completely spoilt as one of the Lions of the country.

May 11 Met a poor woman, very ill, of the name of Hawkins.

May 30 I walked with Col. & Mrs. Macdonall [née Laura Arundell] to Ashcombe. The latter felt <u>much</u> at seeing the place in ruins.

June 20 My cousin, Mrs. Haines [Mary Shelley] was last Friday brought to bed of a daughter.

July 3 I walked to Berwick, called upon Betty Stretch. She has heard that her daughter Fanny who was transported to Botany Bay is dead, & that the ship in which her property to the amount of £700 was sent to England was burnt. Edwards wrote to Lyoids [Lloyds] to ascertain the fact.

July 19 <u>My dear friend</u> Betty Stretch is dead.

Sept 1 Mr. Wm. Helyar is gone to Coker as his father died last night.

Sept 19 We went to Gaunts[D] – Sir R. Glynn's. [After dinner] All the party but my father & mother played at Loo. We read our books.

Oct 23 Harriet rode on her donkey. She made <u>curious noises</u> to get it on.

Nov 5 My uncle [John] Pilfold came, whom we had not seen for 9 years. Received a sad account of uncle James.

Mar. 16 *Sir Charles Grandison* by Samuel Richardson.

May 8 'Lions' in the sense of sights worth seeing (OED). The sudden deterioration of Ashcombe so soon after Tom Grove bought it suggests that like Ferne it developed some radical fault beyond repair.

Nov 6 I heard that a sailor had broken open a poor woman's house on the turnpike road. My uncle called at Charlton. He saw the good humoured Mrs. South & her children.

Dec 8 Visited Dame Pinnock. She is spinning wool to make a blanket for her brother – what she picked from the bushes that the sheep had scattered.

Dec 21 I called on Mrs. Wilkins to engage her as my washer- woman. I then went to Barkers Hill where I saw an old woman of the name of Wadley. Her & her husband great objects of charity both 79 & have only 1 allowance from the parish.

Dec 22 I walked to Talbots to order blankets with Aunt Grove's money for the poor people.

1821

A Letts diary. On a blank page 17 before January 1 she has made four dated entries. Jan 22 – a poetic squib of her father's composition, here transferred to its context in the diary. 5th May – a note of the death of Napoleon Buonaparte 'this great man'. 19th July – A resumé of newspaper accounts of the coronation of George IV and Queen Caroline's attempts to enter the Abbey. Charlotte was passionately hostile to the Queen in the divorce controversy. 7th August – the death of the Queen is recorded without comment.

The end fly-leaf carries a reference to a Bank of England bill of exchange for ten pounds 'received of my father October 16th' – to which the diary adds a comment, relating the payment to her regular personal allowance.

This was an unsettling year for Charlotte. The close association with Sedgehill ended when Harriet's husband inherited Coker Court, near Yeovil. The Knellers were leaving Donhead Hall and there was a political estrangement from Pythouse. The death of Tom's wife, Henrietta, and the desolation of Ashcombe were followed by the even greater tragedy of the loss of little Charles Waddington who had inspired in Charlotte an almost maternal affection.

Jan 6 I whipped Albert [Helyar] as he was very naughty.

Jan 22 My father very witty at breakfast & made some verses.

> They may hang her or drown her,
> Divorce her or crown her,
> But talk not of the Queen,
> For it gives me the spleen.

Nov. 6 Uncle John Pilfold's wife was a daughter of T. South of Donhead.

Feb 1 Dr. Grove returned from Weymouth. Mrs. Thos. Grove has got the mumps.

Feb 5 (Monday) An express arrived early for John from Weymouth as Mrs. Thos. Grove is <u>much worse</u>. We heard after Dr. Grove's arrival that there are no hopes whatever of my dear sister's life.

Feb 6 My father, mother & Waddington went to Weymouth. They called at Langton in their way. I received the sad news that Mrs. Thos. Grove died on Monday morning last [yesterday]. Old Mrs. Farquharson is at Langton & bears it with the greatest resignation.

Feb 7 Wednesday. The funeral is to take place at Langton, and by Henrietta's express desire to be performed by torchlight.

Feb 12 My dear sister Henrietta Ann Grove has left me a present of one large topaz brooch & two small topaz brooches set in pearls. I shall ever keep them for her sake.

Feb 14 John & George walked to Ashcombe to give some orders from Tom to his bailiff. [Later] The gentlemen talked politicks, not a very pleasing subject of conversation as the Dr. [John] is rather a <u>Queenite</u>.

Feb 23 Capt. Haines told us our late neighbour Mrs. Cook & her daughter and son-in-law talk of going abroad.

March 2 Played with little Charles [Waddington]. He is quite diverted with the songs his grandmama & I sing to him & his grandpapa takes a great deal of notice of the darling child.

March 15 I met a poor woman that had been all the way from Alvedistone, heavy laden & only paid 3d for her labour. And so grateful to me for a <u>trifle</u>.

March 20 George went to Salisbury to attend the ball & dance with a certain <u>fair lady</u>. [See April 25 below].

March 21 Mr. & Mrs. Kneller & their family have left Donhead Hall.

March 22 My aunt Jackson etc are coming to live at Coombe in June. My aunt Grove & my dear friend Laetitia Popham came here. We have not seen the latter for nearly four years. I hope she will never be so long a time again from coming to see us. We read Kenilworth.

March 23 Capt. & Mrs. Haines called upon us. They wish to let Donhead Lodge.

March 31 Many of Mr. Kneller's labourers are in great distress for their money.

Feb. 23 Capt Haines had replaced Mrs Cooke as the occupier of Donhead Lodge.

April 3 Called upon Mrs. Pinnock, gave her a commission for my
father to make him 6 pr of yarn stockings out of his wool. My dear
little Charles Waddington's birthday. He is two years old.

April 11 Laetitia read aloud my pocket book [diary] of 1811.

April 18 My cousin Elizabeth Pilfold is dead, daughter of my uncle
James Pilfold.

April 25 George returned from Salisbury <u>disappointed</u> of his <u>fair
partner</u> at the ball.

May 2 [At Sedgehill] Heard that my uncle Capt. Pilfold & his
daughter Emma are arrived at Fern.

May 3 We left Sedgehill with regret, being our last visit to my dear
brother & sister.

May 4 I walked to Upper Donhead, called upon Mrs. Burlton. [She]
shewed me a beautiful present of pearls, watch & shawls from her
son in India.

May 17 My father & George after dinner fancied they had found out
the perpetual motion.

June 1 Emma P[ilfold] rode the donkey & I accompanied her. Called
on Rawlins & found his wife in labour. She was so ill I sent for Mr.
Wills but <u>luckily</u> before he could arrive Christian Wilkins brought
the little girl into the world. E.P.'s <u>exclamations</u> amused me.

June 11 In the evening, being Whit Monday, the Lower Donhead club
came up here & their band played to us upon the Green. My father
sent them a £1 note.

June 19 Charles Jackson & George went to Donhead Hall. Mr.
Kneller's wine sold well.

July 23 Waddington & Tom went to Langton to a turtle & venison
feast.

July 25 My nephew John Waddington arrived from Harrow School.

Aug 9 I walked to Upper Donhead to see a cottage my brother Charles
is going to take.

Aug 16 We left Marwell Hall with regret. Mrs. Long sent her horses
with us to Preshaw. We found a Mr. & Mrs. James Doyle on a
morning visit to Lady Mary. Her ladyship did not give us a very
gracious reception.

Aug 17 My cousin Long has a fine family of seven children. They
showed us a beautiful baby-house Lady Gage made them a present
of.

Aug 20 Mr. Coates & my brother [Dr. John] examined my darling
Charles. It is proved to be the stone, his disorder.

Sept 17 My darling little Charles with his nurses left us for Town. I
fear that I shall never see my dear boy again. He is going to be under
the care of Mr. Abernethy. Waddington went to London by the
coach to procure lodgings for them.

Sept 23 My brother George met with a disappointment, want of
money being the obstacle to his wishes.

Oct 1 My cousin Arabella Jackson was married today to Mr. Walsh,
an excellent match for her.

Oct 2 Walked to Coombe Priory to pay a congratulatory visit to my
aunt Jackson on Arabella's marriage. My cousins went out in their
gig to give away bride cake etc.

Oct 12 I accompanied Eliza [Mrs. Charles Henry Grove] to her
cottage. My sister very much delighted with her new abode. Indeed
she seems a happy temper & pleased with everything.

Oct 16 My father made a <u>mistake</u> in my allowance by which I have
lost a quarter's pay this year.

Oct 17 A letter from Harriet. She wishes to take Sally for her upper
housemaid. [Surprisingly this is the first reference to Harriet since
they 'bade adieu to dear Harriet' in May].

Oct 25 The picture of my father's hunt scene, Lyndhurst, put over the
chimney piece of the dining room.

Nov 6 A letter from Waddington. My darling nephew & godson
Charles Waddington expired last Saturday evening. Most thankful
am I to Almighty God for releasing the little Angel from all his
sufferings.

Nov 7 I put on mourning for my darling child. I walked to Ashcombe
<u>Ruins</u>.

Nov 9 Charles & George went to Tarrant Hinton to see the parsonage
of that place as the former has thoughts of being curate. Mr. Corry
the rector was not there.

Nov 13 Mrs. Charles Grove, her two daughters & Mr. Henry Grove
called in their way from Mr. Tynts.

Nov 23 I enjoy our <u>comfortable</u> little <u>Trio very much</u> <u>indeed.</u>

Nov. 13 This Mrs Charles Grove was not Charlotte's sister-in-law but the widow of
Dr Charles Grove of Salisbury. See previous note Jan 9, 1819. Henry Grove was her son.
Nov. 23 Charlotte was now the only child living at Ferne with her parents.

Nov 28 My dear father's birthday. He has attained 63 years of age, his grand climacterick.

Nov 29 A note from John with the good news that Jane was brought to bed on the 27th inst. of a fine little boy.

Nov 30 I walked with Fanny [Jackson] to Talbots & succeeded at last in getting Lizzy Herring as a kitchen maid for Harriet. Fanny entertained with my strenuous exertions in the cause.

Dec 1 We are all quite provoked at some people's officious interferences.

Dec 2 My father & Charles rode to Tarrant Hinton. It is decided that my brother & sister are to get in there at Xmas.

Dec 4 My dear brother & sister C.H. Grove returned to the cottage to pack up their goods for moving to Tarrant Hinton.

Dec 5 I was caught in a violent storm coming from Berwick. Some of Job Dimmer's house fell down in the night. Both his & Herring's looks in a delapidated state.

Dec 7 Charles rode to Tarrant Hinton to unpack his furniture.

Dec 8 I walked to Ann Herring's to tell her Lizzy is to go to Coker on Monday. Charles has received such presents from Aunt Grove & the noble minded Mrs. Long of Marwell.

Dec 24 Tom called upon us. My mother & him did not agree very well as he rhodomontaded a little.

Dec 27 A note from Aunt Jackson & Fanny. Mr. & Mrs. Walsh [the four following lines are heavily & totally obliterated]

Dec 31 Fanny & Tom Jackson drove over in a gig to pay us a morning visit. [The next word 'I' is crossed through & followed by nearly two lines obliterated]

1822

From 1817 onwards Charlotte used a standard Letts diary each year. No diary for 1822 has survived. On July 8 her cousin Bysshe Shelley was drowned.

1823

In 1823 Charlotte did not use a diary or pocket-book as such but improvised in a blank notebook. This could have allowed her freedom to vary the length of her entries but she disciplined herself to three days per page in equal spaces. As in the Letts diaries she created a separate Sunday section at the back for entries relating to sermons, churchgoing etc.

The book starts with her sketch plan of Avebury and its vicinity and a substantial excerpt from William Stukeley's *Abury* (1743) which she borrowed from the Salisbury Reading Society during December 1822.

1823 brought Charlotte's fortieth birthday and her journal emphasises the changes in the style and direction of her life. The intensity within the family circle of the match-making years and the first births of a new generation has relaxed. The nephews and nieces appear less often as they grow up: young John Waddington now goes off to board at Harrow. The close maidenly friendships with Helen Tregonwell and Laetitia Popham have lost their intimacy. Helen's transformation into 'Mrs. Markland' is much more than a change of name, and a visit from Laetitia leaves little impression on the daily record.

Chance also has played a part. In a family that was so often on horseback Charlotte seems to have been unique in always preferring to walk. She could not command any form of carriage in her own right so her visits beyond her walking range depended on her parents or any relative or friend who would fetch her. Within her more immediate vicinity therefore some recent changes had a particular significance. The Knellers had left Donhead Hall, Mrs. Cooke was no longer at Donhead Lodge, John Helyar and his entertaining wife had moved to Bath, Ashcombe was in ruins and Tom's wife Henrietta was dead; and sister Harriet was lost from Sedgehill to be the mistress of Coker Court.

In these circumstances Charlotte's daily walk led her to a new constituency, the poor, the sick and the illiterate. The old round of social visits, with their pleasures of a gossip and a game of chess became more frequently interspersed with the taking of her mother's medicinal potions and other sustenance to the sick, comforting the poor and the dying, and teaching children religious doctrine and rudimentary skills. In this she was supported by the formidable Aunt Grove, who seems gradually to become a role model for Charlotte as she tacitly accepts her own celibacy.

Jan 1 Waddington & Tom received an invitation from Mr. Wadham Wyndham[B] to dine with Kean the actor at his home & see him perform King Lear in the evening at the Salisbury Theatre.

Jan 10 I walked to Mrs. Dewy's. She has twenty scholars in her school.

Jan 17 I called upon Brockway & paid him another 5s[hillings] of my
aunt's kind donation. The old man seemed pleased to talk of the
Kneller family with whom he lived so many years.

Jan 21 The coach was full & John [Waddington] unable to set out for
Harrow School.

Jan 24 I played 4 games of chess with Emma & she won them all. I
have made a resolution if I continue to play this game, not to mind
being beat.

Feb 3 My brother George has bought a magnet & is going to <u>try</u> to
find out the <u>longitude</u>.

Feb 8 My two pupils Emma Wicks & Harriet Hyscock came again.
They have been very good girls since they were here.

Feb 11 We heard the report that Mr. Portman is dead & that Mr.
Banks is canvassing for the county. Mr. P has a very deserving eldest
son left to inherit his vast property. But as my father says, we shall
now see <u>what</u> he is when he acts for himself.

Feb 14 I walked to Berwick, visited my patient Sarah Pinnock who is
better for the Doveys Powder. Mr. Portman has declined standing
for the county of Dorsetshire in the place of his father.

Feb 16 Many anonymous letters in the Salisbury Journal relative to
the Dorsetshire election. The Freeholders talk of proposing Mr.
Portman.

Feb 18 Nomination Day for the new Member of the county. Two to
one in favor of Mr. Portman.

Feb 19 Mr. Wyndham called at Fern. He says Mr. Portman has a great
majority. He was proposed by Mr. Farquharson.

Feb 20 I called at the farm, saw both Thos. Shere & his wife. They
told me the good news that Mr. Banks has withdrawn his claims &
Mr. Portman is now Member for Dorsetshire.

March 1 George has found out <u>Perpetual Motion</u>. I hope he will attain
the <u>Longitude</u>.

March 5 I went to the parsonage. A <u>large party</u> there. It rather
surprized me as I was in my Meg Merrilies accoutrement this
stormy weather.

March 7 Hunts Powder is a very good substitute for tea to the poor
people. It is much more nourishing & tastes like coffee.

Jan. 17 Brockway had been employed as gardener at Donhead Hall.

March 9 Sunday Snow on the ground. My father read prayers to the family & I preached a sermon, at first felt a little <u>nervous</u> being unused to it.

March 19 George busy finding out the Longitude.

April 14 I left Fern with my dear sister [Harriet] & arrived at Coker Court in very good time. The children all very much grown & glad to see us all.

April 21 Mr. Henry Helyar accompanied me & Harriet to the Book Society at Yeovil. Harriet being the president exerted herself extremely outbidding Mr. Goodford the Secretary in the sale of books & she was quite the life of the party.

May 30 The Womens Club at Coker. We went to church with them. Harriet & I planned a pleasant scheme for the women to dance upon the Green but it was <u>frustrated</u> by Mr. Helyar.

June 6 We dined at Montacute.[D] Silver plate but an <u>ill- dressed</u> dinner.

June 25 I left Coker with regret.

June 27 I heard of the ill behaviour of Widow Bradley - <u>no more</u> visits to her.

July 12 A sailor was screaming ballads in the village, which will not do <u>good</u> to the poor people.

July 13 I begin to be more reconciled to my brother George's wig now he does not wear it so much over his face.

July 30 A poor man, quite exhausted with want, fell down by our gate. My dear father had him taken in, gave him something to eat & sent him to the workhouse for the night.

July 31 I attended Mrs. Lush's school. I selected a class & was very strict with them.

Aug 23 Thos. Shere came in the evening & desired my father & mother to accept a present of a turbot.

Aug 27 Called upon Mrs. John Dewey. She has 15 pupils in the free school & 12 of her own.

Aug 30 My brother & sister C[harles] H[enry] Grove left us in their new carriage with four wheels.

Sept 11 I accompanied my mother to the Abbey [Fonthill]. We went into the sale room but the books do not sell very well.

Sept. 11 William Beckford had sold his pseudo-abbey to a Mr Farquhar.

Oct 1 I visited the school & gave a boy named Burt some instructions
in writing. I intend also to teach some of the boys to cypher.

Oct 2 I walked to Mrs. Lushe's school before breakfast. Afterwards
Jane [Grove] accompanied me. We visited Mrs. White [another
school] where I whipped a little boy that was naughty.

Oct 6 I went by myself to Mrs. White's. I find the little boy I punished
was not in fault: must not be so hasty again.[!]

Nov 9 Mr. John Helyar is dead, uncle to my brother-in-law.

Dec 20 Thos. Shere received the money for my Club at the Saving
Bank. My poor people have 7d each more than last year.

1824

A fresh buoyancy of spirit pervades this year's diary. The melancholy situation of the eldest brother, Tom, widowed and childless, is now yielding to the
prospect of a second marriage. The news arouses in Charlotte a heartfelt
rejoicing and her happiness is buttressed by two other events. The family visit
of earlier years to London is revived by a determined Aunt Grove. The house
in Lincoln's Inn Fields is no longer available: brother John gave it up when
he settled in Salisbury, but John Waddington has arranged rented accommodation for the party in Wimpole Street. Aunt Grove's recent receipt of a
very substantial legacy must have added a celebratory mood to the expedition. A later journey of a different sort was very much to Charlotte's taste
also, taking her for several weeks to Coker Court where Harriet was once
more anticipating the birth of a baby. To be tête-à-tête again was a special
pleasure for the two sisters as they shared their interests and daily activities.
Both enjoyed walking and charitable visiting. Incidentally, when the weather
was inclement they had the benefit at Coker Court of artificial walks. There
are frequent notes that they walked 'on the slate' or 'on the sand' or even
'took our exercise in the great Hall'. A slate walk also existed at Ferne, to
accommodate their commitment to a daily walk, considered essential for
good health.

The journal is written in a plain notebook similar to the previous year's
but slightly larger. The flyleaves, used in her customary way for miscellaneous trivia, tradesmen's addresses etc, contain the following poem – 'On
the marriage of Miss Hill to Thos Grove, jun.'

> That Burnham Wood thro' field & lane
> Came marching down to Dunsinane
> In ominous rank, says Avon's Will -

> But now from Wiltshire speeds a <u>Grove</u>
> To Severn's bank led on by Love
> E'en to the foot of yon sweet Hill -
> But Faith we're told can mountains move
> And, strong as Faith, all powerful Love
> Takes back to Wilts both <u>Hill & Grove</u>.

To this is added 'My Mother's Impromptu' – some further versifying of less merit.

Jan 2   I played a game of chess with George & though I lost the game did not lose my temper at the same time. [A personal triumph following earlier resolutions to self- discipline in defeat at chess].

Jan 5   I sent by Alice Brockway the £1 from my aunt P. Grove to old Brockway.

Jan 19   I played a game of chess with George. I did not keep <u>my resolution</u> but I will try & do so the next time.

Jan 22   I received a nice long letter from Harriet with good accounts of herself & family, particularly little Emma Charlotte.

Feb 17   My father rode in his riding house.

Feb 19   My father has convicted some poachers about here. I hope that they will be <u>punished</u> as it is the <u>ruin</u> of a poor family.

Feb 24   My father received a letter from my dear brother Tom saying he had made an offer to Miss Hill, & was accepted which has pleased us all <u>extremely</u> as she bears a most excellent character.

March 1   James Kelly is sent to jail for deerstealing.

March 3   George joined me in my boudoir & we had two games of chess. He won & I bore the <u>defeat</u> with <u>magnanimity</u>.

March 6   George rode to East Hayes – the first time he has been able to inspect his farm this winter. I met Richard Green – he promised me he would never again pawn his things. My 5 pupils came: my mother has given me permission to keep E. Wicks & H. Hiscock on at school until the haymaking commences.

March 9   A poor man named Crowter has caught the smallpox though he was a few years ago <u>vaccinated</u> & there are many instances of the same at Shaftesbury.

March 11   [Tom's bride-to-be described by him to Charlotte] The lady is a <u>famous rider</u> & <u>very elegant</u> figure. She is just thirty. My brother appears <u>deeply</u> in <u>Love</u>.

March 16 [After meeting Miss Hill] I was nearly <u>mad</u> with <u>joy</u> at the prospect of having such a <u>delightful sister.</u>

March 20 On my return home from my walk before breakfast I found a strange man had got into our library & locked the door. My father, Thomas Shere & George questioned him & he said Lord Eldon had sent him. They walked him out of the park but he returned & kept pacing up & down our road for 2 hours. The constable then took him to Shaftesbury where there was a man in search of him. He proved to be a madman & possessed of great property. I was <u>very much pleased</u> by receiving a letter from <u>dear</u> Bessey my future sister.

March 25 [The will of Mrs. E. Long – recently (March 15) dead, aged 90 – produced legacies for all the family, but principally for Charlotte's Aunt Philippa Grove at Netherhampton]. She will come into a great property & is most truly deserving of it. Has already promised to buy a living for Charles & renew the lease of Dr. Grove's house.

March 29 I called upon Mrs. Herridge at Berry Court – our new tenant's wife.

March 30 Our tenants' feast. The punch opened my dear brother Tom's honest heart. William offered his mare for Miss Hill's use: there's civility.

April 19 Easter Monday. My <u>very dear</u> brother Thomas was married to Elizabeth, daughter of Jere[miah?] Hill of Almondsbury. The servants had a bowl of punch & a dance on this joyful occasion. A large wedding cake arrived - the <u>best</u> I ever tasted.

April 21 Mr. & Mrs. Farquharson, Robert & Frederick rode over to see us. Mr. Farquharson is going to build at Langton a new house.

April 22 George returned from Netherhampton. The doctor [John] proposes pulling down some of the wall of the dining-room at Close Gate. I hope he will be persuaded against it as it may bring down the old house upon his head.

April 24 Mr. Dansey[c] has established a post office at the Glove – no improvement to us.

April 30 My brother & sister Thomas Grove walked to Ashcombe. It was so stormy a day I was fearful lest her <u>sylphlike</u> form might be blown away. My father & brothers went to see the living of Compton Abbas but it will not suit Charles. My mother & aunt [Philippa] drove to Berwick in the carriage to see our monument erected in the church.

May 1 My love for my new sister increases daily. I walked with Eliza to Lower Donhead. We saw the children dancing & the maypole finely dressed up with garlands. William rode to Salisbury to see the Panorama of Algiers.

May 20 Mr. Chafin Grove called upon my father. They now live at Slades.

May 22 I accompanied my mother in visits to Clouds where we found Mr. & Mrs. Still & their daughter at home. Mrs. W.C. Grove was out when we called.

May 26 We left Fern with regret. Arrived at Netherhampton. My aunt rather in a <u>bustle</u> about her journey to London.

May 27 We set out upon our journey. I sometimes was the companion of one carriage, then of the other. We reached Hartford Bridge at night.

May 28 We dined & spent some hours at Staines, arrived at 70 Wimpole Street at seven o'clock: everything very comfortable under the direction of Waddington.

May 29 I accompanied my father & mother in a very pleasant walk. We saw Punch dancing.

May 31 Found a library near our house to my great joy.

June 1 I took a long walk with my father to Leicester Square where we saw the Panorama of Ruins of Pompeii. We dined at Mr. Waddington's, met his family party.

June 4 We went out shopping & afterwards to see Mr. West's pictures which we found it difficult to leave, they are so well worth seeing. 'Christ Rejected' and 'Death on the Pale Horse' beyond anything I ever saw. On our return an invitation from my brother [Tom] to accompany them to the opera. [Subsequently] My mother & I agree we <u>never</u> wish to go to an opera again, so <u>disagreeable</u> it is.

June 9 Bessey told me that most delightful news that they are going to live at Wincombe.

June 18 I accompanied my aunt (Philippa) to the British Museum. We were very much <u>delighted</u> with sculpture. In the evening I accompanied my brother Wm. to Vauxhall. The dazzling brilliancy of the place far <u>exceeded</u> my expectations. A concert, Fantoccini,

May 20 William Chafin Grove (1786-1859) was a nephew of Aunt Chafin. He inherited Zeals in 1851. His wife is indicated, May 22. Slades House was in East Knoyle.
June 4 Benjamin West (1738-1820) became President of the Royal Academy in 1792.
June 9 Tom Grove had rented Wincombe from John Gordon, who was Bessy's uncle.

Chinese Festival. The dancing <u>delightful</u> with the finest fireworks I ever saw concluded the evening. It was the anniversary of the Battle of Waterloo.

June 22 We dined in Town & then proceeded to Staines, the fat cook & Mr. Barnet riding in the barouche.

June 23 We left Staines & dined at Andover. The cook wanted to mount my aunt's box & they had an <u>altercation</u> on the subject. At Winterslow the wheel of my aunt's chariot was broken. William kindly proposed that all the females should proceed in my brother's carriage to Netherhampton.

July 5 I walked to Amy's cottage before breakfast. He went to Rushmore Lodge & brought me £1 from Ld. Rivers to my club. I rewarded him for it.

Aug 19 We visited Dr. Grove in his new house, Close Gate.[D]

Aug 31 Arrived at Coker where I was happy to see Harriet looking so well.

Sept 4 Harriet shewed me her dispensary of medicine for the poor people.

Sept 11 I took Harriet's tickets for blankets etc to some of the poor people. Mr. George Helyar went to Mr. Goodens of Compton & for a fee rent seized a calf.

Sept 15 Harriet gave birth to a very fine little girl.

Sept 24 I walked before breakfast. Mr. Helyar & Mr. Gollop went out coursing. Mr. Helyar called me Ev-g-l because I do not approve of some of his sayings.

Oct 1 I had a conversation with S. Hillier as she has a religious melancholy upon her & gave her my advice to go to the Church only & not to any Meetings. The floods are out all round Coker.

Nov 12 I breakfasted with the gentlemen who went fox-hunting. The ladies had a comfortable <u>late</u> breakfast together. I read the conversation of Ld. Byron to them.

Nov 23 (at Ferne) Last night & this morning was the heaviest gale of wind I ever heard. Some of our trees were blown down & panes of windows broken. Poor old Kimber of Berwick had his house fall in about 10 minutes after he & his daughter had quitted it.

Dec 8 Entered two more women into my penny club. Expelled two for bad behaviour.

Sept. 24 'Ev-g-l' suggests Evangel.

Dec 31 With my aunt's additional bounty I am in hopes now to have 80 in my club. Thus ends this year 1824 with sincerest good wishes of health & happiness to all the family from their affectionate relative Charlotte Grove.

1825

Again a plain notebook has been used but with only two days to each page, allowing her to write in a less cramped manner. The lower middle of the diary has suffered the spillage of some liquid which has soaked the paper and made the writing scarcely legible in places.

The year's events commence with the approaching confinement of Tom's recently married second wife, Bessy. The baby is a girl. This first step in parenthood emphasised the dilemma that besets an heir to an ancestral seat – the need to establish an appropriate residence for the rearing of a young family during the remainder of his father's life, however long or short that may be. That Ferne should eventually be his might influence but did not meet his present needs. Meanwhile it is easy to understand Charlotte's anxiety that Tom & Bessy should remain within what might be considered to be the home territory of the Groves. The lack of any plan to rebuild or renovate Ashcombe remains a mystery; and the loan of Wincombe Park by Bessy's uncle, John Gordon, was only a temporary measure.

The most sensational event of the year was the collapse of the tower at Fonthill Abbey – a landmark in the view from Ferne.

Jan 8 My dear little nephew Cary Helyar died last Thursday evening [the 6th].

Jan 21 I received a present of iron bracelets from my cousins Mr. & Mrs. Jackson. They go to Gravesend tomorrow & hope to sail for the East Indies on Sunday.

Jan 22 The gentlemen hunted. I hope that Sir T. Shelley will attend to my mother's letter.

Jan 25 Mrs. Thos Grove is brought to bed of a little girl.

Jan 26 Tom very much pleased with his little girl. Mrs. Jerry Hill & myself are honoured with being the godmother & Mr. Farquharson godfather. She is to be named after Mrs. Thos. Grove's sister, Mary, who is dead.

Jan. 22 Mrs Grove's letter probably concerned her brother, James Pilfold. See April 22 below.

Jan 28 I accompanied my mother to Wincombe. Tom is so proud of
his child. He is going to build a root house to surprise his wife on
her recovery.

Feb 1 I read aloud to Bessy Harriette Wilson's Life as long as <u>the
Turk</u>, as we call the old nurse, would permit me.
Feb 7 My father reprimanded the housemaids for throwing the
carpets out of the window, and frightened them.
Feb 8 I called upon Mrs. Ailes. Maidment was there. He was just
returned from New South Wales where he was transported 8 years
ago.[N] He gave me some account of the country.
Feb 18 Mr. Wyndham's brother Charles has bought Donhead Hall at
a high price – £10,000 without furniture.
Feb 19 I walked to Mrs. White's. Some naughty boys pelted her door
on Shrove Tuesday.
Feb 28 Tom called & told us the good news that Mr. Gordon is going
to be married to Mrs. Oliver, a widow of large fortune. We talked of
Lower Bridmore in case Mr. G. wishes to live in this country.

March 3 Mrs. Oliver has sent to pay off the mortgate on Wincombe
for Mr. Gordon. The latter has, I think, <u>sold well</u> at his age.
March 13 Mrs. Bingham intends asking Mr. Harvey, Lord Rivers's
Steward, if Rushmore is to be let as my brother & sister Grove wish
to live there.
March 20 I attended the Sunday School & made the children quit the
room <u>regularly</u> by Classes making their bows & curtesies <u>properly</u>.
March 24 Tom has thoughts of purchasing Donhead Lodge. I wish
him to have some fixed residence in this neighbour- hood. The
tenants' dinner – my father & Tom were <u>comfortably happy</u> with
the punch.
March 26 I walked to Donhead Lodge. I met my brother [Tom] &
sister there. The offices etc are so very indifferent & Capt. Haines
asks such an enormous price that it would not by any means suit
them.

Jan. 28 Root house: an ornamental building made principally of tree-roots, especially
in a garden (OED).
Feb. 1 Harriette Wilson's scandalous *Memoirs* had just been published. The names of
some of her alleged lovers and admirers would be familiar to Charlotte.
Feb. 28 Lower Bridmore Farm in Berwick St. John had been bought in 1793 by
Charlotte's father.

March 28 Tom has now thoughts of building at East Hayes,[D] certainly an excellent plan for my brother George.

April 10 Mr. Gordon's marriage to Mrs. Oliver was in the Salisbury paper. They are immediately going abroad for a twelvemonth.

April 11 Aaron is now taken into the house as footman & wears a livery.

April 14 My brother has given up the idea of building at East Hayes & is quite undecided what he shall do.

April 17 My mother drove to Coombe Priory having received a letter from Charles Jackson dated from nearly the Line. They have had a long voyage & do not expect to reach Bombay till June. William left us for Town hoping to get an appointment for promotion.

April 22 My father proposed a good plan for Mr. J.P if Sir T. Shelley will consider it.

April 26 Ld. Rivers is considering whether he shall let Rushmore Lodge to Tom.

April 30 Sir T. Shelley acquiesces with my father in the American plan.

May 2 Emma Weeks who is come home for a few days paid me a visit. She is grown a fine handsome girl. I bought two net caps that she had made. May Day was kept & she was going with a party to dance round the Maypole. I visited Mrs. White, all her school was gone to enjoy the gaieties. William arrived from London in 11 hours in our new phaeton.

May 17 William has neither any chance of promotion or being sent out to sea.

May 27 Our late cook, Mrs. Bugden, & her husband are going to be dipped in the Pool of Bethesda at Semley being of the Society of Dippers – a sort of Methodists.

June 22 We went a grand cavalcade to East Hayes – my aunt's chariot, our phaeton & my brother C.H. Grove's phaeton. It is a most beautiful spot & much improved since I last saw it.

June 26 George has left off his wig.

July 3 I am in hopes by the offer my brother [Tom] intends making Ld. Rivers that they may have Rushmore.

Apr. 17 'the Line' was the imaginary one of the Equator. 'Crossing the line' was a ceremonial occasion.

Apr. 22 Uncle James Pilfold had become a family problem of an unspecified nature.

May 17 William did not go to sea again, but remained on half-pay, and on October 1st 1853 he was promoted to Commander (retired).

July 21 Little Miss Bingham[C] has translated Gulliver's Travels into Latin & only 8 years old.

July 22 Emma [Waddington] <u>dreadfully</u> won of me 7 games of chess, it has quite given me a <u>disgust</u>.

Aug 6 My aunt was so kind as to give me a very pretty Leghorn hat made at the Wilton manufactory.

Aug 7 Tom called. I fear there is not a chance of their having Rushmore.

Sept 21 Mr. King of Alvediston is dead, an <u>irreparable loss</u> to the poor.

Oct 4 I went to see the fish taken out of our pond which has not been drawn for 16 years.

Oct 5 It is settled my uncle James is to go into Wales to reside next week.

Oct 18 A thorough wet day. I went down intending to play chess with George but, his greeting proving not agreeable, I returned to my boudoir. The oftener I read Richardson's works the more I admire them.

Oct 23 A foreigner attended the church without shoes & excited compassion by doing his duty to his God, & got some silver, a pair of shoes & something to eat.

Nov 16 Left Fern with my aunt [Philippa]. We arrived at Bath in excellent time. Mrs. Vashti very ill. Mr. Hay an apothecary sent for who did her a great deal of good. We are comfortably lodged at the York House.

Dec 5 Waddington has thought of buying Upwood in the Chace if they ask a reasonable price.

Dec 8 I received a letter from my cousin Mrs. C. Jackson dated July, written at Bombay.

Dec 15 Dr. Grove returned from Salisbury. A great run on Hetley's Bank. I hope they will stand it.

Dec 21 Fonthill Abbey: the tower of it fell down being built of such very light material. Mr. Farquhar eat his dinner as contentedly as if it had not happened. It is a very great loss in the front view from Fern – remaining as it is, it looks like an old barn with a tower of a church. Fortunate it was when such crowds of people went to see it

Dec. 5 Upwood was a 'gentleman's residence' at Sixpenny Handley built by Edward Buckley Batson c1790.

Dec 21 John Farquhar had paid £330,000 for the entire property when he bought it from William Beckford.

in 1824 & 1823 that it did not fall down when many lives would have been lost.

Dec 26   The bands of singers came. I danced two country dances with my nephew Tom Waddington in the servants hall.

NOTE TO 1825

Feb. 8   In December 1816 John Maidment and his son John, with two other Donhead men, threatened to shoot two of lord Rivers's keepers who caught them poaching deer. The two Maidments escaped but were betrayed by one of their confederates who fell and was captured. See the 1991 edition (p.xxix) of William Chafin's Anecdotes and History of Cranborne Chase.

1826

Charlotte has returned to a printed diary, which allows her less space. The front flyleaf has a recipe for brown spruce beer. The appendix pages have been used for a daily weather report & for sundry items – as follows

Jan [No date]   Mr. Benett of Pyt House has purchased Fonthill of Mr. Farquhar.

[No date]   My father had thrashed out in his barn 347 sacks of wheat, the produce of 26 acres in 1825.

The unexpected death of the rector of Berwick St. John in a road accident brought a newcomer to the rectory, with interesting consequences.

Jan 19   My brother & sister Thos. Grove called here in their way to Mr. H. Hetley's: my brother has taken Holnest, Mr. M. Davies's place nr Sherborne for several years.

Jan 20   A strange story of a person dressed up as a skeleton ghost that walks the streets of Salisbury & frightens the people. It springs some paces when followed.

Feb 5   My mother, George & myself went in the carriage to Wincombe to take leave of my dear brother & sister. Mr. Thomas Gordon[B] there.

Feb 21   That little urchin Cupid has made sad havock amongst the female part of our household. A thorough change is to be effected.

Feb 22   My mother very busy giving warning to the cook, dairymaid & housemaid.

April 16 Sir William Fraser has procured Henry Jackson a cadetship. My aunt Jackson has now four sons in that line of life.

April 20 Charles came here to enquire about the living of Sedgehill which is to be sold.

April 22 William returned from Holnest Lodge. He does not give a very favourable account of the situation.

April 23 Edwards our late butler brought his bride here. She is a very pretty young woman. They keep the Lamb Inn at Hindon.

April 25 My dear father went to Langton to attend the Chace meeting tomorrow, held at Blandford.[N]

May 24 We heard the sad news that Mr. & Mrs. Bingham were overturned from their gig & too much hurt to return home. Particulars we know not.

May 28 Our friend the Rev. P. Bingham died at two o'clock this morning. We had prayers at home. Mrs. Bingham is rather better. She does not yet know of her husband's death. I wish we may have as kind a rector & his wife to the poor as Mr. & Mrs. Bingham have been.

June 16 Dr. Grove came to see Mrs. Bingham & returned with my mother to Netherhampton & most luckily he did, as on their arrival they found my dearest father had been thrown out of the phaeton. He has a black eye & cut his arm but I trust nothing more serious.

June 20 Charles came yesterday. He is very anxious about buying the Sedgehill living.

June 23 Mr. Chitty called in the evening with the delightful news that Charles has the living of Sedgehill. [He took possession of the rectory June 27.]

July 2 Mr. Downes has been to see the living [of Berwick St. John] & if he is elected proposes to behave most liberally to his predecessor's widow.

Aug 24 [At Holnest] Tom shewed Emma P[artridge] all his alterations. She thinks he rhodomontades as much as ever.

Sept 4 Received the sad news that little Emma Helyar was taken ill in the scarlet fever Wednesday & died Saturday [Sept 2].

Sept 8 Mrs. Thos Grove [Bessey] gave birth to a nice little girl – to be named Charlotte in compliment to her grand- mama.

Sept 28 Mr. Downes the new rector seems to be doing a great deal of good in the village.

Nov 29 Mr. Downes called here. My mother being busy writing sent me down to receive him.

Dec 2 Mrs. Lampard arrived yesterday to be my mother's lady's maid.
Dec 3 A letter from my Aunt Jackson, Henry is <u>so silly</u> as to give up his cadetship.
Dec 18 We received the good news that Frederick Jackson is to succeed to the cadetship of his brother Henry.
Dec 24 Mr. Downes has behaved very <u>handsomely</u> about the Penny Club.

NOTE TO 1826

At the Crown Inn, Blandford, the principal landowners in Cranborne Chase agreed to pay collectively an annual compensation to Lord Rivers for the surrender of his ancient right to the preservation of deer within the Chase. A Parliamentary Act of Disfranchisement was to be brought in for the purpose.

1827

No diary for this year has survived, but one event stands out clearly. In June Charlotte married Richard Downes & moved into Berwick St. John rectory. The 'comfortable trio' at Ferne was ended, rather surprisingly but fortunately as Charlotte's mother died a year later. The last of her children was now settled in her own establishment. Otherwise the year passed unremarkably.

1828

She continues to use the printed 'Student's Journal'. There is again some staining in much the same form as in the 1825 diary.

This was a year of adjustment for Charlotte. To be installed in Berwick rectory with a considerate husband was a source of great satisfaction. There was a price to be paid, however, in the loss of all the easy social contacts that had come to her when she lived at Ferne. Even when her brother William attended a service at Berwick church, as was his custom, he did not feel an obligation to call on the rector's wife. Of course she and her husband were welcome at Ferne but as visitors not as inhabitants. Increasingly her diary shows a shrinkage in the range of her interests and a narrowing of attitude. She becomes more circumspect in what she commits to paper, self-censoring anything remotely scandalous. Even signs of pregnancy in Charles's wife

Eliza disappear in a row of dots. The transition from the Regency to Victorian respectability is under way.

Jan 9 We walked out. Richard & I proceeded to Fern. We only staid ten minutes with my mother. Mr. Don told the Foots he never saw any person happier than me. <u>Very true.</u>

Feb 7 Richard's birthday – 51.
Feb 13 Richard walked to Rushmore. Mr. Hervey not there.
Feb 18 Richard attended the Turnpike meeting. Henrietta [his sister] is going to lend £400 to the trustees.

March 27 Mrs. CH Grove, a stillborn daughter.

April 5 This morning my dearest mother died.
April 8 I am now more than ever thankful for what took place 12th June, having a kind husband, as I have lost such an affectionate mother.
April 9 My father spoke in such high praise of my dearest husband. There will now be a great change at Fern.
April 17 Mr. Hervey jun called about the Chace business [see Feb 13 supra]
April 20 The funeral of Robin King. He went into Wales with us when my father lived at Cwm Elan in Radnorshire.
April 22 George has engaged Daniel [Lampard] & his wife to be his servants.
April 24 My uncle [John] Pilfold is appointed to a command at Plymouth.
April 25 George made his calculations about his house- keeping when he lives at East Hayes.
April 26 I gave George a pearl locket & ivory fan that belonged to Louisa that he may present to his wife when he has one.

May 5 My brother & sister Thos Grove, little Mary & their servants arrived to live at Fern which my father has given up to them, reserving the farm for himself.
May 6 I called on Aunt Jackson. Mrs. Budden has left her the house at

Apr. 17 'The Chace business' was the implementation of the agreement reached between the landowners and Lord Rivers over the disfranchisement of the Chase. See note to April 25, 1826. The rector of Berwick St. John was involved as a landowner, albeit in a small way. See Aug 24 and 25 1829 below.

Donhead St. Mary. Fanny in her usual <u>nervous</u> way floating reports of attentions from Sir R. Williams to Mrs. Bingham.

May 10 Richard went to Shaftesbury. Ann Dowding came here. What she said made me <u>excessively nervous</u>. I must put my trust in Almighty God.

May 21 We went to Shaftesbury & did some shopping. We put up at the Grosvenor Arms. Our old servant Edwards now keeps the inn.

June 12 We have been married a twelvemonth & I am blessed with one of the best tempered husbands possible.

June 28 We went to see Norrington House.[D] Lady Gawen lived there at the Restoration, who left it to her lawyer and he sold it.

July 15 Miss Grove of Melbury married to Mr. St. Lo.

Aug 22 Wm has made an offer to Miss Fanny Grove & been accepted by <u>her</u>.

Aug 23 The <u>old lady</u> Mrs. C. Grove <u>demurs</u> about the match. My father's <u>similie</u> <u>curious</u>.

Sept 12 Mr. Downes walked to Rushmore to call on Mr. Williams.

Oct 2 Today my brother Wm was to marry Miss Fanny Grove. We drank their health.

Oct 6 My sister Helyar was yesterday brought to bed of another son.

Oct 17 We called at Odstock, saw Mrs. Charles Grove & her two sons.

Nov 25 We killed our pig: 9 score 17 lbs.

Nov 28 Mr. Downes received a letter from his brother. They are not at all alike in their dispositions.

Dec 2 Mrs. Greenway told us a sad illness that had occurred to a Mr. Greenway from the malevolence of a client.

Dec 8 We went to Sedgehill. Charles & Eliza quite well. I think the latter is. . . . The large trees at Fern much damaged by the hurricane.

Dec 26 We had an excellent Shaston ball. Many families from Shroton. Sir Edward Baker[C] the steward. Henry & Fanny Jackson dined here & went with us.

July 15 Mary Anne Grove, daughter of rev. William Frederick Grove, rector of Melbury Abbas.

Aug. 22 Frances (Fanny) daughter of the late Dr Charles and Mrs Grove of Salisbury.

Oct. 17 Yet another Mrs Charles Grove – wife of rev. Charles Grove (1792-1868) rector of Odstock.

Dec. 2 Witchcraft is indicated.

Dec. 8 'I think' ... wishful thinking perhaps. The first child not born until 1832.

1829

A plain notebook, the boards covered with a decorative paper which is peeling away. The back pages carry verses on a garland of flowers by Richard Downes (and probably in his handwriting) sent to a friend J. S. Duncan, Fellow of New College, Oxford, with Duncan's verse in reply; also an elegy on George IV, recalling his foundation of the Royal Society of Literature. Notes inside the front cover, mainly addresses, include 'to look out London school for Agnes Helyar'. This was a request from Harriet to Charlotte, when she visited London, to inspect and recommend a boarding-school for Harriet's daughter Agnes, now in her fifteenth year. Charlotte was Agnes' godmother. Some correspondence on this subject survives in Somerset Record Office [DD/PH241].

The journal is much occupied with the predictable and monotonous daily routines of pastoral and parochial life in a small rural community. Another visit to London sponsored by Aunt Grove developed into a further tour of the Midlands visiting people and places associated with Charlotte's husband. At home there were changes in domestic staff and some negotiations with Lord Rivers's land steward, Mr. Hervey, involving glebe lands and the Rushmore estate.

Jan 1 We were staying at Fern. Bessey rode on Mary's pony to see my
    father's harriers hunt. He at 70 still enjoys that exercise very much.

Jan 4 We attended the Sunday School. New rules must be made next
    year as some rebellion has been evinced.

Jan 10 We called on Mr. Foot to consult about Mr. Downes buying
    some coal for the poor people.

Jan 13 Mrs. Greenway [née Foot] called. She kindly concurred with
    Mr. Downes in providing coal for the poor at 6d. hundred [weight].
    I am busy making out a list of the old etc.

Jan 21 I walked round the village about the coal tickets. It snowed
    very fast all the time.

Feb 6 Mr. Downes puzzled about Lord Rivers's legacy. Last Monday
    the beautiful York Minster was burnt down.

Feb 8 The King's Speech, Duke of Wellington's, Mr. Peel's - all this
    makes us dread that the Catholick [Emancipation] Bill will be
    gained.

Feb 6 The Rivers legacy provided an annual payment to the thrift club and to subsidize coal for the poor (VCH *Wiltshire*, Vol xiii, p 270).

Feb 13 Bessy told me ... That <u>astonished</u> me <u>extremely</u>. I fear that there will not be <u>an increase of sense</u> in a <u>certain quarter</u>.

April 24 [In London with Aunt Grove] I went with my aunt to Mr. Partington's where she was electrified. We then drove into Regent Park where I took a nice walk. Saw the menagerie.

May 1 Miss Kent recommended some schools for Agnes Helyar. Saw the Woolwich school.

May 6 My Aunt treated Miss Kent & me to The Panorama of Rome, the inside of St. Peter's & Pass of Salsburgh Germany. I visited two establishments for young ladies.

May 15 [In London] I saw Punch, a famous puppet show.

June 14 Sunday. We gave a treat to the School of buns & elder wine in remembrance of our wedding day.

July 30 [At Coker Court] We had a christening of Ann & Ambrose Weston Helyar. Mr. Downes a godfather to the former.

Aug 24 Mr. Hervey came about the Chace. Mr. Downes went to Rushmore to meet Mr. Chitty. He has settled to take nearly 8 acres meadow in exchange for his Chace land & the timber with £15.

Aug 25 Mr. Downes unhappy about his exchange of land in the morning, <u>brightened up</u> when he found Cuttis an excellent water meadow, West Close nice pasture. [NB <u>Cuttis</u> is later rendered as 'Cuthayes']

Sept 24 We went to Holnest to visit my brother & sister, W. Grove. Entertained with the round game of <u>Old Bachelor</u>.

Oct 14 We called on Mr. Gillingham to pay for our cow. I have found in <u>Chess</u> an excellent specific for Richard's drowsiness.

Oct 26 I went round to my Penny Club. A lad named Scammell came to offer but his parents are Methodists. <u>That will not suit</u>.

Oct 27 James Burt formerly servant to Dr. Boys offered (<u>immense</u> wages 36 guineas). I hope his services will compensate.

Nov 2 To Shaftesbury to hear the Tyrolese Minstrels with which we were very much pleased.

Nov 12 Lampard came over to bottle our cyder.

Nov 13 One of the Methodist preachers came yesterday into our little village.

Sept. 24 William Grove took over Holnest Lodge when brother Tom transferred to Ferne (see May 5, 1828).

Nov 15 We attended the Sunday School. We must make an example of
Kelly who has stolen apples from Mr. Foot.

Nov 23 Mr. Hervey sent us a present of some doe venison. The
haunch we sent to my aunt P. Grove, the shoulder to Fern and the
neck & breast for ourselves.

Dec 5 My father has bought a few hounds of Mr. Farquharson & he
has leave to hunt in the Chace.

Dec 15 1st Club Day. 18 tickets given. Attended Mrs. Lathy's shop to
see all right.

Dec 21 I walked about the village in pattens – very slippery it was – to
tell the people about the coal. Snow in the night.

Dec 22 I gave out 70 coal tickets to the poor & reprimanded Charlotte
Longman for an untruth. Took exercise in our corridor above stairs.
Snow deep.

Dec 31 We went to the Shaftesbury Ball. A large party from Fern. My
head caught fire against a lamp. One of the fiddlers very kindly put
it out directly. Frost & snow. We ended the old year very merrily
indeed.

1830

This diary is missing, unfortunately as it must have contained first hand
impressions of the agricultural riots in the autumn – notably at Pythouse.

1831

An unusually substantial volume, allowing space for only two days per page
& still leaving a surplus of unused pages. Some extracts from Chambers
Biographical Dictionary have been added and there are pages devoted to
pencil sketches of flowers. The journal echoes the sombre events of the previous year with the trial and heavy sentences at Salisbury, and acts of arson
and public disorder continuing, in contrast with the more hopeful signs of
political reform. Aunt Grove's decision to rent a house for the London Season
gave Charlotte her longest visit to the Capital, accompanied by her husband
for much of the time. Family news from Sussex brought sorrow: Elizabeth
Shelley dead at the early age of 37 and Uncle John Pilfold lingering with the
after-effects of a stroke.

Jan 1 We killed our large pig. I saw the winnowing in our barn. The judges are now at Salisbury trying the late rioters. My brother Thos. is one of the grand jury.

Jan 4   Tom has succeeded in getting off the farmers at Tisbury whom the mob accused wrongfully.

Jan 9   The Salisbury trials are over. 15 to be transported that went to Pythouse.

Jan 10   Mr. Farquharson has had three ricks burnt of wheat & 1 burnt at Piddletown. How very wicked!!

Jan 13   Fanny Jackson & Mr. Thos. Penruddocke accompanied me to the Shaftesbury Ball. It was well attended. Mrs. Loftus waltzed, a lady above fifty.

Jan 19   We all agree in our sentiments about waltzing.

Jan 24   [Henry Jackson] has got a commission in the Wilts Militia through the interest of Mr. Samuel Foot.

Jan 30   Tom came to church. They had an alarm. Two men with pistols were seen on the road about 4 in the morning Saturday who inquired of Mr. Wyndham's carter if that house was not Mr. Grove's of Ferne, that it looked light then but would look much lighter a few days hence. May the Almighty protect us all from these incendiaries.

Feb 4   The coaches stopped by the depth of the snow. I walked an hour on the terrace in our garden.

Feb 21   I went to see our calf, born yesterday. It is very pleasant to have a farm of one's own.

Feb 22   Capt. Pilfold is very ill having had a parylatick stroke.

March 1   Called at Close Gate & saw my brother Dr. Grove, his wife, little John & Louisa.

March 20   My poor uncle Capt. Pilfold is quite childish from a parylatick stroke.

March 27   Col. Gordon is supposed to have been lost in a steam boat that went down last week between Milford Haven & Bristol.

April 8   Part of the perambulation of the Chace. Richard very fatigued & discomfited: Mr. Wyndham trying to alter the tithe of Norrington. [Aug. 27 below is probably relevant].

April 10   We went in the Traveller [coach] to Salisbury. Master Burlton, a grazier and Mr. Jones bookseller in it. Slept at the White Hart.

April 11   We went by the coach to London, arrived at my Aunt's sumptuous mansion 3 Montagu Square.

April 19 We went into the City, called on Mr. & Mrs. Hodgkinson. Susan Kelly their servant is looking so well & she is delighted with her place.

April 21 We went to Hampton Court to dine & spend the day with Miss Pakington. Met Miss Hawkins there. Richard & myself saw the Palace – beautiful pictures with cartoons by Raphael.

April 28 We heard the Russian Horn Band play. They each play one note on one horn.

May 11 We saw the King & Queen pass in their way to Court. We all went to the opera of Medea. Pasta sung.

May 16 We left Town. Dined at Bagshot. Mrs. Vashti ill.

May 22 Whit Sunday. Tom & George dined with us. They approve the intended Reform Bill.

May 25 Our servants went to the gaiety of Whitsuntide.

May 26 We dined with our new neighbours, Mr. & Mrs. Du Boulay.[B] Mrs. Du Boulay played on the guitar & sung very nicely.

May 27 I walked to Ferne, visited little Mary. She shewed me her silk worms.

June 15 Sad account of Mr. .....'s [Lush's] son obliges his old father to sell great part of his estate in this parish.

July 3 We made a collection at the church for the starving Irish of £7-7s-9½d & my father's £3.

Aug 1 Mr. Samuel Foot has bought Mr. Lush's freehold estate.

Aug 27 The end of next month the boundaries are to be settled between Berwick & Alvediston.

Sept 6 There has been many ricks of wheat & barley burnt at Broad Chalk.

Sept 17 Called on Mrs. Dansey,[C] took her some peaches & had some grapes given us in return.

Oct 20 [At Coker Court] The rioters have been attacking Ld. Digby's & the clergymen at Sherborne.

Oct 21 Riots at Sherborne & Yeovil. Mr. Goodford rode into the latter place & quelled the mob by his eloquence.

Oct 25 [Back at Berwick] A letter from dear Harriet. They are all quite well but have had sad riots at Yeovil & obliged to guard Coker Court & Montacute. The yeomanry at last fired on the mob & dispersed them.

Nov 10 Mr. C. Bowles came here to settle the dispute of tythe between Mr. Wyndham & my husband.

Nov 11 I walked to Ferne took Mr. Bowles's present of seals to my
  father – one a talbot dug up in Upper Donhead, the other my father
  & mother's coat of arms which must have been <u>stolen</u>.

Nov 12 The Cholera Morbis is at Sunderland. Flannel round the loins
  is recommended.

Nov 17 I was busy in the village about my club. A cow in the
  farmyard at Abbots was inclined to run at me.

Dec 21 My father received a letter from Sir Timothy Shelley with an
  account of the death of my dear cousin Elizabeth Shelley.

Dec 28 We walked to the Glove. Ministers of Parish are now charged
  postage.

Dec 29 We began our new plan to prevent sleepiness in RD.

1832

An uneventful year with little distraction from the daily round of parish
affairs. The assessment of tithes is increasingly a matter of controversy and
dispute, particularly where parochial boundaries are ill-defined.

Jan 1 My sister Mrs. Helyar had a son born today.

Jan 18 Poor Col. Brereton shot himself, his conduct being enquired
  into during the late Bristol riots from derangement.

Feb 1 The drawing room chimney is so small at the top that a boy
  cannot get up. Henstridge did it with a rope & straw.

March 10 Miss Ellen Maria Helyar has been <u>burnt</u> to death.

May 20 Tom very much elated that the Reform Bill will pass.

June 2 A letter from the House of Commons to Richard to ascertain
  the boundary.

June 4 Richard walked into the Chace, ascertained the boundary
  between Berwick & Ebbesbourne.

June 14 Dr. Grove has bought Mrs. Medlicot's house in the Close.

June 22 Mr. & Mrs. Shere & family arrived at Berwick & took
  possession of my father's farm. The church bells rung for them. The
  Lushes have left & gone to live near Hounslow.

Nov. 11 The crest of the arms of Grove of Ferne is a black talbot dog.

June 27 We finished carrying our hay in Cuthayes not till 10 o'clock at
night. 14 load from the 4 acres.

July 24 [In Salisbury] We went to Dr. Grove's new house in the Close.
It is very beautiful, Gothick, and a garden & pleasure ground down
to the river, looking into the country.

Sept 19 Richard walked to Rushmore. He saw Mr. & Mrs. Hervey,
the former very polite in offering us tea or coffee there at any time.

Oct 11 We saw the goods of Mr. Baish go by. I fear the publick house
will be a bane to our now peaceful village.

Dec 23 I approve of Mr. Sidney Herbert's speech at the county
election. Mr. Benett & him elected.

1833

She continues to use a plain notebook, adding her own divisions and head-
ings. In her account of the year two events stand out. In the summer she
accompanied her husband in a visit to his sister, Henrietta, at Brighton, which
provided an opportunity to go to Field Place for a few days on their way
home. In the autumn Charlotte was sent to Zeals to attend Aunt Chafin as she
lay dying. The amount of money kept in the house will probably surprise the
modern reader as much as it alarmed Charlotte.

Jan 2 The little pig brought up in our kitchen I shall name "Mrs.
Cinderella" as she is now always in the cinders.

Jan 4 We dined at Mr. C. Foot's, very excellent doe venison.

Jan 24 My brother Tom paid us a long morning visit & kindly invited
us to dine tomorrow at Ferne & meet Mr. & Mrs. Farquharson &
family.

Jan 25 We dined at Ferne. A most lively game of The Knight of the
Whistle.

Jan 29 The clerk's little son James spelt Church, gave him sixpence
for doing so.

Feb 10 My birthday. 50. My dear husband prevented me doing
something wrong & that I should have been sorry for afterwards
(how fortunate to be united to such a good religious man).

Dec. 23 For Sidney Herbert see 1837, August 1st footnote.

Feb 13 They are so <u>long</u> in setting about vaccination in this village that I am fearful the smallpox now at Alvediston will arrive first. Certainly the cowpox does not entirely answer. John Jackson has had the smallpox since in India.

Feb 25 Richard went to the Turnpike meeting at the Glove. My father & brothers there. We do not quite approve of their way of <u>managing</u> it. I walked to Bridemore. Miss Lane rode to Berwick on her donkey.

Feb 28 We have sent my aunt P. Grove a present of a sow. Bradley from Alvedistone bought 8 of our pigs. He was in the Battle of Waterloo.

March 9 We called on Mrs. Foot, took her some griskin & seacale.

March 25 Mr. Waddington, his son George, Mr. Alex Wyndham,[B] my brothers Tom & George dined with us. They <u>all</u> came in <u>one</u> carriage & they were <u>very</u> merry having killed their fox in the Chase that morning.

May 9 Last night some idle men & boys pulled down our wall in parts that is just finished.

May 15 Miss Ribbon the actress has eloped & married Mr. Conduit, leader of the Band at Salisbury.

May 23 A ballot at the Vestry meeting for the labourers. The Grove cottages built by my father portioned out.

June 7 I named the new cottages, built by my dear father, 'Grove Mount' being on a rising ground.

June 13 The cottagers at Grove Mount are digging their gardens.

Aug 3 Called at Ferne. Mr. & Mrs. Grove & Mary are gone to Cwm Elan.

Aug 14 [Visiting Brighton] I walked with Richard on the beautiful chain pier. It is very light & elegant, painted green & hanging in festoons.

Aug 19 [From Brighton] We went to Field Place. My aunt & Sir Timothy Shelley most <u>wonderful old</u> people, the former <u>so very like</u> my <u>dearest mother</u>. Helen & Margaret played to us on the harp & piano. Elizabeth's oil paintings are <u>very beautiful</u>: the dining & drawing room[s] furnished with them.

Aug 20 We walked to Warnham Pond. Mr. Cooke & Mr. Martin called. Mrs. Wm Hutchinson dined here. My brother Charles here & not very well in his old complaint.

Aug 21 Kate Pilfold spent the day with us. I am afraid I have got into a
scrape ... heard of my cousin Mary Trevor ... I hope that she has
repented her misconduct. (I am to ask a question of Mrs. Walsh) A
haunch of venison for dinner. We have been most <u>hospitably
received</u>.

Aug 27 Cwm Elan, my brother & sister say, is very little altered since
we lived there.

Aug 31 [During a visit by the Jacksons] My aunt found it so <u>very</u>
difficult walking up stairs here that she is determined to go home
tomorrow.

Nov 9 Saturday. An express arrived from Zeals. My father & I set off
directly, driven by Tom. My aunt very glad to see us but very ill &
in great pain. Mr. Wm Chafin Grove arrived. I sat up at night.

Nov 10 My aunt remained in a stupor all day. Mr. Newman the
apothecary came. He said hers was quite a decay of constitution
from old age.

Nov 11 My dear Aunt Chafin died without a struggle. Mr. W.C.
Grove a great comfort to both my dear father & myself. The former
is left sole executor to her will.

Nov 12 My father found about £800 in my aunt's bureau. He returned
to Ferne. My aunt told me she left all her wardrobe to me the
Saturday I came. I directed all that was right to be done for her.

Nov 14 In a drawer of the bureau I found the jewels that are left to
Mrs. W.C. Grove & then an heirloom to Zeals; also a quantity of
banknotes & gold which quite frightened me. I wrote to my father
to come immediately & receive it.

Nov 15 My brothers George & Charles came. In the evening we
counted the money which amounted to 19 hundred and 15 pounds.

Nov 19 The funeral. My father chief mourner. We his children
followed. Many poor people attending their late benefactress to her
last home.

Nov 20 My dear father gave us my aunt Chafin Grove's carriage. We
returned home in it driven by her coachman & horses which were
left at Ferne afterwards.

Dec 11 I had my shop for the Penny Club. My <u>customers</u> seemed well
satisfied. Richard put £30 in the Savings Bank for the Penny Club.

Aug. 21 The conduct of Mary Shelley, who left her husband Mr Haynes to elope with
Mr Trevor, was probably not a favoured topic of conversation at Field Place. What
Mrs Walsh, formerly Arabella Jackson, might contribute is not disclosed.

Dec 23 Mr. Ferret came from the Chace to pay Ld. Rivers tithe. A turkey sent to us from Ferne.

1834

The determination of the rector of Donhead St. Andrew, William Dansey, to build a school at his own expense was evidently an inspiration and a challenge to Charlotte & her husband to do likewise. The marriage of her youngest brother, George, completed the marriages of all her surviving brothers and sisters.

Jan 7 My dear father paid us as executor my Aunt Chafin's legacy of £100 deducting £3 tax on it.

Jan 8 My father is having a well opened for the poor people.

Feb 17 I visited the Dissenters & gave them some money from my husband.

Feb 24 I had a letter from my brother George to inform me he is going to be married to Miss Charlotte Eyre, 3rd daughter of the late Mrs. Eyre[B] of Newhouse.

Feb 25 My dear father facetious about the intended marriage.

Feb 26 We walked to Rushmore, saw Mr. George Hervey. He is now living & inspecting the farm there.

March 7 A letter from my cousin & god-daughter Helen Pilfold[A] to announce her marriage with Mr. Leslie, a barrister.

March 13 We came to Netherhampton. Miss Eyre & Miss Popham there, also my brother George. I like my intended sister-in-law very much. She reads well.

March 24 We walked to Donhead St. Andrew. Met Mr. Du Boulay at Mr. Dansey's. The latter wished us to see the site for a new school which his neighbour Mr. Monkland objects to the situation & which Mr. D will build at his own expense.

April 24 We walked to Dickets. He has fenced his garden walks with bones taken out of Ferne kennel 40 years ago. We returned through Dengrove – the wrong way with many watery places to pass.

April 26 Mr. Dansey has obtained a grant of £90 from the National Society for his school.

May 11 A foreigner in church whom we did not know.

June 12 [On a visit to Leamington] A fine view of Warwick Castle. We had our profiles taken by an automaton.

June 22 Passed nr. Aynhoe where the Groves formerly lived.

July 3 I turned Elinor Cull out of the Womens Club for bad conduct.

July 5 My cousin Wm. Jackson expected home. The Donhead St. Mary band went out to meet him.

July 7 Very glad to see my cousin Wm. Jackson after an absence of 15 years. He left at 16 & has now been a Capt. five years.

July 10 My brother George was married to Miss Charlotte Louisa Eyre, 3rd daughter of the late Purvis Eyre of Newhouse. I went shopping to Shaftesbury.

July 12 Lord Arundell died at Rome. Henry Benedict[B] his brother succeeds him.

July 15 We heard of the death of my uncle Capt. Pilfold R.N. He had another parylatic seizure. My husband used the leeches & put on a blister for his cough.

July 18 Dr. Grove & his daughter Henrietta are going to Field Place.

July 22/23 We walked to East Hayes to visit my brother & sister George Grove ... Their house is elegantly furnished & they seem the happiest couple possible.

Aug 7 My dear friend Mrs. Farquharson died yesterday. She had a dream 4 or 5 years ago: in the vault of Langton she saw her coffin dated 1834.

Aug 25 We went to Hanley to visit Capt. & Mrs. Markland who have just got a very pretty house there. The turnpike road by Tollard very rough & the road through the Chace very bad.

Aug 31 Commissioners are appointed for the Poor Laws & the magistrates have no longer anything to do with it.

Sept 4 My dear sister Helyar & her two eldest daughters arrived, their first visit to us.

Sept 13 Went to Norrington. They have rebuilt part of it in the Gothick style.

Sept 23 My brother & sister Wm. Grove left us. I gave the former Miss Austen's novels. We walked to Staplefoot, happy to find Sarah Weeks better than we expected (her daughter rhodomontades)

Sept 26 Mr. Dansey inquired of a house for Mr. Hewit, a curate who is going to serve Anstey on only £22 pay.

Sept. 23 'Staplefoot' was one of the Chase Walks, in each of which a keeper's lodge was located.

Oct 22 Some of the <u>old industrious</u> poor paid only one shilling & three
pence each the week. A <u>wrong way</u> of beginning the new Poor Law I
think.

Dec 11 Had a consultation with Mr. Sharp, Henstridge & Foot about
our school.
Dec 16 We had Sharp, Foot & Henstridge to put down the articles for
roof etc of the school.
Dec 18 We called on Mr. Mrs. Foot considered 5 situations for the
school, fixed on the 1st at last.
Dec 19 My brother Wm. has refused to come to Ferne at Xmas.
Dec 20 Last evening a stone was thrown into our bedroom window, I
<u>hope</u> by accident. We moved into the best bedroom.
Dec 22 My dear father gave us leave to quarry the stone in his quarry.
Dec 29 My cousin Helen Leslie died, the late Capt. Pilfold's youngest
daughter.
Dec 30 I received a letter from Mr. Leslie announcing his wife's death.
My very good husband joined me in sending £10 to him & Emma
Pilfold. A letter from dear Harriet. She is going to take into her
service Ann Weeks & Mary James of our village, both the daughters
<u>of respectable</u> widows.
Dec 31 From her <u>bad</u> behaviour Elinor Cull & her family sent out of
my father's cottage where, being a widow, she had it rent free [for]
some years.

1835

With the coming of Spring work began on the building of the school and it
was quickly completed, with a capacity to accommodate 60 pupils. The new
poor law continued to be disliked and added fresh tensions to the familiar
arguments over tithes. The scale of private entertaining is notable. Charlotte
could cope with a dozen guests at the rectory and when she visited sister
Harriet at Coker Court she was one of eighteen seated at table. Dinner would
often be followed by music-making – songs, pianoforte, an occasional flute or
violin, even Lord Arundell's bass-viol.

Jan 4 Mr. Charles Wyndham is going to give a public breakfast
tomorrow to the Shaftesbury constituents to bring in, I hope, a
Conservative member.

Jan 7 The oat dust makes a very nice servant's mattress.

Jan 19 My brother Grove proposed Mr. [Sidney] Herbert & made a good speech.

Jan 31 I bought some calico at Gouldings, the new shop. He is a dissenter.

Feb 1 We attended the S[unday] School. Anna Foot my 1st teacher is only 8 years old. Last year she deserved it but I thought was too young.

Feb 6 We are going to make our school 10 feet high instead of 9.

Feb 7 The heightening our school will cost £3-s3.d0 more, the wall 1£ and the bank wall 1£.

Feb 10 Mrs. Foot told me the good news that Harriet Foot was last Dec^br very well married to Sir Wm Campbell's grandson in America.

Feb 17 We walked to Ferne & then up Wingreen. We met my dear father riding. He has planted a new clump of trees at the top of the hill.

Feb 24 I heard from Mrs. Dansey that my father had parted with his hounds.

March 3 I received a letter from Harriet & endeavoured to get her an under-housemaid instead of Ann Abbots but <u>three</u> mothers in this village were so <u>silly</u> as to refuse so very good an offer.

March 16 Master Foot is put to school at Sarah Pinnock's. She is very near 85 & says she does it to <u>oblige</u> the <u>gentlefolks.</u>

March 18 We dined & slept at Sedgehill House. The House is now to be let as Miss Helyar & her brother are going to live at Poundisford.

March 21 Henstridge began digging the foundation of our school.

March 27 We walked to Donhead St. Andrew, called at rectory, went into their school. The building is very elegant. We admired it much.

March 30 Mr. King is going to give up the Norrington farm.

April 11 We went to the school. My dear husband got up on the scaffolding – one half of it gave way. <u>Providentially</u> Henstridge was close by & by his <u>exertions</u> saved him from falling for which I shall ever be indebted to him.

April 13 My dear father has in his room two views of Mr. Pleydell's roebuck hunting, done by Mr. Parry Hodges.

April 23 We walked up to Ferne, met Lord Arundell there. He played on the bass viol.

May 23 I walked towards the Glove, met Mr. Dickets <u>rather elevated</u> with the Ferne good cheer. He said he would die like Latimer in favor of his religion.

June 9 Our Whitsun Club. We went to see them dance at the Cross.

June 10 Last day of the Club. I went to see the dancing.

June 12 I gave the keys of the school to Mrs. Lush the Mistress. The glass put into the windows.

June 15 We opened our school. Mrs. Lush is just the schoolmistress I could wish & I have tolerable teachers.

June 17 The children much pleased. Our school succeeds well, 48 scholars in the week & 46 of a Sunday.

Sept 1 [Visiting Coker Court] Mr. & Mrs. Chafin Grove & my brother & sister Wm. Grove called.

Sept 2 We went to Montacute with Harriet. It is uninhabited & looks very <u>desolate</u>. The flower garden & all overgrown.

Sept 19 A letter from Dr. Grove announcing the birth of another daughter.

Sept 26 I looked over our linen with the new housemaid Lucy Gurd.

Sept 29 My new housemaid told me she did not like my place. She leaves tomorrow.

Oct 9 To my Aunt Jackson's quadrille party. I enjoyed it & danced every dance.

Nov 26 We went to a morning concert at Salisbury. Heard Miss Clara Novello, a very good <u>sweet</u> voice.

Dec 6 We fear that there is a beer shop at Mr. B ...s close to our school & gate.

Dec 20 Mr. Downes called on Mr. Rowland to invite him to dinner, but he is engaged to amuse the children with the magick lantern. My kind friends at Ferne sent us a turkey.

Dec 24 A large party arrived at Ferne of <u>all</u> my brothers and their wives & children excepting Mrs. John Grove & her baby.

Dec 25 We dined at Ferne, had convivial games, a raffle, forfeits etc. Mr. Downes sang a song that was much applauded. Tom in high spirits.

Dec 26 We again dined at Ferne. Our Berwick Band played in the evening. We danced quadrilles, reels & country dances: in the last my father joined at 77.

1836

This year was less eventful for Charlotte's brothers than for their cousins, the sons of Aunt Bathia Jackson. Charles Jackson and his wife were reported to be in Egypt on their way home from India after eleven years. William, now a captain, who had returned to a hero's welcome after fifteen years abroad chose a wife to go back with him to India; and Henry, who had returned in the previous year, also married. Travellers of another kind going eastwards were Charlotte's first recorded instance of voluntary immigrants to Australia, not transported there – as the Maidments had been – but seeking better opportunities than they could find at home.

Jan 1 Mr. Rowland does not think we shall have a railroad in our village.

Jan 8 It is settled that Charles is to have the Berwick St. Leonard tithe. The money accompts about it not quite settled.

Jan 12 My brother has had 50 of his trees cut off, out of spite as he is the head of the Poor Union. The railroad to Exeter is, I am happy to say, not to go through our village.

Jan 17 Mr. Frederick Farquharson, cornet of the 7th Hussars, came to church.

Jan 25 Elinor Cull was married to Wm. Herring.

Jan 28 The relieving officer did not bring any bread for the little Culls as their mother's husband, Wm. Herring, is to <u>support</u> them – & he has no work, being idle & worthless. We gave the children a supper.

Jan 29 We called on Mr. Foot. He has taken care, as Guardian, about the little Culls.

Feb 14 Tom is in hopes with my father to do something for the little Culls.

Feb 15 Some ill disposed person has taken up our early broccoli just before it is fit, injuring us & doing no good to themselves.

Feb 18 We walked to Norrington. They are getting it ready for Mrs. Parham.

March 14 Tom sent us 12 books to distribute on migration of large families.

March 18 Walked to Goulds, saw the people measuring for a railway that is unfortunately to go through a water meadow belonging to my husband's glebe & through Mr. Foot's fields & also through Ferne Park.

March 19 Met my father riding at Rowberry. He says if a railroad is made at Ferne he will not live there.

April 14 My dear little niece Lucy Helyar died last Tuesday (12th). She was 11 years old.

April 21 We walked to Norrington, saw Mrs. Parham the farmer's wife there. Mr. Wyndham has quite new done up the old house.

April 23 Lady Arundell died last Tuesday, only 28. She has left 2 sons.

May 5 Mr. Hewitt is turned out of Ansty.

May 15 An annular eclipse of the sun. We looked at it with burnt glass & water in a bucket: had the children from the school to do the same & explained it to them.

May 18 I have 16 frocks made for the school, cut out by Elizth Lush. Gave her 6d each frock.

June 3 We went with Miss Clowes to see Stonehinge. It rained.

June 8 We called at Easton to see old Mr. Lush. He is on a visit to his son. I have engaged to walk with him to Ferne to see my father. My cousins C. Jackson have passed the deserts & were in Egypt in April.

June 14 I went into Maidment's cottage. A woman who keeps a school there is going to leave it.

June 17 With Mr. Lush [senior] to Ferne & saw my dear father. He was very glad to see his old tenant who had lived so many years on his Berwick farm.

July 29 There has been a meeting in the parish of St. Pancras, London, about the Poor Law. Hannah Ridout & child would leave the workhouse & slept last night in a cowpen.

Aug 1 My cousins Capt & Mrs Wm Jackson dined here – I fear the last time I shall see them before they go to India.

Aug 18 Dr. Grove has bought a manor 11 miles from Salisbury.

Aug 23 Our poor-houses are to be sold soon. Mr. Downes hopes that Mr. Foot will buy the one Bugden lives in.

May 5 The provision of regular services at the Ansty chapel was a continuing problem.
June 8 'Easton': a farm in Berwick St. John.

Sept 12 We walked to Ferne Park – met Mary [Grove] & the young Sir Wm Fraser at the little pond fishing for emmets.

Sept 26 Called at Churchill Cottage, saw my cousins C. Jackson who have been in India 11 years.

Sept 30 Sale of the poor-houses here. Mr. D has p^d considerably to prevent a beer shop.

Oct 4 We came to Netherhampton, in our way obliged to have the – [?] wheel greased at the London Elm.[D]

Oct 15 William Herring died that married the Widow Cull.

Oct 22 We gave a Bible & prayer book to Samuel & Ann Wright of Donhead & family on going to New South Wales.

Oct 30 My brother Tom came to church. The rest of the family are afraid of the smallpox now in our village.

Oct 31 Mrs. Baiss is extremely angry at Hannah Baiss being marked for ill conduct & has taken her from school.

Nov 1 Mrs. Baiss very impertinent to me about the school. The children vaccinated in the parish.

Nov 5 Tom has given me 1£ to assist Elinor Herring & the children.

Nov 30 40 of my aunt Grove's elms at Netherhampton blown down in the late hurricane.

Dec 26 A deep snow – so much so that our lane was stopped up & we could not go to Ferne to dine. It was most fortunate we dined there Christmas Day & that we are now comfortable at our own dear home.

1837

She continues to use the standard Letts diary with the Sundays in a separate section at the back. She has adopted a carefully printed script of separate letters – much easier to read than her sloping cursive hand into which she lapses occasionally.

Jan 2 Capt Loring called after taking Mrs. Burlton's house. They are obliged to return to Portsmouth Thursday, his son the Lieut. Navy is ordered to recruit men & he is soon going abroad & is stationed there.

Jan 3 My brother & sister C H Grove kindly sent us a capon that our aunt Lady Shelley sent to them from Field Place.

Jan 10 Mr Mead the clergyman from Swallowcliff dined & slept here
– for one (of that sort) pleasant.

Jan 11 Mr Mead left us (trying to recommend books to me). He is like
Mr. Hewitt in his ideas.

Feb 7 Old Mrs. Farquharson is dead having had this influenza at 84.

Feb 10 [During an influenza epidemic] We went to see some of our
parishioners. The new poor law acts badly with labourers in
sickness. They have no wages nor any remedy in lieu of it.

Feb 18 Mr Downes received a letter from Archdeacon Lear with a
petition against abolishing church rates. He applied at Ferne to get
the signature of my father & eldest brother but could not succeed.

Feb 23 My sister-in-law Mrs. J. Grove was brought to bed of a
daughter last night.

April 5 Mr. James Farquharson is engaged to be married to Miss
Phelips,[B] the present Mrs. Farquharson's daughter, when she
leaves school.

April 18 Mr. Downes called upon Mr. Osborne who is just come to
Rushmore Lodge. He has a wife & 6 children.

April 28 Mr & Mrs Deane read some of Miss Austen's novels whilst it
rained very much, they then returned home.

April 29 Ja^s Kelly is dead, his widow & daughter-in-law are to have
mourning from the Penny Club.

June 3 Mr. Downes called at Rushmore. Ld & Lady Rivers have both
been there. Mr. & Mrs. Harvey are now at Brickseys.

Aug 1 Tom went to Wilton to propose Mr. Sydney Herbert for the
county.

Aug 16 [At Salisbury] We went to the Races with Mrs. Merrick[C] in
my aunt's carriage. Mrs. King's was the next carriage & I got much
information from her about the races. It began at 12 & was not over
till 7. We were quite tired.

Aug 19 Our good & excellent schoolmistress Mrs Lush died to our
very great sorrow & both the children & parents of our village truly
mourn her loss.

Sept 6 Mr. Downes & myself busy picking barberries for preserving.
It is a tedious business.

Aug. 1 Sidney Herbert, Lord Herbert of Lea (1810-1861) became Secretary-at-War in
1845 and again in 1852 and 1859. His reputation as a statesman is inevitably linked
with Florence Nightingale.

Sept 12 Walked to Norrington, saw Mrs. Parham her youngest child
& governess; also saw the banqueting room, chapel etc.

Sept 18 Mr. Downes saw Mr. Lowndes & Mr. Harvey [at Rushmore].
No satisfactory settling of his tythes with them.

Sept 22 We had our Harvest Home & dined at two O'clock. We then
walked as far as the Pond in the Chace. This night our apples were
stolen.

Oct 23 A man about the village singing wrong songs about the Queen,
that we are under petticoat government etc.

Oct 27 Between the storms I went to Mary Ann Kelly. She is not
pleased at her children being dismissed the school, for striking the
mistress.

Dec 5 I wrote a letter to Mr Maffey to try & get John Chowne
reinstated in his work.

Dec 7 My note to Mr. Maffey was of no avail. I now wrote to Mr.
Harvey about John Chowne.

Dec 8 I have succeeded with Mr. Harvey & he has taken John
Chowne which has made me very happy.

Dec 10 Sunday. Miss Wilson came to church, not any other of the
Ferne family. They are going to erect a stove in their seat.

Dec 15 I called on Mr. & Mrs. Shere. We talked a great deal about the
present Poor Laws. They agree with me that the winter & sickness
is very trying to the poor people & private charity is very much
wanted.

Dec 19 My husband rather annoyed about the settlement of his Tythe.
He wishes to do justice to New College but I fear our landlords will
be hard upon the clergyman.

Dec 21 St. Thomas's Day. I gave the school children a holiday that
they might collect pence at the houses. We walked to Ferne gate. I
think it very likely that we shall go to the Commissioners about our
Tythe. My father has offered that we are to have our own
composition which Mr. Downes kindly gave them with heavy
abatements.

A note after Sunday Dec 31 reads 'Civil war in Canada has just broken out
between the Papists & Protestants'.

Sept. 18 The tythes due from the Rushmore estate.
Sept. 22 The pond would presumably be the historic one at Ashmore.
Dec. 10 Miss Wilson was employed at Ferne as governess to Mary Grove.
Dec. 19 New College, Oxford, owned the living.

1838

The diary for this year is missing. Her brother George Grove died during the year, on or about May 31.

1839

She has given up Letts diaries for a smaller plain notebook with an ineffective metal clasp. She has stitched in an almanac at the front and made three entries of varying length per page. The binding is cracking away from the hard cover. Her new-style script writing appears laboured and lacks the earlier sense of spontaneity. The wrangling over tithes emphasises her transition from land-owner's daughter to clergyman's wife.

Jan 21 Mr. Foot called & offered Mr. Downes £475 for our Tithe.

Jan 22 Mr. Downes wrote to Ferne by Mr. Foot to take £490 for our Tithe which the landowners have acceded to, subject to New College.

Jan 23 Mr. Dansey quite angry with my husband for having commuted the tithe. However, it is well worth the peace & happiness it ensures.

Jan 28 A letter from the Warden [of New College] to offer £500 for our living.

Jan 29 The landowners refuse the £500. Another extraordinary letter from the Warden. I was very sorry that the Tithe could not be settled.

Feb 10 A letter from the Warden of New College. I am sorry to say he is going to send a surveyor to value our tithes.

March 13 Mr. Downes walked to Ashmore to call on Mr. Hamilton the curate. He has a great many stuffed birds.

May 20 Mrs. C.H. Grove had another daughter born. She is to be named after our good aunt Philippa.

Feb. 10 The surveyor's figure of £520 led to more haggling until a settlement was reached at £500.

Mar. 13 Mr. Hamilton had been curate at Tollard Royal but joined Mr. Downes at Berwick in November 'to do duty & a sermon in the evening' for a guinea. In 1843 he became Mr. Downes's curate.

June 1 My father & brother very inveterate against the church.

June 7 [At Coker Court] I wish my neices were not so <u>changed</u> in their religion.

June 19 John [Grove, son of Dr. John] is going to be articled to Mr. Still, solicitor, Lincoln's Inn.

July 15 Lord Rivers rode through the village.

July 18 My husband received a very kind letter from Ld Rivers in answer to his, giving Abner Abbot leave to rent his cottage. He will give Mr. Downes £5 to lay out for him for the poor of Berwick.

Oct 17 Fanny & Wm. Grove are likely to have Baverstock with 8 acres of land for £50 a year, very cheap indeed & Mr. Penruddock an <u>excellent</u> landlord.

Nov 9 M. Thompson sold her nuts to us at an <u>enormous</u> price.

Dec 18 Mr. Hamilton came. He accompanied the three Miss Marklands & myself to Ferne where we had a delightful ball & supper, given by my brother in return for a handsome piece of plate presented to him by the Union for the Poor, having done his part as chairman so <u>well</u>. The farmers, their wives & daughters, Sir Edward Baker, ladies & gentlemen of the neighbourhood attended. We danced quadrilles, country dances & waltzes. There were about 150 people present, all in harmony & good humour. We kept it up with great spirit till four in the morning. Ended with Sir Roger de Coverly.

1840

A similar plain notebook to previous years, with again an almanack stitched in. Flyleaf notes include costs of journeys involving turnpike payments & also 'Railroad to Walton £1/5/-'. Journey to Field Place' cost £1/3/4, another 'to Winchester' £0/12/0. A note dealing with servants reads 'Fanny Stainer entered our service March 25, 1840 – to have £9/9/-. Mary Lathy from March 25th to have £11/11/-. Sarah Harman then left us after living with us a good & faithful servant 12 years & a half.'

Blank pages at the back have been used to record an itemised list headed '1841 Relieved Paupers', showing names and cash payments, relating to 30 men, women & children.

At the beginning of June Charlotte abandoned her painfully acquired script and reverted to her cursive hand in a form improved by the script experience.

The death of Aunt Grove removed a powerful influence from Charlotte's life. A visit to Aunt Shelley at Field Place and to Mary Shelley with her second husband at Salisbury reinvigorated the family link.

Jan 12 Poor old Sarah Pinnock died aged 89. She went off <u>easy</u> at last. I shall miss my good old friend <u>much</u>.

Jan 25 [At Netherhampton] My dear & good Aunt expired without a <u>struggle</u>. I attended to the last sad offices for my dear Aunt.

Jan 26 I read prayers & a sermon to the servants. Dr. Grove came. Tom arrived, he read the will. She has acted so kindly towards us all.

Feb 1 Funeral of my very dear aunt. She was buried in the family vault here at Berwick. My dear mother's coffin was as fresh as ever though buried <u>12</u> years ago.

Feb 2 Wm. & F[anny] Grove are likely, I am happy to say, to take the Netherhampton house.

Feb 27 We walked to Rushmore saw Ld & Lady Rivers and her brother Mr. Stewart   pleased with our walk & visit.

March 18 Saw Rose Cottage, a very nice place. We rent [it] from Lady Day at £15 year for our curate.

March 31 Bessy & Miss Wilson walked here to tell us Mr. Grisdale has accepted our curacy.

April 5 A letter from Mr. Grisdale to <u>now refuse</u> being our curate.

April 11 A letter from my sister Fanny Grove with the good news that they are going to live on at Netherhampton & invited us to visit them.

April 14 Fire broke out at 10 o'clock. Little children put burning stick to straw & did it. Women & men very active, through God's mercy we were all saved.

April 15 Sarah Harman [much troubled recently with bad legs] left our house having lived as cook 12 years half & got into her own cottage.

April 29 [The search for a curate continuing, the next candidate being Mr. Rolles] We heard from Mr. Rolles & I very much fear the cottage will not be large enough.

April 30 Mr. Rolles & Mr. Snooke, both very gentlemanly men, arrived to a late dinner. Mr. R. is a gentleman of good fortune, has a pretty carriage & three horses.

Mar. 31 Mr. Grisdale was Miss Wilson's future husband.

May 1   The children came with their garlands, sung God save the
        Queen. We went with the gentlemen to see the cottage. It would not
        do for Mr. Rolles. Went to the Priory. He will take that & be our
        curate if Mr. Foot & him can agree about rent. If not, Mr. Snooke's
        brother is to be our curate at Rose cottage.

May 7   At Dr. Grove's, Louisa's birthday – 13.

May 8   We came home to meet Mr. Rolles. He settled with Mr. Foot
        about the Priory.

July 5   Mr. Rolles began the duty as our curate.

July 27 [Having failed to get on a coach at the Glove Charlotte's
        sister-in-law, Henrietta Downes] went in our open carriage to the
        London Elms [inn] & overtook the Magnet coach in which she went
        to Southampton.

Aug 3   We set off on our journey. Arrived at Dr. Grove's. We went to
        Harnham Cottage saw my cousin Mary Trevor [*née* Shelley] their
        family of 3 girls, her husband a very gentlemanly man. They dined
        with us.

August 8 [At Southampton] We walked down to the station & saw
        some of the trains go out & come in.

Aug 20 We left Marwell, went by the railroad from Winchester to
        Walton. Mr. Robert Downes met us in his carriage & we arrived at
        Fetcham Rectory.

Aug 27 We came to Field Place, found my aunt of 77 & Sir T 87
        wonderfully well, also my cousins, Helen & Margaret.

Aug 28 We went fishing at Warnham Pond, caught 6 jack & 1 eel. Mr.
        [John] Shelley, his son Edward, daughter & young Heavysides went
        with us.

Aug 29 We called on Mrs. Medwin[A] & her daughter & drove as far
        as Home Bush with Lady Shelley.

Aug 31 Accompanied my aunt & cousins to Hale to see Mrs. [John]
        Shelley & their 5 fine children, so humoured [spoilt?] it is sad to
        witness. The eldest, Edward, the best behaved.

Sept 3 We left Field Place & our kind relations with regret. Mr.
        Robert Downes's carriage met us at Dorking.

Sept 7 [Leaving Surrey] We got upon the railroad at Kingston arrived
        at Southampton to dine with our sister H. Downes who was to sail
        in the evening for Havre.

Dec 22 Miss Lane called, brought me a present of a woodcock.

1841 - 1842

A fatter version of the previous volume, covering the events of two years and still with pages to spare. In the absence of equally measured daily spaces she now allows her entries to vary in length, with the happy result that she gives an occasional cameo of village life in some detail and regains some of the quirkiness and lively commentary of earlier years.

After fourteen years of marriage she has become a village institution as the rector's wife, confidently in full command of her duties. The school is now a matter of routine, the penny club and the coal tickets are established customs, the visits to the sick and the poor are taken for granted mutually though in no perfunctory spirit.

There are signs of improving standards of comfort and affluence at the rectory, additional building and furnishing and a higher level of social entertaining. Her love of walking persists but there is now a carriage for longer excursions. She operates as an honorary registry office for village girls wishing to go into domestic service.

And so the years pass, with the finding and keeping of a satisfactory curate a recurring problem.

Flyleaf details include 'Martha James as housemaid 9 guineas a year, Fanny Stainer cook at 11 guineas year'.

Jan 13 The Queen nearly met with a serious accident. The ice on which her sledge was broke. Prince Albert & her were rather immersed in the water.

Jan 28 We accompanied Fanny Grove [from Netherhampton] to Odstock. Saw Mrs. C. Grove, she is very well – the same age as my father. It is a great pleasure to her, F.G. living so near.

Feb 4/5 I never experienced a colder winter. Intensely cold – my father remembers it the same in 1786.

Feb 26 Mr. Downes went to Staplefoot, saw Sarah Weeks and her grandchildren. They are quite wild foresters.

March 23 We went to my brother C.H. Grove. My four nieces – Emily Charlotte, Elizabeth, Julia & Philippa are fine healthy handsome children.

Jan. 28 'Mrs C. Grove', mother of Fanny and of the rector of Odstock, was born in 1758 as Elizabeth Acland.
Feb. 26 For Staplefoot see 23 Sept 1834 (note).

May 12 Sir Timothy Shelley has received his grandson, Percy Shelley & allows him £400 year.

May 26 Mrs. C.H. Grove has another daughter.

May 29 The Election at the [Salisbury] Infirmary for a physician & a chirugeon. Dr. Travers Cox & Mr. Tatum chosen.

June 2 I danced with the Whitsun Club as also did the Miss Sheres & Miss Butcher. It went off quietly & they were all very well behaved.

June 16 I went to visit Eliz^th Dibbin, a melancholy sight to see her & her aged grandmother in the same bed in a miserable cottage too full of inhabitants.

June 29 We walked to Bericourt saw Farmer Sharp & his wife. The former promised me he would give his vote if he wasn't prevented by the Visitation, & his 2 nephews certainly to Capt Mathews.

July 2 The Election at Shaftesbury. Lord Howard got it. My husband went to the Visitation in Mr. Dansey's carriage.

July 26 We went to the school & there were told Henry Kelly had shot Martha Hansford. He took up the gun though told not. Several wounds in her back & arm. We walked to Bridmore where she was. Dr. Foot there. Mr. Downes desired him to continue to attend her & he would pay for it. She came home with her mother riding the donkey. We walked to Ferne & told my father of the circumstances.

July 28 We visited the girl. Dr. Foot thought the wounds rather worse.

July 30 Mr. Downes went up to Ferne to consult about the girl.

Aug 7 Martha Hansford is pronounced by Dr. Foot quite out of danger.

Aug 12 Frederick Jackson arrived from India.

Aug 27 We dined at Ferne, partook of an haunch of venison, but it was unfortunately kept too long. Met Mrs. Burlton. Mr. Rolles accompanied us.

Aug 30 We engaged Mark Hare to come for a month's trial as our servant, 20 guineas [a] year & find his own livery.

Sept 20 Mr. Rolles dined with us, gave an account of Miss Devonshire a pocket-Venus whom he met at Cheltenham - daughter of the ci-devant Miss Cooke who formerly lived at Donhead Lodge.

Oct 1 Tom is much improved by his sojourn abroad, & is a very handsome young man.

June 29 'Farmer Sharp' was the tenant of Higher Berry Court farm. (WRO 743)
Oct. 1 Her nephew Thomas Fraser Grove (1821-1897)

Oct 25 Our Audit. Mr. Lush, Mr. E. Lush, Mr. Shere, Mr. T. Shere, Mr. Thos Lane, Mr Ja^s Lane, Mr. Maffey, Mr. Rolles dined here. A few minutes after they had left the house the policeman came & said the guard-post was down & that he saw Mr. E. L[ush] & two Mr. Lanes run into Easton.

Dec 10 On this day at 9 o'clock in the morning my brother Mr. Helyar died.

Dec 19 Mr. Rolles wants to get leave of absence from his curacy.

Dec 25 My sister Mrs. Helyar has Coker Court during William's life. He is under the management of Trustees.

Dec 27 My father told me I danced as well as ever.

Dec 29 Mr. Downes has allowed Mr. Rolles his curate to have 8 Sundays absence in one year. I hope now it is quite settled.

1842

Jan 2 Mr. South is dead who had a small living of my father [which is] to be given to Mr. Grisdale.

Jan 19 A letter from the Warden of New College. Mr. Downes must go to this election of the Professorship of Poetry to prevent a Puseyite coming in. There is a faint chance of settling it by committee.

Jan 22 The good news that Mr. Garbutt has gained the professorship of poetry. My husband & brother saved their journey to Oxford.

Jan 28 We drove to Shaston,[D] had handbills printed & offered three guineas for the recovery of Miss Stockwell's[C] watch. As soon as they were put up George Kelly brought John Pickford with the watch, having picked it up after meeting us in Jerry Lane yesterday. Alas! that our parishioners should behave so.

Jan 31 Called on Mr. Shere to tell him of the conduct of his shepherd & boy. They met the policeman at 5 o'clock, after they had picked it up at 12, who told them of Miss S's loss. GK said 'I hadn't heard of that watch before'. The boy was silent.

Oct. 25 Annual rent audit suppers, with an accompanying bowl of punch, tended to be high-spirited occasions. The village policeman was an innovation.

Dec. 29 The unexpected absences of this otherwise admirable curate had been a persistent irritation.

Jan. 2 This appointment enabled Mr. Grisdale to marry Miss Wilson, in July.

Feb 15 My father told us that Mr. Foot has sold Berwick Farm to him very dear, he having mortgaged it twice.

April 21 We walked to Rushmore, left our cards. Ld & Lady Rivers now in London. The house is much enlarged, 3 fronts.

May 17 Club Day. Mrs. Foot & party, Mrs. Lane, Mrs. Brine etc came on our green in the evening & made me & Mr. Downes accompany them to the Cross where I & Mrs. Thos Lane led off a country dance.

May 18 Club again. We did not go again to the Cross.

July 17 Mr. Downes kindly got into the pulpit to preach for Mr. Rolles in consequence of his being <u>so inaudible.</u> Afterwards Mr. Rolles sent a letter to Mr. Downes resigning his curacy at the end of 3 months.

Sept 3 My nephew Tom Grove has got a commission in the Army.

Sept 13 Mr. Hodson arrived. The poor people of Wilton gave him a grateful <u>offering</u> of 8 loaves from their gleanings.

Sept 14 We went with Mr. Hodson to Whitesheet Cottage. He has taken two nicely furnished apartments there.

Oct 5 We walked to Staplefoot Lodge, saw Sarah Weeks & her daughter Emma.

Nov 11 My father has bought Mr. Foot's estate at Berwick. Mr F is to be his tenant. Mr. Rolles's servant reports that his master is going to be married to a lady of fortune at Cheltenham.

Nov 17 I heard from Mrs. Markland that Mr. Rolles is going to marry Miss Augusta Devonshire grand-daughter of Mrs. Cooke that formerly lived at Donhead Lodge.

Nov 18 Mrs. Burlton called on us to take leave.

Nov 30 The opening of Donhead St. Mary church. A grand collation at Mr. Blackmore's.

Sept. 3 A cornetcy in the 6th Inniskilling Regiment of Dragoons offered by the C. in C. for £840. His grandfather had advised against it, as 'an idle life at best', and urged him to become a lawyer in the family tradition.

Sept. 14 Mr. Hodson was to replace Mr. Rolles.

Nov. 17 Augusta was described by Mr. Rolles as 'a pocket Venus'.

Nov. 18 Mrs. Burlton was probably going to stay indefinitely with her daughter at Sedgehill.

Nov. 30 Mr. Blackmore was rector of Donhead St. Mary which had been closed for restoration.

1843 - 1844

The brief curacy ended of Mr. Hodgson who had set his sights on the chaplaincy of Salisbury Infirmary. He was succeeded by Mr. Hamilton who brought with him a collection of stuffed birds. The former curate, Mr. Rolles, following his marriage to Mrs. Devonshire's elder daughter, vacated the Priory in favour of his younger brother who married the younger Miss Devonshire. Whether she also were a 'pocket-Venus' is not revealed. Her mother the former Louisa Cooke, made a sentimental journey to Donhead Lodge, her old home where George Grove had courted her thirty years earlier.

The Helyars were adjusting to the death of Harriet's husband and the marriage of their elder son, William Hawker Helyar. Sedgehill House, which had been let, was reoccupied. The elder daughters were contemplating marriage and Charlotte sensed religious tensions when she visited Coker Court.

Bysshe Shelley's father came to the end of his long life. For Aunt Jackson death struck suddenly and cruelly in the prime of her son's life. Tom Grove's persistent ill-health defied diagnosis.

1843

Jan 4 Funeral of our labourer, John Stretch. We have engaged James Blandford to be partly in his place, & partly at his shoemaking.

March 2 Mr. Hodgson gave up our curacy & Mr. Hamilton to my great joy has accepted it.

March 17 Mrs C[harles] H[enry] Grove had another daughter, six daughters living – also having had a still born one.

March 18 Capt Jackson, Capt Henry Jackson & Capt Frederick Jackson called.

March 28 Strange news from Ellen [Helyar. Her eldest brother] Wm H. Helyar is going to be married to Theodora Resuel, orphan neice of Sir I & Lady Bruce.

April 7 We heard the melancholy news that my cousin major [William] Jackson was killed at the battle of Hyderabad Feb^ry. He has left a widow & son.

April 10 Walked to Churchill Cottage saw my aunt who is in sad affliction. Cap[t] John Jackson has behaved most bravely, as also the deceased Major.

April 13 We sent Mrs. W[m] Jackson 20£ draft on Child's [Bank]

May 14 Yesterday arrived bride-cake from Rev. E[dward] & Mrs E. Rolles. She is 2nd daughter of Mrs. Devonshire.

May 25 Cap[t] Tho[s] Jackson is going to France & then I fear to India.

June 4 Mr. Hodgson preached his farewell sermon & quitted our curacy.

June 6 Our Club. In the evening we saw the gaieties at the Cross. Miss Harris Wills & myself danced two country dances with the villagers.

June 23 Mr. Hamilton came to Rose Cottage. He dined & drank tea at our house. The bells rung for him.

June 28 Mr. Trenchard called last evening & proposed wine. Mr. D ordered 2 doz port 40s[hillings] & 2 doz white 45s[hillings]. Mr T very odd.

June 29 Mr. Hamilton very busy arranging his household at Rose Cottage. He has put his museum up in his parlour.

July 22 [While visiting Winchester] Major Shelley has taken a house on this terrace. I know not whether he is brother to Sir T. Shelley or not.

Aug 31 Saw the monument to the memory of Major W[m] Jackson.

Nov 26 Sunday. Mrs, Miss Devonshire, Mr Mrs E. Rolles came in after church. Mrs D looks remarkably well & she was very glad to see me again.

Dec 1 My very dear friend Mrs Burlton died last night.

Dec 8 All the neighbours had scarfs and gloves sent them in memory of Mrs. Burlton.

Dec 10 I set out with Mrs. Devonsher & her two daughters to walk to Donhead St. Andrew. A donkey that they might ride by turns, the young ladies went as far as Clay Lane & then as it rained a little returned. Mrs. D & I waded through the mire to Donhead Lodge which Mrs. D inspected, being her former home.

1844

Feb 1 I walked to Ferne, saw my dear father, Mrs. Grove & Mary. The former gave me some asparagus.

Feb 27 My cousins Capt Thos & Frederick Jackson called, the latter to take leave of me as he is going to join his regiment in India.

March 15 We called at Sedghill. Agnes accompanied us on foot to my brother C.H. Grove's where we took a walk with him, my two neices & Mary Helyar to Sedghill House where we saw dear Harriet, Mr. & Mrs. W. Helyar & took an early dinner there.

March 28 We drove to Sedghill House, took our luncheon there, heard the Hullah singing. I walked with Harriet.

April 11 We went to Coker Court. At Shaftesbury Capt Jackson joined us & we got into a fly. Found my sister with Agnes & Ellen quite well.

Aug. 31 The monument is in Donhead St. Mary Church.

April 12 We drove to Montacute & saw Mr. Phillips old house. In the evening the ladies & Capt Jackson went to hear a lecture by one of the Plymouth Brethren.

April 14 Sunday. Mr. Hewish gave us two good sermons. Agnes didn^t go to church.

April 17 I fear Agnes is a P[lymouth] B[rother] without doubt.

April 26 We heard of the death of my uncle Sir T Shelley at the advanced age of 91.

April 27 Mr. Shere has had a fall from his horse & the horse ran away with his carriage.

April 29 Mr. Shere had another fall from his horse.

May 3 Joseph Lush has been thrown out of a cart & much hurt.

May 4 Mr. Shere rather better. Joseph Lush is hurt on the head.

May 25 I heard from Ann Helyar & her mother that Agnes Helyar is going to be married to Mr. Lambert who was divorced from his wife, a pretty wicked woman.

Oct 27 My dear brother [Tom] taken very ill again. He told his daughter it would soon be all over.

Feb. 1 Asparagus at this date indicates extensive hot-house facilities at Ferne.

Dec 19 Miss Stockwell disappointed of a place in the coach to come to us.

Dec 21 Miss Stockwell came <u>outside</u> the coach.

Dec 28 Capt Thos. Jackson came to take leave of us. He sails for India the 3rd Jan^{ry}.

1845 - 1846

The diary continues her practice of completing two years in a single pocket-book. The early winter months of 1845 were marked by a titanic contest at chess with Miss Stockwell who had arrived before Christmas and didn't end her visit until March 3. Eighty-two times the first white piece moved into action, three times the result was a draw and gradually Charlotte's tally of victories rose to a satisfactory 62, duly recorded in her pocket-book after the return of Miss Stockwell to Wilton with the meagre consolation of 17 games won.

In September Charlotte drove from Coker Court with her sister Harriet to Montacute where Ellen, Charlotte's niece, was now installed with her newly wedded husband, Mr. Phelips.

The dominating event of 1845 was still to come. When she walked to Ferne on November 10 her brother Tom was lying 'in an insensible state'. He rallied briefly but died two days later. In view of their father's advanced age legal arrangements had to be made urgently to designate the new heir to Ferne. The next eldest son was 'Doctor John', whose medical career must perforce be abandoned.

The following year saw the adjustments and stresses that stemmed from Tom's death. His widow, Bessy, was to remain at Ferne for what was left of Mr. Grove's life. Their daughter Mary, now aged 20, was in a restless disturbed state which inspired darkly sibylline comments in Charlotte's diary and provoked some friction between them: Mary switched her churchgoing from Berwick to Donhead St. Mary.

There was no mention of a family reunion at Christmas 1846. Charlotte wrote her briefest ever entry – 'Christmas Day – a sacrament'. On New Year's Eve her brother Charles Henry called for her and they walked together to Ferne to see their father. The ladies were involved in the preparation of soup for the poor.

Jan 31 Capt T. Jackson is going to be married to Miss Mackyllop.

March 29 Ellen Helyar was married to Mr. Phelips of Montacute.

April 17 Walked to Ferne. We went into my father's snuggery. He was reading Latin.

June 11 Mr. Mrs. E. Rolles called to take leave of us. They go to Clifton tomorrow.

Sept 2 [Visiting Coker Court] We went with H[arriet] in the carriage to Montacute, admired the place & environs, climbed up all sorts of stairs. We like our new nephew Mr. Phelips.

Sept 22 We dined at Donhead Hall, played some lively games. Fanny Mackyllop sails for India Wednesday week.

Nov 12 My very dear brother Tom died at three o'clock this morning. My father, tho' feeling most acutely, has great presence of mind – made his will again early in the day.

Nov 14 I walked to Ferne, saw my dear father. He is better. He is become owner of the house & household again. I saw Bessey & Mary, the former quite overpowered. The latter shows great fortitude.

Nov 20 The funeral of my dear brother, Thos. 40 horsemen, 9 carriages and 3 mourning coaches attended.

Nov 22 Dr. Grove is going to give up his profession, having served it 40 years – my father allowing him an income as his eldest [surviving] son.

1846

Feb 15 I heard from my aunt of the death of her son Frederick Jackson after a few days illness.

Feb 26 The election of a physician for the Salisbury Infirmary instead of Dr. Grove. Dr. Moore gained it, a most <u>unfit</u> person.

March 29 Mrs. G. Grove & Mary came to church – a long dissertation about ...

April 19 Mary now goes to Donhead St. Mary church with Mrs. G[eorge] Grove.

June 12 I walked to Ferne, saw the ladies & then my father. Surprised at Mary's behaviour.

July 14 The labourers, some of them, rebelled against their masters. Mr. Shere's cartshed burnt down.

Aug 23 I received the news of my aunt Lady Shelley's death on the 21st inst. at the age of 83.

Sept 23 Heard that T[homas] G[rove] is going to be married to K[athleen] O'G[rady] in Ireland.

Oct 9 My father has given his Norfolk estate to Dr. Grove as his eldest son.

Nov 10 Went to Shaftesbury to hear the Rock & Chinese Steel Band, with which we were much pleased.

Dec 31 Soup given out to the poor at 1d a quart.

1847-1856

The diaries for these years are missing. They are the years that saw the passing of the men who had figured most prominently in Charlotte's life. In 1847 her father died, in his eighty-ninth year. Her husband died in 1855, her brother William in the same year. Leaving the rectory at Berwick St. John she moved to Raleigh Cottage in the village and to the muted life of widowhood that she now shared with her sister Harriet and her three sisters-in-law, Bessy, Fanny and Charlotte Louisa. Aunt Jackson died in 1847, her daughter Fanny in 1854.

Among the nephews and nieces a new generation was emerging. Tom's daughter, Mary, married a naval officer in 1849. Both Dr. John's sons were rearing Grove children, Captain Tom having married in 1847 and his brother John of Mudeford in 1851.

1857-1858

Charlotte's narrative is resumed in a single volume starting in 1857 and continuing through 1858. She has returned to her printed script. Her lifelong iterest in contemporary novelists is unabated: flyleaf notes mention *John Halifax, Gentleman* by Dinah Mulock (1857) and Charlotte Bronte's *Shirley* (1849) and *Villette* (1853).

Inevitably the passage of ten years has brought changes in the social world of friends and acquaintances that she chronicles. The ministers and curates of neighbouring parishes have an unfamiliar ring. In Berwick St. John rectory is the Griffiths family, with Mary Jane Griffiths in particular showing a sensitive consideration for Charlotte. There is a new stage army of faceless names at the many dinner parties but the Mairs are still at Donhead Lodge. The Du Boulays have reappeared, replacing the Wyndhams at Donhead Hall. The Priory is occupied by the Stricklands and among the newest arrivals the most noticeable are the Whiteheads at Oak Cottage.

At Ferne Doctor John is in his tenth year as head of the family. Both his sons and two of his daughters are married; but Helen, aged 21 and Emma, nearly 20, are still at home. For Charlotte Ferne is the last foothold in the network of great houses that she knew so well in her younger days. She has lost contact with Bryanston and Pythouse, with the Tregonwells of Cranborne and Bournemouth, the Farquharsons of Langton, the Arundells of Wardour. Her life is undeniably on a smaller, more parochial scale, but she retains to the full her zest for music-making in the evening, for daily walks and lively conversation, for the pious practices of her religion and for the prospect of yet one more victory at the chess board. Miss Stockwell can be expected to arrive with her cage-birds before the end of the year and to stay until early April.

Jan 1 Circumcision. I having a cold & Miss Stockwell afraid of the damp, we did not go to church. Invited to dine at the Priory, but in the winter I decline it.

Jan 2 A whining needle man came.

Jan 7 Mr. Foot having let Oak Cottage to a Mr. Mrs. Whitehead he came with Sophia Foot to inspect it. They called here.

Jan 17 Mr. & Mrs. Whitehead arrived at Oak Cottage with 4 children & 2 maids.

Jan 20 Marian Stockwell's birthday.

Feb 2 A deep snow. Very comfortable in this dear little cottage.

Feb 10 My birthday 74.

Feb 11 We visited several cottages with Mrs. Whitehead. She is so kind to the poor.

Feb 14 Old Repentance Longman came. I gave her some bread cheese & beer.

Feb 18 I called at Pheasant Lodge, saw Mrs. Wright. She gave a very good charecter of Jane Marchant.

Feb 27 John & Clara Grove [of Mudeford] & their two eldest children called. The former looks very ill.

Feb 28 I walked to Pheasant Lodge, gave Emma Weeks & Jane Marchant their gowns. We kept the school 20 years & [have] given 46 gowns.

March 1 My dear husband died two years ago.

March 2 We called & lunched at Donhead Hall. Saw the white pheasants, peacocks etc. Mrs. du Boulay fed them.

March 5 Mr. Shettle vaccinated my 3 servants and Jane, Miss Stockwell's maid.

March 21 We lunched at Ferne. Helen & Emma [Grove] very chatty. My brother votes for both Mr. Wyndham & Mr. Sydney Herbert.

April 2 My dear companion Miss Stockwell left me, to our mutual regret.

April 4 South Wilts Election – Mr. Sydney Herbert & Mr. Wyndham come in again.

April 20 Very busy in packing up for my visit to Fanny Grove.

April 21 I arrived at the Close Salisbury. F[anny] Grove has a very nice house.

April 22 Our sister Bessy Grove arrived.

April 23 Bessie went to luncheon at L[ord] Nelson's.

April 28 We went to the Horticultural Show – saw many people that remembered me.

April 29 Miss Stockwell came & lunched here. We took her home. Carey [Miss Stockwell's canary] is sitting on one egg.

May 5 I returned to my dear home after a very pleasant visit.

May 23 Mary Jane [Griffith] has kindly desired me to be supplied from the rectory dairy.

June 19 My brother & sister called on us. Jane shewed us many pretty things for the F[erne?] Bazaar done by the Miss Shelleys. Bad account of JG.

June 25 My dear sister Helyar arrived.

June 26 Very hot day. We walked to Ferne Plantation.

June 30 Time goes very fast with dear Harriet.

July 1 Very wet day. Amused ourselves as well as we could.

July 2 We got our walk. We dined at Ferne. John & his wife alone. A very pleasant day. How I do enjoy my sister's dear company.

July 8 We went up to Ferne to luncheon. Mrs. Selwyn [Dr John's daughter, Louisa] & her children there, also saw my brother & sister, Emma & Helen.

July 9 My very dear sister left me to our mutual regret.

Aug 1 I lunched at Ferne, saw my cousins Helen & Margaret Shelley.

Sept 9 Col. Burlton[B] has lost his two eldest sons, officers massacred in India.

Sept 29 We were alarmed at Mr. Whitehead walking off about 4 in the evening and not returning all night.

Sept 30 Mrs. W sent after him. He was heard of at Han[d]ley & Cranbourne, at the latter place about ten o'clock where he could neither get a bed or horse to come home on.

June 19 'Bad account of JG' – see Feb 27 above.

Oct 2 Mr. Whitehead was brought home at night by the policemen.

Oct 3 Alarmed this morning as Mr. Whitehead cut his throat with a clasp knife, luckily being a blunt edge it was not mortal. Mr. Shettle attended him.

Oct 7 Humiliation Day for our sad Indian war. Collection for it to be sent to the Lord Mayor in London.

Oct 12 I called at Oak Cottage. Mr. W[hitehead] is much better. I hope he will persevere & go to the gentleman proposed.

Oct 20 Mr. Whitehead went away with Mr. Stratton of Stratford. I hope it will answer well to him.

Nov 1 Poor Clara Grove is very ill in the measles.

Nov 3 Jane [Mrs. Grove] when she arrived at Mudeford yesterday found Clara had been better all day.

Nov 6 Poor Clara Grove continues very light-headed & in a most dangerous state.

Nov 7 I heard the melancholy news that poor dear Clara expired last Thursday evening, quiet but insensible, an irreparable loss to her husband & 3 children.

Nov 9 Clara Grove before her death said to her husband 'I have lived & die for you'.

Nov 29 My nephew T[homas] F[raser] Grove called & approved of my brougham.

Dec 4 My neices [Helen and Emma] called on me. They go to Mudeford tomorrow.

Dec 22 I went to Shaftesbury with Mrs. Whitehead. She drank tea here. Miss Stockwell arrived with her birds.

Dec 24 Mr. Whitehead came home.

1858

Jan 26 I walked to Ferne, found Henrietta there, also Tom & Kate. Their dear father was taken so much worse on Sunday night.

March 11 I walked to Ferne, saw my brother John. He was in bed in pretty good spirits but swelled with the dropsy.

April 13 Mrs. F.S[trictland] read Shakespeare with me.

April 14 My dear brother John taken ill with sickness. He died about 8 o'clock in the evening.

April 17 My brother John was examined. He had ossification of the heart, adhesion of the lungs & dropsy.

April 21 The funeral of my dear brother, 73 last Dec^{br}. I dined at Ferne. The last of my generation at my once dear home is now passed away.

April 24 Mr. Whitehead returned from Mr. Stratton's after his half year's probation.

April 29 Mrs. Cockram & John Grove [of Mudeford] called. He is very much worse in his mind for his sad propensity. [The last word is inserted above a deletion of what appears to have been 'mania of drinking']

May 12 Kate kindly shewed me the plan of alterations for Ferne House.

May 27 I walked to Ferne. They are in a great bustle packing to leave their dear home.

May 29 I walked to Ferne & took leave of my relations – the last of my own generation living there.

June 1 I walked to Ferne. The footman ushered me into the drawing room with a loud voice as 'Mrs. Downes'. A most cordial reception from my nephew & niece. May they have many years of happiness there together.

June 9 Dear Mary Hamilton [daughter of Charlotte's brother Tom and Bessy] with her two little girls came to spend the day with us. We were so glad to meet again.

June 12 Kate sent me a nice sketch of the new south front of Ferne.

July 8 My nephew & neice Capt. & Mrs. Hamilton arrived.

Aug 13 We drove to Donhead St. Mary. Fanny approved of the tablet she has had erected by Osmond to the memory of dear William. Called on Maria Jackson.

Sept 29 I dined at Ferne. Mr. Hakewell the architect there. Saw the comet to perfection.

Oct 16 I walked to luncheon at Ferne. A long time there seeing the paintings by Mr. Joy.

Oct 21 I dined at Ferne, met my brother Charles & Emily [his daughter]. The former is having his picture taken by Mr. Joy – and very like.

Oct 22 I lunched at Ferne, quite surprised into having my picture painted by Mr. Joy.

Oct. 16-23 For Mr. Joy see Note to 1858 Thomas Grove Diaries below (p 231).

Oct 23 I went up again for another sitting. It is to cost £35. It is a present to my nephew Thomas Fraser Grove to hang up with his other family pictures at Ferne.

Dec 22 Miss Stockwell her birds etc arrived. She has got a young bulfinch.

1859-1860

There are no diaries for these last two years of Charlotte's life. She died in 1860. The hanging of her portrait at Ferne makes a fitting conclusion to a life so closely associated with the house and its fortunes. If the portrait of Charlotte survives its whereabouts are not known. Ferne was demolished in 1966. Her diaries have proved to be the more durable record of her existence.

PART TWO

The Diaries of
Sir Thomas Grove &
Agnes Geraldine, Lady Grove
1855 - 1925

The Principal Characters

The death of 'Doctor John' Grove and the conclusion of Charlotte's narrative usher in a new generation at Ferne, new diarists and a host of fresh names to be added to those familiar ones which survive from earlier years. An additional list of biographies and identifications is accordingly inserted here, supplementing the original groups as follows:

E. Grove Family and Relatives.

F. Friends and Neighbours.

G. Minor Gentry, Servants and Others

H. Family Seats, and other Places of Interest

The original letters of identification A, B, C, D are occasionally added to a name as a reminder that it has appeared in the earlier diaries and is therefore included in the original list (pp. 17-32), not in this supplementary one.

E. *Family & Relatives (1855-1925)*

GROVE of Ferne. Of Sir Thomas's Grove uncles only one – Rev. Charles Henry – survived the year of Charlotte's death, 1860, along with his widowed sister, Harriet Helyar, and the widows of their brothers Thomas, William and George. Attention is now concentrated primarily on the families of Sir Thomas and his deceased brother John of Mudeford.

GROVE, children of Sir Thomas Grove by his first wife Katharine Grace O'Grady:

1. Grace Kathleen (1848-1940) married in 1867 (1) Harvey John de Montmorency (died 1873) and (2) in 1896 General F. Hamilton. Children by her first husband include Kathleen and Tom. After de Montmorency's death she lived at Richmond, Surrey, and was often referred to as 'Mrs de Mont'.

2. Edith Eleanor (1850-1921) m. 1874 Edmund Benson Foster (died 1917) of Clewer Manor near Windsor. Two d., Ruth and Florence, m. Baron Van Heemstra; and a son, Eddy.
3. Walter John (1852-1932) eldest son and heir. See below.
4. Charlotte Augusta (1857-1929) m. Gilbert Davis of Corfe Mullen.
5. Emily Kathleen (1861-1945) known as 'Kat', m. 1885 Edmund Mansel-Pleydell (died 1914). Their children included 2d Vivien & Daphne, 2s Teddy & Harry, both killed in the Great War.
6. Thomas Hele Hooke (1862-1948) m. 1929 Leocadia, widow of Felipe Crosthwaite of Santa Rosa, Mexico.
7. Two boys died in infancy.

GROVE, child of Sir Thomas by his second wife, Frances Hinton Best q.v. married 1882: Olivia Frances (1884-1953) m. 1910 Capt William Blennerhassett, youngest son of 4th bronet.

GROVE, Walter John (1852-1932) succeeded as second baronet 1897, m. 1882 Agnes Geraldine Fox-Pitt, d. of General Augustus Pitt-Rivers. Their children:
1. Honor (1883-1944) also known as Dode or Kiddy. m. 1911 Nicholas Golejewski, Assistant Chief of the Russian Imperial General Staff, died in Moscow 1958, known as 'Koka'. Two daughters Kira and Sonia.
2. Gerald (1886-1962) succeeded as 3rd baronet 1932 dsp.
3. Oenone (1889-1956).
4. Terence (1893-1902) drowned at Tangier.
5. Walter Peel, known as 'Beb' (1904-1944) m. 1926 Elena, d. of Felipe Crosthwaite, divorce 1933. Three sons Walter Philip, known as 'Min', born 1927, died in Philadelphia 1974; Charles Gerald born 1929 and Harold Thomas born 1930. The fourth baronet, Walter Philip, is thought to have died without issue. Of a successor nothing is known.

GROVE, children of John of Mudeford (1823-1859)
1. Aimée Jean (1852-1919) m. 1878 Capt later Sir James de Hoghton (1851-1938).
2. William Henry Warrington (1854-) Lieutenant R.N.
3. Rev. Hubert Farquharson (1855-) vicar of Huish near Marlborough from 1893 after curacies at Ludlow 1886-88, Pewsey 1888-91 and Sixpenny Handley 1891-92.

GROVE, Chafin, of Zeals

As 'Aunt Chafin' had no children the succession at Zeals passed to the children of Dr Charles Grove (1747-1806) a Salisbury doctor residing in the Close:

1. Chafin (1781-1851) succeeded Aunt Chafin. Dsp.
2. William Chafin (1786-1859) m. Eleanor Michell (1799-) d. Thomas Michell of Chitterne. Zeals passed successively to their children -
   (a) William Chafin (1840-1865) Lieutenant Coldstream Guards, died at Poonah dsp.
   (b) Julia Elizabeth (1826-1891) dsp.
3. Maria Caroline (1796-) m. 1826 George Bullock of N. Coker. Their son, George Troyte Bullock (1829-1913) inherited from Miss Julia and adopted the name of Chafin Grove.
4. Harry Thomas (1803-) resided in Salisbury.

GROVE, daughters of Rev Charles Henry of Sedgehill

1. Emily Charlotte, born 1832 m. Charles Townsend 1865.
2. Agnes born 1841 m. John Fraser Hussey 1867.
3. Alice born 1843 m. Charles William Gordon (1819-1897) in 1868.

GROVE, Patrick: not identified, possibly grandson of John of Mudeford.

GROVE FAMILY RELATIONS

ALLHUSEN, Dorothy, d. of John Stanley q.v. She married Henry Allhusen MP for Salisbury 1897-1900.

ARNIM, Mary von, née Beauchamp, m. Count Arnim who died 1910 and (2) Frank Russell in 1916 as his third wife. He became 2nd Earl Russell q.v.

AVEBURY, Lord, see Lubbock, Sir John.

BEST, Edith Anne (1847-1924) m. George, 5th Lord Wynford. Lived at Charlton House, Donhead St. Mary. Memorial in St. John's, Charlton.

Mrs Frances Hinton, widow of Captain Crosse, m. secondly Capt. Hon. Frederick Barnewall Best (1827-1876) in 1870 as his second wife. He was a younger son of the 2nd Baron Wynford. After his death she

m. (3) in 1882 Sir Thomas Grove of Ferne q.v. She died in 1912.

Jane, (1803-1895) wife of 2nd Baron Wynford, married 1821.

Margaret Mary CBE (1872-1941) d. of 5th Baron Wynford.

Marion (1877-) d. of 5th Baron Wynford.

Robert (1834-) Capt. Grenadier Guards. Married. Younger brother of Frederick Barnewall (above).

BRUCE OF STENHOUSE: Lady Bruce and the 1st Lady Grove were sisters.

Sir William Cunningham (1825-1906) 9th baronet (1862) captain 74th regiment, in 1850 m. Charlotte Isabella (died 1873) 3rd d. of Hon. Waller O'Grady, and had issue 1s, 2d, as follows:

William Waller ('Willie') succeeded in 1906 as 10th Bart, born 1856

Grace Katherine (1851-1934) and Corinna Maria (? – 1929)

Frequent visitors to Ferne, the young Bruces had close friendships with their Grove cousins.

BULLOCK, Troyte: see Chafin Grove of Zeals, Maria Caroline.

CONYERS (12th Baron) Sackville George Lane-Fox (1827-1888).

(13th Baroness) Marcia Amelia Mary, succeeded her father as baroness in her own right, married 4th Earl of Yarborough. Known to her Fox-Pitt cousins as 'Mushie'.

CROSSE. The family of the first marriage of Sir Thomas Grove's second wife, Frances Hinton.

Herbert Edward George, Capt 59th Regiment, m. Frances Hinton d. of Henry Northcote of Crediton. They are presumed to be the parents of Herbert, who m. Avis Winn or Wynn in 1895 and of Ella who died in 1885. Mrs Crosse, in 1885, is presumed to be the mother of the late Captain.

DE HOGHTON. see Children of John Grove of Mudeford.

FOSTER, Edmund: see Edith d. Sir Thomas Grove.

FOX, Lane: see Lane-Fox.

FOX: abbreviated form of Lane-Fox.

FOX-PITT. Surname given in 1880 to all the children, except the eldest son, of General Pitt-Rivers.

Alex, see Pitt-Rivers.

St. George (1856-1932) pioneer inventor of electric lighting. His patent of 1878 preceded the work of Edison and Swan. He married 1899 Lady Edith Douglas (born 1874) d. 9th Marquess of Queensberry.

William Augustus (1858-1945) Military career in his father's regiment, Grenadier Guards. Active service in Zulu War, the Sudan, Boer War etc. Married, 1893, Lillie Ethel ('Blossie') d. Arthur F. Payne. Two sons Major-General W.H. and Commander T.H.

Ursula Katherine (1859-1942) m. 1880 William Charles Scott of Thorpe, Chertsey. They had at least three children. Willie Scott's mother, Hon. Harriet Alethea Stanley (1805-1888) was Ursula's great-aunt: she m. 1835 General William Henry Scott, who died 1868.

Lionel Charles (1860-1937) m. 1898 Nesta d. J.C. Blackett of Egham. Divorce 1920 and second marriage, to Elspeth Phelps.

Alice Augusta Laurentia (1862-1947) m. 1884 as his second wife Rt. Hon. Sir John Lubbock P.C., FRS, 4th Baronet, later Lord Avebury of Farnborough, Kent. Several children, including Harold Lubbock q.v.

Agnes Geraldine (1863-1926) m. Walter, son of Sir Thomas Grove q.v.

Douglas Henry (1864-1922) probably dsp unmarried. A painter of professional standard.

Arthur (1866-1895) nicknamed 'Carrots'. Progressive mental disorder. Certified insane 1891.

FRASER, Georgina or Georgiana (1807-1891). An aunt of Sir Thomas Grove. Certified insane in 1874.

GOLEJEWSKI: see Grove, Honor, d. of Sir Walter Grove.

HEEMSTRA. Baron van: married Florence Foster, grand-daughter of Sir Thomas Grove.

HELYAR. Children of Harriet Grove and William Helyar.

William Hawker (1812-1880) succeeded by his son Horace Augustus (1853-1893) who m. his cousin Violet Wedderburn

Agnes Grove, born 1814, married 1844 William Charles Lambert of Stepleton Manor, Dorset, as his 2nd wife.

Edwin, named in his father's will, 1841, as 4th eldest surviving son (1832-1868) married 9 May 1855.

Ellen Harriet (1816-1911) in 1845 m. William Phelips (1823-1889) and had issue. See Phelips below (F).

HOGHTON: see Children of John Grove of Mudeford.

HOZIER, Blanche (1852-1925), d. of Rosalind (Stanley) Countess of Airlie 'Aunt Ros', m. 1873 Col. Sir Henry M. Hozier & had issue.
    Clementine ('Clemmy') their daughter m. 1908 Winston Churchill M.P.

HUSSEY. Family of Sir Thomas's sister Henrietta (1819-1893) who m. James Hussey in 1839.
    Anthony (1842? –) served in 53rd Regiment.
    John Fraser (1840? –) m. 1867 Agnes d. Rev. Charles Henry Grove of Sedgehill.
    Henrietta.
    Grace m. – Heathcote 1876.
    Margaret (1851-1941)
    Agnes married 22 April 1890 to R. Hussey Freke.

JEUNE, Sir Francis (later Baron St Helier) m. Mary, widow of John Stanley q.v.

LANE-FOX the birth-name of General Augustus Pitt-Rivers and his children q.v.
    Charlotte.
    Hon. Edith m. 1893 Reginald Wentworth Fitzwilliam, s. Earl Fitzwilliam.
    Kathleen m. April 1884.
    Marcia ('Mushie') see Conyers.
    Sackville George see Conyers.
    Violet.

LUBBOCK, Harold, son of Alice Fox-Pitt and Sir John Lubbock. He married Dorothy elder d. of Lord and Lady Forster, whose younger d. Rachel m. George Pitt-Rivers. In April 1918 he was killed in action with the Grenadier Guards.

MANSEL-PLEYDELL of Whatcombe and Longthorns, near Blandford. Three brothers.
    1. Edmund ('Eddy') m. Kate d. Sir Thomas Grove. Served in India
        with 12th Lancers. Died 1914. Four children:
        (a) Teddy (1886-1915) Killed on active service in Great War.

(b) Vivien (1889-1977) m. 1919 George Railstone.

(c) Daphne (1893-1989) m. 1919 J. Arnold-Forster.

(d) Harry (1895-1916) Killed at Thiepval on active service.

2. Harry (1852-1886) 1st Royal Fusiliers.

3. John Clavell, rector of Sturminster Newton.

MONT or de Mont, Mrs: see Grace Kathleen, d. Sir Thomas Grove.

PAYNE, 'Blossie': see Fox-Pitt, William.

PITT-RIVERS. Name assumed in 1880 by General Augustus Lane Fox, his wife and his eldest son, all the other children assuming the name Fox-Pitt q.v.

PITT-RIVERS. General Augustus Lane Fox (1827-1900) F.R.S., Grenadier Guards, Staff Officer at battle of Alma (Crimea), m. 1853 Alice, d. 2nd Lord Stanley of Alderley, inherited in 1880 the Rivers estate of 29,000 acres under the will of his great-uncle George Pitt, 2nd Baron Rivers and assumed by royal licence the surname of Pitt-Rivers. An Act of Parliament appointed him as the first Inspector of Ancient Monuments. His influence on British archaeology was profound. His widow died in 1910. For their children see Fox-Pitt, except for the eldest son and heir, who was Pitt-Rivers, Alex (1855-1927) Sheriff of Dorset 1909, m. 1889 Ruth Hermione, d. of Rt. Hon. Henry F. Thynne P.C. Two children, a daughter, Marcia, and the male heir:

George H.L. (1890-1966) Capt. 1st Royal Dragoons, known as 'Joe' (i.e. Geo), in 1915 he married Hon. Rachel Forster, d. of Lord and Lady Forster. Rachel was better known by her stage name as the actress Mary Hinton. The marriage was dissolved and he married again.

PLEYDELL: abbreviated form of Mansel-Pleydell q.v.

RIVERS: George Pitt (1751-1828) succeeded as 2nd Baron 1803.

George Pitt (1810-1866) succeeded as 4th Baron 1831.

Horace Pitt (1814-1880) succeeded as 6th Baron 1867.

ROSS, Major John (died 1896) in 1865 m. Helen Sophia, sister of Sir Thomas Grove and had issue 2d and 1s.

RUSSELL: Agnes Geraldine Grove had Russell cousins in consequence of the marriage of her aunt, Hon. Kate Stanley, with Lord John Russell's son, Viscount Amberley.

Bertrand, 3rd Earl. Philosopher. Visited Rushmore, corresponded with Agnes.

Sir Claud (1871-1959) 2nd son of Lord Arthur Russell, m. Athenais Iphigenia Atchley in 1920. A career diplomat and one of Agnes's more turbulent flirtations.

Frank, 2nd Earl (1865-1931) A barrister, who represented Agnes on one occasion. His third wife was Mary von Arnim, author of *Elizabeth and her German Garden* and for that reason sometimes called 'Elizabeth'.

Rt. Hon. George William Erskine P.C. (1853-1919). Liberal undersecretary and author. A grandson of 6th Duke of Bedford.

Lady: in context probably widow of 1st Earl ('Lord John').

Other: there are passing references to Conrad, Gilbert and Lady Victoria Russell.

ST. HELIER, Baron: see Jeune.

SCOTT, William Charles, s. of General William Henry Scott and Hon. Harriett Alethea Stanley (1805-1888), m. 1880 Ursula Fox-Pitt and had issue. His mother was Ursula's great-aunt.

SELWYN, Frederic m. Louisa Jane Grove, sister of Sir Thomas.

Reginald, s. of Frederic & Louisa, born 1857.

Arthur, probably son or grandson of Frederic.

SHELLEY. Grandsons of Sir Timothy.[A]

Percy Florence (1819-1889) 3rd Baronet. Resided at Boscombe Manor. Son of Percy Bysshe. Dsp.

Edward (1827-1890) 4th Baronet. Son of Shelley's younger brother, John (1806-1866). Dsp.

Charles (1838-1902) 5th Baronet. Son of Shelley's younger brother, John (1806-1866). Dsp.

John, Sir (1848-1931): not a direct descendant of Sir Timothy. Holder of a collateral baronetcy.

STANLEY. Mrs Pitt-Rivers was eldest d. 2nd Baron Stanley of Alderley, who died 1869, survived by his widow until 1896. Their nine children were, in order of age:

1. Henry (1827-1903) 3rd Baron m. Fabia.
2. Alice (1828-1910) m. General Pitt-Rivers q.v. in 1853.
3. Blanche (1829-1921) m. Earl of Airlie.
4. Maude (1832-1915) did not marry.
5. John (1837-1878) m. Mary Stewart-Mackenzie and had two d., Madeleine and Dorothy, who m. Henry Allhusen q.v. (John's widow m. Francis Jeune, q.v.)
6. Lyulph (1839-1929) 4th Baron. m. Miss Bell.
7. Kate (1842-1874) m. Viscount Amberley.
8. Algernon (1843-1928) Bishop of Emmaus.
9. Rosalind (1844-1921) m. 1864 George Howard, Earl of Carlisle. Their two eldest children were Mary and Charles.
   Rianette (1797-1882), a sister of 1st Lord Stanley.
   Oliver (1879-1952) 3rd son of Edward Lyulph 4th Baron, m. 1919 Lady (Alice) Kathleen Violet Thynne eldest d. 5th Marquess of Bath.

THYNNE Rt. Hon. Henry F. Thynne P.C. (1832-1904) younger son of 3rd Marquess of Bath. His d. Ruth m. Alex Pitt-Rivers q.v.
   Alex (1873-1918) younger brother of 5th Marquess of Bath. Killed in action.

TROYTE-BULLOCK: see Bullock

WINN or Wynn, Avis: see Crosse.

WYNFORD: see Best.

YARBOROUGH: see Conyers, Marcia.

F. *Friends & Neighbours*

ADEANE, Hon. Marie: maid of honour to Queen Victoria, m. Sir Bernard Mallet 1891, had issue and died 1934.

AIDÉ, Hamilton (1830-1906) poet & novelist, lived in the New Forest.

AILESBURY, 3rd Marquis: Sir Ernest Bruce PC (1811-1886) MP Marlborough 1832-78. In 1878 succeeded his brother (1804-78) who m. a d. of Earl of Pembroke. dsp

ALINGTON, 1st Baron, Henry Gerard Sturt (1825-1904) MP Dorchester 1841-56, Dorset 1856-76, created Baron 1876 m. his cousin Lady Augusta Bingham eldest d. Earl of Lucan 1853.

2nd Baron, Humphrey Napier Sturt (1859-1919) MP East Dorset 1891-1904.

ALLENBY, Edmund (1861-1936) captain, later 1st Viscount (1919), Field-Marshal and High Commissioner for Egypt (1919-25) m. Adelaide Mabel d. Horace Chapman, rector of Donhead St. Andrew, in 1896. She died 1942.

ARNOTT, Hermione Mary Louisa (1885-1923) *née* Cooper, sister of Alfred Duff Cooper, 1st Viscount Norwich, m. 1904 Neil Arnott who divorced her in 1921 citing Gerald Grove as co-respondent.

ARUNDELL. Family of Wardour (B) continued.

John (1831-1906) the 12th Baron, was succeeded briefly by his brother,

Everard (1834-1907) as 13th Baron, and then by a cousin.

Edgar (1859-1921) 14th Baron, whose brother, Gerald (1861-1939) became the 15th Baron Arundell.

BANKES, 'Ada' – possibly Adelaide Anne, sister of Walter Ralph (1853-1904).

Albert (1840-1913) D.L., J.P., barrister, of Wolfeton House, Dorchester.

'Florrie' – not identified.

Walter Ralph (1853-1904) of Kingston Lacy, m. 1897 Henrietta Jenny Fraser and had issue 1s 2d.

BEAUFOY, Mark (1854-1922) MP Kennington 1889-95, married, resident Donhead St. Mary (Coombe House, built 1886).

BENETT of Pythouse [B] continued:

BENETT-STANFORD, Col. Vere Fane (1840-1894) was born Vere Fane, s. of Rev. Arthur Fane, whose mother was Anna Maria Benett. Arthur m. 1832 his cousin Lucy, d. John Benett MP. Vere Fane adopted the family name of Benett and, when he m. the wealthy Ellen Stanford, he was obliged to add her surname. After his death she married again and died in 1932.

Col. J.M. (1870-1947) – known as 'Mad Jack' - inherited Pythouse in 1894. His only son Vere died in 1922.

BLANCHE, Jacques-Emile: French portrait-painter resident in London. Painted Thomas Hardy and published gossipy reminiscences of Hardy's circle of friends in London (*Mes Modèles*).

BONTINE, Mrs (1828-1925) born Hon. Anne Elizabeth, sister of 14th Baron Elphinstone, she married William Cunninghame Graham who adopted the surname Bontine to comply with a legacy. The name was dropped by her son Robert Cunninghame Graham q.v.

'BOOB'. A close friend of Walter Grove's, alternatively 'Booby'. Diary contexts suggest he became a cleric and a magistrate. Identity not known, but 'Booby' could be a comical corruption of 'Bouverie' and might therefore refer to the Earl of Radnor's 4th son – Rev. Hon. Bertrand Pleydell-Bouverie (1845-1926) who was a Wiltshire J.P. and rector of Pewsey 1880-1910. In 1870 he married a sister of Lord Trafalgar, who was one of Walter Grove's friends.

BRUCE, Lord Henry: succeeded as 5th Marquess of Ailesbury in 1894 and died 1911.

CAMPBELL, Mrs Patrick: famous actress. Developed an enduring friendship with Agnes Grove.
    Stella: Mrs Pat's daughter, later Mrs Beech.

CARLOW, Viscount: George Lionel Henry Seymour Dawson-Damer (1858-1900) in 1892 succeeded his father as Earl of Portarlington. He married, 1881, Emma Andalusia Frere.

CHAPMAN, Rev. Horace Edward (1842-1907) rector Donhead St. Andrew, married d. Sir Henry Fletcher. Their children:
    Horace Bruce (1866-1937); 'Nelly' (Helen Mary) m. 1890 Rev. Daryl Tupper Cary; Florence, m. 1902; Adelaide Mabel m. 1896 Capt. Allenby q.v. Mary Edith m. 1901 Admiral Charles Lionel Napier.
    Kyrle Alfred of Roehampton (1838-1891) a distant kinsman and occasional guest at Ferne, sometimes with Louisa Chapman.

COCKBURN, Sir Alexander (1802-1880) Liberal M.P. Attorney

General 1851, succeeded an uncle as baronet 1858, became Lord Chief Justice 1859.

COOPER, Lady Agnes, wife of Sir Alfred Cooper FRCS and sister of 1st Duke of Fife. Her children included Hermione Arnott, q.v.

CRAIGIE, Mrs Pearl Mary Teresa (1867-1906). Wrote under pseudonym 'John Oliver Hobbes'.

CREWE, Lord: Robert Offley Ashburton Crewe Milnes (1858-1945) succeeded his father Richard Monckton Milnes in 1885 as 2nd Lord Houghton, was subsequently created Earl (1895) and Marquis (1911) of Crewe. Lord-Lieutenant ('Viceroy') of Ireland (1892-95). Married Lady Margaret Primrose, d. of Lord Rosebery. Two sisters of Lord Crewe were Florence Henniker q.v. and Amy, Lady Gerald Fitzgerald.

CUNNINGHAM GRAHAM: see Graham.
DAWSON-DAMER: see Carlow.

DOUGLAS, John Sholto, 9th Marquis of Queensberry, died 1900.
    Sybil, his wife 1866, divorced him 1887, died 1935: 'Sybil Q'. Their children:
    Francis Archibald, Viscount Drumlanrig (1867-1894).
    Percy Sholto, 10th Marquis (1868-1920) m. 1893 and had issue, 2s, 1d.
    Alfred (1870-1945).
    Sholto George (1872-1942).
    Edith Gertrude (1874-1963) m. St. George Fox-Pitt 1899.

DUGDALE, Florence (1879-1937) second wife of Thomas Hardy q.v. married 1914.

ELCHO, Lady: see Wyndham (of 'Clouds') Mary, below.

FARQUHARSON FAMILY [B] continued: grandchildren of 'Squire' J. J. Farquharson (1784-1871).
FARQUHARSON, Archibald James, R.N. (1852-1925) s. of James John Farquharson (1806-1896).
    Grace Mabel (-1928) daughter.
    Henry Richard (1857-1895) MP West Dorset 1885-95, s. of Henry of

Langton St. Leonards (1816-). He m. 1878 his cousin Constance (died 1898) and they lived (1885) at Westbury House, Tarrant Gunville.
    Robert: identity (1881) uncertain.
    Ronald James (1855-1934) of Tilshead where he trained horses.

FITZGERALD: Amicia ('Amy') Lady – see Crewe.

FORSTER, Rachel: see Pitt-Rivers, George.

FOLKESTONE, Viscount: Jacob (1815-1889) son and heir of the 3rd Earl of Radnor.

GLYN of Gaunts House, near Wimborne. Sir Richard George Glyn, bart (1831-1918) Dep.-Lieut. Dorset, High Sheriff 1869, succeeded his uncle in 1863. He married a Fitzgerald and had issue, Fizgerald (1875-1960) and Geraldine Mary.

GLYN of Iwerne Minster (Barons Wolverton). George Carr Glyn, 1st Baron (1797-1873) was 4th s. Sir Richard Carr Glyn, bart. In 1823 m. Marianne d. Pascoe Grenfell MP and had issue George Grenfell (1824-1887) 2nd Baron, and 10 others including.
    (a) Henry Carr C.B., father of Henry Richard (1861- 1888) 3rd Baron and Frederic (1864-1930) 4th Baron.
    (b) Hon. Pascoe Charles (1833-1904).
    (c) Hon. Sidney Carr MP, Capt. Rifle Brigade (1835-1916) whose children included Arthur (1870-1922) and George Carr (1872-1905).

GRAHAM, Cunninghame: sons of Mrs Bontine q.v.
    Charles Cunninghame (1853-1917) R.N., later deputy chief inspector RNLI.
    Robert Bontine Cunninghame (1852-1936) author, MP North Lanarkshire 1886-92.

GROSSMITH, George (1847-1912) actor, particularly in Gilbert & Sullivan operas.

GUEST (Lord Wimborne) 1. Sir Ivor Bertie Guest of Canford Manor (1835-1914) cr. 1st Baron Wimborne 1880, m. 1868 eldest d. 6th Duke of Marlborough & had 4s & 4d including:

(a) Ivor Churchill (1873-1939) succeeded his father 1914, in 1920 m. younger d. 2nd Lord Ebury & had issue.
(b) Henry, Captain (1874-1957) MP 1910.
2. Thomas Merthyr of Henstridge, Blandford (1838-1904) younger brother of 1st Baron, in 1877 m. Lady Theodora Grosvenor, youngest d. 2nd Marquess of Westminster.

HAMILTON, General Frank, in 1896 m. Sir Thomas Grove's widowed d. Grace, 'Mrs de Mont'.

HAMILTON, Mary Baillie, d. Thomas Grove junior (1783-1845) [A] q.v.

HARDY, Thomas (1840-1928) novelist and poet. Encouraged Agnes Grove as a writer, correcting her proofs, accepting her dedication of *The Social Fetich* and describing her as 'my good little pupil'. She is the subject of his poem 'Concerning Agnes'.

HAWKINS, Anthony Hope (1863-1933) Kt 1918. Author of Ruritanian novels, *The Dolly Dialogues* etc.

HENNIKER, Hon. Florence Ellen Hungerford, *née* Milnes (1855-1923) sister of Lord Crewe q.v. In 1882 she m. Hon. Arthur Henry Henniker-Major, s. of 4th Lord Henniker. He became a Major General, Coldstream Guards and died 1912. Her friendship with Thomas Hardy extended over 30 years and they collaborated in the writing of a short story. She published half a dozen novels which were well received.

HERBERT, Rt. Hon. Sidney (1810-1861) s. of 11th Earl of Pembroke. Several periods as Secretary-at-War, notably during Crimean War. MP for S. Wilts, in 1861 became Lord Herbert of Lea.
    Sidney junior, son of above (1853-1913) MP 1877-85 and 1886-95, succeeded as 14th Earl of Pembroke. In 1877 he married Lady Beatrix Lambton, who could be identified as 'Beatie Herbert' in 1893.

HOPE, Anthony: pseudonym of Anthony Hope Hawkins q.v.

HOUGHTON, Lord: see Crewe.

HULSE, Sir Edward (1809-1899) 5th Bart., of Breamore House, near Ringwood.
Sir Henry (1859-1903) 6th. Bart
Sir Henry (1889-1915) 7th. Bart, killed in action.

KIPLING, John Lockwood (1837-1911) and his wife Alice (died 1910) lived in Tisbury at 'The Gables'. There are memorials to them in Tisbury church.
Rudyard, their son, was an occasional visitor to the district.

MATTHEWS, Lieut. George R.N. known as Billy.
Mrs. his mother – Oenone's London landlady.

MORRISON, Alfred (1821-1897) of Fonthill House, Hindon.
Hugh his son (1868-1931), married 1892 Lady Sophia Castalia Mary (died 1931) 2nd d. of 2nd Earl of Granville.

MUNRO, Lieutenant-commander Edward Lionel (1862-1920) 2nd son of 3rd Baronet, wounded in the Sudan. In 1887 he m. wealthy heiress Mabel Zoe Walker (1866-1924) of Eastwood Hall, Nottinghamshire, and added her name to his – Walker-Munro. They built Rhinefield House in Brockenhurst and also St. Saviour's Church there, where they are both buried.

NOVIKOV, Olga: Russian journalist, friend of Gladstone and Campbell-Bannerman.

PEEL, William Robert Wellesley (1867-1937) succeeded as Viscount Peel 1912, cr. Earl 1929. In 1899 m. Hon. Ella Williamson. First recorded acquaintance with Agnes 1898. The christening of her youngest son Walter Peel in 1904 suggests that Peel was a godfather, but this is not so. He took her to a Buckingham Palace ball three months later and their friendship persisted until 1918 or later.

PELLY, Lady, née Anna Maria Poore of Salisbury, m. 1889 Sir Harold Pelly of Gillingham, 4th Bart, had issue 2s, 3d and died 1939.

PEMBROKE, 13th Earl, George Robert Charles Herbert (1850-1895 dsp) succeeded his uncle 1862.
14th Earl, Sidney Herbert (1853-1913) succeeded 1895.

PHELIPS of Montacute.

Mary Anne (1797-1869) widow of John Phelips (1784- 1834) m. c1837 J.J. Farquharson (1784-1871) of Langton Long as his second wife.

Mary, only child of John Phelips and Mary Anne, m. 1837 J.J. Farquharson junior.

William (1823-1889) m. 1845 Ellen Helyar of Coker Court, d. of Harriet, *née* Grove.

Richard (1825-1889) Capt. R.A., brother of William (preceding).

William (1846-1919) son of William and Ellen (above), accompanied Agnes and Walter Grove to New York in 1882.

PORTMAN FAMILY [B]continued:
PORTMAN, Edward Berkeley (1799-1888) created Baron 1837, Viscount 1873. His children included, by his first marriage, Edwin Berkeley (1830-1921) MP N. Dorset 1885-92, and by his second marriage Rev. Walter (1836-1903) rector of Corton Denham, Sherborne; and Lucy Ella who died unmarried in 1908. The first Viscount was succeeded by his son

William Henry Berkeley (1829-1919) whose children included Edward ('Teddy') William Berkeley J.P. (1856-1911 dsp) and Henry Berkeley J.P. (1860-1923).

QUEENSBERRY, Sybil Marchioness of (died 1935) Her period of residence at Hatch, near Tisbury, gave Agnes a neighbour with shared interests in amateur theatricals and the arts generally. She was godmother to Agnes's youngest son and sculpted a bust of Agnes. Her daughter Edith married Agnes's brother, St. George. See also Douglas.

TENNANT, Pamela: see Wyndham (following page).

VACHELL, Horace Annesley (1861-1955) Novelist and dramatist: author of *Quinneys* etc.

WADDINGTON: see Grove, Emma Philippa (1788-1819) [A]

WALKER, Mabel Zoe: see Munro.

WOLVERTON: see Glyn of Iwerne Minster.

WYNDHAM of 'Clouds', East Knoyle.

Percy Scawen (1835-1911) son of George, Baron Leconfield (1787-1869).

Rt. Hon. George P.C. (1863-1913) Under-Secretary for War 1898-1900, Chief Secretary for Ireland 1900-1905, m. 1887 Mary, Countess Grosvenor. Their son Percy Lyulph killed in action 1914.

Guy Percy (1865-1933) married twice.

Mary (1862-1937) m. 1883 Hugo Charteris, Lord Elcho, 11th Earl of Wemyss.

Pamela A.G. (-1928) (1) m. Edward Tennant, cr. Baron Glenconner 1911. They had 3 sons – Christopher, 2nd Baron Glenconner; Edward Wyndham 'Bim' (1897-1916); and David Pax who m. Hermione Baddeley. Pamela m (2) Earl Grey of Fallodon.

5. *Minor Gentry, Servants and others*

Beaumont, Fred: commissioned by General Pitt-Rivers to paint portrait of Agnes, exhibited at Royal Academy 1892 (catalogue no. 196) and also portrait of himself.

Blackmore, Richard White: rector of Donhead St. Mary 1847-1882.

Cary, rev. Tupper, vicar of Ebbesbourne Wake in 1870s and '80s. His son, rev. Daryl Tupper Cary m. 1890 Nelly Chapman q.v. [F].

Dixon, Miss: children's governess taken by Agnes to Morocco in 1901.

Hakewill, John Henry [?] (1811-1880): architect responsible for additions to Ferne House.

Hawkins: horse-dealer.

Kemble, rev. Arthur, rector of Berwick St. John 1880-'89.

King, Walter Edward, Donhead Lodge, Donhead St. Andrew.

Nixon, Miss: a nursery governess 1890.

Raymond, John Gatehouse: Sir Thomas Grove's land-agent.

Rutter, Clarence: Sir Thomas Grove's political agent in 1885.

Spurgeon, Charles Haddon (1834-1892): popular nonconformist preacher. His Tabernacle in London seated 6000.

Waterfall, rev. George W. rector of Tollard Royal.

West, rev. John: rector of Chettle, founder of the Gypsy School,

Farnham. See 1890 Note (Sir Thomas Grove's diary), p.256.
Wilkinson, Canon G.H: rector of St. Peter's, Eaton Square, London.

H. *Family Seats, and other Places of Interest*

Boscombe Manor: residence of Sir Percy Florence Shelley (1819-1889).
Branksea Island (modern Brownsea Island). The largest island in Poole
  Harbour, with a long history of habitation.

Canford. Family seat of Guest family, barons Wimborne, SE of Wimborne Minster, now Canford School.
Clewer Manor: residence near Windsor of Sir Thomas Grove's
  daughter Edith and her husband, Edmund Benson Foster.

Donhead House: formerly Donhead St. Andrew rectory, purchased as
  his private residence by the rector, Horace Chapman (1842-1907)
  when he resigned his living.

Ensenada: Mexican town on the Pacific coast of Baja California. Trad-
  ing centre for the ranching activities of Tom Grove.

Fernditch: see Vernditch.

Ferne: under its final resident Grove owner, Si Thomas, the house
  was substantially altered and developed. It was purchased in 1902
  by Major Albany Charlesworth. Following his death in 1914 his
  executors sold it to the Duke of Hamilton, who died in 1940.
  Nina, Duchess of Hamilton (died 1951) converted Ferne into an
  animal sanctuary. The house was demolished in 1966. The residual
  property is now in private ownership.

Gypsy School: see 1890 note (Sir Thomas Grove's diary), p.256.

Hatch House, Tisbury: since 1841 a part of the Pythouse estate.
High Cliff (modern Highcliffe-on-Sea) east of Christchurch, Dorset.

Iwerne Minster village 5 miles N of Blandford. Family seat of Glyn,
  barons Wolverton, now Clayesmore School.

Larmer Tree Gardens: pleasure grounds created at Tollard Royal by
  General Pitt-Rivers. A popular attraction in the 1890s, with annual
  attendances reaching 10,000.
Longleat: family seat, near Warminster, Wilts, of the Marquess of Bath.

Longthorns: a residence built c. 1855 by John Mansel-Pleydell about 5 miles S.W. of Blandford. It became the home of Sir Thomas's daughter Kathleen ('Kat') when she married Edmund Mansel-Pleydell in 1885.

Ludwell: a hamlet within Donhead St. Mary on the A30 about 3 miles east of Shaftesbury.

Matajanal: stock-raising ranch in the vicinity of Ensenada, Mexico, managed or owned by Tom Grove. Contemporary snapshots show a hilly boulder-strewn landscape with typical 'cowboy' scenes. After the death of Sir Thomas Grove and the departure from Ferne in 1897 Charlotte joined her brother Tom here. Walter paid a visit in 1899 and again during the period 1908-1914 with Agnes. In 1922 Gerald, having lost his employment in Australia, arrived at Tom's ranch and became involved in the export of onyx before going on to Hollywood. Later that year 'Beb' arrived, became a permanent resident and married locally in due course. Kathleen Pleydell paid a visit, her nephew Eddy Foster joined the work-force and increasingly this Grove colony became the family's more dynamic centre. After Agnes's death in 1925 Walter stayed at Sedgehill until 1928 when he set out with Oenone for Baja California. He also visited Gerald at Hollywood and died there. In the new generation the name and title of 'Grove of Ferne' disappeared from Wiltshire. It survived only in the increasing anonymity of Mexican and American life.

Ox Drove: a section of the Ridgeway running eastwards from Win Green.

Pitt-Rivers Museum: a subsequent use of the Gypsy School, to present the educational collection made by General Pitt-Rivers, at Tollard Farnham. More recently the collection has been dispersed and the site redeveloped.

Quaker Burial Ground, Tollard Royal: located in Chilvercombe Bottom, Higher Ashgrove Farm. See footnote 25 October 1895 (Sir Thomas Grove's diary).

Savernake Forest: between Marlborough, Wilts and Hungerford, Berks.

Vernditch: historically one of the administrative Walks of Cranborne Chase; more specifically a substantial woodland north-west of Martin Down.

West Lodge: the keeper's lodge for the West Walk of Cranborne Chase, gentrified in the eighteenth century with skill and taste, and now a private residence.

Whatcombe House: Family seat of the Pleydells at Winterborne Whitechurch, c. 5 miles SW of Blandford.

Willis's Rooms: formerly Almack's in St. James's, London.

Winterslow: a scattered farming village six miles east of Salisbury.

III

The Diaries of Sir Thomas Grove
1855 - 1897

INTRODUCTION

In her record of 1857 Charlotte entered against the date November 29 'my nephew T.F. Grove called & <u>approved</u> of my brougham'. The brougham was newly made for her and its construction had been the cause of some anxiety. On the same date – it was a Sunday – her nephew wrote in his diary 'Went to Berwick church. Called on Mrs Downes afterwards'.

That linking of the two diarists neatly marks the point of transition from the generation which had emerged from the eighteenth century to its successor which reached the threshold of the twentieth. Charlotte's formative world was the England of George III and the Regency. When her nephew was born the future Queen Victoria was two years old: he lived and died within her life-span, and he assimilated effortlessly the imperial delusions of grandeur of the Victorian heyday.

His earliest surviving diary is for 1855. It is a *Gentleman's Pocket Diary or Memorandum Book* of the kind that he used for the next forty years. Pages on the right hand side record payments and other financial matters. In 1855 he allowed himself £25 monthly for incidental spending. The left hand pages are mainly devoted to hunting and shooting: he makes a cross beside days when he hunted – three or four times a week, sometimes six. The day's bag from shooting was regularly itemised and an unusual quarry – a landrail or corncrake, for example – was singled out. References to family matters, personal friends and other human activities are sparse and laconic. There is no trace of the curiosity, voicing of opinions, gossipy chat and personal striving that bring Charlotte's world to life.

This first diary is inscribed 'T. Fraser Grove, Seagry House, Wilts'. The name 'Fraser' recalled that he was the grandson of Sir William Fraser and not only of T. Grove. Seagry lies a few miles north-east of Chippenham, conveniently placed for his role as an officer in the

Chippenham troop of the Wiltshire Yeomanry. Ferne was about 40 miles away and frequently visited. On January 8 he noted that 'Kate and the children arrived from Ferne'. Kate was his wife, a child of the Irish aristocracy and at this time the mother of two daughters and a son, Walter. Married in 1847 they had lived at Seagry since 1850.

The three diaries of the Seagry period, 1855-57, give some insights into his way of life. His writing is difficult to decipher and many of the entries are no more than a monotonous catalogue of shooting bags and hunting conditions.

1855

March 7 I went to Ferne after hunting. Got there at 12.
Waddingtons[A] and John [his brother] were there.

March 8 Attended Mr Downes funeral. Walked about Ferne.

March 9 The Waddingtons[E] left. I left at 3 for Seagry. Got home to
dinner.

March 26 Lord H. Thynne[E] came to stay.

April 19 Fished in the lake at Longleat[H].

April 23 Hunted at Fernditch[H] with Farquharson's[B] hounds.
Indifferent sport. Rode Midnight.

April 25 Rode Sion into Shaftesbury. Kate drove in with [his sisters]
Helen[A] and Emma[A].

May 2 Went to Plymouth to see launch of Conqueror, 101 guns.

May 8 To Dawlish to Edwin Helyar's[E] wedding.

May 19 Came to Ferne. Lunched at Sedgehill en route. Shot 17 rooks.

May 21 Shot 35 rooks with rifle. My father, brother & aunt Eliza
came from Mudeford[D].

June 3 Went Berwick church & afterwards went over the Priory
House and called on Mrs Downes.

Aug 25 [After a continental tour of some weeks in France, Germany
and Switzerland] Went into Bath to a concert. Met Chafyn Groves
etc. Dined at the Clutterbucks afterwards.

Sept 14 Chafyn Groves[E] came & slept.

Sept 15 Chafyn Groves left.

Oct 13 [While visiting Exmoor] I shot on Haddon, killed 1 grey hen
etc.

1856

[A note reads – £650 paid to my account in London & Westminster
[Bank] between 16th Aug' 55 & 1st Jan '56]

May 14 Took house [in London] from 1st June for 1 month at £42-
No. 19 Portman Street.

May 20 Was gazetted Captain of the Chippenham troop.

1857

April 4 Polling for county. [Sidney] Herbert[F] and [William]
   Wyndham returned. Thynne beaten by 178.
July 19, Sunday [In London]. Went to Music Hall in Surrey Gardens,
   heard Mr Spurgeon [G] preach.
Nov 25 Kate was confined at 5 a.m. of a girl.

The year ended with no further reference to the girl.

1858 - 59

THE NEW MASTER OF FERNE

Thomas's father, 'Doctor John', died in April 1858 and the very different
character of the new regime was quickly apparent. On the day of his
final departure from Seagry Thomas collected his chosen architect Mr
Hakewill[G] en route to Ferne and immediately put in hand extensive
alterations. In little more than a week the preliminary demolition work
began. The enlarged Ferne that gradually took shape was to be altogether more imposing than its predecessor, capable eventually of
serving as a political headquarters where supporters in their thousands
could rally to hear speeches by leading party spokesmen. The bill for
his improvements was not far short of ten thousand pounds.

His new social position, combined with his prowess in field sports,
gave him the entrée to the influential house-parties which nourished
his political ambitions. A case in point is his visit to Lord Ailesbury[F]
at Savernake.[H] In three days Captain Grove was one of the seven
guns returning daily bags of 619, 667 and 663 head of game, with
Grove's personal contribution on one day amounting to 104. Incidentally the tips paid by him were £4 to the keeper and ten shillings each
to the butler and the man who cleaned the guns.

The London season had its regular place in his social programme. In
1858 he attended three operas in London – *Lucrezia Borgia* and *Don
Giovanni* at the Haymarket and *Otello* at Covent Garden. He also saw
Miss Sedgewick in *The School for Scandal* and went to a grand concert
at the Crystal Palace.

1858

[Fly-leaf note] Wine at Ferne May 14 – 69 doz port 13 doz sherry 2 doz champagne

Feb 2 Heavy snow. Had the baby christened Charlotte Augusta [E] at Donhead.

April 15 Went to Salisbury by train. Met Smith who told me of my poor father's death yesterday. Went on to Ferne.

May 21 Sale of stock at Ferne. Total amount £1174.

May 31 Left Seagry, the whole household. I met Mr Hakewill [G] at Wilton & came in Jackson's coach to Ferne. My mother etc left same day. Kate & children arrived later.

June 1 Looked over the house etc. Mrs Downes called.

June 9 Began pulling down offices.

Aug 30 My mother & John [his brother] went to Mudeford.

Sept 8 Sale of stock on the farm. Gross amount £2314.

Oct 14 Mr Joy came to stay.

Oct 15 Uncle Charles & [his daughter] Emily Grove [E] came to lunch.

Oct 18 Mr Joy began to paint Walter [N].

Nov 4 Kate, self & Walter[E] drove in barouche to Mudeford to stay. Left at 12 arrived at 5.

Nov 5 Walked on the shore. Drove in my mother's carriage to see church etc.

Nov 6 Drove to Bournemouth in barouche.

Nov 7 Went to Christchurch in morning. Walked High Cliff[H] in afternoon.

NOTE TO 1858

The likely identification of 'Mr Joy' (Oct 14) is as Thomas Musgrove Joy (1812-1866), who had exhibited a portrait of Grove's Irish wife at the Royal Academy in 1849. Grove invited Joy to Ferne to paint Walter, aged six, the next heir to Ferne. The luncheon meeting with 'Uncle Charles' seems to have prompted the decision to add portraits of the two local survivors from the previous generation, Charles Henry Grove and his sister, Charlotte Downes. See her diary Oct 16-23, 1858. Grove's Accounts include in mid-November 'Mr Joy 2 pictures £40, frames £18'. If the portraits have survived, their present ownership is not known. Joy spent a fortnight at Ferne and a friendly

relationship persisted. In a note of some London addresses Grove included
'Joy, 32 St George Square' and his 1859 diary records on May 4 'Called on Mr
Joy & went to Exhibition'.

1859

Jan 25 Went to Lord Ailesbury[F] at Savernake[H] to stay.

Jan 27 7 guns shot 663 head, 197 pheasants.

Feb 18 Heard of John's death on the 16th.

Jan 23 Attended John's funeral. [at Mudeford]

March 1 Mr Corben comes as bailiff to Ferne.

March 4 Engaged Wm Coles as butler.

March 5 Lent W.C. Bruce[E] cheque for £50 as a loan.

March 11 Got I.O.U. from Bruce.

April 11 Helen [his sister] came from Salisbury.

April 26 Mr Holmes from Huddersfield came with Miller, gave me an
estimate for the gas – £130.

May 2 [General Election] Thynne and Herbert returned without
opposition.

May 7 Went to Wilton House[D] to stay. Marched into Salisbury with
troop for Yeomanry meeting.

May 14 Went by new line to Ferne.

May 28 Bought two pictures at Christie's by Giordano for £35.

June 16 Coles left [after only 3 months. He was paid £16/7/2 and
Frederick Toosey replaced him as butler]

June 24 Heard of Chafyn Grove's death.

June 28 Went to Sir A. Cockburn's[F] ball at Willis's Rooms.[H]

July 2 Kate Walter & myself went to Folkestone. Dined at my
mother's.

July 7 [Back in London] Went to opera in the evening. Drury Lane –
Norma.

July 12 La Traviata.

July 29 [At Ferne] Had the dining-room fitted up & dined in it. Mrs
Downes & Wm. Grove[E] called.

Sept 30 [William] Chafyn Grove[E] [1840-65] came.

Oct 20 H[enrietta] Hussey[E] came & left the two girls [probably the
two eldest of her four daughters]

May 14. The London-Salisbury railway-line was extended in 1859 to Tisbury and
Semley, reaching Sherborne in 1860.

1860 - 1869

The diaries for this decade are missing. Like those for subsequent decades they were presumably tied together in a bundle which went astray in the final dispersal of family papers. Fortunately some correspondence and other papers are preserved which shed light on the principal events in this period when his political career began.

The starting point is in fact an entry in the previous year's diary (above) – May 7, 1859 'Went to Wilton House to stay'. Ever since the Dissolution of the Monasteries Wilton has been the seat of the Herberts, Earls of Pembroke. Five days before Grove's visit Sidney Herbert had been returned unopposed to Parliament in the general election, and the bond between the two men was clearly a political one. Their families had a long history of association dating back to Elizabethan times and Sidney Herbert had had the support of the Groves throughout his career. In 1835 Charlotte Grove noted, Jan 19, 'My brother [Tom] Grove proposed Mr Herbert and made a good speech'; and again in 1837 she noted, August 1, 'Tom went to Wilton to propose Mr Sydney Herbert for the county'. Now in 1859 the immediate business was Herbert's growing inclination to resign his Ministry and go to the House of Lords, which in turn raised the question of his successor in the Commons. He evidently saw Captain Grove in that light.

A year later, as his health worsened, Herbert made his decision and encouraged Grove to make his first private moves. In a letter of 13 December 1860 he wrote to Grove:

> I think your view of your own position is quite a fair and reasonable one. I would confidentially sound two or three such men as Wyndham, Matcham and Hinxman . . . I wd not engage an agent or do anything to publish your intention till the vacancy occurs.
>
> If you have the support of the men I have mentioned you need not fear any contest. I mean there will be none.

Within a fortnight Herbert wrote again -

> I hope by a day's post or two at the outside to be enabled to announce my retirement, and then the ground will be open for any step you like to take. In the ordinary course of things the election couldn't take place till about the middle of February. Would that suit you?
>
> It will I think be important that you shouldn't appear to have

had any prior information from me, as it will be seized upon as
unfair etc etc etc.

The unexpected nomination of an opponent did not diminish Herbert's
confidence and he comforted Grove with the assurance that the Duke of
Somerset had urged his agent to 'use every effort' in Grove's cause, and so had
Lords Clarendon, Ashburton and Ailesbury. To no avail, however. It was
Captain Bathurst who was elected by the voters of South Wilts.

Following this check to his ambitions Grove decided to enhance his status
as a landowner by purchasing the Winterslow[H] estate, about 30 miles from
Ferne to the east of Salisbury. Comprising 2138 acres it cost him fifty
thousand guineas, half of which he raised on a mortgage that he never repaid.

In 1865 he invested over five thousand pounds in the electoral expenses
required to promote a second attempt to enter Parliament, and this time
he succeeded. When the record of his diaries is resumed in 1870 he is a
prosperous and influential figure in the prime of life, in his forty-ninth year,
father of two sons and four daughters, much in demand as the local M.P. for
the laying of foundation stones – particularly of non-conformist chapels,
where much of his political support was concentrated – and recognised as a
major landowner of unimpeachable lineage who might expect the eventual
reward of a baronetcy for his political services. He was riding the crest of the
wave.

1870

Jan 12 Hunted with the Duke of Beaufort at Titherley.

Feb 14 Went to London & to House of Commons.

Feb 15 Mr. Gladstone brought in Irish land bill.

March 11 Attended levee at Buckingham Palace & went to House [his
  fourth day's attendance this week]

May 2 Walter left early for Switzerland.

June 20 Went with Edith[E] [his daughter] & Kate to Mr Gilletts
  fancy ball at Willis's Rooms.

July 19 Went to Salisbury & stayed with Harry Grove.[E] Dined with
  the Bishop.

Oct 24 Went to Avington to stay. Mr Edgecumbe & Sir J. Shelley.[E]

Dec 1 Willie Grove[E] [his nephew] came.

Dec 10 Filled the ice house.

Dec 23 Aimée[E] & Hubert[E] Grove [his niece & nephew] came.

1871

Nothing of note. Terse and often illegible entries record the familiar round of hunting, shooting, attending the House of Commons and the Church Synod at Salisbury, and very little else.

1872

Jan 19 Hall ball in the house. 200 people present.

July 30 Walter went into Salisbury to dance at Jacobs. Shot at Wardour[D] – 133 pheasants, 90 hares, 41 partridges, 2 woodcock, 5 duck.

Feb 24 Walter went to London & back to get measured for his [Yeomanry] uniform.

March 4 Came to London & slept at 62 Portland Place. More of the servants came up.

Oct 11 Bought chestnut colt of Hawkins,[G] 3 yr old £45.

1873

Early in the year his eldest daughter, Grace Kathleen de Montmorency,[E] was widowed after only six years of marriage. She returned to England with her young children from their Irish home.

Jan 20 Heard by telegram of Harvey's death this day.

Jan 25 Harvey de Montmorency[E] was buried at 8.00 a.m.

April 30 Women's suffrage lost by 60 [votes]

May 1 Tom[E] [his younger son] went to school.

July 13 Drove to Rushmore[D] to call on Lord & Lady Rivers.[E]

July 14 Laid memorial stone at Wesleyan chapel at Berwick [St. John]

July 23 Oddfellows' Fete at Ferne. 6000 people were present.

Sept 9 Walter came of age.

Sept 22 Sir E & Lady Hulse, [F] Brymer & E. Shelley[E] came [for a week's shooting]

1874

The name of John Gatehouse Raymond,[G] which appears here for the first time, will become increasingly prominent as Grove's estate agent coping with a worsening financial position. The Norfolk properties mentioned had been held by the Groves since about 1766. A hundred years later they were for sale.

Politically Grove's term as M.P. ended with the dissolution and his failure to win re-election. Mr Gladstone responded to the pressure of Grove's influential friends and gave him the coveted baronetcy in recognition of his services.

Socially he cultivated the ties of kinship between Ferne and the Shelley family who had forsaken Field Place for Boscombe Manor,[H] in the vicinity of Bournemouth, where the poet's son Sir Percy Florence Shelley[E] devoted himself to his hobby of amateur theatricals.

Jan 10 Raymond called. Signed deed for Norfolk manor.

Jan 24 Heard that Parliament was to be dissolved. Went into Salisbury & saw Kelsey.

Feb 7 Poll declared [*smudge*] [Viscount] Folkestone[F] elected.

Feb 19 Mr Gladstone offering me a baronetcy which accepted.

March 3 Was in the gazette as baronet.

March 7 Hunted staghounds, Fifehead. Very good run to Deadmore, deer killed.

March 11 [Lord] Wolverton's[F] staghounds, Ferne. Good run to Motcombe.

April 7 Quarter Sessions. Went into Salisbury & to Bournemouth afterwards to Sir P. Shelley's theatricals.

June 11 Marriage settled between Edith [his daughter] & Mr Foster[E]

Aug 4 Edith was married to Edmund Foster. All went off well.

Lady Grove's Diary, 1874

As a supplement to the record of 1874 the only surviving diary written by Sir Thomas's wife adds some interesting details.

There are no entries in January or December. The diary was a Christmas present from her daughter, Edith. The rigours of a 'Drawing-room' at Buckingham Palace are chronicled with feeling.

Feb 6 Polling day. Tom turned out by 900.

Feb 9 Walter & Edith go to the Shelleys for a ball.

March 11 Lord Wolverton's hounds. White Melville & several people came. The Deer was let out in the Park.

April 10 Tom Julia Agnes Philis & John went to the Shelleys' Theatre at Boscombe.

April 22 Heard the Co-coo for first time.

May 5 Drawing room! Started at half past one returned ½ past seven! Dreadful!

June 11 Edith accepted E[dmund] F[oster]

June 12 Sir Tom went to Town, Mr Foster Home, & we all felt upside down.

June 13 A sharp frost, ice as thick as sixpence!

Aug 4 Dear Edith was married & left her home today, went to London on their way to Killarney.

Sept 2 Miss Pit & lady Rivers called.

Sept 15 Called at Rushmore.

Sept 21 Dined & slept at Rushmore.

Oct 14 Went to Maskelyne & Cook's Anti-Spiritualists Exhibition.

March 11. G.J. Whyte-Melville (1821-78) wrote novels about hunting life and a celebrated manual on riding. He was killed in a hunting accident.

1875

This was an uneventful year during which he 'settled about investments' for the children of his deceased brother John of Mudeford – Aimée aged 23, Willie 21 and Hubert 20. Aimée was soon to marry, Willie to become a naval officer and Hubert to enter the Church.

1876

He was promoted to major in the Royal Wiltshire Yeomanry Cavalry and spent July at Weymouth where the Yeomanry customarily held manoeuvres and organised social festivities. August was reserved for shooting grouse in Scotland and by September he was back at Ferne for the shooting season there.

July 1 All went to Weymouth, to 8 Victoria Terrace.
July 3 Barouche arrived from Ferne.
July 29 We all left Weymouth, Kate & I returned to Ferne by Blandford.
Sept 2 Began shoot round Ferne. Medlycott got entangled in reaping machine & badly cut. Left off shooting. Dr Thompson attended.
Sept 3 Sir W. Medlycott & son came to see his son.
Sept 9 Sir W. Medlycott sent me haunch of venison.
Oct 13 Hubert left for Oxford.

1877

Sir Thomas did not contest a seat at the General Election. Sidney Herbert's younger son (also named Sidney) was returned for Wilton.
    The newly invented game of lawn tennis was the fashionable craze among the young Groves and a court was marked out at Ferne.

Feb 19 Sidney Herbert [junior][F] returned for Wilton.
Feb 26 Attended levee & presented Sir George Clay [the successor to his shooting host in Scotland]
July 6 Glyns,[F] Gordons[B] etc came for lawn tennis.

Aug 23 [Touring Cornwall] Drove to Lands End. Called on my tenant at St. Just.

Dec 10 Went to the Shelleys at Brighton.

Dec 13 Went with Onslow to Cuckfield Park[D] to call on Sergison.

1878

Three years earlier Donhead St. Andrew had welcomed a new rector, Horace Chapman,[F] whose introduction of High Church or 'Romish' practices had increasingly aroused Sir Thomas's hostility to the point where he now took action. To launch a formal complaint a minimum of three parishioners had to give their signatures. Sir Thomas had no difficulty in adding to his own those of his son Walter and the postman. As a seasoned campaigner he then took an active interest in the parish vestry. The bishop showed no eagerness to intervene in any decisive way but Chapman eventually had a mental breakdown, resigned his living, became a Roman Catholic and bought the rectory as his private residence, renaming it Donhead House.[H]

During the year the last of Harriet's and Charlotte's brothers, Charles Henry, died; and the Shelley papers he had preserved with Harriet's diaries at Sedgehill passed to his descendants.

March 10 Sunday. Went to early service at Donhead St Andrew 8 a.m. with Singleton. Mr Chapman & Butt present.

March 22 Declaration about Donhead St Andrew came & was signed by all three parishioners.

March 24 Went to Berwick church. Charlotte, Kathleen & Tom went to Donhead.

March 25 Mr Berridge came & signed Representation. Sent it off. Attended vestry.

March 27 Received receipt of petition from Bishop.

April 22 Vestry at Donhead St Andrew. Was elected church warden.

May 2 Went into Salisbury & attended synod.

June 16 Signed power of attorney for sale of Aimée's money £6,076.

June 27 Early to Town to Aimée's wedding to Mr [later Sir James] de Hoghton.[E]

July 12 Went to Salisbury, dined with Bishop to meet judges.

July 13 Was foreman of Grand Jury, dined with judges.

Dec. 10. Presumably the Edward Shelleys[E] with whom the Groves had spent some days in France in the summer.

July 14　Uncle Charles died, aged 83.

July 22　[At Weymouth] Went out for sail with R. Phelips[F] in his steam yacht.

Aug 22　Had lawn tennis party.

Oct 20, Sunday Went to Donhead St Andrew, volunteers went to church there.

1879

An uneventful year, except for the death of his wife at 4.30 a.m. on June 8 – recorded without comment.

1880

Following the dissolution of Parliament in March Sir Thomas showed no inclination to unseat Lord Folkestone who continued to represent South Wilts; instead he gave active support to Sidney Glyn[F] in his contest at Shaftesbury.

Just before polling day the sixth and last Baron Rivers died. The vast Rushmore estate passed to General Augustus Lane Fox who was denied the barony but permitted to adopt the surname Pitt-Rivers for himself and his heir. His other children were to be styled Fox-Pitt. After years of ill-health and general decline at Rushmore the arrival of this vigorous young family was noted at Ferne as a welcome event – six sons and three daughters, all as yet unmarried.

Feb 17　[In London] Called on Lord Rivers & Mrs Halyburton.

March 14　[In London] Called on Lord Rivers & Mrs Haliburton.

March 18　Mr & Mrs S[idney] Glyn[F] called. Canvassed with him, attended meeting at Donhead & spoke.

March 20　Attended meeting at Shaftesbury & spoke.

March 22　Went to Sedgehill. Walked over Mrs G[eorge] Grove's[A] farm.

March 27　Went into Shaftesbury & spoke from Town Hall with Glyn & party.

April 2　Polling day. Glyn won by 34 votes. Great row at night.

April 3　Point-to-point steeplechase. 9 started. Walter won on Harboro'.

Dr. John Grove (1784-1858): he inherited Ferne in 1847. Portrait by Margaret Carpenter.

Berwick St. John rectory: where Charlotte spent her years of marriage to Rev. Richard Downes.

Pythouse: north of Donhead, the seat of John Benett MP (1773-1852) and his descendants.

The sign of The Glove Inn: On the Shaftesbury to Salisbury road the recognised stopping place for the mail-coach in Donhead was the Glove. Neighbourly balls were also held there. It is now a farmhouse.

Rev. Charles Henry Grove (1794-1878) rector of Sedgehill: Shelley's closest friend and confidante among his male Grove cousins.

Major William Chafyn Grove of Zeals (1786-1859) a nephew of 'Aunt Chafin', inherited Zeals House in 1851.

Lady de Hoghton: Aimée Jean, born 1852, daughter of John Grove of Mudeford, married in 1878 Captain, later Sir James de Hoghton.

Thomas Fraser Grove (1821-1897): in his early military career as an officer in the Inniskilling Dragoons. He inherited Ferne on the death of his father, 'Doctor John', in 1858.

Mrs Thomas Fraser Grove: Katherine Grace, daughter of Waller O'Grady, 3rd Lord Massy, married Captain Grove in 1847. This portrait of her, by Thomas Musgrove Joy, was exhibited at The Royal Academy in 1849. She died in 1879.

The Ferne Lawn Tennis Club 1879: Kate Grove (left) her sister Charlotte (standing) with their cousins Corinna and Grace Bruce. With its appropriate emblem of a frond of fern, this is the earliest example of the special outfits developed by clubs in the first years of the game.

Ferne House.

The Hall at Ferne House: In December 1839 Charlotte recorded 'a delightful ball & supper...about 150 people present'.

Sir Thomas Fraser Grove MP: created a
baronet by Mr Gladstone in 1874.

A political rally at Ferne in the Liberal
interest in September 1890.

Left Lord Rivers: Horace Pitt (1814-1880) the sixth and last Baron Rivers.

Below Rushmore: as it was when Agnes's father, General Pitt-Rivers, inherited it in 1880.

April 27 Petty Sessions Shaftesbury: trial of 10 men for riot at election [seven were committed].

May 7 Went to London & attended Levee: presented Walter & William. [his nephew]

May 18 Attended Petty Sessions Shaftesbury about perjury of police at Election.

May 19 Went again to Shaftesbury. Police acquitted.

May 28 [In London] Charlotte, Kathleen and self went to Lyceum. Merchant of Venice & Iolanthe.

May 31 Went to Gaiety: Frou Frou.

June 22 Went to Sanderstead Court to stay with Mr & Mrs Haliburton.

June 30 Went to Dorchester Quarter Sessions. 4 of rioters sentenced to 6 weeks hard labour.

Oct 17 [Visiting his married daughter, Edith Foster, at Clewer[H] manor near Windsor] Went to Clewer church & called on the Shelleys.

Dec 3 Mrs & Miss Pitt-Rivers dined.

Dec 24 [His daughters] Charlotte, Grace [and Grace's children] Tom[E] & Kathleen[E] de Mont came. Dined at Rushmore. Christmas Tree.

1881

This, his sixtieth year, was hardly a memorable one for Sir Thomas but for his elder son Walter it was to become so. In January the visitors' book at Ferne received three new signatures from the younger generation at Rushmore – Alice, Lionel and Agnes G. Fox-Pitt. In her family circle Agnes was known by her second name, Geraldine. At this time she was seventeen, vivacious, a budding beauty, hot-tempered and ready to rebel against the parental constraints imposed on young women of her generation. It was thoughts of Miss Geraldine that preoccupied Walter Grove during the early months of 1881.

During the London season both families were in residence there. In his new affluence General Pitt-Rivers now occupied an impressive mansion, 4 Grosvenor Gardens, with ample facilities for giving a ball. In his diary, on July 7, Sir Thomas Grove wrote in his usual succinct manner 'Mrs Pitt Rivers ball'. His son wrote rather more, in the form of a letter next day to 'My dear Miss Geraldine':

Do write me a line if you are going to ride in the Park

tomorrow, and what time; as I should so like to ride the same time. So do write to me like a dear.

I liked your ball last night because you were kind to me and spoke to me severall times.

You are very nice indeed.

Not powerfully eloquent but it was a start: they evidently rode together in Hyde Park and other meetings followed. None of this though was yet noticed by Sir Thomas in his chronicle of his daily activities.

Jan 6 Hunted with Portman. Duke and Duchess of Connaught out.

Jan 7 Called on Robt Farquharson[F] and Lord Portman.[F] Went to Ball at Crichel,[D] drove my own horses.

Jan 8 Walter came from Kingston Lacy[D]. Returned to Ferne.

Jan 16 Pitts lunched. Went to London in evening.

Jan 17 Went to theatre Pirates of Penzance.

Jan 18 Heavy snow. Tried to go to Brighton but line blocked with snow, no trains.

Jan 20 Went to Brighton to Miss Shelley.

Jan 21 Snow.

Jan 22 Shelleys had dinner party.

Jan 25 Returned to Ferne. Frost. Came out in sledge.

Jan 26 Miss Pitts lunched & stayed the night. Snow.

March 29 Met Raymond in Shaftesbury & went to Bank, signed mortgage deeds for 25,000. 18,000 left due to Bank.

April 29 Alex Fox Pitt[E] came. Walter rode to Troop drill.

May 7 H. Farquharson[F] came to lunch. Sold him 12 pigs at 24/-.

May 14 Walter & Pitt went to Devizes for Yeomanry drills.

May 19 Arranged to take 51 Eaton Square from 30th to 30th July for 150 guineas.

July 18 Went to Winterslow agreed with Compton to go on with his farm at £60 for this year from Michaelmas. Returned to London – dined with Sidney Glyn.

Sept 19 Tom returned to his tutor.

Dec 14 Shot home beat Rushmore, dined there.

Dec 27 Kathleen,[E] Charlotte & Walter went to Rushmore.

That final item, Dec 27, was amplified in another diary or journal which commenced at this point, though out of synchronisation with Sir Thomas by

Jan 20.   Presumably Shelley's sister Hellen[A] (1799-1885). The younger sister Margaret[A] (1801-1887) was probably living with her.

one day. This was a stout notebook with a brass lock acquired by Agnes
Grove, who incidentally will be referred to as Agnes, not as Geraldine except
where contemporary verbatim contexts use 'Geraldine'. In her last year at
school, 1879, Agnes had used a diary sporadically but none has survived for
1880 or 1881. She was approaching 1882 with a new resolution to chronicle
her life in close detail and she warmed to her task with a preliminary canter
over the last days of 1881:

> On the 26th [December] I hunted with Alex, L[ionel][E] and
> D[ouglas].[E] Groves out [i.e. hunting] On the 27th the Blandford
> ball enjoyed it immensely. W[alter] gave me some flowers. On
> 26th also Christmas tree. Rather slow but for talking to W. who
> had been rather nice at Ferne when we went in to luncheon.

By January 25 Agnes was confiding to her journal 'I love Walter with all
my heart' and it must have become increasingly obvious, at Rushmore and at
Ferne, that a marriage alliance between these two neighbouring dynasties was
a distinct possibility. It might even be considered a matter for unalloyed
rejoicing, but this was not the case. General Pitt-Rivers intended to provide
an annual income of £300 p.a. for each of his daughters in their marriage
settlements, in return for binding assurances that their prospective husbands
were men of substance making provision for the possibility that they might
predecease their wives. As heir to Ferne and the baronetcy Walter appeared to
be fully eligible but the General was disinclined to accept verbal assurances
from Sir Thomas, preferring written words drafted by solicitors. And Sir
Thomas had no liking for documents that restricted his financial stratagems.
He found it easier to promise than to sign.

His attitude to Agnes was brutally simple. Whatever her merits might be
she lacked the crucial one – she was not an heiress and could never hope to
be. Her dowry would be 'pin-money' only. It had always been Sir Thomas's
intention that Walter should marry an heiress or a wealthy young widow. He
therefore temporized and quibbled and obstructed, even when the date of the
wedding had been fixed. So great was the tension that Walter and Agnes were
forbidden to meet or to correspond. The two fathers locked horns grimly and
refused to give ground.

The day-to-day dramas of this period are detailed later in Agnes's journal
(pp 271-82). They are barely noticed in Sir Thomas's 1882 diary, nor does he
give any but the very slightest indication of the sub-plot which was running
concurrently. Practising what he preached to Walter Sir Thomas was in pursuit of a wealthy widow to become his second wife and bring much needed
succour to the struggling finances of Ferne. She was a Mrs Fenwick, enjoying an annual income of £5000 p.a. It was Walter's hope that such a marriage would make it possible for his father to give him a sufficient allowance
to leave Ferne and marry Agnes. In a letter to Agnes he wrote, 'Grovie's

marriage is really our only hope for the present. I daily pray for it. Grovie writes to her almost every day and has hardly missed a week without going up to London.'

Few stepmothers can have been so eagerly awaited as the future Lady Grove. In Sir Thomas's 1882 diary, which follows, Mrs Fenwick's name appears only once; and they did not marry. He had to look elsewhere.

1882

Jan 10 Went to Rushmore to dance.

Jan 11 Had dance at Ferne.

Jan 15 Sunday. Went to Berwick. The Pitts came to lunch.

Feb 7 I went to London. Dined at Mrs Fenwick's.

March 2 Point to point race near Castle Hill. Went there by train. Walter won on Harboro'.

March 3 Went to London by first train & to Savoy Theatre, saw Patience.

March 20 Attended Agri[cultura]l Association in London & went on to Brighton to the Shelley's, met Charlotte & Kathleen there.

March 23 Shelleys had dinner party.

March 24 Left Brighton, went to London. Charlotte went to [her sister Grace at] Richmond & Kathleen to Ferne.

April 4 Attended Quarter Sessions at Salisbury. Walter qualified as magistrate for Dorset.

April 25 Mrs George Grove[A] died.

May 17 I went to Weymouth stayed at Bardon Hotel.

May 18 Went to see drill of Dorset Yeomanry. Dined at their mess.

May 19 Went to Inspection of Reg^t. Went to ball.

May 20 Returned to Ferne. Went to East Hayes.[D]

June 1 Went to Crystal Palace to see electric light.

June 16 Called on Mr Farrer about settlements.

June 18 Lunched at the Pitt Rivers.

March 3, July 19. *Patience*: the Gilbert and Sullivan opera.

20 May. The death of George Grove's childless widow at East Hayes required Sir Thomas's superintendance of future arrangements for the property, which reverted to the Ferne Estate.

June 16. Mr Farrer had the unenviable task of drafting the marriage settlement for the wedding of Walter and Agnes, in terms acceptable to Sir Thomas and General Pitt-Rivers.

June 20   Called on Mr Farrer & lunched at Pitt Rivers.

June 26   Went to Weymouth. Dined with Mrs Best.[E]

June 27   Took 11 Gloucester Place from Monday 3rd for a fortnight [at Weymouth].

July 3   Charlotte & Kathleen went to Weymouth.

July 4   I attended Mr Blackmore's[G] funeral & went to East Hayes & to Weymouth afterwards.

July 7   Dined Mrs Best.

July 12   Went to garden party at the barracks.

July 17   Left Weymouth called at East Hayes on the way.

July 19   I went to London, signed settlements, saw Patience.

July 20   Attended Walter's wedding at St Peter's Eaton Square. Dined at Grosvenor Gardens.

July 28   Mrs Best came [to Ferne] had dinner party.

July 31   Dinner party, Du Boulays,[B] Milfords etc.

Aug 1   Lawn tennis party.

Aug 2   Mrs Best left.

Aug 6   Sunday. Went to Berwick church.

Aug 7   Went to Weymouth, dined with Mrs Best.

Aug 8   Dined Mrs Best.

Aug 9   Left Weymouth.

Aug 15   Herbert Cross[E] came.

Aug 16   Cross rode with Charlotte & Kathleen.

Aug 21   Went to London, called Grosvenor Gardens, saw Walter & his wife.

Aug 22   Walter, Agnes & self went to Ferne.

Aug 24   Went to Weymouth.

Sept 13   Walter & Agnes went to Kingston Lacy.

Sept 16   Went to Weymouth to 2 Belvedere.

Sept 19   Was married [to Frances Best] at St John's church [Weymouth]. Went to London, to York Street, Portman Square.

Sept 20   Went to Lyceum & saw Irving in Romeo & Juliet.

Sept 21   Went to Savoy & saw Patience.

Sept 22   Called on Lady Wynford.[E]

Aug 16. Herbert Crosse was evidently related to Mrs Best by her first marriage to Capt. Crosse, and was probably her son.

Sept 22. Frances Best's second husband, Capt. Hon. Frederick Barnewell Best (1827-1876) was the second son of Lord Wynford.

Sept 23　Returned to Ferne.

Sept 25　Herbert Cross came.

Oct 10　Tom & Herbert shot Rushmore. Frances & self went to party at Morison's.

Oct 11　Attended Petty Sessions Hindon. Frances Tom & Herbert went to Weymouth.

Oct 17　Frances, Herbert & Tom returned from Weymouth. Edmund [Foster] & Edith came. Traction engine arrived.

Oct 19　Traction [engine] fetched van with goods from Weymouth.

It was Sir Thomas's custom to reserve the foot of the left hand pages of his diary for records of payments received, usually from sales of livestock or as rent due to him. In the week ending November 4 he noted 'Lady Grove 100£', and in the week ending December 23 '£136.12.9 from Lady Grove.' Frances was making the expected contribution.

1883

A year of family adjustments. Walter and Agnes had left Ferne as soon as Sir Thomas married Frances Best. After an extensive tour in the United States they returned, with Agnes pregnant. Sir Thomas incidentally had now adopted Geraldine as her name. She and Walter were to move into Easton House, Berwick St John in May.

Walter's younger brother, Tom, is seldom mentioned by his father except as one of a shooting party. The paternal policy now seemed to be to ship Tom across the Atlantic and let him find his own opportunities there.

Payments from Lady Grove are regularly noted. Her contribution was worth about £1500 p.a. Socially the year followed a familiar pattern – hunting and shooting, theatregoing in the London season, Ascot races, country house-parties enlivened with cricket matches and lawn tennis, sailing at Weymouth.

Feb 1　Walter & Geraldine came.

Feb 8　Walter & Herbert hunted Henstridge. Harboro' broke his back at a brook.

Feb 9　Walter & Geraldine returned from Pyt House.[D]

March 20　Tom left for Canada.

March 30　Geraldine was confined of a girl.

April 17　Mrs T[homas] Grove died.

April 20　Herbert & Ella[E][Crosse] left.

April 27 Miss [Maude] Stanley[E] & St George Lane Fox[E] came.

April 28 Walter's child was christened Honor[E] at Berwick.

May 11 Frances self & servants went to Weymouth. Walter went to join Wilts yeomanry. Geraldine & Kathleen to Berwick.

July 10 Set the [new] hay dryer at work. Did well.

July 11 Making hay, a great success. Geraldine came up from Berwick.

Sept 15 Herbert played cricket at Pyt House. I shot Jeffery's farm with De Hoghton.

Oct 10 Frances & self went to Maiden Bradley to stay with Ld H. Thynne[E].

Nov 9 Heard Gen Pitt Rivers would take traction engine.

1884

Jan 1 Walter & wife came & Harry Pleydell.[E]

Jan 17 Kathleen went to Tupper Cary's[G] for theatricals.

Feb 4 John & Helen Ross[E] came.

March 29 Received £75 from Beaufoy[F] for field at Combe & paid it into bank with £350 from Frances.

April 23 Went to London, did shopping with Tom.

April 24 Returned to Ferne. Attended Synod at Salisbury. Tom sailed for Canada.

May 2 Capt & Mrs Robert Best[E] came.

May 8 Signed agreement for advance of £400 to Walter from Nat. Prov. Bank.

May 13 Went to Salisbury, took command of yeomanry for permanent duty.

May 14 Drilled on Homington Down.

May 18 Church parade at Cathedral.

May 30 Went to London & dined at the Albion at Inniskilling [regimental] dinner.

June 2 Was at sale of Sir R. Glyn's[F] horses at Tattersall's, bought Tyrone for 46 guineas.

June 3 Went to the Savoy & saw Princess Ida.

Apr 28. Agnes's Aunt Maude and her brother St George had come to attend the christening. St George was refusing to change his surname to Fox-Pitt.

Aug 17 Sunday. Went to Berwick church. Walter & Geraldine dined.
Frances confined of a girl.

Oct 3 Baby was christened at Donhead St Andrew – Olivia
Frances.[E]

Oct 6 Rent day. Paid 1609/17/9 into bank.

Dec 13 Shot Wiltshire Wood with Rushmore party – 11 woodcock.

Dec 25 Walter & wife dined & slept.

1885

There is a striking contrast between the first half of this year and the second.
The early months are mostly concerned with his usual field sports and
occasional family matters. The question of how much extra money Lady
Grove should contribute to the maintenance of baby Olivia was settled, to the
nearest penny. A scarcely noticed relative of Lady Grove's, Ella Crosse, died;
and Herbert Crosse became a closer companion to Sir Thomas through their
shared interests in horses and yachts. The children of Sir Thomas's deceased
brother, John of Mudeford, reappear at Ferne and Weymouth – Aimée with
her husband Captain de Hoghton for a few days' shooting, William in the
course of his duties as a naval officer, and Hubert after a voyage round the
world, perhaps as a ship's chaplain and, according to Agnes, 'much improved' by the experience.

The marriage of Sir Thomas's daughter Kathleen to Edmund Mansel-
Pleydell[E] of Whatcombe is mentioned in a surprisingly casual way in the
Spring. Summer brings a shift from Ferne to Weymouth and the pleasures of
sailing.

In early autumn there are the first signs of a reawakened political interest
at a meeting in Blandford with Sir William Harcourt, a future Chancellor of
the Exchequer who resided in the New Forest and took an interest in neighbouring constituencies. Four days later Sir Thomas had a public meeting at
Wilton, followed by a daily round of meetings throughout south Wiltshire as
he developed his campaign for re-election to the House of Commons. Ironically his opponent was the son and namesake of his original sponsor, Sidney
Herbert. The traditional alliance of Grove and Pembroke was broken.

Jan 18 Arranged with Frances to allow half of £53/14/1 on account of
infant's expenses up to this date, & she to pay me £100 per annum
for her cost from Jan 1st.

Jan 21 Went to Bournemouth & back, to Ella's funeral.

Feb 7 Hubert came back.

Feb 27 Hubert left.

Feb 28 Herbert came.

March 6 Went with Frances to Shaftesbury to sign Ella's administration deeds. Herbert met us.

April 4 From Lady Grove 375.0.0 to bank.

April 6 Rent Day took 923.0.0.

April 23 Heard Kathleen was engaged to Eddie Pleydell.[E]

April 25 E. Pleydell came.

May 3 General Rivers called.

June 6 Kathleen married to Eddie Pleydell at Donhead church. Husseys, John Pleydell,[E] Mr Colville, Chapmans etc came to breakfast.

July 20 [at Weymouth] The Fleet came to Portland. Sailed in the Puffin to see them come in. William [Grove] dined.

Aug 23 Sailed at Daybreak from Weymouth & got to Torquay in afternoon late.

Aug 24 [at Torquay] Called on Robert Best & Mrs Crosse.[E]

Sept 28 Went with Frances & Walter to Blandford to meeting for Sir W. Harcourt.

Oct 2 Had public meeting at Wilton. [the first of many]

Dec 1 Went to Wilton. Was elected by majority of 822 over [Sidney] Herbert.[N]

Dec 2 Declaration of poll at Wilton, returned to Ferne.

NOTE TO 1885

Dec 1. *The defeat of Sidney Herbert was received at Wilton with bitterness and anger. In a letter to Sir Thomas his political agent Clarence Rutter[G] wrote 'Lord Pembroke could hardly contain his rage and vexation when the Poll was declared. His steward incited the mob by the Pembroke Arms to duck you in the river. Carse an understeward made a determined attack on you and a policeman knocked him into the gutter. This Carse is a town councillor but his evil passions quite got the mastery of him. He formed one of a mob who howled round James Lander's house and he shook his fist through the window at him and hissed 'It's because of you damned Methodists'.'*

Much of Grove's support had indeed come from the Nonconformists and the various associations of small tradesmen and craftsmen, many of whom were qualified to vote for the first time as a result of electoral reform introduced by Gladstone in his previous administration. Rutter's letter emphasised the importance of this new element, commenting that 'the labouring men are of course extremely glad; it is their victory and has been won in spite of intimidation and pressure. Tom Cory the thatcher said 'You may 'pend on't this will give all us chaps a good heart and we'd make the majority a good 500 more another time'.'

[See also Edith Olivier's account of the declaration at Wilton in her book Without Knowing Mr. Walkley.]

1886

The New Year began with some light-hearted theatricals at Rushmore before Sir Thomas returned to the House of Commons and resumed his political career, spending two or three days a week in the House and attending a torchlight procession and other functions in the constituency with his supporters. The one ominous note appeared in the week when he dined with the Speaker. Several of his tenants stayed away from the annual audit and his rents were showing a decline.

June brought a sensation when the Home Rule legislation for Ireland, on which Gladstone had pinned his hopes, was defeated by the defection of Liberal support. Sir Thomas was one of those who voted their Leader to defeat and resignation. After only six months the nation faced the unwelcome prospect of a fresh Election. Some of the Liberals condemned Sir Thomas for voting with the Tories and wanted to replace him. Lord Pembroke had no stomach for a second contest so soon after the previous debacle, but needed an assurance that Sir Thomas, if unopposed, would stay firm on the Irish question. There were doubtless many urgent and impassioned discussions of what to do. In all the circumstances Sir Thomas's succinct notes in his diary are a masterpiece of economical compression, if nothing else. By harvest-time he was again the sitting member.

Before the end of the year he acquired two grandsons – one by Walter, the other by Kathleen in India where her husband was a serving officer and her sister Charlotte had joined her.

Jan 4 Theatricals at Rushmore.

Jan 20 Went to London for day. Was sworn in in H[ouse] of Commons.

March 3 Went to Mere & to public meeting there with torch-light procession.

March 24 Walter, Geraldine, Col. Best & self drove to Charlton Horethorn to Point to Point race.

March 25 Went to London & to H of Commons.

March 29 Rent day received 734£   several did not come.

March 31 Went to London & House. Dined with the Speaker. Paid to Bank 1102.11.9.

April 3 Went down to Berwick about Humby's house.

May 8 Gladstone brought forward Irish local government bill.

May 13 Govt introduced Home Rule Bill.

May 28 Theatricals at Rushmore. Went with whole party.

June 7 Returned to London. Division on Irish gov^{nt} Bill 2nd reading rejected by 30. I voted against bill.

June 8 Went to Downton to meeting of Baptists slept at Mr Kemp Welch's house.

June 11 Saw Ld Pembroke abt election.

June 15 Went into Salisbury met Ld Pembroke about Election & attended Agricultural Society Show – agreed to support me.

June 17 Attended Victoria Friendly Socy meeting Donhead St Andrew & dined with them.

June 18 Walked to Berwick heard from & answered Ld Pembroke.

June 24 Heard Hanham was going to stand for S. Wilts.

June 25 Drove to Mere & saw Hanham & C. Rutter with Chapman & Walter.

June 26 Meeting of delegates at Wilton. Hanham & self attended. Hanham retired from contest.

July 6 Went to Wilton with Chapman & was re-elected MP for S. Wilts.

Aug 12 Charlotte sailed in P&O s.s. Nepaul for Madras.

Aug 23 Began harvest. Returned from Weymouth.

Aug 26 Went to London took my seat House of Commons.

Oct 27 Herbert went to Horse Show at Shaftesbury, won 1st prize with Baron, 2nd with Grey Cob.

Dec 15 Lionel Pitt came home [from Canada] & called.

Dec 18 Geraldine confined with a boy [Gerald][E].

Dec 23 Heard that Kathleen had a son in India.

3 April. Joseph Humby occupied Manor Farm, which became the new home of Walter and Agnes Geraldine in July.

June 25. It is not clear if Chapman, frequently mentioned as a gun in shooting parties, is Rev Horace Chapman rector of Donhead St Andrew or a namesake.

1887

In this year's diary there is little of interest. Attendance at the House of Commons is noted daily, with no mention of the business engaging the house. Some days are left blank entirely. There are the usual summaries of a day's shooting or hunting, the names of those who 'came' or 'left' and sometimes 'dined', and little else worth reproducing. Lady Grove's financial contributions continue in a regular pattern.

March 26 [In London] Engaged to take 94 Queens Gate for 13 weeks from 21st April for £167/10/-.

March 31 Went to child's party at Walter's for Honor's birthday – 4 yrs old.

April 13 Willie Bruce,[E] Walter & wife, 2 Fox Pitts & self went to Sherborne for Point to Point race which was won by Herbert on Baron.

May 5 [In London] Drove with Frances to buy carpets etc for Weymouth.

June 14 Dined at Willis's Rooms at dinner to Mr Chamberlain.

June 28 Geraldine & self went to Ball at Guildhall. All the royalties present. [celebration of Queen Victoria's Golden Jubilee]

June 29 I went to Garden Party in Buckingham Palace.

July 16 Attended Levee.

July 30 Mr Compton called. Agreed to add 50 acres to his farm at present rent.

Aug 9 Frances, Miss Weld & Husseys with self went to lunch at Rushmore to meet Archaeological Society. They had tea at Ferne.

Aug 10 Went to Larmer Tree[H] after dinner which was illuminated.

Aug 16 Frances Herbert Best Geraldine & self drove to Blandford & thence went to Brownsea[H] Island to garden party, back by 8 p.m.

Oct 3 All went to theatricals at Wardour. Merchant of Venice acted. Lady Arundell – Portia.

Oct 21 My rent day. Took 1065.15.2.

Oct 27 Went to Winterslow, took chair at Oddfellows' dinner. Dined afterwards at Mayor's banquet at Salisbury. Slept at Hussey's.

Nov 7 Frances went to Weymouth as Mrs Crosse[E] was very ill.

Nov 26 Mrs Crosse died.

Nov 29 Went into Salisbury arranged to let field called Sodom at

Winterslow to Thomas Collins at £1 per acre with 10 pence off for
first year.

Dec 8 Went into Shaftesbury. --- deed from Bank to Raymond.

Dec 19 Tom arrived from Canada.

1888

Less prominence given to his attendance at the House of Commons and to
London life. He seems to have lost his enthusiasm for Gilbert & Sullivan
operas at the Savoy. It is his home ground with its guns and its horses that
receives most attention. Herbert Crosse appears to replace the younger Walter of earlier years who now is noticed less frequently, as 'Walter & wife'.
Tom's return to Canada is not mentioned.

May 9 Frances went to Drawing-room.

May 29 [At Weymouth] Dined at Militia Mess with Herbert.

June 23 [In London] Frances & Herbert went to opera. I went to
    Vaudeville & saw Joseph.

June 30 Left London, came to Ferne, presented silver bowl to H.
    Chapman from parish.

July 18 Herbert went to Southsea & back. I went to Lyceum to see La
    Tosca, S. Bernhard[t]

Aug 22 Returned to Ferne. Dinner party – Bests, Du Boulays, Mrs
    Pitt-Rivers & sons, Geraldine.

Sept 4 Sold 202 sheep to Mr Jeffery for 335£.

Sept 26 Gave Walter £25.

Oct 17 Had rent day. Received £924/18/9 leaving due £624/2/6.

Nov 23 Went to Collingbourne to stay with Lord H[enry] Bruce.[F]

Dec 2 Tom arrived from Manitoba.

1889

This was the year of the first elections to the newly created county councils.
Walter hoped to join his father as a member. Liberal politics locally were far
from tranquil. Some Liberals could not forgive Sir Thomas for having voted
with the Tories on the Irish question, and General Pitt-Rivers was enraged by
the radical sympathies of his son St. George, who attended Liberal meetings.

Tom Grove, now aged 27, was off to the New World again – not Canada this time but Argentina, with a premium paid and £20 in his pocket. In March heavy snow brought the sledge into use again.

The diary continues to reflect the traditional life of the great house where the pursuit of private pleasure blends with the duties of public office, but there is increasingly a new element – the background murmur of distress and anxiety among the farming tenants as British agriculture goes into decline.

Jan 7 Heard Clouds[D] was burnt down.
Jan 23 Election to County Council took place. Walter was defeated by Mr Carpenter.
Jan 30 Went by early train to Devizes & attended first meeting of County Council.
Feb 15 Went into Salisbury took Chair at political meeting. Great row. Slept at Husseys.
Feb 26 Went into Salisbury to Liberal meeting. Great row, meeting did not take place. St. George came to it.
March 1 I went to London. Heavy snow. House of Commons division on amendment to Address. Geraldine had a daughter. [Oenone][E]
March 3 Went Berwick church [his regular custom]. Heavy snow at night.
March 5 Frances went in sledge to Berwick.
April 6 Rent day took £846/7/2. Unpaid 801/11/8.
May 27 Frances & self went to State Ball.
May 28 Went to Lyceum, Macbeth.
May 29 Came to Weymouth.
June 8 Gladstone had address presented. Was in procession.
June 15 Chapman called about address to Gladstone. Walter & wife dined.
June 17 Drove the coach to Shaftesbury & Gillingham to meet Gladstone.
July 11 Called & lunched with Marryat. Paid him £100 premium for Tom.
July 18 Tithe Bill second reading carried, 59. I spoke against. Tom sailed for Argentine.
Aug 10 Agreed with Mr Sims to keep on his farm, he to pay 300£ a year from Mic[haelmas] next & I to allow 40£ of rent now due.
Aug 12 Voted against Tithe Bill.
Aug 16 Tithe Bill withdrawn.
Sept 26 Cooper gave me notice to quit his farm.
Oct 3 Braye from Winterslow called. Reduced his rent from 20£ to

16£ if paid in 10 days. Attended meeting in Salisbury. Dr Roberts in chair. Sir Wm Harcourt, Ld Wolverton,[F] Hanham came to Ferne after.

Oct 4 Wolverton & Harcourt left.

1890

The year began with the familiar winter sports of hunting and shooting. In mid-February he spent a week in London, attending the House of Commons every day, returning to Ferne with what he described as influenza and cold. A more serious illness developed. After noting political meetings at Mere and Tisbury that he could not attend, the diary becomes almost blank through the month of March apart from a note when he 'came downstairs for the first time' and arranged to pair in the House of Commons until Easter because of his inability to attend. By late April he was able to go into Salisbury for a family wedding and to resume his normal journeys to the Agricultural Association at Deptford and the House of Commons.

The end of August brought Tom to Ferne, not entirely expected to judge from Agnes's hearing of his 'having turned up from Argentina'. He did tend to appear annually at Ferne at the start of the shooting season and was promptly out with his gun after partridges.

The principal autumn event was a great Liberal open-air demonstration in the park at Ferne, with T.D. Sullivan MP as the main speaker supported by Sir Thomas's personal friends, Sir William Bruce and Mark Beaufoy. The usual October entry for Rent Day records no details but was immediately followed by a payment into the bank of £1174/8/4. Among the many financial transactions, great and small, noted on the right hand pages of the diary is one unusual one in early December – 'Percy Shelley's portrait with frame 1/2/6'. This would be an engraving of a miniature by A. Easton based on the well-known Curran portrait and still retained by Grove descendants. By coincidence or not Sir Charles Shelley, the poet's nephew, came to Ferne at this time for a day's shooting.

With the approach of Christmas heavy falls of snow threatened what was to become a winter of exceptional severity. Throughout Christmas week the sledge was in daily use as roads were blocked.

March 19 S.W. [Wilts] Point to Point race. Capt Challoner won, Walter second on Tyrone.

April 22 Went to Salisbury & back to Agnes Hussey's[E] wedding.

Aug 30 Tom came.

Sept 2 Tom, Herbert & self shot at Gipsey's School.[N]

Sept 13 Had Liberal meeting in Park. T D Sullivan MP spoke also Beaufoy [et al].

Oct 11 Rent Day.

Oct 16 Laid foundation of Primitive Methodist chapel at Salisbury, attended Odd Fellows' dinner with Beaufoy.

Dec 16 Sir Charles Shelley[E] came.

Dec 17 Shelley, Capt Noel, Herbert, Tom, Walter & self shot part of Ferne 125 ph[easants] 56 rab[bits] 3 hares = 183 [or preferably 184]. Heavy snow.

Dec 22 Snow & frost Frances went to Shaftesbury in sledge.

Dec 25 Went to [Berwick] church in sledge. Lunched at Walter's.

NOTE TO 1890

Sept 2 *The Gipsy School* [H] *at Tollard Farnham* [D] *owed its existence to the missionary enthusiasm of Rev. John West,* [G] *who became rector of Chettle in 1820 and left a curate in charge while he went to Canada as chaplain to the Hudson's Bay Company. At the Red River settlement (today's Winnipeg) he built a church and a school. Returning to Chettle finally in 1828 he was given Farnham in plurality with Chettle and raised enough money to start the building there in 1845 of a school for gipsy children. The school was completed in 1852 but West did not live to see it. Without his drive and leadership the project languished and the building was eventually acquired by General Pitt-Rivers as his specialised museum. In this new form it attracted many visitors, for whom a hotel was built nearby. Today Gipsy School and Museum alike are only memories.*

1891

The New Year brought no respite from the severe weather. Freezing conditions persisted for weeks and the sledge continued in constant use as drifting snow filled the steeply banked downland lanes and roads. When the frost finally broke on January 29 it was said to have been the longest and hardest known throughout the century.

January also brought news of an expected legacy, following the death of one of the sisters of Sir Thomas's mother. Georgina Fraser,[E] certified insane in 1874, died at Brighton aged 84. A departure of another sort was that of Tom who sailed to New York to meet Willie Bruce[E] and travel on with him to southern California, intending together to start a new life there on a ranch.

Wintry weather returned in March when some newly purchased calves were stranded for a week at Shaftesbury because the road to Donhead was again blocked by snow. On Good Friday, March 27, still more snow prevented the Ferne party from going to church.

The shooting of a fallow deer in the autumn is a reminder that this deer which, before the disfranchisement of Cranborne Chase,[D] was numbered in hundreds, possibly thousands, was now a rarity.

Jan 13 My Aunt Georgina[E] died at Brighton age 84.

Jan 19 Drove with Frances in sledge to East Hayes.

Jan 29 Tom left for South California.

Feb 6 Heard of death of Kyrle Chapman[F] out hunting today.

March 9 Went with Miller to Gillingham to sale of calves, bought 22. Heavy snow, could not get the calves further than Shaftesbury.

March 10 Heavy snow could not fetch calves.

March 11 Roads still blocked.

March 13 Snow in the night.

March 14 Road open to Shaftesbury. Sent for my calves.

March 26 Paid into Bank 3,500 legacy money.

March 27 Good Friday Heavy snow could not go to church.

April 4 Rent day.

April 6 Paid to Bank cheques 916.16.1.

May 30 Frances & self drove to East Hayes, agreed to let Capt Noel 54 acres of land from Michaelmas at 70£.

June 13 [At Weymouth] Herbert's yacht Aziola arrived. I went on board with Frances.

Sept 9 Paid 350 thro' Mr Sanders to Willie Bruce for balance of Tom's share of Ranch, also 100 to Tom.

Oct 17 Held Rent Audit took 767/18/11½.

Nov 19 Wright shot fallow deer, doe, in Pickets Close.

Feb 6. Kyrle Alfred Chapman (1838-91) of Roehampton was killed instantaneously at Doncliffe, his horse 'getting away with him' and falling over a gate. Walter Grove was taking part in the hunt, which was abandoned.

1892

It was in this year, his seventy-first, that Sir Thomas's fortunes took a distinct turn for the worse. He lost his seat in Parliament and he also lost the confidence of his bank manager. In July he was warned that the payment of £100 due to Walter as part of his allowance would be with-held until new funds were paid in. For a man in his social position this was not the treatment expected from a bank, but it was to become an increasingly persistent feature in his life as his weak financial position came under pressure.

In 1850 the Ferne rental was worth about £1500 for a half-year and would probably have remained at about that figure eight years later when Sir Thomas inherited Ferne. His investment in 1869 of fifty thousand guineas in over two thousand acres of farmland at Winterslow was clearly intended to raise his gross rental substantially. In the absence of detailed accounts his diary notes give only partial information but the trend is unmistakable. He notes the two half-yearly rent days, in April and October, though with no indication of whether the Winterslow payments have been amalgamated with the original Ferne rental. The April rent-day is given little attention in the diaries, the October one was evidently more important and shows declining revenue and concessions needed to maintain tenancies. His political instinct failed to recognise that the virgin soils of the old colonial empire, combined with faster refrigerated shipping, were revolutionising Britain's internal market for cereals, meat and dairy products. As land values fell, so did the security on his mortgage of the Winterslow acres and the ability of tenant-farmers to pay uneconomic rents.

For instant if temporary relief he could sell disposable assets. The inherited Grove properties included estates in Cornwall, at Zennor. They were now up for sale.

Jan 15 Miller went to Winterslow & collected 328.0.11 on acct rent.
April 2 Rent Day took 570.18.7.
April 27 Went to London to H of C, voted against Woman Suffrage.
June 13 Went to meeting at Wylye [the first of more than two dozen before polling day]
July 16 Attended County votes counting Folkestone 3746 Grove 3339 = 407 Went to Weymouth
July 22 Deed of conveyance of Zennor came, signed & returned it.
July 26 Went to Salisbury & to Liberal Delegates meeting.
Oct 12 Rent Day took 839.15.3.

Nov 5 Frances & self signed note of hand to bank for 1,000£.

Nov 11 Uncle William's picture came.

1893

No longer a Member of Parliament his London visits were few and mainly connected with agricultural meetings at Deptford. The bulk of his time was spent at Ferne, shooting indefatigably, hunting only occasionally and maintaining his Liberal contacts locally; or at Weymouth sailing with Herbert Crosse and going to the Regatta week at Cowes.

The sale of his property in Cornwall came in instalments totalling £1400, to offset the continuing fall in rents.

His political career was given a graceful ending when the South West Liberal Association – which had withdrawn its support in 1887 over his Irish vote – presented him with an illuminated address. It was tacitly understood that he would not make a second attempt to regain the seat.

Jan 7 Went to Beaufoy's & skated.

Jan 20 Mr Humby came to see me about Easton House & stables.

Feb 6 Mr Humby came & agreed to take house & stables at Easton from Lady Day next at £80 per annum.

Feb 24 Charlotte got a fall hunting & could not return home.

Feb 25 Charlotte came back none the worse.

March 4 Settled with Woodford to take Miller's place at 80£ per annum.

March 12 Henrietta Hussey [his sister] died at 8.00 pm.

April 7 Rent Day. Took chair at Liberal meeting at Tisbury.

April 10 Paid to Bank 390.16.8 in cheques.

May 3 Horace Chapman & daughter Florence[F] came.

May 5 Drove with Frances to West Lodge[H] & called on Mr Cleveland.

May 25 [Near Devizes] Went to Kings Down to play goff.

June 2 Renewed bill for £1000 for 6 months.

July 18 Went to Salisbury attended meeting of S.W. Lib Assocn was presented with Illuminated address.

Aug 21 Geraldine held Woman's [Suffrage] meeting at Berwick. Attended it.

March 4. Miller seems to have been in day-to-day charge of farm management.

Sept 6   Went to fete at Larmer Tree.

Sept 28   H. Chapman was taken to lunatic asylum[N]. Walter went to Scotland.

Oct 17   Renewed Walter's bill for £50 on bank.

Oct 20   Rent day 795.1.3.

Nov 14   William & wife came.

Dec 11   Frances & self signed bill to bank.

NOTE TO 1893

28 Sept. *Horace Chapman, rector of Donhead St Andrew, became a Roman Catholic in 1891, gave up the ministry but bought the rectory. In a letter to Walter in Scotland, Agnes wrote 'poor Chapman has gone clean mad, was taken on Wednesday to Salisbury, to the Asylum. His mania is that he is ruined. Bruce Chapman* [F] *[his son] enquired into his whole financial position & brought the lawyer to try & persuade him he was never less ruined in his life but he could not get the idea out of his head & became very excited, so they got 2 doctors. He was got off quietly, Mrs Chapman saying "You know, Horace, it will be better for me if you go for a little change & better for you, better for both of us." Poor poor man. It's very sad'.*

1894

Preliminary memoranda pages show taxation on 9 servants at 15/- each, 4 carriages at 2 guineas each, armorial bearings at 2 guineas, and also Winterslow rents at Jan 24 itemising 6 tenants and a collective item for allotments and cottages, altogether totalling 208.9.6, with one of the tenants, Whitlock, an exceptionally large contributor at £100.

An unpropitious year started miserably with a swelling of Sir Thomas's face, neck and ear which developed as an abscess. Over five months various doctors lanced it indecisively before the discharge was halted.

In April the bank refused to give him any further credit and stopped payments of Walter's quarterly allowance and of interest due to Mr Raymond. By June 30 his private account was overdrawn £2958 and the Loan account stood at £6500. Early in December Equitable Life threatened to foreclose unless overdue interest on the £25,000 Winterslow mortgage was paid by return of post. The financial outlook could hardly be more bleak.

March 8   Heard that Herbert had broken his leg hunting.

April 6   Miller came, went over Upton Farm with him, gave him terms

1£ arable, 30/- pasture, 20£ for farmhouse, he paying tithe.

April 12   Let Miller Upton Farm from Mich[aelmas] '95 at 158.10.0 [terms as preceding entry except reduction of farmhouse rent to £10]

April 18   Rent day took 834.6.7.

April 21   Paid to bank in cheques 656.7.10.

Aug 1   Lady Queensberry[F] and [daughter] Lady Edith Douglas[F] came to stay. Meeting in tent in park took place. 3000 people present.

Aug 2   I went to Montacute.[D]

Aug 3   Went to Coker Court[D] with W. Phelips.[F]

Aug 8   Went to Blandford & there met Kathleen. Went to fete at Branksea Island & back to Longthorns.[H]

Aug 17   Signed promissory note with Walter for £225 & returned it to bank.

Sept 5   All attended fete at Larmer [Tree Gardens]

Sept 7   Loan affair completed.

Oct 3   Called at Bank. Renewed bill with Frances.

Oct 12   Rent day took 897.10.0.

Dec 4   Went into Shaftesbury & saw Mr Chaloner at Bank.

Dec 14   Called on Mr Chaloner at Bank.

Dec 17   Tapper came to cut hair.

Dec 27   W. Bruce, Grace,[E] Corinna[E] [Bruce] & self went to Rushmore & to Larmer Tree, King John's House[D] etc.

1895

A spell of ill-health in the Spring emphasised a general slowing-down in his activities but he continued to play a prominent part in local affairs as magistrate, county councillor and chairman of political meetings. When a Government defeat in June brought a General Election he gave friendly support to his successor as the Liberal candidate for S.W. Wilts.

His financial position worsened as further reductions in farm-rents became unavoidable. Quarterly allowances to his children were paid in instalments, in cash and one of Lady Grove's cheques to Kathleen, and to Walter an item in January reading 'To Walter on acct 15.0.0 in notes, 1.0.0 gold'. There was apparently a danger that his own cheques might not be honoured.

Aug 3.   Willie Phelips was a grandson of Harriet Grove.

Jan 10 All the party went to Morrison's ball at Fonthill.[D]

Jan 11 Went into Shaftesbury to Bank signed papers about paying
Raymond & Equitable.

Feb 25 Heard that Lady Wynford[E] died on Saturday aged 92.

Feb 26 Walked to Easton lambing yard 34 twins.

March 1 Was re-elected to County Council.

April 3 Rent day. Received 753.7.11.

April 5 Paid into bank 686.1.10. Settled with Frances up to date.

May 20 [Weymouth] Went by train with Herbert Frances & Olivia to
Southampton & sailed back in his steam yacht Albion.

June 3 Attended Assizes at Dorchester. Was foreman of Grand Jury.

June 24 Govt minority of 7 [Lord Rosebery resigned]

July 2 [Liberal] meeting at Salisbury. Pyke adopted as candidate.

July 3 Attended Capt Thomas's sale bought 6 vols Don Quixote 15/-.

July 23 Election took place went to Donhead St Mary & Berwick
polling places.

July 24 Pyke was beaten by 268 votes.

July 30 Made arrangements to take off Sharpe's farm to balance his
debt.

Sept 23 Mr Humby called & gave me notice.

Oct 5 Herbert engaged to Miss Winn.[E]

Oct 7 My Rent day took 814.13.11. Agreed to remit 20£ off Bayford's
rent.

Oct 20 Frances & self signed promissory note.

Oct 21 Henry Jeffery came arranged to reduce his rent to 230£ from
Mic[haelmas] last. Also E. Barter to 130£.

Oct 23 Settled with Penny to reduce rent to 100£.

Oct 25 Beaufoy Walter Mr Eustace & self shot Quakers burial
ground.[H] 86 rabbits.

Dec 22 Tom came home.

Dec 31 Frances & self went to look over Donhead Hall.[D]

Oct 25. The burial ground was established at Chilvercombe Bottom on Higher
Ashgrove Farm by an early Quaker, William Fry, who was himself buried there in
1708. He established a right of way to it for Quakers who still preserve it by a
procession at the start of each decade.

1896

In the face of his impending ruin Sir Thomas seems not to have considered that his social standing and his inherited life-style might not be as impregnable as he had always assumed. The diary still suggests that outwardly Ferne must have seemed to pass the days and weeks in the familiar manner with its shooting parties and dinner parties, its continual coming and going of well-heeled friends and relatives. The son and heir, Walter, followed his accustomed carefree round of hunting, point-to-point races, visits to the Scottish grouse moors and countryhouse weekends.

When the threats of creditors could no longer be ignored Sir Thomas's strategy was to look round for some short-term relief. At various times he had sold off the outlying properties of his inheritance, in more distant parts of England. The last to go was the Zennor sale, in Cornwall in 1892. He turned now to family heirlooms, disposing of the Romney portraits of his grandmother and 'Aunt Chafin' and replacing them with copies of the originals. This discreet transaction had its moments of comedy when he tried to extricate himself from his agreement with the first buyer because a second buyer offered a higher price. A threat of legal action put an end to this manoeuvre.

Jan 8 Attended Hubert's wedding at West Coker church. W. Phelips and self met H. Batten afterwards on Trustee matters.

March 9 Tom & Herbert went to S. Wilts Point to Point. Walter won heavyweight.

March 10 Went out of doors first time [after illness]

March 30 Rent day.

March 31 Paid into bank 516.1.0.

April 27 Herbert was married in London [to Avis Winn]

May 2 Attended woman's meeting in Easton barn at Berwick, Geraldine in the chair. Lady Queensberry & our party present. Mrs Phillips & I spoke.

May 5 Olivia [now aged 12] drove me to Berwick & over farms in pony trap.

May 19 Tom went to stay at Wardour.

June 13 Tom left for Lower California via Southampton.

Aug 27 Wertheimer Renton came [about the Romney portraits]

Sept 11 Mr Maclean & Mr Borgen called & looked at pictures.

Sept 17 Mr Renton came about pictures. Canini came over early before Renton & they did not meet.

Sept 19 Canini came in morning with Mr Vicars; agreed to sell 2 Romneys for £2900 & safe copies.

Sept 20 Mr Renton came about pictures.

Sept 21 Mr Wertheimer came & bought two Romneys for £3500. Sent money to bank.

Sept 24 Went to London called on Mr Wertheimer.

Sept 25 Called on Mr Beecham, saw Mr Groves, lunched with Wertheimer.

Sept 26 Saw Mr Danby & Groves about pictures. Returned to Ferne.

Oct 7 Grace married General F. Hamilton[F] in Guernsey. Went to London. Called on Vicars.

Oct 12 Held Rent Audit took 601.13.5.

Oct 14 Canini came to clean pictures.

Oct 21 Herbert & Avis came.

Oct 31 Arthur Selwyn[E] came from Salisbury on bicycle & lunched [probably the first luncheon guest whose arrival was not assisted by a horse]

Nov 12 James Farquharson[F] died at Langton at 91.

Nov 14 I went to London, called on Vicars & saw pictures [copies]

Nov 17 The pictures came from Vicars.

Nov 18 The pictures were hung in the dining-room.

Nov 19 Portrait of Mr Gladstone came from Mr Stewart. Wrote to accept it.

Dec 1 Read Chapman's book about Donhead St Andrew career etc.

Dec 6 Capt [later Viscount] Allenby[F] & Mabel Chapman,[F] young Best & sister called to tea.

Dec 14 Canini sent picture to Sykes fetched it & returned it.

Dec 30 Frances & self went to Mabel Chapman's wedding [to Allenby] at Donhead.

Dec 1. *Why I became a Catholic* by Horace Chapman 20pp 1897.

1897

January began normally with some local shooting, his usual Sunday attendance at Berwick church, discussion with a possible tenant for Corner Farm in Tollard Royal and visits to amateur theatricals in Shaftesbury and Berwick. On the 7th he attended Petty Sessions at Gillingham & pencilled in a note to do the same at Tisbury a week later. However he made a brief visit before then to his daughter Edith at Clewer, and it was there, on January 14, that he died suddenly.

The funeral procession which made its solemn departure from Ferne on January 19 broke the family connection with the house which had begun when William Grove bought it in 1563. The estate was now so encumbered with debts that the only course was to vacate Ferne and put it on the open market, with the hope that it might sell at a high price.

It quickly became apparent that Sir Thomas had made no will, nor any provision for his widow and their daughter. Letters of administration were granted to his son and heir, Walter, and to Frances who surrendered her rights in favour of Walter. In a letter to the family solicitor she wrote:

'Although the loss of my Husband, to whom I *was very much attached*, makes *mine* a far greater loss in some ways than this sad occurrence is to Walter, yet, in other ways, *his* is the hardest to bear as I am free from *pressing anxieties*, though I do not pretend to say, that I do not (in addition to my *loss* & the *heart-lonely* life before me) feel very much being suddenly turned out of this dear house where I had so thoroughly taken root ... pray keep my grumbling to yourself; Walter looks so ill and careworn I should be very grieved to add to his troubles'.

In a second letter, referring to the effect of Sir Thomas's intestacy, she commented, 'I wonder if widows are usually treated in this manner ... more than £21,000 have I paid my late husband, and this is my return – directly he is dead, unless I pack up my things & leave, a few days after the funeral, I have to pay for my maintenance'.

To carry the course of events ahead to the next century, but also to retrace the almost two decades when Frances had lived at Ferne and Walter was embarked on married life in the shadow of his dominating father, a further set of diaries is to hand – those of Frances's successor to the title of Lady Grove, Agnes Geraldine Lane Fox Pitt.

IV

The Diaries of Agnes Geraldine, Lady Grove
1882 - 1925

INTRODUCTION

Born in July 1863, Agnes was a boarder at Oxford High School when she wrote in her earliest surviving diary, 1879. The entries are spasmodic with long blank periods. During school holidays the family elders who took her in hand were on her mother's side – the Stanleys. The London residence, 40 Dover Street, Piccadilly, of her grandmother the dowager Lady Stanley[E] was a typical salon of the Whig aristocracy where the young Agnes met lively ideas, impassioned argument and a formidable moral code. The Stanley women married into noble families, took an active part in public life and championed worthy causes. Aunt Blanche[E] was Countess of Airlie, Aunt Rosalind[E] Countess of Carlisle and a champion of the temperance cause, Aunt Kate[E] Viscountess Amberley – daughter-in-law therefore of the great statesman Lord John Russell[E] and mother of Bertrand Russell. The only one not to marry was Aunt Maude[E] who pioneered clubs for working girls and was a stern but kindly influence on Agnes. When it was time for Agnes to return to her boarding school it was Aunt Maude who escorted her to the railway-station, pausing on the way to buy her a Bible.

If there were diaries for 1880 and 1881 they are lost. It is in 1882, in all the novelty and excitement of her new life at Rushmore, that Agnes makes her diary a close confidante of her innermost thoughts and feelings. She is caught by that fear which haunts adolescence, that time is slipping past wastefully and every endeavour must be made to turn each fleeting minute into some good purpose. As Agnes's pen runs across the page the secret presence is unmistakeably Aunt Maude, frowning on a tendency to 'moon'.

1882

Jan 1 Sunday. Went to church. No sermon. No visits all day.
Farquharsons expected. No New Years festivities nor presents!

Jan 2 Monday. 9-10 Prayers – breakfast. 10-11 practising and seeing
others off riding – 11.10-12.15 reading in my room, my hour and
mooning – thinking of W[alter]. Blaming myself really must not
moon. 12-12.15 still in room, went down to drawing room
pretended to read to M[ama]. Talked, about allowance. 1.
luncheon, still allowance 2. doctor came, 3. went out driving in
pony carriage with M. Went to see News, Rose, Bennett etc.
gardeners wife child ill – 4.30 measured my room talked to Douglas
5. wrote to Aunt M[aude]. tea. 6. talked to Alice about people
coming here – and what she had done at Ferne – W[alter] wanted
some girls I thought quite natural. I could not dance with him the
whole time – went down stairs, came up again, went to work room
– went to drawing room, talked about servants wanted them sent
away. 7 o'clock dinner, after dinner Mummers came we all laughed
- still making a noise downstairs 11.30 Shant be able to sleep in the
meantime I talked to Lionel – girls. Went and reread Aunt Maude's
letter at 11.

Jan 3 9-10 Prayers – breakfast Letter from Aunt M[aude]. Did not
settle as I had intended to, to work till 10. Music, talked Lionel etc.
about dance – he settled to have one - Groves too. 11 came up stairs
my hour, till past 12. 1. luncheon, till 3 nothing particular must
make use of that spare time working for Aunt Maude. 3 went out in
pony carriage. Mama and Alice to Ferne. Sir T[homas] and
K[athleen]. 5 Waterfall[G] girl came to tea we played duet to her. 6
Alice's room, talked, went to bed early but waited up to get my
allowance which I never got till next morning.

Jan 4 9. Prayers breakfast. Felt unsettled not having got my allowance
so did not make as much use of my time as I might - 10-11 practising
but did not get my hour in was very sorry made up for it in
afternoon. Wrote to Aunt Maude about Chintz. Wasted heaps of
time read Soll und Haben also tonight till 10. Must manage better in
morning tomorrow.

Jan 5 Disappointment again this morning. I did know that I was going to Wilton only I had forgotten. 9-10 prayers, good, etc. 10-11 practising duet with A[lice]. 11 till we started about 11.45 reading and dressing and waiting. Wilton we had luncheon with Lady Pembroke. Baroness von Hugel and Mrs. Ellins, came in train with the rich Mr. Morrison. Lovely place Wilton. Lady P. showed us all over it. 'Carrots' [her youngest brother, Arthur][E] conversational as usual. Came home about 6.45 dinner dressing and going to Tollard concert great success Alice and my duet much applause also A's solos. Came home – 10 – bed.

Jan 6 9-10 Prayers. Mama late made breakfast late. So did not begin as early as I should have liked. Read played arranged room intend beginning tomorrow.

Jan 7 9. Prayers. 10 we started for Bower Chalk where Lord Pembroke's harriers met, jolly ride only I rode the little beast of a brown cob which had not been exercised for about a year and which pulled and kicked etc. Rained a little and we stopped in two sheds, but after it was simply a beautiful day. Lord P[embroke] introduced himself separately first to Alice then to me. Handsome man – several good runs got in at 3. Eat large luncheon. I was fearfully tired. I could do nothing all the rest of the day went to bed early 9 oclock.

Jan 8 Sunday. 9 breakfast missed prayers sorry first time this year – must turn over a new leaf next week! Went church, my patterns came for room, measured and sent for them. Wrote to Aunt Maude.

Jan 9 Prayers but owing to some cause or other extreme unsatisfaction in morning. Preparation for our dance.

Jan 10 Prayers – still did not do all I should have done in the morning – (P[apa] went to London, in evening won 6d! at billiards, played rather well with Lionel). No that was on Monday – dance in the evening enjoyed myself very much thought I should not at first and felt very blank when they first told me W[alter] was not coming – wonder why he didn't! They said his leg was bad. However got on very fairly without him – dance a great success I think everyone enjoyed themselves. L. went away with Grace F. caused commotion.

Jan 11 Down early at prayers – but I read, and played a little but not as I should have liked, rode with Douglas to Larmer Tree. Pretty place I thought. Then rode towards Handley.[D] Dance in evening at Ferne. Perfect bliss! Danced very often with the Napier boy and Walter. Went up to gallery with W. for one or two dances Fools made a commotion, I got angry but it was well worth it. I felt angry with him though, I l[ove] him. Napier was insolent.

Jan 12 Down at 11. Of course an unsatisfactory day. Tried to ride etc. but sent in carriage Yesterday Alice's birthday.

Jan 13 Prayers 9.45. Music till 10.45 Read German till 11. Came up punctually and wrote this. Must read all I have been missing, mean to do some work for A[unt] M's poor. Read again till 12 to 1 luncheon rode to Ferne. Groves (W. & C[harlotte]) came on with us to Shaftesbury. Bought pres[ent] for Alice.

Jan 14 Missed prayers sorry so tired in morning – practised till 11. Read till 12. Read B. till 1. Went out for a walk to Mrs. King's.[G]

Jan 15 Sunday. No prayers. So did not <u>miss</u> them last S[unday]. Went to the Berwick church. Groves came in one by one, Sir T, Ch. T[om] then W. Walked home with him, then had luncheon and went out rabiting. Walked and talked with W. Then had tea and went home.

Jan 16 Prayers. 10 went out hunting. Groves late as usual did not appear at Broad Chalk (Ld Radnor's hounds) till after 1st run. My hat came off. W. brought me violets and held my horse etc. rode with me.

Jan 17 Prayers. Wrote letters. Read. Afternoon went for a walk with L[ionel] to Mrs. King's. Evening played bil[liards] won 1/-!

Jan 18 Prayers. Did not do much. Went out for walk L and Alice, very little incident.

Jan 22 Sunday. Tollard – Ch. Tom and Booby[F] came to luncheon. Walter appeared later on. Went out for a walk Woodcuts Common.

Jan 23 Were not allowed to go to Ferne. Meet at Rushmore.

Jan 24 Alice and I drove over to Ferne to luncheon. No we were not allowed. Groves came to dinner.

Jan 25 Alice and I did drive over to F. Walter and I became greater and more open friends than ever. This should be the happiest day of my life because I love Walter with all my heart.

Jan 27 Walter came here at 5 or 6. Stayed till this morning Saturday. Dear darling boy.

Jan 29 Sunday. Kat[hleen] came all drove to Tollard to church. Came home found Walter who had been wet through. Willy's clothes on fitted beautifully. Happiest day in my life hitherto Talked to him all the afternoon – They stayed to dinner went away at 9. I went to bed.

Jan 30 Went to Larmer Tree to Walter went on found hounds at Chettle wood. Lovely. Great fun. Walter there and rode home with us at 3 stayed till 5. Happy day till then after that <u>very</u> unhappy.

Loved Walter all the more, better than ever. Letter from
Grandmother.

The doubly underlined 'very unhappy' marks an abrupt change of mood
following the first indication that Sir Thomas intended to raise difficulties
over the marriage settlement, although at this stage there was a general presumption that a further exchange of letters between the two fathers would
reach a satisfactory conclusion eventually.

Feb 1 Miserable day. Did not see W. In morning letter from Sir T. to
Papa. Very unsatisfactory. Wrote to W. said we could not come to
luncheon. No news of them all day. Made more miserable by
reading his dear letter to Mama of the day before. Felt I loved him
better than anything. Only I do wish he would write.

Feb 2 Prayers Letter from dear Kat. Such a nice one. Went to
Wardour to luncheon on my way left letter for Kat. at Ferne. All
morning read Kingsley. Heavenly book. On way back from
Wardour went to Ferne. W. gave me a letter he had written. Would
not at first but I made him – came with us as far as the gates. Read
letter when I got home. Oh such a heavenly dear kind beautiful
letter. I felt I had never really loved him till then. Wrote a long one
in return. Wrote to Aunt Maude and Lionel. Willy[E] not much
better. Selfish horror that I am I never went to see him all day. Hope
he did not notice it. I am afraid he did not miss me!

Feb 3 Missed prayers. At breakfast Willy remarked upon the neglect
we had shown him yesterday. In afternoon Lady Aylesbury came,
she went to Larmer tree with M.   Alice and I drove there, in dog
cart, then on to Ferne left note. Went in, Sir T. & W out hunting. In
evening answered letters wrote to Aunt M. & Lionel. They wanted
me to write to Sir. T but I do not think I will. No.

Feb 4 Letter from W. Played. Papa came up and spoke to me in Alice's
room. Said couldn't give me more [as marriage allowance]. Hope
tomorrow's interview with Sir T. will be satisfactory. Have my
misgivings. So sorry for my poor darling – fretting himself ill.

Feb 5 Sunday. Went to Tollard church found Walter already there.
Walked part of the way home with him. Did not go in to the house
stayed in the conservatory. Bliss! After luncheon he talk to Papa. No
results. It was decided it must be off. I felt miserable but could
hardly realize it. Then we went into the hothouse and talked there
till past 5. Then I came in and cut off my hair and wrote to him as he
asked me. Then I felt simply wretched I would not go to tea of

course. Mama came in. Passed a miserable night. Thinking of him and being separated from him.

Feb 6 Got up early. Dressed at ½ past 8. Thought of nothing but my hopes of seeing him at station, finished writing my letter to him. Settled about my room. By the bye must write to Charlotte about that colour – had luncheon, went to station only just in time No Walter – last hope cut off. Misery. Gave my letter to be posted. Felt that off my mind.

Arrived in London about 6. Foggy and horrid – Missed beautiful country air – unpacking my private ornaments thought of Walter.

Feb 7 Headache, came down to breakfast. Disturbance felt miserable vented my feelings by writing to Walter. Felt better, then spoke to Mama. Arranged flowers for her Then went to Dover St. Aunt M. out waited about 20 minutes then she came, showed her photographs. Read her some of W's letters about the money, abroad etc. She liked him of course. When I said he said he was sorry he had said anything she said – oh no I am very glad he proposed! Its much better. We were then interupted by the entrance of the grandmother, who said she was sorry etc. but felt sure all would come right like my dear Walter himself says. He must know best so I am bright and hopeful too. Then we had luncheon, and Aunt Maude left soon and Mama came and we went to a lecture at the R[oyal] I[nstitute] on the Senses.

Feb 8 In morning went with Augustine to Gros[venor] School of Art. 10-1 Aunt Maude came to Luncheon. Then we went to Covent Garden Market – Then to see some poor people, Aunt M. would not drive up to their doors because she said it would look ostentatious!

Feb 9 Arranged my room and played most of the morning. Mrs. Bontein [Bontine][F] told us her son Charley Graham[F] was going to be married to Miss B. A lovely girl they say and a friend of the Prince of Wales! and on less than £700 a year!!!

Feb 11 Letter from Lionel – went drawing class 10-1. Went Dover St. Aunt Maude out so came home to luncheon 2. 3. Went to Royal Institution: Pauer on Beethoven. Played. Then joined by Alex and we went to Borheim's studio. Beautiful sculptures. Then to Conyer's.[E] Mushie[E] looking lovely. Then home. Great crowd at top of Prince's Gate on account of the assault of Arm's at The Albert Hall.

Feb 12 Sunday. Went to Sunday School 10-11. 11. Church at St.

Peters. Luncheon at home. Then went out with Mama. I spent from
6 to 7 alone with Walter today. Sweet communings with my own
heart and his in the spirit. I wonder whether he is thinking of me!
Perhaps! Oh yes there is affinity of spirit between those who love
one another.

Feb 13 Went to drawing class all morning. In the evening we went to
the Halfords ball but although I enjoyed it immensely because I
danced and it was fun and the people were appreciative (!) and
above all because I could look at Dawson Damer[F] still I thought I
loved my own more than ever and I did yearn oh so so much for my
darling to come to me. Oh won't he? I think my yearning is more
intense than anything.

Feb 14 I got no valentines by the first post, only one or two later on.
Mama and Alex went to dinner at Dover St. and we had dinner at
home and after dinner I talked to K. Alice wrote a rather inane letter
to W. I felt in the evening that I loved Kathleen passionately and we
were lying on the sofa together and I simply hugged her and felt oh
so in love with her and I found out after it was only Walter I was
thinking of the whole time! – that I was yearning longingly for him.
But of course I do love K too for her own sake and especially
because she's his brother and more especially because she is his
favourite. Oh I do at this moment I am writing long inexpressibly to
see to hear to feel my Walter's presence.

Feb 16 3 A.M. Great fun at ball – they all abused me for dancing so
much! I said I "did not really care" etc. etc. Walter K and I know
better! Dear Walter darling Kat – she's a perfect love. Oh my Walter
do come and see me. Foolish child that I am – 12 P.M. It's very late
but I must write to my darling in this book which is to be our
common property some day. To go through first of all, all I did all
day which is the commonplace uninteresting part of this book, but
which must all be told as the connecting link between that and the
real part. I looked anxiously to see if there were any letters for
Kathleen scribed in his hand – but there were none. I rode with
Alice at 12. Before which we had played the fool in my room
downstairs. Then after luncheon I went to a lecture and then to
Dover St. Aunt Maude talked nonsense about my not caring either.
How little they all understand but Kat and I propose going and telling
her because we think if she were explained she would understand but
not the others we are afraid. Then we went home. Then Alex and I
cabbed to the Conyer's and had tea there and talked – we walked the

whole way back! Good for me. Then I came upstairs and like an idiot
that I am I was offended with my Kathleen for not going upstairs with
me when I asked her, so I tried to be cold to her the whole time till
dinner and after till we went to bed!! Then she came up and the dear
sweet girl was so nice I do think Kathleen has got about as much tact
and as kind feelings as anyone I know. Then after we were undressed
we talked till late into the night. We talked about Willy and his
coolness to her after his open evident flirting etc. etc. and of course
Walter! I don't think anything <u>could</u> make us quarrel. Dear girl – well
I have eulogized her enough. I will now end, this has been a long day's
writing. I must be less prolix in future.

Feb 20 I came down quick, a letter from Walter in Mama's. It was so
nice to see the dear thing's writing again to <u>me</u>. (I answered it all
day at intervals). Then we went to some shops and then took K to
the station. So sad her going! I really felt quite sad and
'missing-like'.

Feb 21 I went to Dover St. with Mama and a few other uninteresting
places. In the evening Pascoe Grenfells ball.

Feb 23 Had a row with that insolent maid. Sorry. But not my fault. 12.
went in carriage with Mama till 2. Read and played music. Tea
rows. Rowy day. I felt miserable. I can't think why but whenever
I'm wretched I long for him to comfort me perhaps. I <u>do</u> wish he'd
come.

Feb 26 Sunday. Alice went to church. I did not. Came back just as I
was starting for Sunday School. Got abused for going. Shameful. 11
church. After luncheon we all went for a long walk came home, to
church 5.

Feb 27 Late for breakfast considerable disturbance. I got <u>very</u> angry.
Really angry. With the Man too. Went to drawing class. Did panels
etc. Came home. Felt better after I had sympathised with Alice.
Much. Mr. Wilkinson[G] wrote to me to say he wished to see me. I
said alas I could not. But will some day.

March 1 Drawing till one, then after luncheon Alice and I (and Doug)
wanted to go to Barkers [shop], and M said she did not <u>choose</u> us to
go. We said we would as we were not babies to be ordered about
like rats. So the Man joined in and swore like – anything at Alice, <u>of</u>
<u>course</u> I took A's part so he began at me, so we went out of the
room, when it was over straight to Barker. There I ordered a gown

Feb 27. She now refers frequently to her father as 'the Man'.

and different things and then we came back – a gloomy dinner! Poor
Alice, I have a faint chance of escape from this tyrany and misery
but she seems to have none as yet but I am certain Providence could
not in justice allow her to go on much longer in this place. I only
wish oh so much that my fate could be decided – we will pray &
hope for the best.

March 2 I arranged my room till dressmaker came and then there was
a row about that. Its so degrading – Fancy not being allowed to
order what one likes. We did not go to the Speakers in the evening
because of Aunt Rianette's[E] death. She left Aunt Maude £4,000. If
only some one would die and leave me some.

March 3 After luncheon Alice and I had a long walk all down Oxford
Street. I bought a 'lot'. I had a row in the afternoon because M said
she would not take me to the play on account of my conduct . I
wished to know what conduct. However, Alice and I did not go and
what's more we had to have our dinner upstairs. More fun. In the
evening I was so delighted and excited and mad with joy. A letter to
Alice from dear Walter saying he would be in London on Saturday.
It was all a failure I cant write about it. It makes me cry now.

March 4 Drawing in the morning an almond sprig in blossom from
nature. Nearly finished. All the time I was only thinking of meeting
him after it was over and refused the offer of a lift from Marie
Adeane,[F] but I never saw him, and I walked to the lecture with M.
and all the time hoping and after the lecture I was so tantalized
because she drove about all over the place. I was wanting to get
home and see if – when we did get home Alice nearly drove me mad
by saying W. had been here. I said very little but inwardly – oh
misery. Then I read and re read a 100 times his letter. Then we
wrote to him. Then I wrote. Alice had made friends with Papa in the
meantime. I felt oh so so utterly wretched. To think of having been
so near yet missing. Oh it was misery.

March 11 Drawing – afternoon. Grand row. The Man swore etc. I
had dinner up in my sitting room.

March 12 Sunday. I came down to breakfast – began again so I was
very angry but restrained myself which made him more angry and
then went out of the room. Then to Sunday School - also in
afternoon. Oh the misery of these two days. I shall never forget.

March 13 Drawing. Hurah! Man went to Rushmore – Now letter
from Walter [addressed to] Kat, so on my way home went to Aunt

M. and left note. Answer came in evening, telegraphed to K.

March 14 Luncheon at 35, Dover St. On to 40 met strangely enough
to my joy Walter at the door! after that to Royal I. He came in and
sat by me Dear thing!

March 15 Drawing. Walter walked back with me. I got into a row
because that horrible maid told.

March 17 Letter from W. to Al[ice]. Char[lotte] sent me some violets.
Alice and I went up Grosvenor Place by ourselves and tremblingly
into the Park. Met Walter half way down. Bogie [Alice's pet dog]
ran away. W. fetched it and we walked home together. In afternoon
we went out for a walk Douglas Alice and I to Harvey & Nicholls
[shop] and that wretched dog ran away. Alice was in agonies and
sent everyone flying about the place till after dinner. The dog was
brought by a small boy and had been found at the Serpentine.

March 18 We started early and met W. at the Park gates like a dear
good faithful soul waiting for us. Then we walked the whole way
and Alice and he came in and Miss W. took him for Alice's
husband! and asked me after they had gone if that gentleman was
my brother-in-law. I said 'Yes'!!

Towards the end of March it became clear that negotiations for a marriage
settlement were at a standstill. The General would not allow Agnes more
than £300 p.a. and Walter could not expect more than £400 from Sir Thomas.
It would be possible, as Walter remarked in a letter, to manage on £700 if they
chose to 'live abroad in some cheap place', but Sir Thomas crushed this idea
by saying, 'I won't allow you to marry on £700 a year, and I'm certain
the General won't allow his daughter to do so'. At the age of thirty, Walter's continuing dependence on his father was brutally underlined. 'I simply
haven't got a brass farthing' he admitted ruefully and his ability to earn an
income did not inspire confidence, 'I was never a clever boy at school [Eton],
never took any trouble about learning anything, and now it's perfectly impossible for me to earn more than £100 a year as a clerk in an office'. Aunt
Maude hoped he might become one of the new inspectors of factories but
Walter knew that 'all government offices are closed to me because I couldn't
pass an examination for them'. As for the thought that the depth and strength
of their love might soften Sir Thomas's heart, Walter had no such illusion: 'he
thinks a man an egregious ass who marries for anything but money, and
looks upon being in love with a woman like a slight cold in the head – a
fortnight will cure it'.

It followed, then, that Walter could not continue to enjoy the privileged

March 15. Agnes had evidently been forbidden to have secret meetings with Walter.

position of Agnes's 'intended' and must conform with the etiquette of the time as no more than a friendly neighbour and possible suitor. Walter himself recognised that 'a woman must marry, but a man need n't'. It fell to Mrs Pitt-Rivers to decide where the line was to be drawn: hence the family frictions, the secret assignations, the use of sisters as the addressees for forbidden correspondence. In these circumstances Agnes hit on an ingenious strategy. She persuaded Walter to start writing a daily journal, similar to her own, so that they could exchange books at intervals and replace the difficulties of letter-writing with a continuous narrative of the thoughts and feelings of their daily lives. Walter's journal reached her on March 30, and he received hers on April 2. Each then made continuing daily entries until the time came for the next exchange.

Much of what they wrote is a mixture of teasing and tender avowals of their love, but occasionally they reveal something more of their underlying characters, as for example when Agnes wrote on April 10 (which she wrongly dated as March 10):

I feel rather sick at heart and a-weary of life at this present moment. I do get downhearted at intervals because I feel so helpless and I think if only *I* were a man, how different things would be. I would have long since quitted the paternal roof and wandered out alone like St. George has done, and made my fortune by some gigantic stroke of genius which is now pent up in my unfathomable brain and senselessly thrown away upon a female *woman*! Bah! I can't think why men are so fond of women. I can see nothing at all attractive in most of them. Anymore than I can see anything attractive for women in the generality of these nimminy-pimminy men that one sees. Can you? I like those ancient heroes who always had done something brave and were upright honest warlike men; but of course in these peaceable civilized times all that sort of thing has been given place to by bravery, not in shedding blood, but in fighting against the Power of Evil.

Warming to her task Agnes covered several more pages with a powerful sermon, commending virtue and high principle to Walter and assuring him of the reformative power of religion. What is so endearing about her is the way her moods of rather ponderous Victorian moralising suddenly break up, as on this occasion, into a sort of pirouetting gaiety:

There is, there can be, no sham about real religion. Can there? I don't know how long I have been writing for but I do believe that for the few minutes I did forget self, and really and truly mean everything I say. I feel that if you are good, and me good, we shall be so much happier and we shall be able to trust each other so implicitly. I could never be

jealous of anything you did because I should know that your duty
and your principle, as well as your love for me, would prevent your
doing anything I should not like, you wicked thing. You must not
write to that horrid person who wanted to kick you. She can't be
nice, or she wouldn't have wanted. Besides, she's a nasty horrid
untruthful person to call herself *your* Elsie, because *I'm yours* so she
can't be too. See?

But *I'm* not jealous – if you think I am, you're most wonderfully
mistaken. It's very lucky, if you care to hear all this, that I take it into my
head to *write* it because we never *talk* anything but fearful nonsense
when we get together. I wonder why – but one does write more seriously
than one talks, as a rule. Well, if we wrote down some of the things that
we talked, and showed it to any 3rd person, they would simply call a cab
and have us both off to the nearest lunatic asylum.

But now I must finish simply. Good night, dearest.

Walter got home from Wales, where he had been competing in steeplechases,
little more than a day before Agnes was due to leave Rushmore. His successes
as an amateur jockey had evidently encouraged him to stay longer than he at
first intended or she expected. There was a deeper quarrel than the sudden
little tiffs that could always flare up with Agnes's unpredictable temperament.
His changes of address in Wales had confused the exchange of journals so
that for a week Agnes had neither volume in which to confide her thoughts –
and this had aggravated her impatience. As usual Walter bowed to the storm.
He justified his absence in Wales as a means of sparing them both from
the 'sneaking underhand' methods they would have had to employ to meet
each other daily near Rushmore. 'You see', he explained, 'I am in such an
unpleasant position as all the difficulty against the marriage is on my side
(my father's side rather) and with somewhat doubtful prospects'. As for the
sharply worded letters that reached him before he left Wales, he conceded:

> You are quite right as to yr. scolding me for my casual *laisser aller*
> indolence. That is indeed my besetting sin, there is no doubt it's a
> good deal constitutional. I'm afraid I shall never quite get rid of it
> entirely but I have always looked forward to you as my helper
> in that matter. Yr. energetic character and dear little flashes of
> temper will hustle and make me less indolent. I think the life I
> have led, simply pleasure seeking with no particular aim beyond
> getting through the time with as little trouble and with as much
> excitement as possible, rather conducive to indolent habits.

A more immediate fault was his bungling of the exchange of journals so
that Agnes was left for days with neither book in which to recount events

and relieve pent-up emotions. The stratagem was tacitly abandoned. When she received her original book she retained it as her continuing journal and stopped using it as a sharing of confidences although she still refers to Walter sometimes as 'you', expecting to show him the diary some day. Through May her entries were often compressed and perfunctory, noting the routine visits of 'Chev' (Mlle Chevalier, presumably a teacher of French) attendances at the Grosvenor School of Art, the lectures on various subjects at the Royal Institute and the names of friends and acquaintances she met; but occasionally the tensions explode in a vivid account of family life at 4 Grosvenor Gardens:

May 4 Got up rather late. Had intended going for a walk on account of hearing a row going on when on the stairs. I refrained from going down further, therefore went without breakfast but it did not do much good. I was flown at, at luncheon and bored to death almost. Having already had it pretty severely from the minor one [Mama] all the morning. I was told to write and tell you not to come to the ball which I did, but I was in hopes you would, so I went. I danced a good deal with a Russian, who said he wished he could dance with me all the evening, after having been down at supper about an hour with him. I don't care. You flirt with dear Mrs. Hellyar. In the afternoon I was just going to the lecture when Mama who had been hatching stories to Papa all the time suddenly hit upon an unfortunate phrase of mine 'The Man has no heart'. He tramped up and said 'you go to not a single place the whole of this season', about a dozen times nothing else varied it. Occasionally 'you don't go out once this season, mind you' etc. etc. I am seldom amused at his rows but this did amuse me and as he was tramping down again, I was all trembling with the suddenness and unexpectedness of the whole thing. I tried to stammer out something about his being so good and kind on the contrary when the sense of the ludicrous presented itself to me, and I broke down in a hopeless giggle! Its about the only time I've not flown into a temper when he's been violent, and made matters ten times worse, but this did seem so ridiculous I couldn't be angry. So I made up!

At other times she finds almost nothing to record -

May 21 Sunday. 10 School. Al[ice] too ill. 11 church Bishop [of] Ely preached. Evening Mr Wil[kinson] preached 7.

It was a time of dull despair. The negotiations became increasingly cluttered with fresh objections and intransigent demands. The General wanted an absolute guarantee that Walter would inherit the Ferne estate, by entail if necessary. Sir Thomas demanded a guarantee of £7500, payable on the General's death, to support the continuance of Agnes's annual allowance. In the meantime Mrs Pitt-Rivers wrote formally to Walter requiring him to refrain from writing to Agnes 'until all is settled'.

The brighter moments came from Agnes's brother, St. George, whom Bertrand Russell described as 'combining saintliness and company promoting in about equal proportions'. Both were in evidence in his offer to appoint Walter to a post in one of his companies at £300 p.a. or to pledge the £7500, if the General broke off the negotiations. This undoubtedly gave St. George the pleasure of irritating his father, which was one of his constant pursuits, but it did at least provoke fresh discussions. On May 30 letters were delivered from Sir Thomas and Walter, and a family conference followed -

May 30 A day of importance. Chev. morning. Didn't go out. Late for R.I. 'Digestion'. Very hot morning. After R.I. came home found a letter from Sir Thomas. Then Willy S[cott][E] came and brought one from Walter to Mama. Unsatisfactory at first but soon St. George came in and put quite a different face on matters. P[apa] Stealthy says he could not do any more for us. As it is I am not feeling alright at all. Long discussions with the rest of the family. All thought of course that P. ought to give more but if he won't what's to be done. St. George offers to satisfy Sir Thomas, on the question of settlements, but is it right to accept it. I don't mind and no one could the way he does it. He says it might look ostentatious but he has the most generous kind heart and noble charitable disposition in existence, I am sure, and I simply think he is an angel brought down to benefit mankind! If only tomorrow would settle all. I'm simply ill.

May 31 I went downstairs last night to Mama and she told me that she had told Walter to be here at 11 so I slept in peace and joy. At 20 past 11 he came. I talked to him very little, at 20 past 1 Sir Thomas appeared by orders. He did not talk nicely I was furious with all he said, so wrote a letter gave it to Kathleen. After spent a miserable afternoon crying my eyes out and expecting him. St. George came at 5. I talked to him he reproved me and rightly. Then I saw them come in one by one. Still no news I was distracted. Till Alice came told me the joyful news that my own true dear love was coming tomorrow at 11. I bounded upstairs a different person.

June 1 They all went to the trooping of colours at 11, and soon after Walter came and we made him speak to Papa. Then he went away and chaos and darkness ensued in my heart and was not lessened by

Papa's coming up and saying 'It's no use, Sir Thomas refuses his consent so there's an end of it'. I rushed away couldn't answer and till they came back was miserable. Then I was informed that he had gone in search of Sir Thomas and was coming back at 7 so I waited in anxiety till the others returned from their walk and then I was happy because he came. Then all was apparently settled and the 20 July fixed! Hurah! Hurah!

June 2 Blessed heavenly day. Rather anxious morning as a letter had been expected last night and had not even come this morning but Chev. rather whiled away the time. And at 12.30 he [Walter] came, no letter. So he was sent away and he went to Lowndes Sq. and got it but it was not what was wanted so he was made to write another and then they all went in the carriage and left me with him. So we talked and wrote together in the room downstairs till nearly 5 and then Alex came in and we went to see his horse which he is going to get [for] £100. Had dinner at half past 6. and they went to the Crystal Palace. I wanted to go but not to any parties or balls. Tonight it would spoil the remembrances of the blissfully happy afternoon I spent with my darling Walter. Walter was coming to dinner but told not to – is coming tomorrow instead. Mama is very nice to him and I am sure likes him very very much. Of which I am glad.

As the month of June progressed preparations for the wedding gathered momentum. There were social visits with Walter in attendance, appointments with the makers of the bride's trousseau and a general atmosphere of relief and approval. Agnes's entry for June 14 is typical of this period:

June 14 Walter came about 12. Went for a little walk. Then luncheon. Then a beautiful ring came for me. Then we walked to Russell & Allen. I tried on my gown, then we walked to photographers. Met Aunt Maude in the [Burlington] Arcade. Then went home & rode. W. came to dinner. Heavenly day.

On the same day Mr. F.W. Farrer, a solicitor of 66 Lincolns Inn Fields, informed Sir Thomas that he was awaiting the General's instructions to put into a formal agreement the terms now considered to be agreed for the marriage settlement. For this purpose he needed to make the customary inspection of the Ferne estate's rentals, land deeds etc in order to establish the soundness of Walter's future prospects. Sir Thomas's assurance that he had made a will bequeathing Ferne to Walter was not quite what Mr Farrer wanted. As the difficulty of acting for both parties became apparent Mr

Farrer asked Sir Thomas 'to get some other solicitor to act on your behalf', and on June 22 he warned Sir Thomas that 'it will be impossible for the marriage to take place by the 20th of next month unless every exertion is made'. Writing on June 26 he again pressed Sir Thomas for the financial details of the Ferne estate.

Sir Thomas, however, was preoccupied with another and even more pressing matter. On June 26 he was not at Ferne, sorting through his estate papers. He was at Weymouth dining with someone mentioned in his diary for the first time – the widowed Frances Best. On the following day he rented 11 Gloucester Place in Weymouth for a fortnight, to give himself long enough to bring this promising courtship to a decision.

By July 7 Farrer, in some desperation, was telling Sir Thomas that what the General wanted was simply the guarantee that 'your eldest son (and his eldest son if he has one) shall at your death be in the position that an eldest son ought to be'. Sir Thomas continued to evade the issue and to stall until the wedding was little more than a week away, when a compromise was reached by his offer to covenant an income of £2000 p.a. chargeable on the Ferne estate after his death. He did not sign the settlement until he visited Farrer's office the day before the wedding. It is against this background that Agnes's July journal can be understood.

July 7 Walter came at about 10 and then went to Farrer. After luncheon we all went in the carriage and then to the dress-maker's and ordered several gowns.

July 8 Walter came at 1 and went away directly after and came again at about 3. The glove man came. I had 3 doz. pair took back one doz. The Munro girl came and Al[ice] and she went away and played lawn-tennis at St. George's. Walter and I had intended to go to Hurlingham but it was too bad a day. So we stayed at home. We intended to ride but we did not. So we stayed till dinner. Then we counted presents and stayed down after the rest for which there was stealth.

July 9 Sunday. Went to S[unday] School. Met W. after and then he went home and about half an hour after he appeared with 'Harry' [Pleydell] and we all went to Berkley Chapel. Then we came home and Papa talked to Walter – and he is not to be allowed to come here again till all is settled! Several more presents yesterday.

July 10 I wrote to W. and he wrote to me. The short separation came to an end very soon at about half past one Walter came with the news that Sir Thomas would settle £2,000 a year only [in the event of his death], but they were satisfied and Papa wrote a letter. W and

I called to Farrer. Then to Harvey & Nicholls. Rained all day. Walked back in it.

July 11 I have left off here more than 3 weeks ago and now I am a settled down married woman. It does seem odd. I must try and remember what we did. Today is August 1st. Walter went out in the carriage with us and dined too.

July 12 Several more presents and what with letter-writing present thanking, trousseauing and going out with and talking to Walter my time was fully occupied.

July 13 To-day week the wedding day. I got quite tired of trying on things etc. but I got a pretty good 'kit' especially of shoes. Walter went to Ferne so I had plenty of time to myself to do everything in.

July 14 I was out nearly all day continually trying on, buying etc. etc. and in the afternoon went to Moyall and had my photograph taken in my black gown.

July 15 I had four letters from my W. all the time he was away and today to say he was coming back today this evening in time for dinner which he was at 6. Then we rode and had dinner and talked.

July 16 Sunday. I went to the Sunday School for the last time and Mr. Thessiger asked me if I would come to the Sunday School treat on Thursday! [her wedding day]

July 17 We arranged the presents in the afternoon some people came to tea. Walter dined with us.

July 20 My wedding day. Today a great step in my life. The great step of one's whole life. I got up very early and went to church and met Aunt Maude and then after breakfast I went out again and saw Mr. Wilkinson. He talked to me and I am sure helped me a good deal. He gave me several books. Then the usual thing. I dressed and at half past eleven was in church and married. We signed everything and came home to breakfast then I talked and laughed and felt very gay and so was Walter after it was all over but before he was dreadfully nervous, and then we went off in the carriage and Harry P[leydell] had gone before with Walter's luggage and Tawny [pet dog]. They met us at the station again and we went off and got to Clewer at about 5 we had tea and went out again. Then had dinner.

July 21 We walked into Windsor & bought a few things & looked at the Castle & walked about & did nothing particular.

July 22 We went on the river & were towed along & someone saw us under one umbrella! It was lovely.

July 23 Sunday. Got up too late to go to church so we wrote more letters & read & sat out in the garden. In the afternoon we went to the chapel [St. George's] at Windsor & got very good seats. The singing was lovely.

From Clewer they moved on to a sort of freewheeling opportunist tour, after a visit to Agnes's married sister, Ursula Scott,[E] where they celebrated Agnes's nineteenth birthday. At Brighton they met the Benett-Stanfords[F] of Pythouse and spent some days with them before taking a sea-passage to Plymouth and an impulsive train-journey to Penzance and Land's End. A visit to the Scillies occasioned a chance encounter with the owner of Tresco who invited them to spend some days there with his family.

One month after the wedding they were back in London and travelled down to Ferne with Sir Thomas. On September 21st they heard of his marriage at Weymouth two days previously to Frances Best. They left Ferne immediately to stay with the Benett-Stanfords at Pythouse for a few days before going on to Clewer. Their next destination was the Phelips family-seat at Montacute where Willy Phelips[F] decided to join them in a lengthy visit to the United States. Agnes's brother Lionel was already in Canada and was expected to meet them at some stage. Before their departure Agnes spent a couple of nights at Rushmore without Walter. The guests at a dinner-party included Sir Thomas, his new wife, his son Tom and – in Agnes's words – 'the Crossboy' [Herbert]. Rejoining Walter in London at 4 Grosvenor Gardens she was busy with last-minute packing.

Oct 20 Very busy packing. Went out & bought rug with £10 Papa gave me. Left Gros. G. about 5 missed one train, rather [a] bustle for next, all my fault. Felt parting with dear old Al[ice] very much. Arrived Liverpool 11. Aunt Maude was at station dear old thing. Went round the place stopped finally at the Adelphi.

Oct 21 Willy Phelips came and hustled us and we got everything ready and then went by the two oclock boat to the [s.s.] Servia and started at about 4 p.m. calm.

Oct 22 Sunday. Calm. No service. Stopped at Queenstown.

Oct 23 Calm. Felt a little sick on account of swell.

Oct 24 Walter very poorly. We stayed downstairs, rather rough. Food beastly!

Oct 25 Still rough. I came up for a little in the evening.

Oct 26 Much better, but not calm. Most people very ill. Spoke to Dr. MacKellar and L[or]d. Tarbat.

Oct 27 Felt quite well. Nice fine day. In evening a woman sang.

Oct 29 Sunday. 2nd off[icer] read prayers. Missionary man preached we stayed for prayers then went up beautiful day. Patti [the celebrated prima donna] (with Nicolini) appeared they sat opposite us – made acquaintance with Mrs. Thurber.

Oct 30 Great excitement landing tomorrow. Finished Vice Versa Very good. Read Browning.

Oct 31 Landed at 11. People up at 5. Band for Patti – went to Brunswick hotel. Had luncheon and dined at del Monico's with McKellar and T[arbat].

Nov 1 Looked at New York. Bad streets noisy and dirty. We did not like our rooms so we looked for others with no success.

Nov 2 Wrote letters and Lord Tarbat came to luncheon. We walked about.

Nov 4 Moved in morning to Westminster [hotel]. Lovely rooms. But shocking bad food. I was tired. Called on Mrs. Thurber.

Nov 5 Sunday. Did not go to church. Afternoon went for a little walk and Mrs. Thurber called.

Nov 6 I looked after a piano on Saturday and it came.

Nov 7 Letters from Mama Alice Aunt Maude etc.

Nov 8 Mr. Hewitt and Miss called and they asked us to go and stay with them Friday.

Nov 9 We dined with the Thurbers. Went to the opera.

Nov 10 Mr. Hewitt called, a friend died. They were going to funeral so we could not go till tomorrow. Opera was L'Africaine.

Nov 11 Decided to leave the Westminster. So we took rooms at the Buckingham hotel. Missed our train in consequence of packing: went by 4. Arrived after dark driven by a black coachman. Nice wooden house. Nice people. Charming room.

Nov 12 Sunday. Mr. Hitchcock staying there. Only person. No church. But Miss Hewitt drove us out and we saw the most lovely view. In a valley with high hills behind beautiful wild rocky scenery. We had tea in a log cabin belonging to the youngest girl. Great fun.

Nov 13 Returned home, drive perfectly lovely. We arrived at New York about 5. Went and had tea at Hewitts and in the evening they kindly gave us tickets for the opera. Patti sang in Faust.

Nov 15 Went to Christie Minstrels, went to fire brigade with the Thurbers and after to Dorlan's and had an oyster supper excellent.

Nov 18 Mrs. Thurber called had luncheon and went to call on Miss Coddington and bought a chest preserver. In evening went to Mrs. Botta's party. Mr. Story the sculptor read his poems. Was introduced to Mrs. Story who knows the family. Oscar Wild was there.

Nov 19 Sunday. Miss Coddington came and fetched me and we drove to Grace's church.

Nov 20 4 months [married]. Heard from Mama and W. fr. Charlotte. In evening Col. Hazard dined.

Nov 22 Very ill with coughing last night. Much better this morning. Did not do much. Wrote letters.

Nov 23 We lunched at Delmonico's & dined with the Butlers.

Nov 24 The Butler's (homoeopathic) doctor came to see me on account of my bad cough. Said change of air would do me good. Gave me powders. Left New York about 10. Had small carriage to ourselves and arrived at Rochester in evening.

Nov 25 Left Rochester saw little and arrived Niagara about 8. Went to Prospect House. Canada side. Very much struck. Looked lovely by moonlight. We telegraphed to L[ionel].

Nov 26 Sunday. Went to table rock underneath the falls. All dressed up in oilskins etc. spray very violent but quite wonderful. Went on to burning spring. Whirlpool rapids.

Nov 27 Decided not to go. So drove again first to Park island. To see the falls quite close from above, these are the American falls and one crosses over the bridge for which one has to pay enormous sums and then down by the tramway to see the Falls from below. Both equally marvellous and beautiful and then we went to goat island. I got a Canadian fox's head the other side. We went round everything and saw everything and one thing delighted us more than another as we went on.

Nov 28 We left Niagara for Cleveland about 12 and arrived about 10. Went to [blank] but we did not like it because it was a temperance place. This is one of the prettiest cities we have seen and Euclid Avenue is quite lovely. Nice quaint houses.

Nov 29 Today met a Mr. who took us out in his carriage and showed us round the town. It snowed very hard and the tall electric light looked lovely by night on the snow and trees in the square in front of us.

Nov 18. William Wetmore Story DCL (1819-1895) published volumes of poems 1847, '56, '86. His *Life* by Henry James was published 1903. His wife described New York social life in 1882 as like 'the whirl of a London season'.

Oscar Wilde had recently returned to New York after his extensive tour of America.

Nov 30 We left Cleveland at 2 but our train was 2 hours late so we drove about in the town to wait for it and saw the sleighing in Euclid Avenue and arrived in Toledo, where we broke our journey for Chicago at about 7.30 Boody's Hotel which they were ornamenting – they gave us nice rooms but Elizabeth [her English maid] had bugs. Willy Phelips left us at Cleveland and went back to New York.

Dec 1 We missed our morning train so we walked about Toledo dirty uninteresting city all the morning and had dinner at 7 and left in the night train for Chicago and arrived at 6 on

Dec 2 and after breakfast we were downstairs when a person with a beard came up and shook hands with us who turned out to be Lionel. We went upstairs and talked and then went out for a walk. I do not know what to make of Lionel he seemed to talk very sensibly and well and we thought he had been hardly treated but since then something has happened to make me suspiscious.

Dec 3 Sunday. We did not go to church because we got up too late. Chicago is a wonderful place when one thinks that less than 10 years ago it was nothing and was burnt down 5 years ago.

Dec 4 We settled not to go till next day. Money from New York not yet arrived, in evening went to play. Adrienne Le Couvreur Mslle Rhea acted extremely well.

Dec 5 Money came and Walter and Lionel went off to see slaughter house, where they kill 15,000 pigs a day. We left Chicago at 5 oclock next day.

Dec 6 Express train very fast. But very jolty. I felt very sore. Had meals in train not bad. Passed through huge prairie by night and arrived at New York at 7.30 in the evening.

Dec 7 Met Willy Phelips who had only got our letter half an hour before and had got one room for us.

Dec 10 Sunday – too late for church. Wrote all morning. Walter and W.P. went to club. The something that happened that I mentioned a few days ago concerning Lionel is simply that he telegraphed to Walter for 100 dollars, we know he had £100 in his possession but Walter sent it to him, and yesterday a letter came from him to Walter and Walter won't tell me a word about it not even yes or no and Lionel at the end said don't tell anyone. Not even Agnes. I wonder what it can be. When I asked Walter if he had done anything wrong he doesn't answer anything.

I have since found out that he lost his money to a horrid man who took him to his house and made him gamble it all away after having stood him several drinks at the bar he has now gone back – I wrote to him. Walter told me because he thought I might say something rash about it at home. Of course I do not intend to mention it.

Dec 12 We changed into our present rooms on the 1st floor today. Very nice rooms. Mrs. Thurber came.

Now installed in a suitable apartment with her personal maid Elizabeth at hand Agnes was able to entertain her new American friends and she entered wholeheartedly into the social life of New York, attending tea-parties and dinner-parties, calling and leaving cards and attending balls at Del Monico's where the master of ceremonies, Ward McAllister, was reputedly the 'ring-master' of wealthy New York socialites such as the Vanderbilts, Astors etc. Her diary catalogues the names of new acquaintances and little else, though Mrs Thurber, whom she had first met on board the s.s. *Servia*, became a closer friend.

Dec 14 Went out walking with Walter in morning and ball in evening at del Monico's 1st. Assembly. Rather amusing. Several English men.

Dec 18 Went to Patriarch's ball at Del Monico's – McAllister asked me to lead Cottillon. Danced Major Slade.

Dec 22 Walked out in morning with Walter, who bought me lovely present coloured dragon fly brooch. Went to Mrs. Th[urber] who gave me luncheon Miss Coddington there and then to shops.

Dec 25 Monday Christmas Day. A very joyous day to me. We went to church and Walter and I stayed together for the Comunion. I felt so extremely happy – It joined us together more than ever. Then we lunched with Miss Butler and she gave me a book of Aldrich's poems. And he Emerson essays. In afternoon we went to tea with the Mariés. In evening we dined with Thurbers. Mrs. Th: gave me a banjo and he a croqodile and some shells.

Dec 26 Mrs Th: came and fetched me out driving. Called on banjo man and went shopping.

Dec 27 Went to dressmaker. Had gown made. Banjo man came [to instruct her].

Dec 28 Coddingtons to tea – ball Cottillon in evening.

Dec 29 Elizabeth went to see the doctor. Banjo master came.

1883

Jan 1 Went in morning to Brooklyn. Prospect Park etc. had lunch in a little inn.

Jan 2 Banjo master and afternoon Mr. Marié called and we went to see Vanderbilts house. Very fine but gaudy and bad taste. In evening ball. F.C.D.C. McCallister sent me a bouquet. Gown came fitted badly. Sent it back next day.

Jan 6 Still heavy snow. Practised banjo, afternoon went out sleighing with Thurbers.

Jan 7 Sunday. Went to church. St. Thomas's. Met Mr. Marié, dined in evening with Mrs. Stephens. Lady Mandeville. Mrs. Vanderbilt. Met Mr. Parker Mr. Pelham Clinton.

Jan 10 Went out sleigh driving with Thurbers. Banjo man came.

Jan 12 Left cards etc. Went out sleighing with P[elham] Clinton.

Jan 13 Left for Albany at 11. Arrived 3 had luncheon and then went out sleighing. Saw Capitol and Palmer's studio. Dinner party in evening rather tired.

Jan 14 Sunday. Went to church and saw plate and windows.

Jan 15 Left Albany at 11. Arrived N.Y. at 6. Had dinner Went to ball at Del Monico's.

Jan 16 Mrs. Thurber sent things etc. People came in afternoon. Miss Marié in morning, dined in evening with Thurbers.

Jan 17 Went off in carriage to ship. Paronia. When nearly there our wheel came off Got out and walked and got boys to carry our things. Found Thurbers, Butlers, Firman etc. on board seeing us off. Sailed at 12. Calm all day. Eat our oysters and butter – given us.

Jan 18 On the ocean. Rather rough. Very ill. Got up beautiful sun.

Jan 19 Still sick. Very rough. But got up.

Jan 20 Better. Stewardess charming person took great care of me.

Jan 23 Got up and played chess with Col. Warburton.

Jan 24 Calm and sun. Played draughts, backgammon and chess with W. and Col. Warburton.

Jan 26 Arrived Queenstown. Wrote several letters. Rather squally.

Jan 27 Rather cold and drizzly. Arrived Liverpool 12, but did not get in till past 5 in tug: raining & cold. Started at 6 dinner at station. arrived G.G. 12. Mama up.

Agnes was now in her seventh month of pregnancy and as yet had no home of her own. Easton Farm at Berwick St. John was being renovated for her and Walter to live in but was not ready for them. The immediate plan was to find suitable accommodation within range of her London doctor where she could await her confinement. Walter spent days in London house-hunting but with no firm result and the departure of Agnes's maid Elizabeth to be married came at an unfortunate moment.

Lionel had returned to England and spent some time at Ferne reviving his flirtation with Kate Grove before setting off again with young Tom Grove to Halifax, Nova Scotia. During March Agnes and Lady Grove must have been forced by circumstances into each other's company, and the older woman – conscious that they both were newly married Grove wives – had no wish to stand on ceremony and desired to be called by her christian name, Frances. To Walter and Agnes, with their liking for nicknames, she was already known privately as Grovina. It is noticeable that Agnes's diary almost ignores her until a sudden dramatic occasion at the end of March -

March 29 Thursday – was a marvellous day for me. Walter had gone
    to Crewkerne races. Charlotte and Kathleen were staying with the
    Troyte Bullocks.[E] Frances & I went over to Rushmore to
    luncheon, came back about 4, the roads were very rough & jolted
    me a good deal. That afternoon providentially Fran & I became
    great friends & she insisted again upon my calling her Frances &
    kissed me. At 5 I went down to tea after having conversed with Ella
    [Crosse] on my drawing which I was painting in the schoolroom. I
    did not go up again till 7.30 having talked to Grovina all that time.
    After I had laid down a little Walter came home. I did not go down
    to dinner as I felt rather uneasy. Time went on & it grew worse. At
    ½ past two on Friday morning my baby was born. I was quite alone
    & it came in about 5 minutes. I was very well & Mrs Wright came
    up & delivered the child. Soon after, the doctor came. Poor Walter
    was then happier, but during the time he was fetching Jane the baby
    came & no one knew. Kind Frances sat up nearly all night with me.

Aunt Maude and St. George came as godparents to the Christening, when the baby was named Honor though she soon acquired the pet-name of Dode or Dod. Agnes was unable to attend as she had contracted measles and her health continued to be poor at times. In May the removal began to Easton farmhouse, breaking off for a visit to Sandown, Isle of Wight, where various relatives and friends were staying. She was now ready to join in the usual activities of the London season during June and it was not until July that she began to settle down to her new home-life at Berwick. Walter was frequently absent as he resumed his familiar pursuit of the pleasures of saddle and gun, and Agnes evidently missed the general bustle and activity of a large establishment with its constant comings and goings of brothers, sisters and ever-changing visitors – something that she evidently relished during the Christmas party at Rushmore.

May 10 Walter went out with his Yeomanry. They went to Weymouth. Kathleen & I went into Berwick. Everything in great disorder. I slept on the Ferne bedding on my spring mattress on the floor. I did nothing much but lie on the sofa till Kathleen left for Weymouth. She arranged everything.

May 15 Walter came back. We arranged the rooms a little & went out. I got gradually stronger & better. My babe flourished & was happy.

May 20 Sunday. Sir Thomas came church time & brought his silver teapot & coffee pot – very beautiful. I went to church for the first time [since the birth] & was churched. Sir T lunched with us & looked at everything, attics & all.

July 19 I do dislike being alone all day. I have no horse or anything, a wretched cook, no food hardly, no-one to see. My baby asleep & when awake I am too busy to do anything. I am getting the house much more straight. I heard from my dear boy. Oh how I do miss him, no one knows. Tomorrow is our first wedding day.

July 20 <u>Anniversary</u>. Walter arrived at about 2. We spent a lovely happy day together.

July 25 My birthday. Met Walter at Tisbury at 11. Went to - Horse Show, saw Lord Alington,[F] had tea at the hotel, came back in train with Benyon.

July 26 Ld Alington had the train stopped at Tisbury, picked up us & Benyons. Harry Pleydell in the train. Went to Sandown.

Nov 2 Going to hunt at Iwerne, on Alice's horse, feel a sort of presentiment of evil have not slept all night. Hope nothing will happen to me for the sake of my beloveds. My dear dear treasures. [Added later] We got to the meet & my horse was waiting for me. I jumped the first fence, then I had a stupid fall the first I have ever had. I got hung up by my stirrup but I got on alright again & joined them afterwards. We walked home quietly.

Dec 8 I lunched at Rushmore. All this time a disgusting scandal is circulating about Mrs Benett[-Stanford][F] & her groom. Not yet cleared up, hope it will be soon.

Dec 10 We drove to Pythouse. Harry P[leydell] & Chapman there.

Dec 11 Poor N[elly] B[enett] looks very ill & worried. We left about 2.

Dec 24 Went to luncheon Pythouse. Poor N.B. talked to me a long time, is much distressed about the loathsome scandal about her.

Dec 25 [Christmas Day] We went to Rushmore after luncheon. Met them all. Papa had gone to London. We had great fun & played romps.

Dec 31 Last day of this year I finish this dear old book & I bequeath it to my precious Dod.

1884

The journal just completed had exactly covered two years. Its successor is slightly smaller but no less substantial – well-bound in leather with, again, a brass lock which has at some time been forced, presumably because the key was lost. Agnes's entries run through to June 1888 in this volume.

As wife and mother with her own establishment at Easton House, Berwick St. John, Agnes now enjoyed the larger family life that flowed between Rushmore, Ferne and Easton. With no pressing anxieties she and Walter developed the texture of their married life and created their own circle of friends – the Pleydell brothers of Whatcombe,[H] the Bankses of Kingston Lacy, Nelly Benett and her husband at Pythouse, Lord Alington at Crichel, Lord Wolverton and the Glyn family at Iwerne Minster.[H] In their company she danced at fashionable balls, rode to hounds and interspersed the pleasures of country life with visits to London – notably for Alice's marriage to Sir John Lubbock[E].

Jan 10 W., Alice & I went to Dorchester to the King's Arms Hotel for the Hunt Ball. Perfectly delightful.

Jan 21 Drove from Rushmore. Alice W. & I to Whatcombe. Lord Conyers at Rushmore.

Jan 22 Rained all day. Blandford ball in evening <u>most</u> enjoyable.

Jan 23 Left Whatcombe after lunch, arr[ived] Rushmore for the night.

Jan 24 Left Rushmore for Kingston Lacy. Went to a ball at Mr & Mrs Lees. Harry P[leydell] was there. Delightful.

Feb 11 Tom [Grove] came home from Manitoba.

March 12 I rode Athlone & hunted at Minchington. Had a bad fall, horse went head over heels.

April 1 We wrote fool's letters to Edith [Walter's sister], Mr

Hutchinson & Mr King to arrive today.

April 7 We all went out foxhunting. I rode Jacob, Walter Romeo. We had a lovely day. Two good runs, 30 & 45 minutes, killed two foxes. I got one brush.

April 21 I went to Rushmore to talk about the land Papa wants Sir T to sell. He won't.

May 30 Lionel & Douglas left for Canada.

June 19 Walter left for Heligoland on his summer cruise with William Grove [his cousin].

June 29 Sunday. [In London] Did not go to church. Tried St. Peter's but found it too crowded. Bishop of Truro preached.

July 9 Went to Holland House with Mama.

July 15 Walter & I dined at the Jaunes [Jeunes][E]

July 20 Sunday. Today is my 2nd wedding anniversary. We did not celebrate it particularly.

July 21 Mama drove to Aunt Loo's & stopped & saw the great National Liberal Demonstration. My heart was with the 'people'. After dinner Walter, Willy & I went to the Philosophical Society, saw Madame Blavatzki [founder of modern Theosophy]

July 25 My birthday. I am 21. I had luncheon with the Hambros. Mr Guest there. I sent off to I. Halford for an invitation for Mr [Ivor] Guest.[F] We went to the Halfords' ball in the evening. I danced the cotillon with Mr. Guest & we came home about 5 in the morning.

July 26 Last night was the most enjoyable birthday I think I have ever spent except perhaps the one on my honeymoon.

Aug 1 I drove W & Burt to play cricket at Alva Distan [Alvediston]. Mrs Parran [Mrs Parham] who lives at Norrington [House][D] where they were playing is a most beautiful old house showed us all over it & a curious cellar with beautiful stone-work ceiling.

Aug 17 Sunday. We did not go to church but Sir T & Charlotte went & afterwards announced to us the astonishing news of the birth of a daughter of Frances [Olivia][E].

1885

Two events stand out – the marriage of Walter's sister Kate to Eddy Pleydell, and the decision of Sir Thomas to stand for Parliament at the General Election.

Jan 4 Bracelet came from H[arry] P[leydell] <u>lovely</u>.

Jan 20 Walt & Alex hunted but the huntsman broke his ribs so Lady Theodora Guest[F] had the hounds called off.

March 12 I rode grey cob at Gunville. Lord Wolverton hunted a deer but did not catch it.

March 19 Walt & I drove to Iwerne to the meet. They hunted a deer.

April 23 I heard of Kathleen Grove's engagement to Eddy Pleydell. Great rejoicings in the family.

May 13 Went to the Drawing-Room, great crowd.

May 14 Saw L[ionel] Monro[F] just back from the Soudan wounded.

June 1 Had very bad news of Harry Pleydell who came back from Gibraltar very ill.

June 3 Harry P worse. Wedding put off.

June 4 Harry a little better. Wedding put on.

June 6 Kathleen was married, without a wedding gown as it had not arrived.

June 9 [In London] We dined with the Foxes. Mr Chandos Pole took me into dinner. I liked him.

Oct 27 Charlotte & I drove to [East] Knoyle – excellent meeting. Walt in chair. Saw Mr & Mrs P[ercy] Wyndham[B] [of Clouds]. Sir T spoke well. Capt Waly proposed to Ch.

Nov 23 Meeting at Berwick. Most enthusiastic. Excellent. Mr Chapman spoke, capital speech.

Nov 30 The Election tomorrow. Greatest possible excitement.

Dec 1 Charlotte came down & she & Walt drove to the different polling places. I drove to Woodcuts to try & get King to vote but he would not.

Dec 2 Walt went off at 7 to Wilton. At 1.30 I got a telegram saying that Sir T had got in with a majority of 832. We went up to Ferne, greatest excitement Sir T & Mr Chap[man] & Walt made speeches outside the house, when the band played & there was beer, dancing & [?] bread.

1886

Feb 9 We, Walt, Ch. Honor & I, went 3rd class to London. We went to Clewer & Ch. to Twickenham.

Feb 11 Walt & I drove over to Brackens to fetch Grace Bruce for the dinner party. Bruces all in a dreadful state having lost all their money or gone smash in some way. Looking most disconsolate. 24 to dinner.

Feb 12 Very seedy. Edith took Grace Bruce back to Brackens. Walt went to London. Edmund [Foster] gave the Bruces a house rent free for 3 years.

Feb 22 I heard the sad sad news of the death of dear Harry Pleydell. I can hardly realize it now.

March 15 We lunched at Ferne & went into Humby afterwards. Delightful house.

Joseph Humby was Sir Thomas's tenant at Manor farmhouse in Berwick St. John, which he was intending to vacate. Agnes and Walter decided to move into it & began transferring some of their furniture in late May after their return from Ascot races. This new activity accounts for a loss of interest in her journal. The last May entry is on the 21st, there are only six entries during June, and in July only five. In this period Gladstone was defeated over Irish Home Rule, Parliament was dissolved & Sir Thomas was re-elected unopposed.

July 5 We went to 33 Belgrave Square to stay with Alice.

July 12 We went to Ferne whilst moving into our new house.

July 20 Went to Goodwood, our party Trafalgars & R. Bankes.[F]

Aug 12 We went to Windsor races. Edith went to see Charlotte off to India [where their sister Kate was expecting a child]. I wrote her a note.

Aug 31 Great gaps & inaccuracies are unfortunately caused in the last three months owing to my having stopped entry while at Berwick in May as we were doing nothing particular but remove furniture.

Dec 1 In evening we went to a P. Reading [? Poetry] in Berwick. Willy recited.

Dec 11 Walter hunted with Wolverton's harriers – stag.

Dec 17 After dinner at about 9 o'clock I suddenly felt the waters break inside me & I ran upstairs with streaming from me & sent for the doctor & Mrs Lush.

Dec 18 At 2 o'clock my boy [Gerald] was born. I had a much worse
    time of it than the last, but he was alright and I also.
Dec 26 St George came & sat in my room. Heavy snow storm.
Dec 30 The country completely snowed up.

1887

The year of Queen Victoria's Golden Jubilee. Agnes was in London during
the celebrations but found little to record in her journal. Surprisingly she
makes no reference to the Ball at the Guildhall, with 'all the royalties present',
to which Sir Thomas in his diary says he took her. For her the high spot of the
year was her triumphant ride with Mr Gladstone and his entourage past the
cheering crowds at Nottingham and Derby in the autumn. This yielded one of
the most detailed accounts in any of her journals.

She had planned a rendezvous with Walter at Nottingham on his return
journey from a shooting holiday in Scotland – the sort of plan that generates
more hope than confidence.

Jan 4 Walter went Lockeridge to stay with Sir H. Meux, to shoot.
Jan 27 We went to Sherborne for the Sherborne ball & stayed in
    Herbert's rooms.
Feb 18 [In London] Walt, St G, Willy & I went to Faust. Irving &
    Ellen Terry excellent, the whole thing beautiful.
March 3 Walt & I went out hunting at East Stour. I rode Arabic.
    Lovely day. Warm sun, lots of people out.
March 14 Heavy fall of snow.
March 16 Mrs Best was coming to luncheon but the snow was too
    deep.
May 16 Walt went to London to ride a horse for R[onald]
    Farquharson called 'Filter' at the Olympia horse-show.
June   Insolent maid left.
June 21 Queen's Jubilee day. Saw it from Lombard Street Phoenix
    Fire Insurance Office.
Aug 10 Fete at Larmer Tree. We danced about & had claret cup. Band
    & lights.
Aug 12 Rushmore came to Berwick & we all went on to Ferne.
Aug 29 Went to Rushmore where they played cricket & served tea. F
    objectionable.
Sept 9 Went to Penruddockes at 1. They did not offer us luncheon.

Sept 16 I arranged my room. Walt is taking lessons every evening in carpentering from Fry, so a great deal of knocking goes on every night.

Sept 26 Walt went to Bamborough Castle where the Lubbocks are staying. I felt so sad at parting from the dear kind sweet thing.

Oct 19 Left Berwick about 8 for Nottingham to hear that great grand old man W.E.G. speak. Arrived Nottingham at 4.30 at which time I had told both St George & Walt to meet me. Arrived at Station, no one there. Utter loneliness & desolation of feeling indescribable. Got a cab, went to George Hotel, saw landlady [who] said no-one had been there. Went to lodgings she had taken for me, left bag & rug there & drove back to Station. No one there. Then went back to George Hotel. Landlady gave me some tea. I was all this time without money & had lost my ticket for the platform [i.e. the meeting] on the way, so thought I should have to give up the meeting when suddenly I determined not to & got a cab & drove to the meeting.

After telling my story to several people I suddenly saw Lord Wolverton who simultaneously saw me. He then took me in hand & we went boldly in & took seats on Gladstone's little private platform, on which eventually the chairman, Alderman Gripper, the Mayor & Mayoress, Mr Arnold Morley & one or two other speakers besides Mr & Mrs Gladstone were. And then I heard the grandest speech ever heard. Mr A. Morley also spoke. Then Lord W. & Mr Morley suggested that I should come to Mrs Farmer's instead of staying by myself in lodgings; so I went there to dinner, nice kind woman, & sat at dinner between Mr Morley & another M.P. whose name I did not make out. I found Mr Morley very interesting & charming.

Oct 20 Having met Mr Henry Gladstone last night, he & Lord W. settled between them that I should go to Derby next day in Mr G's private special saloon train so about 11 next day Mrs Gladstone came in, I was introduced to her & then Mr & Mrs Farmer, Lord W., Mr Morley & I were photographed in a group. Then we got in the carriage & the procession of carriages went through the crowded town with the people cheering & waving as we passed. Mr Gladstone & Mrs & the Mayor were in one, & Mrs Farmer & myself & Ld. W & Mr H. Gladstone in another. We arrived at the station and there the Mayor presented G. with an address, to which he replied in a touching speech. Then, after about half a dozen

people had shaken hands with him, he got into his carriage & I then
was introduced to him. He shook me warmly by the hand & hoped
I was not tired to which I replied, no, I would do still more to hear
what I had heard. Then Mrs Gladstone forbade him to talk & after
one or two remarks he colapsed into silence till we reached Derby.
There again we rode in procession through the town. In my carriage
was Lord Buxton & Lord Wolverton & Mr H. Gladstone. The
streets were crowded & the enthusiasm was enormous. We drove
first to the Derby China Factory: I was there introduced to Sir
William Harcourt & I was made to sign my name in the book
between Mr Gladstone & Mrs Gladstone [who] had asked me in the
train if it would interest me to see it. Then we again drove through
the surging presses of cheering people to the town-hall where Mr
Gladstone made another speech & Sir W. Harcourt also spoke
there. G again – at the end of the 2nd he shook hands 1st with Lord
Wolverton & then with me, which made me feel very proud.

   Then we had luncheon behind the room. I sat next to Ld. Wn &
Mr H. Gladstone & opposite Mr G & Sir W. Harcourt. We settled
that I couldnt get back to Berwick that night I had better go to
London, so I went up with Lord Wolverton & Mr H. Gladstone &
stayed the night with Lady W. in London. Mr Pascoe Glyn[F] & Mr
A. Morley also dined & Lady W came down after dinner, she had
had an operation in her head but was better.

Oct 21 After breakfast next morning I drove in their brougham to a
few shops & then went to see Ursula who was out: then
immediately after luncheon I left for home. All this time I had not
heard how Walter missed me, but it appears he had arrived at
Nottingham the morning of the 19th & had asked at the George
Hotel & been told there that all rooms [were] taken; had then
driven round the town & they had told him none could be got so
had telegraphed to me not to come; had then got home, found I had
gone, telegraphed to Edwin Portman[F] – which telegram passed
through my hands on the platform. Then he telegraphed to me as I
had telegraphed to Kathleen to send me some money. When I
arrived home safely at 4 found Walter at the Tisbury station. Drove
me home & we had a long talk – dear children with slight colds – so
pleased to see that dear sweet kind boy again after his long absence
in Scotland.

Oct 25 I had promised to go to Lord Wolverton's meeting at
Wimborne but did not go as Walt wanted me to stay with him.

Nov 7 Honor & I had luncheon with Mrs Best & there I heard the sad
    sad news of dear Lord Wolverton's sudden death. It seemed so sad
    after having seen him such a short time before.

1888

Agnes continued to write in her existing journal, begun in 1884, until she
reached June 17 on the final page. For the remainder of the year she used a
diary printed and published by William Whiteley, Universal Provider at the
celebrated Bayswater store. This set out seven days to a page interleaved with
blotting paper and thereby inhibited greatly her freedom to write expansively if
she chose to do so. Her writing deteriorates at times into a scrawl which
becomes illegible and is perhaps an indication of emotional stress. She was
troubled with a rash – a persistent ailment of hers – and her readiness to take
offence appears in sudden flashes of anger. Walter's frequent absences in
pursuit of his sporting pleasures depress her morale which finds consolation in
the attentions of Dawson Damer and Chandos Pole at Ascot and Weymouth.
    Always in the background is the tension between an acceptable life-style
and an inadequate income, which fuels her feeling that the two fathers might
contribute more. Some notes at the end of this diary provide details of her
domestic establishment – Governess (£20) Nurse (£12) Maid (£20) Parlour
maid (£16) and Cook (£22) per annum. Outdoor male staff, groom etc are
probably represented by Burt (£52) and Trowbridge (£34). Another list
names the women as Estelle (£22) Alice (£22) Clare (£15) & Elisa (£10) – an
annual cost of £69, which is confirmed by another note 'wages quarterly
£17/5/-'. Estelle was the governess.
    A letter written in December by Agnes to her father, and published pp76-
78 in Concerning Agnes (Alan Sutton, Gloucester, 1982) reveals that she already faced several summonses for outstanding debts.

Jan 10 My rash began to come out again. I did not go out much these
    days – but we went to the Morrissons' ball. They had a cottilion.
    Rather a grand ball.
May 21 We left for Weymouth. Went to a play.
May 22 Went to [Yeomanry] Sports. Talked to Mr D[awson]
    D[amer][F]
May 23 Yeomanry Ball. Danced Mr D. Damer.
May 24 Ball in Jubilee Hall. Danced Mr Chandos Pole, Mr D. Damer.
June 14 [at Ascot] Tea [in] G[uar]ds tent Mr D. Damer.
June 15 Pouring rain but most fun had luncheon Gds tent D.D.

June 16 Went to London.

June 25 Caledonian ball. Enjoyed it [? more] than any other ball. D.D. there.

Aug 9 [Staying at Clewer] Went to Windsor. Grace [Bruce?] offensive & objectionable at dinner.

Aug 27 Played cricket at Donhead. Cricket ball in the eye - black eye in consequence.

Aug 31 Cricket match at Rushmore. Women against the men left-handed with broomsticks. Women won.

Oct 9 Eliza Smith came.

Nov 2 Eliza Smith left suddenly in most insolent manner.

Dec 1 I lunched at Rushmore & had talk £P [i.e. about money with Papa]

Dec 7 We lunched at Rushmore & went to Ferne, talked to Sir T about money matters.

Dec 9 I drove children up to Ferne. They were insulted.

1889

A Renshaw's Diary in cloth boards which have come away from the book. Cost one shilling. Six day entries in open spread with a separate section of Sundays at the back. The end fly-leaf has a lightly sketched head of a girl – possibly Honor, or 'Kiddy' as she is now frequently named, drawn by Agnes. Her third child Oenone was born in March.

This was a low-key year with periods of illness – some serious – resulting in blank entries and generally perfunctory writing. She did however go to Ascot and to Yeomanry Week at Weymouth, renewing her friendship with Dawson Damer who had become Lord Carlow in the meantime.

Jan 15 St George came to help Walt at meetings for his County Council for which he is standing for Wylye division.

Jan 23 Telegram came announcing Carpenter's victory. He got 594 votes to Walter's 131. Great blow.

March 30 Kiddy's birthday 6 years old. Oenone was christened. They had a little party after.

May 27 Left at 10 for Weymouth. Went ball, Yeomanry. Saw G D Damer now Lord ['and Lady' inserted] Carlow & Mr C. Pole.

May 29 Ball in evening in Jubillee Hall, danced Ld C.

June 20 [at Ascot] Had tea Ld Carlow. Walked down to the booths, he played the fool & insisted on our being photographed.

July [First week blank]

Aug 6 Still feeling ill, got out of bed & drove to a party at Dalhousies
... Grossmith. Felt very ill.

Aug 7 Doctor Wilkinson came & found I had inflammation of lung.

Aug 9 Both lungs now affected. Temperature 104.

Subsequently the diary was largely neglected until September 10 when Agnes went to Longthorns to be with Walter's sister, Kathleen Pleydell, who gave birth to a daughter. In the concluding months of the year nothing of note was recorded.

1890

A diary of superior quality – T. J. & J. Smith's Post Diary, two days per page octavo, strongly bound in cloth boards. With more space available Agnes's writing becomes more controlled and easier to decipher. Her health has improved and the family finances are also about to do so. Her customary zest for life is more in evidence. The year's most disturbing feature is the revelation of the decline in the mental health of her youngest brother Arthur.

Papa's detachment from family life is illustrated by his first visit to what has been Agnes's home – two miles from Rushmore – for the past four years.

Jan 17 [staying at Kingston Lacy] In evening we went to the
entertainment at Canford. Prince of Wales there ... sat at same table
[at supper], saw Lord Portman,[F] Marcia Yarborough,[E] Percy
Wyndham.

Jan 21 M drove me to St Giles to see Tableaux Vivants, saw Sturts,
Ashleys etc. Lord Shaftesbury sang, beautiful voice, seems a nice
boy.

Feb 4 We all went up to a phonograph lecture given by a Mr Lind at
Rushmore.

March 19 We all drove to Semley where Charlotte & I got on to
horses & rode to see the start of the point to point race. Walter rode
Tyrone & came in 2nd which was splendid considering who he rode
against. Captain Chaloner won. Mr. George Wyndham[B] was 3rd.
We lunched with the Wyndhams [at Clouds].

March 28 I visited poor & sick.

May 5 A day in which, owing to a letter from Sir T, we were relieved of much anxiety as he has undertaken to allow us £200 a year more. The pony & donkey got loose, strayed away & could be found nowhere. Herb came down in afternoon who had seen a man who had seen them going past Rushmore.

May 11 We all went to church. Boob[F] preached & came to tea.

May 13 Boob came to stay.

May 15 Walt & Boob drove to Tisbury Petty Sessions.

June 5 I had yesterday the most dreadful letter from Alice telling me of Arthur's terrible condition, & I waited at Tisbury, hearing P was coming. He told me much sad news that I had not heard before. How the poor boy has constantly to have 2 keepers with him & how he tries to escape. I can think of nothing else, it quite upsets me. I so long to get to him & try what I can do, if they could only get him into the country it would be so much better for him.

June 23 We went London in evening, found Arthur when I arrived. Saw him nearly every day.

June 24 Papa came up to London, St George came after luncheon & they had an interview, Arthur here.

June 25 M[ama] & I went to Dr Vimaces to see Arthur.

June 27 Saw Arthur luncheon & tea, talked to him.

June 28 Went with Lord C[arlow] to Aquarium [theatre] to see The Mesmerist, very funny & entertaining.

June 29 Sunday. Went to Brompton Oratory morning with Lord Carlow, walked back after & lunched with him. Dined Bachelors Club evening with Mr Guest.

July 1 Walt & I went to Halfords ball. Came back with Mr Guest.

July 2 Dr Blake examined me & said I was thoroughly out of health.

July 8 I went with M to Blake again. Dined with Mr Hambro. This was my last dinner out & I lay up from this day all day & every day.

Sept 10 I read quietly all afternoon in hammock. P came down with Mama for the 1st time & looked over the house.

Oct 1 Walter left for Scotland to stay with Sir H. Meux in Ross-shire.

Dec 1 to 11 [No entries]

Dec 18 Sir Charles Shelley[E] & I left Ferne driving to Rushmore for luncheon – stayed there & joined by children & Miss Nixon [their governess] in evening.

Dec 19 Snow storm began.

Dec 20 Snow continued to fall heavily.

Dec 22 We all left Rushmore after luncheon – Gerald & Oenone in panniers on the pony, Honor riding the donkey, the luggage in pack saddles. I went with P as far as the top of the hill, Miss Nixon[G] rode my horse to there & then I rode the rest of the way home. The road was completely blocked in parts.

Dec 25 Christmas Day. Took Honor to church. Sir T, Frances & Herb lunched. Gave children presents.

1891

A Charles Letts diary, open spread of six days, poor binding, front cover lost. Advertisements for patent medicines etc.

The exceptionally severe winter weather continued. The decline in Arthur's condition did not respond to efforts to check it. Agnes became more active on horseback and her father commissioned a distinguished artist, Fred Beaumont, to paint an Academy portrait of her.

A recurrence of her rash perhaps accounts for some outbursts of anger.

Jan 25 Break-up of frost, longest & hardest known this century.

Jan 29 Heard from Mr Bright from Algiers where he went a week or so ago with Arthur for change of air & scene which it is to be hoped will do him good.

Feb 16 I went out hunting on Arabic, with Walter on J. Bennett's chestnut, at Iwerne. Most exciting day. Arabic went beautifully, enjoyed myself very much, got bad cut under chin when jumping high blind fence, many of which I went over during the day.

Feb 21 I heard Arthur & Bright were coming home. Their trip seems to have been more or less a failure.

March 9 Violent snow storm.

March 10 Was going to London by 11.51 train but the snow had completely blocked the roads so I was obliged to give up going, much to my annoyance.

March 11 Snow worse than ever, drifts 20 or 30 feet high.

March 16 Walt & I rode to Tisbury & caught the 11.45 train. Maid & luggage went by road amid great difficulties. Arthur went today to Dumfries by himself to an institution voluntarily.

April 22 Heard that poor Arthur had tried to escape from Institution at Dumfries, & been recaptured after 2 days unhurt but shaken after falling down railway embankment. Is now certified.

May 13 Walt & I drove in pony cart, shot rooks & had tea in woods.

May 14 Picked up rooks Walt had shot yesterday in Ferne Park.

May 16 Walter went otter hunting.

May 25 Came London 11.5 found Papa who immediately took me off to see Mr. Beaumont[G] artist by whom he is going to have me painted. We then went to the Academy.

May 27 Went 11.30 to Mr Beaumont for my 1st sitting [sittings continued through June & July]

May 29 Tea Dover St. Blanche Hozier[E] came in. She is separated from her husband. It created a sensation.

May 30 In evening Hedda Gabler [Ibsen play] Very good indeed. Went with Charlotte.

May 31 Went to see Blanche.

June 25 Bad rash all over my face, stayed indoors. Saw [doctor] McClagan who said it was eczema.

June 26 Rash still bad.

June 27 Rash rather better. Stayed in all day, was prevented from going to water party.

June 28 Went out in park with thick veil on. Met Kathleen & Co. & Molly Langley who was offensive.

July 4 Went with M. & Ursula to Holland House after Beaumont & saw Mr. Balfour playing lawn tennis.

July 7 Saw K. & E. Pleyd[ell] in morning & had a row but they all lied so I am quit of the lot for good which is a good thing.

July 9 Went with P to Beaumont & was severely photographed!

July 15 Sara Woodbine black nurse came seems nice.

Aug 11 Walt & I went to London again & tried unsuccessfully to get cooks. I sat to Mr. Beaumont, Walt very pleased with picture.

Sept 1 Walt & I dined at Rushmore. Edith & Kathleen from Ferne, did not speak to latter.

Nov 30 Went up to Rushmore & rode Arabic with Willy & Douglas to Fontmell, did not stay out & then rode him home to keep, Willy having kindly given him to me.

Dec 4 Hunted Park Farm. Most delightful day. Arabic a great joy to me.

1892

Pettitt's Annual Diary, cloth boards, some pages loose where binding staples have rusted. This year saw Agnes's first active move to become involved in politics, with some guidance from Aunt Rosalind, Countess of Carlisle.[E]

She also found time for singing and dancing lessons and set aside a period for reading in the early morning.

The Beaumont portrait of her was exhibited at the Royal Academy but did not please her. Midsummer brought a gradual worsening of her health culminating in peritonitis. Through July her diary went blank except for a few brief entries. In August she was in a bath-chair, and a further severe illness while she was staying at Clewer in October and November brought the year to a melancholy close.

March 26 Am reading in mornings from 6.30 now. Have got through 2 of Lang's books.

May 15 Went to see Aunt Ros as I have been appointed a delegate for the Women's Liberal Association.

May 17 Ursula & I went at 10 to the Memorial Hall Farrington St. Aunt R[os] made speech. Proceedings generally harmonious.

May 18 Went to great meeting in St James Hall, Lady Aberdeen in chair.

May 19 I went to party given by Lord & Lady Aberdeen. Mr Gladstone there.

June 6 Whit Monday. Great demonstration & speeches in Iwerne park [Lord Wolverton's]

June 27 [In London] Was moved into Mama's room & a nurse came.

June 28 Peritonitis set up. High fever 105.2.

July 22 Walter went down to vote for his father.

July 23 We heard sad news of Sir T's defeat.

Aug 19 Mrs du Boulay lent me her bath chair to drive about in.

Dec 14 Walt came back from seeing Arthur [in Dumfries asylum] & thought him much the same.

Dec 28 Bell rang in drawing room. No one rang it.

1893

Pettitt's Foolscap Folio Scribbling Diary, one week to a page. Cover detached, binding staples rusted. As the year progressed Agnes, again pregnant, spent more time at home with her three children in a calm atmosphere of local tea-parties, croquet in the garden and cricket matches at Rushmore. With nothing of note to mention in her diary she sometimes left days blank.

Jan 2 We were going to stay at Clouds with the Percy Wyndhams but one of Lady Elcho's[F] children had died & the rest had scarlet fever.

Jan 10 We started by 3.29 train for Rhinefield [House] Brockenhurst in the New Forest: the Walker Munros.[F] Found Beatie Herbert[F] & her brother-in-law, Lady Carew, Mr & Mrs Wood [et al.] Lionel Munro took me into dinner by fair choosing. We were 17 at dinner.

Jan 11 All the party were photographed. Had political argument with Lady Carew & Mr Wood. A ball in the evening which was very good.

Jan 12 Went out for walk in afternoon with Lionel Munro, Beatie Herbert & Wood. L. & I went off for fun to take a 'short cut' & got lost & did not come back till after tea. Walter & the Baron & Capt Herbert shot rabbits at Brockenhurst. I enjoyed my walk. Played [illegible] in the evening & rehearsed tableaux.

Jan 13 Listened to the rehearsals of the play that was played in the evening called *The Duchess of Bayswater* by Beatie as Duchess, Wood as Duke. Then there were tableaux - [illegible] & Beauty (Mrs W. Munro!) & the Beast. Then Antoinette which I did. Then we danced.

Jan 14 Left Rhinefield, arrived home & found all children well.

Feb 2 Honor & I had lunch with the Verschoyles. I waited there for the skirt of my gown which did not come. Went in an old grey tweed on the same body! to Edith [Fox]'s[E] wedding. Got there in good time & found Reggie Fitzwilliam [her bridegroom] already there & Lord H. Vane Tempest as best man. [Honor was a bridesmaid]

Feb 3 Arthur who was being transferred from Dumfries to Malling Place escaped then & slept in the house [4 Grosvenor Gardens] for a short time – escaped again early this morning & was brought back. Then we had a terrible morning. He locked himself in twice & was finally got off at about 12. I was with him about an hour. He looks terribly changed & ill but went off happily. Douglas & Walt went to the station with him.

April 13 Willy was married at St Mary's Chelsea. Blossie [Payne][E] looked very nice.

April 30 Went with Walter to hear Dr. Stenton Coit on Walt Whitman.

May 30 Went to the Council meeting of the Women's Liberal Federation at Holborn Town Hall.

June 1 Went to the tableaux at Queen's Gate Hall in aid of Women's Suffrage in which I appeared. Saw Aunt Rosalind.

June 3 Walt & I went to the Foreign Office party.

July 19 Moved into my own bedroom.

July 20 My wedding day. Married 11 years.

Aug 21 We gave a tea on the lawn to about 40 or 50 women & started a WLA [Women's Liberal Association] for BSJ [Berwick St. John]

Oct 20 To luncheon at Rushmore. Drove on to Handley[D] to see [at archaeological excavation] the skeletons, 2 side by side without heads.

Nov 4 Saw Florence Chapman whose marriage is quite off. She has just come back from seeing her father who has quite recovered & leaves the asylum on Friday. [See Sir Thomas Grove's diary 1893 Note. p. 260]

Nov 14 At Ferne met William Grove & his bride, an elderly rather handsome person.

Dec 9 At 9.30 my baby [Terence] was born, a beautiful boy weighing nearly 9 lbs.

1894

The foolscap diary of the previous year was probably too unwieldy in use: Agnes now went to the other extreme, choosing a little pocket diary with one day per page. During the year she made two new friendships which figure prominently in subsequent years. At a dinner-party given by one of her Stanley aunts, Lady Jeune, Agnes met Lord Houghton who became Earl and later Marquis of Crewe [F]. In 1894 Lord Houghton was Lord Lieutenant of Ireland (at a salary, incidentally, four times that of the Prime Minister). He and his sister, Florence Henniker [F], belonged to the literary aristocratic circle, to which Agnes was instinctively drawn.

The other new friend was Sybil, Lady Queensberry [F], whose marriage had ended in divorce in 1884 and who ten years later now took up residence in Tisbury, at Hatch House[H] close to Pythouse. Her eldest son, Lord Drumlanrig, appears among Agnes's luncheon guests at Berwick Manor. Sybil Queensberry shared Agnes's artistic interests and sculpted a bust of Agnes.

April 14 Met Papa Tisbury went with him as far as Salisbury. Great reconciliation.

April 29 I went to luncheon at Rushmore. I drove with P[apa] to King John's House. We had coffee & drove back.

April 30 I took Terence to London by the 11.5 train. Saw Lord Drumlanrig [F] who travelled up with us.

May 9 Went with Willy Scott to National Liberal Club, heard Lord
    Rosebery & Sir W. Harcourt.

[May 22 to June 10 Blank]

June 11 Walt & I dined with the Jeunes, met Lord Houghton, Duke of
    Teck, the Ribblesdales, Lady Malmesbury.

July 9 Went to Lyndhurst, to the Queen's House, to stay with the
    G[erald] Lascelles.

Aug 1 Demonstration at Ferne. Lord Ribblesdale, Mr Pyke [Liberal
    candidate] Lady Queensberry & daughter dined & slept at Ferne.

Aug 10 Lord Drumlanrig & St G came to luncheon.

Aug 15 With Gerald & Oenone went to tea Hatch House, taken by
    Lady Queensberry. Found Wyndham party there.

Aug 30 I took the 2 eldest children to luncheon at Rushmore. Willy &
    Blossie there. Most unpleasant & disgraceful scenes took place.

Sept 4 Lady E[dith] Douglas[F] & [her brother] Lord Drumlanrig
    came to stay.

Sept 16 I drove children to Larmer Tree, met Mr & Mrs R[udyard]
    Kipling[F].

Sept 26 Aunt Maude came to stay, taught us basket-making.

Oct 9 Heard from Lord Drumlanrig that he is engaged to marry Miss
    Alice Ellis.

Oct 19 Saw in paper the most sad death of Lord Drumlanrig who
    accidentally shot himself out shooting in Devonshire yesterday.

Nov 1 Drove with Walter to Sedgehill to see a horse[?]

[After mid-November the diary peters out]

1895

Army & Navy Pocket Diary, seven day open spread, 6½ x 4 inch interleaved
with blotting paper, cloth boards, cost tenpence halfpenny, still in remarkably
good condition, bears Agnes G. Grove signature.

This year gave a strong impetus to her development as a spokeswoman for
women's interests. The Local Government Act of 1894 was a fresh stage in
the political emancipation of women, of which Agnes was quick to avail
herself. Starting the year with a visit to Montacute it was Agnes and not
Walter who left early to return to the first meeting of the new district council.
The participation of women in local government was recognised as a step
forward in the national campaign for women's suffrage; it led Agnes to the
presidency later of the Forward Suffrage Union.

Last year's meeting with Lord Houghton was now followed by an invitation to the Vice-regal Lodge in Dublin, and the autumn brought her first acquaintance with the author of *Jude the Obscure*. Near the year's end the words in her diary 'I lunched at my club' suggest that the much discussed 'New Woman' was quietly changing the social scene.

Jan 3 I left Montacute to attend 1st meeting of District Council.

Jan 4 Walt came back from Montacute.

Jan 31 Went to Board of Guardians & carried the Brabazon scheme.

Feb 6 I sang at Tisbury at a village concert & attended meeting at Mrs Ensor.

Feb 11 Left Euston 9.30 with Ruth & Alex for Dublin. Maids got out at Chester, got left. Arrived 6 next morning, went straight to our rooms.

Feb 12 Breakfast 10 saw party consisting [among others] of Mary Jeune, Lord Inchiquin, Lady Fitzgerald,[F] 2 Miss O'Briens, Lord Houghton. I sat next to him at supper. Levee. Band.

Feb 13 Long talk in morning with his Ex[cellency]! Drove Vice Regal Lodge in afternoon. Drove back with Lord H. Drawing room in evening.

Feb 14 Went to Lord H's room. He gave me his book of poems.

Feb 15 Looked at photographs in library, chose one. Dinner & dance in evening in St Patrick's Hall. Most delightful evening of all.

Feb 16 Sat next to Lord H at dinner.

Feb 17 Sunday. Read in morning, went for walk – stables & round gardens after, then to see books. Went in to dinner with his Exc. played games in evening.

Feb 18 Left Dublin 9 morning, felt very ill, arrived Hoghton Towers about 8 very tired.

Hoghton, near Blackburn, was the Lancashire home of Walter's cousin Aimée. Agnes was now far advanced in pregnancy and the Irish sea-crossing probably aggravated her general malaise. Her ill-health continued after her return to Berwick, where she received an unexpected gift from Lord Houghton of one of his books. On March 25 she gave birth to a boy who died within 48 hours. In the following weeks her diary contains little more than the names of those who came to comfort her and the words 'I went through much misery'.

It was well into May before she resumed her normal activities, going to London to spend three days at the Liberal women's conference and seeing her redoubtable Stanley aunts, Rosalind and Maude.

May 13 Arrived London 5. Went to party at Inst. Aunt Rosalind.

May 14 Went to Conference of W.L.F. luncheon Welsh delegates.

May 22 I went to the drawing-room.

May 28 Went to House [of Commons] to Grand Committee on the Factory bill. Heard Burns, Asquith, G[eorge] Wyndham.

June 23 Lord H [? Houghton] came to see me in afternoon.

June 26 Garden party Holland House afternoon, great crowd.

June 27 Went evening to Blavatsky to hear Mrs Besant.

June 28 Miss E [? Elinor] Glyn came to tea & then I drove with Alice to leave cards at Holland House.

July 25 Aunt Maude had tea-party. Lady Fitzgerald, Mrs Henniker [two sisters of Lord Houghton who had now become Lord Crewe] came.

July 26 Had luncheon 64 Cadogan Gardens with Lady Fitzgerald, Lord Crewe & Mrs. Henniker. Then he walked back to Smith Square with me.

Aug 13 Arrived Hoghton Towers about 8. Children tired. I got Gerald shoes at Euston & got wet through.

Aug 14 Walter & J[ames] de H[oghton] went grouse shooting.

Aug 20 Children left directly after luncheon for London & we left for Windermere.

Aug 21 We went in a boat on the Lake. Was entranced with the scenery.

Aug 24 Arrived at Bramham about 7 spending an hour in Leeds.

Aug 25 Sunday. Went to church in morning!

Aug 29 York races. Saw Lord Crewe, enjoyed the day.

Sept 4 [Back at Berwick] Went to Larmer Tree Sports, met & talked to Thomas Hardy [F], found him interesting, dined there.[N]

Sept 5 Left by 11.50 train for London.

Sept 6 I left with Davis [her maid] for Newhaven, Dieppe, Paris. Most unpleasant journey after Paris.

Sept 7 Arrived Geneva.

For the rest of the month Agnes enjoyed an alpine holiday, meeting the Lubbocks at Chamonix and making expeditions with them by mule or on foot in the vicinity of Mont Blanc. She returned home on October 8 and neglected her diary during the second half of the month.

Oct 30 I heard from Ursula telling me Arthur was very ill, the 1st I had heard.

Nov 6 I went into Salisbury. A telegram was sent on to me, telling me of Arthur's death.

Nov 13   Walt & I drove with Frances to the funeral. I brought a
wreath. Inexpressibly sad. Had luncheon at Rushmore. Made
friends with Willy [see 30 Aug 1894 above]

Nov 26   Drove with Walter to Tisbury. I attended Visitors' Committee
meeting at Union [workhouse]. Found drains all right.

Dec 10   I went to London. I lunched at my club.

NOTE TO 1895

*Sept 4. The Larmer Tree Sports, instituted by General Pitt-Rivers and held
annually in the first week of September, were a revival in popular Victorian
terms of the Tollard Hunt which had been a festive event at this season of the
year in earlier centuries. Instead of a deer-hunt there were races on horseback
and on foot, and the permanent sporting amenities included a golf course,
lawn-tennis courts and a bowling green. In the evening there was dancing in
the open air, by the light of many hundreds of Vauxhall lamps hung in the
trees.*

*The General would have known Thomas Hardy as a fellow-member of the
Athenaeum, and Hardy had been entertained at 4 Grosvenor Gardens in
1894. The General evidently wanted Hardy to see the Larmer Tree Gardens
in full swing and invited him & Mrs Hardy to visit Rushmore for a few days
at this time.*

*Hardy was impressed, writing later in his autobiography 'the dancing
on the green was a great success'. He preserved and reprinted a local
newspaper's description of the scene, which mentioned that the dances were
mostly polka-mazurka and schottische 'though some country dances were
started by the house-party, and led off by the beautiful Mrs Grove'. To this
Hardy added the rather tart comment that it was he who started the
country dances, 'his partner being the above-mentioned Mrs (afterwards
Lady) Grove'. It was a romantic moment, stored in his memory for thirty
years until the death of Agnes inspired the poem which evoked that evening*

> When the wide-faced moon looked through
> The boughs at the faery lamps of the Larmer Avenue.

*The entry in Agnes's diary was matter-of-fact. The house-party at Rush-
more drove to the Gardens to have dinner there and to stay for the dancing
afterwards. Next morning she travelled to London. There is no subsequent
reference to Hardy in this year's diary. Nevertheless their encounter had
made a lasting impression on them both.*

*Agnes was already wrestling with the problem of what a mother should
teach her children in a radical period of changing values and beliefs. It was
that circumstance which established a rapport between them and brought*

Hardy's encouragement to her to publish her thoughts. She drafted an article in controversial terms and sent it to him. Two months after their conversation in the Larmer Tree Gardens she received a copy of Jude the Obscure, *just published, with a letter from Hardy commenting in detail on her article, offering to mark it with suggestions for revision, and suggesting that she should send him a rewritten version which he would forward to a suitable editor. His letter concluded:*

> I have often thought of the pleasant conversation we had at the Larmer, and shall hope to renew it some day.
> I am sending, as I promised, a copy of my new book *Jude the Obscure* for your acceptance. You are, I know, sufficiently broad of view to estimate without bias a tragedy of very unconventional lives.

He evidently hoped that Agnes might represent a younger and more enlightened generation of readers than those of his usually staunch supporters who had been shocked by attitudes to sexual mores and religious belief expressed in JUDE. *Her reply was prompt. She liked* Jude *and she wanted Hardy to correct her article in the way he proposed. He did so, adding 'I am sure that the person who had intelligence enough to write it will know quite well that, if she goes in for literature – where competition is so keen and ruthless – it is truest friendship which points out faults frankly at starting'. A week later he had her rewritten article and forwarded it to the editor of the* Atlantic Monthly. *This was a form of sponsorship that Hardy had previously given to some of the short stories of Mrs Henniker.*

1896

T.J. & J. Smith's Large Quarto Diary, signed Agnes G. Grove. Entries mostly in a less hurried and more legible style, but dying out in mid-October. In the early winter months she stayed quietly at home, involved in nothing more exacting than children's parties and the usual interchange of social visits. Politically she tried unsuccessfully to open up local government to Press reporting and developed her friendship with the Asquiths. Friendship of another kind was that which blossomed so vigorously with Lady Queensberry. Together they went to Bayreuth to attend the full Ring cycle twice, while at Tisbury in the garden of Hatch House they prepared an ambitious hybrid of amateur and professional theatricals which Mrs Patrick Campbell[F] was persuaded to attend and indeed to support by sending down two young London actors in advance to undertake the male roles: the female roles were played by Lady Queensberry, her daughter Edith Douglas and

Muriel Douglas[F] with Agnes and Honor. The play was W.S. Gilbert's
Broken Hearts, in three acts of blank verse. One of the actors, aged 19 at the
time, was Harley Granville Barker. For Agnes it was an introduction to the
fashionable back-stage life of the London theatre world, where she continued
to meet 'Mrs Pat'.

Her first attempt at authorship ended in failure. When Hardy wrote to tell
her of the *Atlantic Monthly*'s rejection he proposed that she should try again,
concentrating specifically on the theme of 'What should children be told?'
Early in April he sent her a reminder, mentioning that – in accordance with
his usual custom – he had taken a London address in Kensington for the
Season and hoped to see her there. A rapid exchange of letters followed with
Hardy applying his professional skill to Agnes's drafts. This time she tasted
success, seeing her essay in the final form in which Hardy had sent it to the
Free Review, though she was less than pleased with the editor who gave the
author's name as Mrs Walter Grove and not as she had wished as Agnes G.
Grove. More pleasing, when she thanked Hardy for his help, was his reply
that 'The trouble has been nothing. You are such a good little pupil that it is a
pleasure to offer you suggestions'. During the summer she became a member
of Hardy's London tea-party circle of friends.

Jan 1 I went to concert at Hussey's in Salisbury. Lady Radnor sang.
    Found letter from H on my return.
Jan 2 Received by morning's post 2 vols of Rossetti's poems from
    Lord Crewe.
Jan 11 Children's party at Ferne. About 70 children.
Jan 30 Went to Board [of Guardians] meeting. Moved admission of
    Press. defeated by large majority.
March 8 Walt & I arrived at Pyt House.
March 9 Felt too ill to go to the Pt to Pt so stayed in & sent to ask
    Lady Queensberry to come & see me. Walter won the Heavyweight
    Race – much to everyone's joy.
March 25 [In London] Mr Thomas Hardy came to see me.
May 18 I went London by 11.50 train. Took Edith Douglas to
    Suffrage party, was staying with [her mother] Lady Queensberry 18
    Cadogan Place, so kind & loving.
May 21 Went to tea with the Hardys, met Mr Macmillan, Mr
    Hamilton Aidé, Lady Fitzgerald.
May 22 Wyndhams, Pamela [Tennant] [F], Hardys, Mr Boyd came to
    tea. Went to 'For the Crown', saw Mrs Patrick Campbell & Mr
    Forbes Robertson after.
June 4 Went to Board Meeting, rained in torrents, hat spoilt.

June 5   Arrived in London, 18 Cadogan Place, went out with Lady Queensberry driving. Took Edith Douglas in evening to Asquiths' party, met Mr Anthony Hope Hawkins [F], met Hardys.

June 6   Tea party at Lady Queensberry's Mrs Patrick Campbell Pamela Urs[ula] & Alice went in evening to 'Magda' & went behind the scenes.

June 9   My speech day, was very nervous. Went to Council meeting about 11, my speech came on in afternoon. Success!

June 10   Went Council meeting. Had luncheon with the Asquiths.

June 11   Went to tea at the Hardys, met the Henry Normans, Mr Hamilton Aidé, Mr [Hamo] Thornycroft, Mrs Henniker, Lady Fitgerald, Lady Wynford & Mr Lionel Johnson.

June 21   Received *Free Review*. [My] signature wrong.

June 26   Went to Suffrage annual meeting, was elected on the Committee.

June 27   Lord C[rewe] came to see me about 12.

July 6   I went to see Mrs Henniker in morning & then had luncheon with Theresa Verschoyle & returned to Smith Square at the same time as Lord C came to see me. We talked till 4.30 when he went to House of Lords. Walter & I went with Aunt Maude to 'The Sign of the Cross' at the Haymarket. Good.

July 21   Lord C came to see me before luncheon. After luncheon we went to Dorothy Stanley[E] & Mr Allhusen's[E] wedding. Saw Mr Anthony Hope[F], Mr Hardy, G[eorge] Alexander the actor, Grossmith[F] etc & much family.

On July 23 Agnes travelled to Cologne and Bayreuth, meeting Lady Queensberry on the way. They attended two complete performances of the Ring cycle and were guests at a party given by Madame Wagner. Agnes's comments on each opera are full of enthusiasm and delight. They left Bayreuth on August 6 and travelled straight through without incident 'beyond Giovanni the footman being left behind'. A fortnight later they were together again at Hatch when rehearsals began in readiness for Mrs Pat's arrival.

Aug 21   I went Hatch & found Mr Foss & Mr Barker the actors. It rained, so we had our first rehearsal in the house.

June 11. Hamilton Aidé (1830-1906) poet & novelist; Sir William Hamo Thornycroft (1850-1925. Kt 1917) sculptor; Lionel Johnson (1867-1902) published a critical appreciation of Hardy. Henry Norman was assistant-editor, *Daily Chronicle*; his wife wrote under pseudonym of Menie Muriel Dowie.

Aug 23 We rehearsed all the morning.

Aug 27 Mrs Patrick Campbell came and in the evening we had a dress rehearsal.

Aug 28 The play took place in the evening at 9, went off really extremely well. My song was much liked.

Sept 24 I went to luncheon at Hatch House. Went to Tisbury after to the Board of Guardians & then to tea with the Kiplings[F] with Lady Q & the girls.

Sept 26 I sat for Lady Q to model me.

In October the diary began to peter out and was left totally blank in November and December, which is a pity as she was starting to have some success as a writer. In a letter of December 30 to Mrs Henniker Hardy wrote 'Agnes Grove has another article about to appear – did she tell you?' And in an exchange of New Year greetings he congratulated Agnes on her progress, commenting 'You have obtained a firmer hold upon the pen, and are in a fair way of being well known as a writer'.

1897

Army & Navy Octavo Scribbling Diary, interleaved blotting paper, hard back, with a week on opening. In good condition. The page June 3-9 has been cut away with scissors but left in place.

This was a momentous year, starting with the death of Sir Thomas, followed in April by the departure of the last of the Groves from Ferne, and in October by the removal of Agnes and Walter from Berwick St. John to Sedgehill. As a chronicle of these events and their implications her diary is disappointing, partly because the ill-health that seemed to dog her came to a climax in May with some major surgery performed by Sir Frederick Treves. Apart from a period of four weeks shortly after Easter this diary does not really get under way until late July. Following Sir Thomas's funeral on Jan 19 there are no entries at all until April 28, and Treves's operation on May 26 was understandably followed by a long quiet convalescence.

Nevertheless the hard facts of Agnes's life during the first half of this year are that the presumption that she would in due course become the mistress of Ferne House was destroyed; and that, with Sir Thomas gone, Walter was now compelled to act as the master of a sinking ship. To satisfy the estate's creditors his first step was to put Ferne on the market and to look among the Grove possessions for an alternative family-seat of more modest pretensions. Ready to hand was the farmhouse in Sedgehill known as 'East Hayes'[D] since Walter's great-uncle George Grove retired from his seafaring life and developed the Sedgehill farm in the eighteen twenties. For George and his wife, who were childless, the house was large enough. Now, with four growing children, Walter planned to spend the winter adding five new rooms.

Agnes took very little practical interest in her future home. With returning health in the autumn she was more likely to be found at Hatch with Sybil Queensberry or at Sybil's London residence 18 Cadogan Place. This was the address Agnes gave with her order for next year's diary. Through the unsettling events of 1897 she seems to have turned to Sybil for stability.

By December she had adopted the fashionable practice of wintering on the French Riviera, where the children joined her.

Jan 15 Had telegram telling us of Sir Thomas's death [at Clewer]. I drove Walter to the station & then went up & broke the news to Charlotte. Spent the day with her.

Jan 19 The funeral took place at 2.30. Great many people there. Willy Bruce stayed at Ferne. Walt & I still staying there.

April 28 S.Q [Sybil Queensberry] came to tea. Great pleasure to see her again.

April 30 S.Q came to spend the afternoon.

May 3 Went to Hatch with Gerald to stay for a week.

May 4 Honor rode over in the morning & brought the letters. S & I went for drive.

May 5 Children came over to tea, also Walter. S. wrote to Mr S[t]anford [headmaster] at Rottingdean asking him to take Gerald.

May 11 Drove to East Hayes.

May 12 Left Hatch, arrived London.

May 13 Went to Conference of Poor Law at Adelphi. Dined with Aunt Maude.

May 15 Walt & I took darling Gerald to Rottingdean, to Mr Stanford's school.

May 18 Went to W.L.F. Council Meeting. I spoke. Letter from Mr Stanford objecting to my religious views.

May 20 Afternoon meeting of Practical Suffragists.

May 21 I went to Committee Meeting of W.L.F. came home about 1, felt very ill & was soon in agonies. [Doctor] MacClagan injected morphia.

May 22 MacClagan came in morning and a nurse. SQ came to see me & Alice. Dr MacClagan said an operation was imperative.

May 26 On this day I was tried for my life & acquitted. The 2nd nurse arrived in the morning. Mr Treves arrived at 2 o'clock. They

anaesthetised me in the drawing room and I recovered
consciousness at about 3.30. Inconceivable agony I suffered till 9
then MacClagan came & injected morphia.

May 27 I was suffering great pain all day. Treves came & MacClagan.

May 29 Still pain & discomfort. MacClagan & Treves came, latter
dressed wounds.

May 31 Sibyl Q came to see me. Great delight. Alice later.

June 2 From this time on people came to see me every day. Dear Aunt
Maude came nearly every day. Lord Crewe came [and many others
named] but not least dear Sybil and Edith Douglas who came often,
also dear Alice whenever she was in London, she was so helpful and
kind.

July 3 Went for my 1st drive.

July 4 Went in park in bath chair with Walter.

July 22 Sir Charles Tupper, Lord Crewe, Sibyl & St George came to
luncheon. I had tea Cadogan Pl.

July 24 To Clewer to see Charlotte, found her fairly well.

July 25 Walter & I had luncheon with Mrs Henniker at the Close,
Eton.

July 26 Left Clewer, said Goodbye to dear old Charlotte & travelled
to London with Mrs. Henniker.

Aug 7 I came home.

Aug 12 Mrs Patrick Campbell brought her two children to tea.

Aug 17 I took Honor & Gerald to Maperton to stay with Frances.
Olivia & Miss Bond [governess] there. Nice house & pretty garden
& surroundings about 4 miles from Templecombe & Wincanton
which is the post town. Olivia's birthday but we arrived too late for
tea.

Aug 18 Herbert drove over in the afternoon. Walter arrived in the
evening.

Aug 21 Walter left Maperton early, went home & then to London on
his way to Dublin for the Horse Show.

Aug 25 Frances drove me to Sherborne to see the Crosses' nice little
house.

May 18. Agnes had published her rejection of the religion in which she was brought
up in favour of the teachings 'of such modern thinkers as Mill, Spencer, Huxley, Kant
and Fichte'.

July 26. At this point Charlotte departs with no further mention for many years. She
probably joined her younger brother Tom in Lower California, where she was known
to be in 1899.

Aug 29 Walter & I went to Ferne in the pony cart. House empty and examined the windows etc.

Oct 11 Walter's sale at Ferne [of his father's farming stock and equipment]. Fine day luckily.

Oct 17 Sibyl drove over & fetched Oenone & Terence who left Berwick for good.

Oct 20 I went to Hatch House and LEFT BERWICK for good.

Oct 30 [From Hatch] Went to Luncheon Sedgehill. Walter very comfortable [there].

Nov 18 Went to Sedgehill.

Nov 20 Walter & I went to Pyt House.

Nov 22 I came to London.

Nov 24 Went to luncheon party Garrick Club with Mrs P.C. then saw Hamlet again.

Nov 28 to Dec 11 Blank.

Dec 18 I left London with my maid at 11. Perfectly smooth passage. Letter from Mr L. de Rothschild secured me great attention at Calais.

Dec 19 Arrived Mentone about 4. Beautiful scenery after Cannes.

Dec 20 Went to call on English Vice Consul about villas. Went in search of one.

Dec 21 Think of taking Villa St Vincent, most attractive little place, house very small but we can just squeeze in.

Dec 22 Took possession of Villa St Vincent after having had drains examined by local architect.

Dec 23 Prepared rooms for children & got everything ready.

Dec 24 I went to the station to meet the children.

Dec 25 Christmas Day. Children delighted with everything. All went out. Shops all open.

1898

For this year Agnes chose a hard back diary published by the well-known London drapery store Peter Robinson Ltd. The front cover bears the initials AGG.

Wintering in the mild Mediterranean climate was not so advantageous to the family's health as Agnes might have wished. A succession of ailments afflicted the children or herself and she was too ill to return with them on April 25.

Sybil Queensberry arrived at Mentone in early February, stayed for a week before moving on to Monte Carlo and spent a month there. No news from England of Walter is recorded. He arrived in late March and went with Agnes almost daily into Monte Carlo to visit the casino, where they won or lost a few louis.

Returning to England Agnes concentrated on the events of the London season. In the autumn there was a visit to Lord Crewe at Fryston. Her diary indicates no interest in her new home East Hayes, later re-named Sedgehill Manor, and she seems to have spent very little time there, preferring Hatch or Rushmore when not in London.

Jan 10 Went into the town to Book Club. Walked about & bicycled. Honor still feverish.

Jan 12 Letter from S.Q. rather depressing.

Jan 19 Went at 9 to the Palais de Justice & fought over the price of bicycle & won my case!

Feb 4 Went to station & met Sibyl & Edith, went with former to Belle Vue.

Feb 11 S[ybil] & Edith left Belle Vue & went to stay at Monte Carlo.

Feb 12 [I] went to Monte Carlo, played & won about £5. S. persuaded me to stay the night at M.C.

March 2 Did a good day's writing till 3.

March 21 Walt arrived.

March 23 I took Walt to the Hanburys' garden [La Mortola].

April 14 Walt & I went with the Tighs[?] to Monte C had luncheon & I went into rooms for one minute & won 3 louis. Then we all went on to Nice & Walter went on. I went back to Monte Carlo, dined there & I won 6 louis.

April 25 Too ill to leave Mentone so decided to send children with Fraulein.

May 1 Walter arrived.

May 14 Left Mentone about 2, arrived Marseilles very tired about 8.

May 15 Kept quiet all day. Walter ran about.

May 21 Arrived Plymouth. Heard of the death of the Greatest Man [Gladstone].

May 26 Walt & I left London with Kirk, housemaid I engaged to wait on me. Arrived Rushmore found Oenone & Terence well.

June 17 Went to cotillon at 18 Cad. Pl. very successful & pleasant.

June 18 Took Oenone & Terence to stay with Frank Russell[E] at Amberley Castle. Aunt Maude staying there.

June 27 Flo Henniker, Duke of Abercorn & Mr Walker came to Rheingold in box lent me by the [?] Carries. Walter took [his Hussey cousin] Grace Heathcote who dined with us.

June 29 Went to the opera Walkure.

June 30 Went to 'Siegfried', rushed home to dress, went after the opera to supper at the Savoy with Mrs P. Campbell, Sarah Bernhardt, the Trees, Forbes R, Mrs Schuster, Mr G[eorge] Wyndham. Sarah B delightful.

July 1 St George & I drove to opera, then had dinner between the acts at the Holborn Restaurant. Walter took the children to the Aquarium [theatre].

July 27 Mr Alfred Austin, Mrs Craigie [F], Mr Peel[F] lunched. I went to 1st meeting of Nat[ional] Anti Viv[isection] Soc[iety] then went with Lady Wynford to Mr Savage Landor, then to Sesame Club dined alone & went to the Asquiths' party.

Aug 3 Walter & I went to Southampton to join the Fletchers on their yacht.

Aug 5 [At Cowes] We went on board the Royal yacht.

Aug 27 I went to Eton to stay with the Hennikers in a house they had taken in the Close.

Sept 12 [At Rushmore] Lubbocks arrived with Harold [their son][E]. I went to Sedgehill with Honor, 1st taking Mr Peel to Wardour.

Sept 14 Larmer Tree fete. Lubbock & Scott children danced & played. We dined there & danced after.

Sept 20 [at Salisbury] Went one o'clock to Sedgehill. Train punctual so we missed the 12. Left Sedgehill by the 5 train arrived Cadogan Place & found letters from Sybil & Edith announcing latter's engagement to St. G.

Sept 21 Left Kings X for Fryston having had telegram from Lord C[rewe] saying he was all alone. Found him very well. No children.

Sept 22 We walked & talked all day with Lord Crewe.

Sept 29 [At Cadogan Place] Mrs Patrick Campbell came to luncheon. At 5 Sybil & I left London for Hatch.

Sept 30 Walter came to tea.

Oct 1 I went over to Sedgehill.

Oct 4 Lionel came to luncheon & announced his engagement to Nesta Blackett. I drove him to Sedgehill after.

Oct 22 I left Hatch & came to stay Sedgehill.

General Augustus Pitt-Rivers: the father of modern British archaeology – and of Agnes.

Agnes Grove: a pencil sketch by an unknown artist.

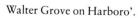
Walter Grove on Harboro'.

Agnes Grove in Court dress: she attended
several of Queen Victoria's 'Drawing-Rooms'.

Sedgehill Manor: the Wiltshire home of Agnes and Walter Grove from 1897.

Sedgehill Manor, the Hall: the copy of the Romney portrait of Aunt Chafin, commissioned by Sir Thomas when he sold the original, is just visible on the right-hand wall.

Kate Grove: Sir Thomas's daughter (1861-1945) m. in 1885 Edmund Mansel-Pleydell.

Sir Thomas Grove with Olivia, the only child of his second marriage.

From left to right: Walter Grove, Charlotte Grove, Alex Pitt-Rivers, Sir Thomas Grove.

Agnes Grove with her younger daughter Oenone.

Honor Grove: Agnes's eldest daughter, who in *1911* married Colonel Nikolas Golejewski.

Left The Larmer Tree Grounds, Tollard Royal, where in 1895 Agnes Grove and Thomas Hardy first met, and danced together.

Below left A proof page of *The Social Fetich*: Thomas Hardy wrote his corrections and suggestions in the margins. The book was dedicated to him by his 'good little pupil'.

Below Agnes Grove in 1906, when she was writing *The Social Fetich*.

Bottom Thomas Hardy: an etching 'from the life' by W. Strang (1893).

SOCIAL SOLECISMS

Miss Cholmondeley objects, if my memory is correct, to "pillow-shams" and "bed-spreads." Upon my word I have never heard of either; but I have heard, and I confess it, *seen* nightgown-cases. The people who use them will, if I may be pardoned for mentioning so intimate a portion of a lady's toilette, substitute the French "chemise" for the homely English "shift," call that portion of the outer garment that covers the body a "bodice," talk about a "dress" when they mean "gown," and being "gowned" when they mean "dressed," and at meals make use of an unnecessary "serviette" instead of an honest napkin. They would also no doubt "ride" in a "trap," a carriage, a train, or a cab. And if the latter were a hansom and one of these were its sole occupant, he or she would possibly betray him or herself by sitting in the middle (or, as they would say, "the centre") of the seat.

You may be sure that their ladies will call upon you with their card-cases held

13

above Lady Lubbock: Agnes's sister Alice
(1862-1947) married 1884 Sir John Lubbock (later
Lord Avebury).

above right Mrs Thurber: Danish wife of
Francis B. Thurber, a prominent figure in the
commercial and social life of New York, formed a
friendship with Agnes and Walter Grove on their
honeymoon visit to America.

right 'Sybil Q': Sybil, Marchioness of
Queensberry.

On Tom Grove's ranch, Matajanal: Walter Grove, Charlotte and her husband, Gilbert Davis, and Tom Grove (far right).

Ensenada: focal point of the new Grove settlement in Baja California, Mexico.

Early in November Agnes was in London for committee meetings of her Liberal and Suffrage interests. Her diary entries became increasingly slight and ceased in early December.

1899

Agnes's attitude to her diary now shows a marked change. She has always seemed to be honouring a tacit obligation to give each day some narrative of events, with only occasional lapses for short periods due to illness or some other passing handicap. Her choice of diary for this year is a little volume of the 'pocket' variety which is more suited to brief notes of engagements and is treated generally in an off-hand manner.

The first entry is not made until Feb 17 and is of a single sentence followed by six blank days. From mid-March to early August is virtually blank and so are the autumn months, September to November. Altogether it provides a very inadequate account of Agnes's year.

Fortunately another diary for this year has survived to fill one important gap. This is a small 'Pacific Coast Diary' used by Walter during a visit to California in the early part of the year. His purpose was evidently to see his younger brother Tom who was farming at Ensenada.[H] A subsequent letter from Tom refers to this visit and indicates that Walter was accompanied by their sister Charlotte. No date is given for their arrival in California but Walter recorded on March 21 'Leave Ensenada' and on the next day 'leave San Diego'. He travelled via Chicago to New York, sailed on March 28 and arrived at Southampton April 3. Subsequently there are very few entries, limited to engagements. He notes 'AGG St James Hall' on May 9 which corresponds with Agnes's entry on that day. Next day he writes 'AGG D-Room' – presumably a royal Drawing room – which Agnes's diary neither confirms nor denies, being left blank.

Feb 17 Went to London 9.40 Cadogan Place.
Feb 24 Went to stay at Sherborne [with Herbert and Avis Crosse], went to Sedgehill on way, found children well.
May 9 Meeting at St James's Hall on Anti-Vivisect. I spoke.
Aug 12 Walt & Ger[ald] went to Berwick riding.
Aug 13 I read to the children.
Aug 19 Frances & Olivia came to stay with us.
Aug 20 I drove Frances to Bests, Ferne, Chapmans & to see Robert.
Aug 23 I drove Frances to Hambros & Gordons.[B]
Aug 24 Frances & Olivia went to Sherborne to their new house, The Beeches.

Aug 25 Gerald & I drove over to Rushmore to see P[apa] who is very
   ill. Found him little better but at loggerheads with the nurse.

Aug 26 Sibyl came to stay with us.

Aug 29 I drove Sibyl over to Maiden Bradley where she stays. Duke
   Duchess showed me garden, stables.

Aug 30 Went to Salisbury with Honor to meeting of Soc. Protection of
   Children.

Sept 2 I sent off my article to Sir A. West.

Dec 17 Went London 46 Eaton Place. John Waldegrave dined with
   me.

Dec 19 Lunched Alex Thynne dined Ridleys I.G. [presumed to be
   Ivor Guest] came home with me.

Dec 25 Went for a walk with St. G.

1900

Collins Portable Diary, French morocco, limp, signed 'Agnes Grove,
Sedgehill'. There are blank sections – after July 8 continuing through most of
August, and from October 21 to November 9 – but her entries are generally
more informative than in the previous year. She had fresh plans for her older
children: Honor, now sixteen, was to go to Cheltenham Ladies College while
Gerald, thirteen, would move to a fresh school for preparation to enter the
Royal Navy. Agnes's visits to London concentrate more narrowly on political
activities, less on socialising. The friendships with Mrs Patrick Campbell &
Sybil Queensberry continue though the latter's association with Hatch seems
to have lapsed or been terminated. It is not mentioned. In March Sybil was
staying at Smedmore House in the Isle of Purbeck.

The relationship with Thomas Hardy switched from London to Dorchester where she twice visited him at Max Gate. Her feminist views made
her a welcome guest to Hardy's wife who was an avowed suffragette. In the
autumn Agnes attended an international congress in Paris on women's rights,
for which she prepared a paper, later incorporated in her book *The Human
Woman*.

The year ended with a decision to spend the winter months in Morocco
with Walter's sister Kathleen & her husband Eddy Pleydell. In the general
bustle and activity of their arrival at Tangier the diary was neglected.

Jan 29 [In London] Left Browns Hotel went to 143 Sloane St & stayed
   night with Sibyl Q.

Feb 1 Arrived Dorchester. Went for walk with Ivor Guest who dined at Captain Foster's where Walter & I stayed.

Feb 2 I drove with Ivor Guest to Mr Hardy & had luncheon with I.G.
Heard of death of Lord Queensberry. Wrote to S[ybil].

March 15 Had luncheon Peels, left London 3 arrived Dorchester 6.30.
Mrs Hardy met me at station, pleasant dinner & long talk after with
Hardy.

March 16 Arrived Smedmore, found Sibyl & Douglas children, fine
little boys.

March 24 Received Cornhill [Magazine] with my article in ['On
Fads'].

May 4 Had a telegram first thing from Lionel saying poor Papa died
quite peacefully at 1.45 this morning. I drove over to Rushmore &
saw him. He looked quite beautiful.

May 22 Walter & I went to Salisbury to S.W. Lib Assn, selected Mr
White as candidate & he declared in favour of W[omen's]
S[uffrage].

May 23 I went to London, stayed 24 Clerida [?] Place. Lunched &
dined Cad. Pl.

May 29 Went play Mrs Campbell 1st performance of 'Fantasticks'.
Guest boy called.

June 2 [at Sedgehill] S.Q. came to stay.

June 14 [In London] Drove with Sibyl. Went to Westminster Abbey,
heard Clara Butt.

June 25 Gentle quiet uneventful week. I did several drawings of
myself.

Sept 7 [In Paris] Went to Congress [Congrès International de la
Condition et des Droits des Femmes] Could not get anything
definite about my paper out of Mme Durand.

Sept 8 Went to Congress. Had my paper ready but did not read it.
However, made short speech in French.

Oct 19 Gardener Brockway dismissed.

Dec 11 [Arriving at Tangier] Landed about 9. Kathleen with her
children met us. We came to New York Hotel. I arranged my sitting
room quite nicely. Walter went off with Kathleen to the Pigsticking.
[The hunting of the wild boar with a spear. OED]

Dec 25 Christmas Day. K & I went to church.

1901

Collins' Portable diary, as previous year but not signed. Starting the year in Morocco, as a refuge from the British winter, Agnes was intending to follow the conventional course by returning to London for the Season, more particularly to present Honor as a *débutante* at Court. The death of Queen Victoria in January and the national mourning which followed meant – as Agnes wrote later – that 'the daughter for whose sake we would have returned home made her first functional curtsey in the presence of Royalty to the Sultan of Morocco, instead of to the Queen of England'. The Grove family therefore remained with the Pleydells throughout the year though Walter and Agnes made visits to England to attend to practical matters, not the least being the future of Ferne. Following Sir Thomas's death the house had been let, with sporting rights, to a member of the Cabinet, Lord James of Hereford, for a tenancy which was now expiring. Walter's visit in March was probably connected with the decision to offer for sale by public auction in July, when he and Agnes both returned. Presumably the reserve price was not reached as the house was then let for the winter's shooting to a London merchant, Mr Schwann.

Life in Morocco was rich in contrasts. Tangier offered an extension of orthodox social life within the British community, observing the rituals of parties for tea, luncheon and dinner, lavish balls in fancy dress, calls to leave visiting-cards and playing polo. The hunting and shooting expeditions that ventured into the wilder areas had to face hardships at times and needed the practised military leadership of someone like Eddy Pleydell, drawing on his experience in India, to set up and move camp, organise supplies and equipment on pack-mules etc. Their wanderings took them into the Atlas mountains and as far from Tangier as Marrakesh and Mogador.

Jan 19 Heard the Queen was ill. Went round leaving cards with
    Kathleen. All went to dull dance at Hotel Cecil.
Jan 23 Heard of Queen's death. Went to British Legation.
Feb 25 Walt & I went to Hamara camping for the Pig-sticking week.
Feb 26 Went out, found nothing.
Feb 27 Went out pig-sticking early, found nothing.
March 6 Dined at Brit[ish] Leg[ation]. Went in with Cunningham
    Graham.[F]

March 6. In 1898 Cunninghame Graham had published *Mogreb-el-Acksa: a journey in Morocco*.

March 11 Walter left for England.

March 20 Went for ride with Pleydells met 2 Miss Oakleys who showed us the Sewell's house in the mountains which fascinated me so I decided to take it.

March 21 Telegraphed to Sewell offering £5 a month for his house.

March 22 Mr Cameron brought answer to telegram "accept" so I rode up to the house & made arrangements.

March 26 Went to meet Walter by 2.30 boat, then took him to Sewell house. Walter very much pleased.

March 28 Went out pig-sticking at Sidi Cassim [?] rode with Mr Russell part of the time & found him pleasant.

April 1 Saw Mr C[laud] Russell[E] off quite sad.

April 25 Walter went into the town early to try & buy mules.

June 5 Went out mouflon hunting, of course saw nothing.

June 26 Wrote all the morning. Looked at Mogador from high roof.

June 28 Wrote assiduously all day long.

That was her last entry in the diary until October when her visit to England, begun in July, was coming to an end. In the final days before sailing she looked in at Sedgehill, visited Frances, collected a new governess for Terence and heard that her book on camping in Morocco had been accepted for publication by Longmans.

Oct 29 Arrived Gibraltar early. Sir George White came on board to take us off.

Nov 1 We left Gibraltar in Torpedo-Destroyer Ariel. Arrived Tangier about 12. Came straight up to Ravens Rock. Walter away pigsticking.

Nov 21 Went with Walt luncheon Pleydells. Walt then played polo, very well. E.P. rode home with me. I rode his horse the Kaid, beautiful horse. Corrected proofs.

1902

Again a Collins Portable Diary. A memo page at the end itemises incidental expenditure in Germany. The final blank page has been used to copy out passages from Emerson, Ruskin, Goethe etc.

This second winter in Morocco was spent in much the same way as the first. Boar hunts, fancy dress balls, polo matches and children's parties made up the social calendar, from which Agnes reserved her private time to devote to her writing. Walter teamed up with Meade Waldo, who was collecting specimens of rare birds, of which the skins were wanted by the British Museum. With a third man serving as interpreter and taxidermist they sailed to Casablanca to hunt in the Forest of Marmora. On his return Walter decided to go back to England for a fresh attempt to sell Ferne, and now a buyer was found, Colonel Albany Charlesworth.

By a tragic coincidence at this moment their youngest child was lost in a drowning accident. They left Morocco immediately and never returned. In her grief Agnes wrote and published privately a haunting allegory in which Terence became a sort of Peter Pan figure. She had a large mural of Terence and herself, based on a photograph, painted on the chimney-breast above the fireplace of the drawing-room at Sedgehill. Her diary paid little attention to the outward circumstances of life in England during the summer. In the autumn she travelled with Walter to a German spa where Sybil Queensberry joined them.

Feb 17 Walt & I took Miss Dixon[G] [governess] down to the Tia's to see about rooms. On her return she found all her money had been stolen, £9.

Feb 18 We all went down to see the Eng[lish] Consul & told him to arrest Abder Rhamena who had been in our employ and was suspected.

Feb 20 No one came to tea although I sat at home.

March 21 Went down to the pier to see Walter off with Mr Meade Waldo to Casablanca.

April 9 Hunted cork woods. Killed 2 pigs. I stuck the 1st pig several times.

May 1 Walt decided to go to England.

May 7 Wrote hard all day & sent off article to 'Cornhill'.

May 8 Got letters, 2 reviews, 1 good in Field, 1 Athenaeum partly irritating, which I answered [Her first book, *Seventy-one Days Camping in Morocco*, had just been published].

May 14 Telegram came from Walter saying Ferne all sold, which

May 15 was only given me on the morning of this awful day. The children all came to me & then I sent them away & told Gerald to order my horse. He forgot. I called him up from the garden where I heard my blessed's laugh. Gerald went up to the stable & Oenone too, it appears, though I did not see her. Then I went off about 12 to luncheon with the [?] Bacharapts [Russian minister] & while there they telephoned for me to say he had had a fatal accident. I galloped up & found the light of my life had been drowned [in a garden pool] and had died.

May 16   They buried my beautiful baby in the cemetery. I went down in the evening to Kathleen who has been so kind & considerate as has everyone else.

May 19   Left for Gibraltar with Kathleen, Gerald & Oenone.

May 20   Walter arrived.

June Arrived in England, came to Sedgehill. Great pain.

July 16   I wrote letters, one cruel one. Played croquet after tea with children.

July 24   I drove to Gillingham to look for a Catholic church in which I was unsuccessful.

July 31   Gerald went to sale at Ferne.

Aug 23   Left Sedgehill with Walt & went via Flushing to Cologne.

Aug 24   Arrived Schlangenbad, found Sibyl & Edith here.

Aug 30   Walt left for England.

Sept 7   Went to Catholic church in morning.

At this point the diary falters and, apart from a brief spell during November, is almost entirely blank.

1903

A change from the Collins Portable diary to the smaller Walker's Diary, containing the minimum of general information. Memoranda pages list several book titles that Agnes chose to note including *The Children's Book of London* and *Journalism as a Profession* – indicators of the direction in which her thoughts were turning.

This year brought her fortieth birthday. It began quietly at Sedgehill in the familiar activities of family life, riding to hounds with Walter and Oenone, taking Gerald to the Salisbury dentist, visiting locally and receiving visitors. What is conspicuously lacking is the stimulating vitality that filled the great houses of the previous decade. Charlotte, Kathleen and Tom Grove are no longer at Ferne. Agnes's mother left Rushmore when the General died, and its inheritor, Alex, had no urgent desire to leave his beautiful manor-house at Hinton St. Mary. He let Rushmore to a disagreeable tenant and was having difficulty in regaining possession. It was Frances and Herbert at Sherborne who became Agnes's link with the earlier years. Thomas Hardy and Emma were twice expected to visit Sedgehill but were prevented by Hardy's minor ailments.

Away from Sedgehill Agnes followed her special interests in London, and a springtime visit to Norwich produced one of those sudden impromptu flirtations to which she was temperamentally subject – this time with Ivor Guest's younger brother Henry [F]. After this episode the diary was left blank from June 9 to September 6, with a brief revival in November and a blank December. With Walter and the children she ended the year in Paris.

Feb 11　Walt, I & Oenone went out hunting. I rode the little mare.

Feb 14　Heard that Lionel had gone to London to begin his 'cure'.

Feb 16　Frances & I went to Sherborne to see The Red House – house she has taken.

March 9　Sibyl & I went to Sherborne to the opening by Lord Londonderry of the new Sherborne School for girls to which we have decided to send Oenone.

April 22　Went to London alone. Went on to Norwich, arrived at Freethorpe to stay with Corin Rodney.

April 23　We all went out in motor after luncheon. Capt. H. Fraser came.

April 25　Capt. Guest arrived. I liked him at once. Had embroglio with Capt. Fraser.

April 27　Drove to Haviland [?] with Captain Guest & played chess (?) with him in the evening. Was almost happy.

April 28　Left Freethorpe with Capt Guest & Mr Grosvenor, had breakfast in train & arrived Hotel Metropole. Met Walter there. We dined with Ridleys & went to The Marriage of Kitty. Then Capt Guest came to supper with us.

April 29　Went to Zoo with Captain Guest. He & W. Peel had luncheon.

April 30　Capt Guest called in morning. I bought him my book, then returned home & found Gerald in bed with mumps.

May 2　Arrangements had been made for Mr Grosvenor & Capt Guest to come here & have a golf match but owing to letters Gerald's illness Mr Grosvenor never turned up.

May 3　Gerald seemed much worse, his temperature very high.

May 6　Capt Guest arrived in his motor. He had luncheon. A servant arrived later with Mr Grosvenor's luggage.

May 7　I drove after luncheon to Canford[H] with C.G. [Captain Guest] Had tea there & returned.

May 9　Drove in motor with C.G. to Wardour & then into Tisbury.

May 11　Arrived London with Honor, went to Smith Square [Aunt Maude].

May 16　Luncheon at Sesame with W. Peel. Telephoned to Guest who came about 6 to see me.

May 17 After luncheon I went to Windsor, motored with Capt Guest, dined with him, returned home about 10.30.

Next day Agnes went back to Sedgehill and her diary became blank. There is no further mention of Captain Guest, nor indeed of anything much else except an interview with the editor of *New Review* who offered her 10 guineas a month for a regular contribution.

1904

A John Walker's diary of the same format as the previous year's. Signed 'Agnes Grove'. The diary commences in Paris, with family sightseeing and shopping. On their return to London Walter and Agnes, who was pregnant, had evidently decided not to go back to Sedgehill. They began looking for a suitable London house to rent and chose 51 Bedford Square. Before they moved in, however, Agnes gave birth to a son, Walter Peel Grove, at Kensington.

The choice of the name Peel for the baby is not easily explained. It was not a family name. Its association is with a friend of Agnes's, Willy Peel, who re-appeared in the previous year as a rival to Captain Guest – though at a more leisurely tempo. He is identified as William Robert Wellesley Peel (1867-1937) succeeded as Viscount 1912 and Earl Peel 1929. He married in 1899. The presumption that he was a godfather to the infant Walter Peel is false. The godfathers were Agnes's brother Lionel and a Dutch friend from their Moroccan days, Major van Heemstra [E], who later married Walter's niece, Florence Foster [E]. What is certain is that Willy Peel continued to be an important element in Agnes's life, vying with the diplomat she had first met in Morocco, Claud Russell, whose departure from Tangier had left her 'quite sad'.

Jan 2 Went to Bon Marché with Honor.

Jan 4 Went with Honor & Oenone to Mag[asin] Louvre. Bought Honor a hideous gown through fatigue.

Jan 5 Walt took Honor & Gerald to Versailles.

Jan 7 Walt & Honor left for England. The children made a regular day of it, sight-seeing.

Jan 12 Walter turned up.

Jan 26 Left Paris in the evening after having been about all day at furniture shops.

Jan 27 Arrived London. Parted with dear children at Southampton.

Went to Hurst Lea to see Mama.

Feb 1 [In London] Went to play with Willy Peel & Walt Joseph entangled. W. Peel came to tea. Went Bedford Square.

Feb 2 Walter went Sedgehill for day. We left Brown's hotel. Arrived 35 Courtfield Road [Kensington]

Feb 21 Went in morning to see Sybil & after luncheon to see her house.

Feb 25 Walt & I went Bedford Estate Office. Party in evening – Dinner & Music Uncle Alg[ernon][E] Mrs Craigie Duke of Abercorn Mr [Hilaire] Belloc.

March 14 May Morrison sent her carriage for me & we went to Bedford Square.

March 21 W. Peel came to tea. Suddenly Walter returned with dear Heemstra! – great rejoicing.

March 22 Drove Heemstra afternoon in Alice's carriage, took him to Bedford Square & to see Sibyl Q.

March 30 At 4 my sweet little baby Walter was born. Thanks be to God from whom all Blessings flow. Peaceful quiet day.

April 26 Willy Peel came to tea.

April 29 My babe was christened at Westminster Abbey <u>Walter</u> <u>Peel</u>. Salten Heemstra & Lionel godfathers, Sibyl Queensberry & Honor godmothers.

May 14 Eve of the anniversary of my best beloved little angel boy. Death or New Birth. My blessed baby Terence my ever beloved & ever mourned.

At that point the diary halted and remained blank until July 8. In late May and June Agnes would have been engaged in the handover of Sedgehill Manor to Lady Grant, the incoming tenant on a four year lease, later extended to July 1909. Perhaps Charlotte's marriage took place at this time, an event not recorded by Agnes. In July a ball at Buckingham Palace and the attentions of W.P. and C.R. restored some vitality to the diary.

July 8 W.P. & Claud Russell dined & W.P. took me to Buckingham Palace ball.

July 9 Claud Russell came to tea.

July 25 My birthday, lots of people. W. Peel & Claud Russell came later.

July 29 St. G came to luncheon, C.R. came to tea & he & Conrad R[ussell][E] dined & St G & we all went to the Palace.

Aug 6 Walt & I started in motor at about 10.30 via Basingstoke &

Andover. Between Andover & Salisbury, near Winterslow, oil ran
out & we were taken after waiting 3 hours into Salisbury by a hired
motor. Left Salisbury after dinner intending to go Shaftesbury
reached Tisbury 12.30 where we stayed the night.

The rest of August was uneventful, with a few days of family holiday at
Clacton-on-Sea, and the diary was abandoned after the first week of September.
However a letter from Conrad Russell [E], Claud's brother, writing from
the Colonial Office to Flora Russell, gives a lively impression of Agnes in
December, installed in her London *salon* at Bedford Square -

Gilbert [Russell][E] and I dined at the Grove's on Sunday [Dec 18] where I
met Miss Clemmy Hozier [E] for the first time – she is very beautiful and nice
too. There was the usual stormy debate of the sexes, which goes on in that
house. It is tedious and makes real conversation impossible. However it is
great fun for a bit.

1905

Collins' Gentleman's Diary, No. 25: long grained roan, gusset and card pockets
back and front, gilt edges, one day to a page.

Their new style of life was now settling down to its first full year at 51
Bedford Square, exchanging country life and the horse for the London scene
and the motorcar. The effect on Walter must have been severe. He could no
longer shoot and hunt except by the invitation of friends, and he had no
reciprocal opportunities to offer them. There is no mention now of the grouse
moors of Scotland, the pheasant coverts of Severnake Forest or the rooks and
rabbits of Ferne; and no riding to hounds or point-to-point races. He had no
positive part to play in Agnes's literary and political activities. The diary gives
scarcely a hint of how he passed his days in London.

Agnes apparently devoted less time to Liberal and suffrage committees, or
no longer chose to mention them. She was enjoying her success as an essayist
and commentator on social topics, and began to attract literary celebrities to
her dinner-parties. Another new address on the social map was 99 Kensington
Church Street, to which Sybil Queensberry had moved. Following the death
of Sybil's ex-husband there was a new Marchioness of Queensberry.

After the long stay – almost exile – in Morocco there were old friendships
to mend. Hardy is not mentioned in this year's diary but the relationship was
only temporarily suspended. During the months of May and June when the
Hardys resumed their customary seasonal residence in London Agnes's diary
was left blank.

The attentions of Willy Peel and Claud Russell continued unabated, with
W.P. visiting Agnes for tea or dinner on six days out of a consecutive seven in

March. C.R.'s posting to Paris might account for her decision to break her journey there on her way back from Bordeaux after a holiday on the Franco-Spanish border with Walter.

Jan 2 Walt went by train to Sedgehill to arrange something. Heard from Sibyl. Claud R. came to tea. I took Gerald & Honor to Peter Pan.

Jan 5 C.R. left London for Paris.

Jan 12 Theresa [Verschoyle] came to luncheon. Afterwards having noticed his condition I gave Atkin the choice of either going through the Oppenheimer treatment or leaving at once. I took him on the box of a 4 wheeler & he began the treatment.

Jan 19 I took Oenone in the morning to Queen's College, listened to a lecture & then went to the White Steam & saw the engine. At luncheon met Mr Raymond Asquith. Then afternoon went lecture Roy[al] So[ciety of] Arts. Came home in a bus.

Jan 21 Went by twopenny tube [London's underground railway] to see Mrs Craigie.

Jan 23 Honor came home. W. Peel came to luncheon.

Feb 2 Went to see Lady Alfred Douglas & brought Lady Sholto [Douglas][F] back to tea. Went in car to Peels to dinner, went to Henry V, went back to supper & they sent me home. Dinner 4 Peels & Lord St. Cyr.

Feb 6 I took Honor to hear Mr Antony Hope lecture on Realism in Fiction & brought him home in the motor.

Feb 13 Went to geographical Soc, too full to get in so we all went to Sesame [Club] & then to Lansdowne House. Then I took W.P. in my motor to the House of Commons.

Feb 15 Mr Percy Wyndham & W. Peel dined here. We took them to St James's Square to a dance. We then drove home & round London in my motor.

March 2 I went to lecture at 3 at the Womens Institute where the [? Cobden] Sandersons "misbehaved" themselves outrageously & then Walt & I went to see Fuchs' exhibition at the Grafton Galleries.

March 10 W.P. dined. Girls went in his motor to King Lear.

March 18 Walter & I left London by the St[eam] Nav[igation] Co. steamer for Bordeaux. My precious Babe went with Russ to Clewer. I took him in my bed about 6.

March 22 Left [Bordeaux] for St. Jean de Luz.

April 4 Went after luncheon to Biarritz. Drove to Mr Hambro's villa.

April 6 I went for a donkey ride. Walter walked with me & we explored the country which is lovely.

April 7 Went to Bordeaux where we stayed the night. I telephoned to Paris.

April 8 I bought a veil in Bordeaux [a rash was again troubling her] & Walter saw me into the train. I arrived at Paris at about 6. Claud R. met me & we dined together at the hotel where I stayed.

April 9 Claud came & fetched me to go to luncheon at Voisin, after that we went to the races, came back, dined at the hotel & then went to a play about Napoleon.

April 12 Had luncheon at the Ritz with Claud & met there Mr J- & Lord Berwick who are both at the Eng[lish] Embassy. Then I finished packing, paid my bill & went to the station. C.R. came to Boulogne with me. Gerald met me at Charing X.

April 13 Found my [illegible] on servants ignored by Honor.

April 28 Lady Queensberry[F] & her 3 children came to tea.

As in the two previous years there is a blank in the May-June period, extending this year from the start of May to the first week of July. There are a few entries in high summer but from September onwards the pages are almost entirely empty.

July 13 Mr G[eorge] Wyndham, Mrs Craigie, Mrs Meynell & Mr Max Beerbohm came to luncheon.

Aug 10 Oenone & I left London at 11 & arrived Wadebridge [Cornwall] at 5 with Annie. Walt & Atkin met us [Atkin having survived the Oppenheimer treatment: see Jan 12 above].

1906

Collins' Gentleman's Diary, as in the previous year. Wintering abroad is now a settled policy, choosing the Bernese Oberland this year, for its winter sports and a climate suited to Agnes's suspected tuberculosis. In a letter to Florence Henniker in February Thomas Hardy indicated that Agnes had gone for treatment of a lung complaint. She was clearly worried about her health, recording her temperature almost daily and complaining of pain and bad nights. A recurring squiggle, sometimes with a number, and mention of the English chemist locally, may indicate a medicament or drug of some kind – possibly morphine. Her brother Alex with his wife and son George[E] were also there for a time. Accompanying Agnes were Walter, Oenone and the infant Walter with nurse Johnson. Walter senior departed on January 20 and his presence is not recorded anywhere until he arrived at the port of Liverpool on May 27. Agnes occupied herself with extensive reading, a little skating and writing letters and articles. Feeling lonely she sent distress signals to Willy Peel and Claud Russell, who responded.

In March she moved to Genoa and Alassio for a couple of months, taking Italian lessons with Oenone and living quietly. Returning to Southampton she sent the children to the Shaftesbury home of her brother Lionel, Cliff House, while she went to Sybil Queensberry and had reunions with her London circle, including Thomas Hardy who was to play an important part in the book she was now completing, *The Social Fetich*. After a few days at Shaftesbury and a week at Folkestone with assorted Peels and Russells she settled into 51 Bedford Square which had been let or lent to Lady Pelly.

To separate husband and son she now uses nicknames – 'Fard' for Sir Walter, 'Beb' for their child.

Jan 1 Left Clewer, arrived Victoria where Walter met us with Oenone & Atkin. Arrived Boulogne about 5.30 & came straight on to Bale where we changed.

Jan 2 Changed again at Bern, Spietz and Frutigen where we had luncheon & came on up in a sleigh to Adelboden.

Jan 16 Balfour defeated, great Lib victories [in General Election].

Jan 19 Snow fell heavily all day. I did not go out. Alex, Ruth & the Horace Wests dined with us. Walt & Oenone went out skiing in the afternoon.

Jan 20 Walter left at 3.50 in the dilligence. Very unhappy & depressed at being left. Temp 99.6.

Jan 23 Telegram from Walt. Willy Peel beaten.

Jan 24 Papers. W.P. minority 416. St. George's polling day at Wimbledon.

Jan 25 Got telegram about 6 saying St George had been badly beaten. Dreadful disappointment.

Feb 1 Went skating with Oenone. Got no one to help me. Letter from Honor & cheque from Westminster [Gazette].

Feb 5 Interminable snow. Cold. Did not go out. Wrote letters. My erythema [rash] appeared.

Feb 6 Rash worse. No sun. German gov[erness] came in morning for Oenone.

Feb 11 Reading Plays Pleasant & Unpleasant [Bernard Shaw]. Posted art[icle] from D.M. [? *Daily Mail* continental edition] about Adelboden to C.R. & W.P.

Feb 17 I went to see Dr Schaer & he told me to stay indoors till my fever went. Dr S said my left lung is affected too.

Feb 20 Telegram from C.R. saying coming as soon as possible.

Feb 22 Dr Schaer came to see me, said my case is one of tuberculosis unmistakably.

March 3 Letter & telegram from W.P. saying he was coming which much cheered me.

March 4 W.P. arrived about 5, seemed very well. I was very glad to see him.

March 8 We all left Adelboden & arrived Bern at the Schweizehof about 6. WP & OE & I went for a drive round the town & then we had dinner & champagne. I was rather tired but not very. Went to bed early.

March 9 W.P. left at 6.30.

March 11 Left Milan for Alassio after Genoa.

March 15 Italian mistress came to give Oenone & me lessons in Italian at 50 lira the month.

March 23 Heard from C.R.

March 25 Expected Gilbert Russell and a party for luncheon, had a telegram at 5 to say they could not get over the frontier.

April 11 Oenone & I went to the station to meet Claud Russell who arrived looking very thin & with a cold.

April 12 C[laud], O[enone] & I went for a drive & then had tea in the Eng[lish] tea garden.

April 13 Walked about & did nothing in particular.

April 14 Telegraphed for Gerald, wrote to him & sent him a cheque.

April 16 Claud left. Oenone went with him to the station. Beb bathed in the sea with only his little jersey on. Telegram from C. saying he had enjoyed visit! [see May 19 below]

April 19 Went out with Oenone into the town, sent O back for something & when she reappeared lo, there was Gerald. Great delight at having the dear boy.

May 4 Left Alassio by 3.30 train, arrived Genoa 6.30.

May 15 Arrived at Southampton, all went to South Western Hotel for the night.

May 16 Gerald & Oenone went to Cliff House [Shaftesbury], I went to London & Church Street, found S.Q very well.

May 18 S[ybil] went out to dinner & I dined alone.

May 19 Claud R came to see me early in the morning & we had an agreeable reconciliation. W. Peel came afterwards. St. G also came in.

May 20 Went to luncheon with Lady Pelly[F] in 51 Bedford Square,
then went back to Church Street in motor.

May 21 S & I went to tea with the Hardys, met several people.

May 22 Went Times Book Club morning. Ruth, Lady Pelly, Mr
Wyndham & Mr Hardy came to tea at Ch[urch] St[reet].

May 23 Left Church St. with Beb for 3.30 train. Found Oenone &
Nesta [Lionel's wife] at Cliff House.

May 25 Nesta & I went to Sedgehill. I went in. Lady Grant [tenant] a
nice woman.

May 26 Heard from Sibyl Q by telegram that Walter had telegraphed
from Liverpool to say he wd be there at 5.

May 27 Walter arrived from London looking very well.

May 29 I went to Lady Wynford's to lunch. She drove me through
Ferne park to look at the house, saw some terrible iron balconies
they had put up for the first floor windows. Also porte cochere.

May 30 Left Cliff House for Folkestone.

May 31 Walter & I & Honor went for a walk & I went in bath chair
to Registry Office.

June 1 W.P. came to tea.

June 2 Claud & Conrad [Russell] came to see me.

June 3 Claud & W.P. came after luncheon. After tea W.P. drove Walt
& Honor in his motor to Canterbury. C & I walked on cliff.

June 4 We went to the sports of the Beds Yeomanry. Talked Col. Lord
A. Compton, Peels, Russells etc, rather fun.

June 7 Walt left by 2 train, we went 5.18. I went to Church St,
children & servants went Bed Sq.

June 8 Left Church St. with S in her motor, went to see Mr Algy Burke
& his Italian things, came straight Bedford Square where motor
refused to go on. S left in 4 wheeler. Miss A[gnes] Tobin came to tea
having given me a surprise visit as she arrived from San Francisco.
Described earthquake to me & was very amusing.

At this point the diary goes blank for several weeks and recaptures Agnes's
attention for little more than a dozen entries in the remainder of the year. She
spent the rest of the summer mainly in London with minor excursions to her
mother at Caterham and to Clewer for the wedding of Florence Foster and
Van Heemstra. She met Thomas Hardy at Lady Burghclere's on June 29 and
is among the guests he listed at his own tea-parties at Hyde Park Mansions. Another of his guests at this time was the French artist Jacques-Emile
Blanche[F] who was painting a portrait of Hardy: in his reminiscences, *Mes
Modèles*, Blanche wrote:

C'est lady Grove qui semblait recevoir, lors de petites tea-parties où nous fûmes convoqués, au flat meublé du cher ménage provincial. Mrs Hardy la laissait minauder avec les plumatifs.

Emma Hardy was finding it increasingly onerous to manage two establishments, in London and Dorchester, so she may have been relieved to let Agnes exercise her skill as a hostess. The association with Hardy was particularly strong at this time as he had accepted Agnes's dedication to him of her forthcoming book and had undertaken to correct the proofs in his meticulous way. She was still a favoured pupil.

In September the Groves *en famille* were at Littlehampton where friends had lent them a house. The last quarter of the year is blank in the diary but Agnes was certainly in London in November when, according to a letter of Conrad Russell's, Eddie Marsh – the patron of the Georgian poets – had 'been to stay two Sundays with Lady Grove'. By the year's end she was established, with Walter & the children, in Spain in the vicinity of Malaga.

1907

A Walker's Diary No 3, of the type she used in 1903 and '04, opening to a one-week spread. As usual the pencil supplied with the diary is lost but it was unfortunately used to write the very faint entries which are now so difficult to read.

As a record of Agnes's year the diary is woefully incomplete. The winter-abroad section occupies the early months up to March 16 in southern Spain, where her artist brother Douglas joined them to do some sketching. There is the familiar chronicle of ailments and an air of debility and boredom in Agnes's account which halts before their return to England. A visit to Alex and Ruth at Hinton St. Mary occupies a few days in May; and in mid-August the family disperses from London, with Agnes going to visit her mother, Oenone to visit her aunt Ursula at Thorpe, and Walter and Gerald intent on yachting at Poole. All the rest is left blank. There is no mention of Willy Peel or Claud Russell, no mention even of Thomas Hardy although *The Social Fetich* was published during the year and he included Agnes and Walter in his list of friends received at Hyde Park Mansions. The friendly response of the critics to her book must have been gratifying to master and pupil alike. The fact that the event is not noticed in the diary indicates the extent to which her keeping of a diary had deteriorated into a spasmodic and superficial habit. It is as likely that she now gave up the habit for several years as that the next sequence – 1908 to 1914 – did exist but has not survived. She was pouring her thoughts and experiences into her published writings.

Jan 1 Shops all shut. We did not go anywhere.

Jan 6 Walter & I & the girls went to a ball at the 'Club'. Honor & Oenone danced. I was bored.

Jan 7 Walter & I went into Malaga. Theresa housemaid came.

March 12 Went for a drive with W, saw Douglas & Taylor sketching. Girls had dancing lesson.

May 17 Went to Hinton [St Mary] with Walter & Oenone.

May 20 Ruth & I went for a drive.

May 21 Dance in the barn, very successful.

May 22 Returned to London.

1908 - 1909

During 1908 Agnes and Walter had to consider the future of Sedgehill Manor, where the tenancy was due to expire, and the cost of maintaining their London residence. Walter had an approved overdraft of £900, secured on deposited bonds: during 1907 it had risen to £2285 and was causing some anxiety to the Shaftesbury bank, if not to Walter. Since his father's death and the disposal of Ferne and Winterslow Walter had sold a pub in Ludwell [H], another in Berwick St. John and some land in Sedgehill – a method of buying time that the diminished Ferne estate could not stand indefinitely. One line of action would be to leave London and retire to Sedgehill. The immediate decision was to extend Lady Grant's tenancy of Sedgehill for a further year.

For Agnes London was certainly the place to be in 1908. The success of *The Social Fetich* prompted editors of periodicals to commission from her the sort of witty, anecdotal yet penetrating comment on social topics that she could contribute so entertainingly. Early in 1908 *The Daily Chronicle* asked for more on the lines of her book. *The Daily Dispatch* followed, suggesting 'a severe criticism of Provincial manners' – a subject 'raised by Mr Pinero's recent play'. Other invitations ranged from the Northern Newspaper Syndicate to *The Lady's Realm*, and she was able to demand five guineas for 1200 words.

There were no Hardy tea-parties in 1908 as Emma did not feel up to housekeeping in London. In August Agnes was staying at Bishops Waltham, south of Winchester, and invited Hardy to visit her there, but he was unable to do so. In the autumn her book *The Human Woman* was published and strengthened her reputation. In the words of a Scottish reviewer 'Lady Grove's latest book will do more than all the antics of the Shrieking Sisterhood to advance the cause of Women's Suffrage among reasonable people'. In November the *Daily Mail* invited her to 'write occasionally for our leader page columns on subjects of interest to women'.

1910 - 1914

By the end of 1909 the decision had been taken to give up 51 Bedford Square and move back to Sedgehill Manor. In April 1910 Mary Arnim[E] wrote in a letter to Agnes 'I wish you still lived in London' and in May Hardy used the words 'If you are coming to Town' in his invitation to the flat he and Emma had taken in Maida Vale until July. When he left London at the end of July he pressed her to motor over to Max Gate on the August Bank Holiday, saying she would be 'a godsend' and could drive from Sedgehill in an hour. Earlier in the year, in April, she had sent him her latest book *On Fads* which he greeted with a judicious blend of commendation and a scolding for the careless way her ideas came 'tumbling out in such a torrent'. In June, writing to her on hearing of her mother's death, he commented on Agnes's healthier appearance since she left the London atmosphere.

There were of course friendly houses in London where she could still participate in social parties and base herself for a visit of several days – her sister Alice, Aunt Maude and Sybil Queensberry suggest themselves at once – but she was no longer the queen of her own *salon* inviting whom she pleased. She had to come to terms with a rural Wiltshire community in which the name of Grove had lost much of its lustre.

Within her family there were important changes. In 1911 Gerald, having found no career prospects in England, joined the British South African Police in Rhodesia. In the same year Honor, now twenty-eight, married 'the military attaché at the Russian embassy in London' Colonel Golejewski[E] who subsequently became Assistant Chief of the Russian Imperial General Staff. It was the kind of fashionable wedding that must have pleased Agnes. 'What a wedding,' Sybil Q wrote, 'with all the Russian Grand Dukes!' It was the epilogue however to the golden Edwardian years when Agnes had enjoyed her celebrity as the beautiful, witty and influential daughter of the Whig aristocracy. After 1910 she published no new book. The outbreak of war in 1914 drew a concluding line. Her day was over.

1915

C. & J. Penny's London Almanack and Diary 6″ x 3″ roan pocket book, seven day spread. Signed 'Agnes Grove'. Entries written in pencil.

The most striking difference from the preceding diary (1907) is the impact of the war, with its mounting lists of casualties. Aimée de Hoghton's son Guy was killed and so was Teddy Pleydell. Agnes's nephew Billy Fox-Pitt was wounded. Rushmore had been converted by Ruth to provide hospital beds for wounded soldiers. Oenone was nursing at Rushmore or at Tisbury Red Cross.

There was little social life. Agnes spent much of her time bicycling or walking, with Oenone as her constant companion. Beb was at boarding-school at East Grinstead, Honor abroad with her Russian husband and their two young daughters, Gerald in Africa. The bicycle had replaced the horse in Agnes's life and was more reliable than the motorcar. Her own motor was sold and Walter's was of a somewhat haphazard nature.

Her poor health was Agnes's constant preoccupation. She installed a Turkish bath, frequently recorded 'very tired, much pain' and made coded entries which probably refer to medicaments. The letters FP and LM appear several times written in ink, in advance of the day's pencilled entry.

Jan 12 Feeling ill and depressed.

Jan 16 General Flint called. I asked him about a commission for Gerald.

Jan 17 Sunday. Took Beb to church.

Jan 19 St. G took Beb back to school.

Jan 24 Oenone & I bicycled to Semley & got a paper. I did not smoke after 10.00 a.m. Throat still sore.

Jan 27 Oenone went to London to stay with Mrs Matthews[F] at Windsor Hotel, Vic[toria] St. 2 people came to see house.

Feb 5 Went motor afternoon intending to go to Shaftesbury but it would not go up the hill.

Feb 28 Went out in wood with F[ard] & OE & marked trees for felling.

March 2 My Turkish bath came.

March 18 Heard of poor Teddy Pleydell[E] being killed in the war.

March 20 Fard went to stay with poor Kathleen [Pleydell] who sent motor for him.

April 11 Oenone & Beb went church. Fard & I motored Knoyle. Wheel came off.

May 5 Oenone took Beb to Shaftesbury but there was no cinematograph.

May 10 Went round hospital which Ruth has got at Rushmore - 20 beds. Saw soldiers. Went to tea at Athelhampton, Mr [de] Lafontaine's place, perfectly lovely. Jacobean house, garden etc all done up by him in 20 years.

May 28 Fard & I motored to Croft House Botley to stay with Kathleen Pleydell. Vivien[E] there.

July 17 Saw in paper of Aunt Maude's death on Wednesday [14th] Wrote to Uncle Lyulph [Stanley][E] felt very much upset & miserable.

Sept 11 Charlotte & G. Davis [her husband] came in their motor bicycle & trailer to stay.

Sept 25 Cleaned my head with petrol. Some went into my ear, very painful.

Oct 24 Oenone went to Tisbury to her hospital. F[ard] fetched her in his motor. They got back at 10 after bursting 2 tyres.

Nov 21 Ruth brought Oenone back [from Rushmore] & announced George's engagement to Rachel Forster[F].

Nov 29 I cleaned my head with petrol and spoilt it with Peroxide of Hy[drogen].

Dec 21 Fard & I went in rain to Semley in motor which broke down & refused to move, so it was left at Semley at Bignalls & we walked home.

Dec 25 Fard worked at his motor.

1916

'Gossamer' Pocket Diary No 48, one day to a page. Written in pencil, mostly clear and legible. Mood and circumstance much as in preceding year. Agnes continued to use her Turkish bath and check her temperature regularly but the serious ailment this year was Walter's appendicitis, necessitating an urgent operation while they were visiting Kathleen to give her support in a harrowing time. Widowed in 1913 and losing one of her sons in 1915 she now knew that her other son, Harry [E], was reported 'missing'.

Oenone's readiness to marry Lieutenant Billy Matthews RN[F] was checked by his lack of the private means to give her security for life in the sort of marriage settlement that Agnes regarded as indispensable.

Jan 22 In the afternoon F[ard] & I went into the wood and chopped wood. I wrote to Claud Russell.

Feb 16 Billy Matthews came to stay, arrived same train as Oenone.

Feb 24 Walt was going to Mere but could not get the motor to go.

Feb 28 Walt walked to Mere to his Tribunal over 11 miles there and back.

March 3 I sent off Gerald's letter from the lawyers in which they informed him that Aunt Maude had left him £200.

April 26 Frank [Russell] & his wife motored here about 12.30, stayed
    & spent time on their way home from their honeymoon trip.

May 23 Heard that Harry Pleydell[E] was 'missing'.

June 6 Had my head washed, Fard helping with Lux.

June 8 F.P. 12 left. We went to Shaftesbury & saw Dr. Harris who told
    us where 'Bob Grey' in Harry [Pleydell]'s regiment lived & we went
    to see him. He told us all he knew about the last time Harry was
    seen.

June 10 Walter Oenone & I went by train to Croft House Botley to
    stay with Kathleen.

June 13 Vivien came from Notley for her ½ holiday.

June 14 Walter was taken with pains in the stomach in the night. We
    sent for the doctor.

June 19 Walter no better so Dr Keel [?] came from Southampton to
    have a consultation with the other doctor. They did not either of
    them know what was the matter but spoke of an operation.

June 20 Kathleen & I were playing croquet when the letters were
    brought out. She opened one with O.H.M.S. on it & after reading a
    few lines said in a whisper 'Oh my God'. I went to her & read that
    Harry had been found dead near Thiepval - identified by his disc.
    Poor Kathleen behaved wonderfully, so brave & wonderful but it
    [is] too heartbreakingly sad.

June 21 I wrote letters for Kathleen & did what I could.

June 25 Walt had a bad pain again so we sent for Dr Pern [?]. After
    examination [he] said that he was convinced that it was the
    appendix & that an operation would be necessary. So that same
    evening Kathleen ordered it was to be done here.

June 28 Vivien went back to her hospital & Kathleen went to London
    and two nurses came from London.

June 29 Walter had his operation. It was perfectly successful. I saw W.
    directly he recovered consciousness & he was very sweet & happy
    over it. Daphne [Pleydell][E] arrived in the morning from France.

July 5 Oenone came back from London & told me that Billy
    Matthews had proposed to her & that she was actually thinking it
    possible to accept him. Stupendous blow. Incredible.

July 6 Heard from Gerald that he had seen the Buxtons & had been
    transferred to the Native Rhodesian regiment which was going up
    to German East Africa.

July 10 [Oenone] has daily letters from B.M. whom she has decided to
    accept.

July 16 Billy Matthews came to see us. Had long talk & explanation. Finance not very satisfactory.

July 22 Lady Wynford & Marion came to tea.

July 31 All the Gooseberries disappeared. Note for next year.

Oct 2 Got telegram from Honor to say they had sailed on the 'Czaritza' & would telegraph again from Petrograd.

Oct 3 Walt & OE & I went to Brighton to stay with Taylor.

Oct 4 Prince Kropotkin & wife & Miss Lucas came to luncheon & Douglas came to tea. Oenone heard from B. Matthews & sent him a telegram. The engagement is off as there is not enough to live on. Poor little Oeno not happy.

Oct 13 [At Clewer] All 3 went with Edith to see Bruces.

Oct 27 [The words 'I washed my Head' are set out boldly, one beneath the other at three-line intervals].

Nov 4 Oenone went to Tisbury Hos[pital] heard from B. Matthews probably for the last time. He seems very miserable.

1917

There is no diary for this year but Agnes's letters to Oenone supply some information. At Clewer Edith's husband died and the future of the house, which had been so hospitable to Agnes since the earliest days of her honeymoon, was uncertain. A letter of Walter's identifies 'Billy' Matthews as George Matthews R.N. commanding HMS *Cockatrice*: his sister was one of Oenone's friends at Queen's College. Agnes began to favour the match, Billy's mother guaranteed an allowance of £200 p.a. but then changed her mind. Feeling that she should do something for Oenone Agnes urged her remaining society contacts – Willy Peel (now Lord Peel) Claud Russell and Lady Jeune – to draw Oenone into their circles.

Agnes's other daughter Honor was in Russia and did not write letters but in December an alarming telegram came from Honor's husband 'Koka' in Odessa. They had all had typhoid fever and the younger daughter, Kira, had died of it. Money was urgently needed. Agnes was inevitably overdrawn and appealed to her sister Alice Lubbock for the loan of £100 to be sent to the British consulate in Odessa. Alice responded at once.

On the last day of the year a very depressed Agnes wrote 'the future looks rather hopeless'.

1918

The Universal Pocket Book, Diary and Almanack, seven day spread. Signed 'Please return to Lady Grove Sedgehill Manor Shaftesbury'.

As the Russian situation worsened Agnes turned to Claud Russell for diplomatic assistance to Honor when she met him during a brief visit to London in January. Another source of maternal anxiety was Beb's retarded development. In letters to Oenone, who had joined the nursing staff of St Thomas's in London, Agnes described Beb as 'very very young', wondered if he was 'mentally deficient' and did not know 'what on earth is the best thing to do for him'.

Agnes herself seems to suffer from a lack of the stimulus of conversation and political controversy. She has withdrawn completely from public life and has found no wartime outlet for her talents, even within the local community. Her immediate concerns are the regulation of her coal and coke supplies so that each delivery lasts until the next arrives, and the making of jam by the hundredweight. She decides to sell her diamonds – 'the last things I have to sell'.

Jan 16 Beb & I went to London & to Alice at Grosv[enor] St for tea, large party for the Christening of Harold's baby. Claud R[ussell] there.

Jan 17 Oenone came about 9, went out with Beb & me. Saw Beb off Victoria.

Jan 18 Went to tea with Aunt Blanche & Claud came to see me about 6. Had dinner in the hotel.

Feb 7 Coal 2 tons. Head washed. Fard went Tisbury Petty Sessions.

Feb 16 Received long most interesting & wonderfully written letter from Koka.

Feb 18 Received letters from Honor dated Odessa Dec 21st, Jan 3, 18.

Feb 21 Went to London, went to dentist, then to Charing X Hotel where Oenone met me.

Feb 22 Luncheon with Alice. Dinner meatless at Savoy with Ld Peel & the play there Nothing but the Truth. Saw Marsh & Mrs Pat.

Feb 23 I went to luncheon with Mrs Pat Campbell & went with her to '13th Chair', saw Stella [her] daughter.[F] Then to see Oenone at St. Thomas's.

Feb 25 W received telegram from Honor saying use all influence with F[oreign] O[ffice] to get permit for all 3 to leave for England. Fard wrote same day to Balfour [Foreign Secretary].

March 13 Fard received an answer to his letter to F.O. saying they had telegraphed on Feb 27 but that he [the British Consul] had had to abandon his post and they couldn't do anything more.

April 4 Harold Lubbock[E] killed.

April 25 Beb collected for Wilts Prisoners of War.

May 11 Telegram from Gerald saying that he had landed at Plymouth & was going on to London to report.

May 15 Gerald arrived. Looks thin & rather ill but it is a joy to have him.

May 22 Coal lasted till today, nearly twice as long as the last. 30 cwt arrived.

May 24 New coal was begun.

May 27 Gerald went to London to see doctor, stayed 52 Portland Place with Mary St. Helier.[E]

June 18 We all picked strawberries in the morning & made 10¼ lb jam with 7lb 2oz fruit & 5 ½ sugar.

July 2 St George left. Dorothy Allhusen came by 4.40 [train]. Walter broke down on way to fetch her.

July 9 Heard from Gerald sending cheque for £130 for which he had sold my diamonds.

July 13 Made 52lbs gooseberry jam altogether. Gerald returned. Fard & I bicycled to station to meet him as the tyre was off the motor.

July 31 30 cwt coal came today & was begun today. The other came 70 days ago & lasted 68 days.

Sept 9 Fard Beb & I left for Clewer to stay with Edith in her new home Manor Farm.

Nov 11 Armistice signed. Peace at last.

1919

Again a Universal pocket-book, diary & almanack. Unsigned. End flyleaf records the year's jam-making in detail – a grand total of 505 pounds of jam, absorbing 293 lbs fruit and 222 lbs sugar.

January and February have only one entry each, March very few and many later pages are blank. The happiest event was the safe arrival of Honor with Koka and their daughter Sonia.[E]

March 13 Honor Koka & Sonia arrived after dinner.

April 6 Beb went to church with Sonia.

April 19 Frank Russell brought Mr Stephen McKenna to luncheon, quite pleasant. Frank told me his wife Elizabeth (Armin that was) had again left him.

June 16 Lucy Watson [servant] asked leave to go to Dinton & did not return.

June 17 Telegram from Lucy W to say she had married her Sergeant, return tomorrow! 2 cwt of sugar came.

June 25 Went in motor with Charlotte to Daphne Pleydell's[E] wedding. Sonia bridesmaid.

July 5 Mr Arundell came to see me. Went Comittee meeting Sedgehill school.

July 7 Left for London to stay with Honor.

July 8 Went to Oliver Stanley's[E] wedding.

July 11 Fard & I & Oenone went to the garden party at Buckingham Palace.

1920

No change in her choice of diary. The new year starts with signs of peacetime life opening up. In some of the great houses there is music for dancing again. Similarly in September the Larmer Tree Fete revives its prewar customs, and old friends reappear – notably Sybil Queensberry. Walt's motor is replaced by a motor-bike and sidecar.

Jan 5 Fard went to London. George & Ray [Rachel] Pitt-Rivers came to luncheon & tea.

Jan 6 Gerald came & he OE Beb & I went to ½ & ½ dance at Fonthill, very pleasant.

Jan 7 Fard returned & Honor Koka Gerald Oen Beb & I all went to ½ & ½ dance at Longleat.

Jan 9 Honor Koka Sonia Beb & I went to childrens party at Wardour & Gerald OE & Beb went to a dance at Zeals.

Jan 10 Honor Koka & Sonia left & went to Hinton [St. Mary].

Jan 13 OE Beb & I went party at Pyt House.

Jan 14 Oenone went to London again to 4B Warrington Crescent.

March 23 [In London] Went to see Aunt Blanche[E]. She is nearly 90 & quite wonderful. Then I had luncheon with Sybil Queensberry & Edith & tea with Honor.

May 18 F & I went Salisbury, lunched Husseys, went cathedral to see Bimbo Tennant's plaque [*Edward Wyndham Tennant*[F] (*1897-1916*) *Grenadier Guards, killed in the Battle of the Somme.*]

July 22 Oenone & I went to Buckingham Palace Garden party.

July 27 Went to stay Sibyl Queensberry at Shelley's Folly, Lewes. Edith, St G & Dorothy Douglas [Sybil Q's grand-daughter] only staying here. Nice little place.

Sept 1 We all went to Rushmore to luncheon, Duke & Duchess of Somerset, 3 Sturdys etc Then Larmer Tree for Fete for Nursing Home.

Sept 25 Oenone sailed with Mrs Matthews on board the Somali for China.

Nov 17 Went into Salisbury with Fard in motor-bi.

Dec 30 Beb went to Salisbury to stay with Husseys for Wilton & another dance.

1921

There is no diary for this year. Oenone was in Hong-Kong in January and returned to England during the year. In November *The Times* published a list of 118 divorce decrees made absolute, including Arnott v. Arnott and Grove. The Grove in question was Gerald who was shortly due to take up an appointment in Australia and did not relish publicity as the co-respondent in a divorce case. Writing to Oenone in December he told her that Mrs Arnott sent him a telegram saying 'Mother adamant regarding engagement & subsequent marriage of co-respondent & respondent thinks it most important you should come at once to London love from Hermione.' Gerald replied that 'the great thing was to keep things quiet' and he was 'much too broke to keep running up to London'; that she must 'disillusion her mother if she thought I was heir to a rich baronet with many broad acres'. He told her 'she could marry any day somebody with money enough to keep her in comfort,' that he has got the chance of a pleasant job and 'she must not upset the applecart'. 'Then', he concluded, 'I ended up in a friendly cheery way.'

1922

The same Universal pocket diary as in previous years, but with more and fuller entries. There was certainly more to write about, arising principally from her children's problems. With Gerald safely away on the high seas it was Agnes who faced the barrage of telegrams and letters from 'the woman A'. When Agnes tried to overawe her she was discomforted to find that Mrs A's mother, who joined in the fray, was the sister of a Duke. Divorce in different circumstances was threatening Honor, whose Russian husband wanted to end their marriage. And all the time the lovable enigmatic Beb posed questions to which Agnes had no confident answer. He was a keen Boy Scout, he enjoyed reading the lessons in church services, people liked his general demeanour but he was evidently unemployable. Kathleen's daughter Vivien and her husband, Mr Railstone, tried to take Beb in hand but described him regretfully as 'hopeless'. There was a hint also of addiction to alcohol.

Before the year ended the final Grove tactic was employed. He was shipped off to Lower California to join his uncle Tom who, a generation earlier, had made the same voyage. As Gerald left Australia and also took temporary refuge with uncle Tom there seemed to be a sort of higher logic or destiny about it all. 'California, here we come!'

Jan 4　Gerald sailed on s.s. Demosthenes for Melbourne Australia as private secretary to Lord Stradbroke, state governor of Victoria. From Tilbury he sent a telegram to me.

Jan 5　Letter from Mrs A[rnott].

Jan 7　Telegram came for Gerald from the woman A, returned to sender, addressee being away.

Jan 8　Telegram came for Fard from the woman A.

Feb 10　Beb turned up during luncheon & went back to Longthorns.

Jan 12　Wrote to Gerald enclosing letter to Fard from the l.w.

Jan 13　The servants went to the village tea & play to which F & I went & Sonia acted & Honor spoke & wrote prologue.

Jan 20　Fard & I went to Shaftesbury & I took Gerald's receipt for registered letter [and] sent [it] to Lady A. Cooper[F] [mother of Mrs A].

Jan 24　Gerald's medals came by registered post & were forwarded re-registered. Letter from Gerald from Tenerife Madeira.

Jan 25　Ruth wrote to Honor to say she would have Sonia for a year. She also heard from Koka.

Jan 28　Fard & I went to luncheon at Fonthill with May Morrison, after to tea at Wardour. Lord & Lady Arundell[F] both there. Letters from Railstone & Kathleen saying Beb was 'hopeless' & from Mrs A threatening to go out to Australia. Bad night.

Feb 18　Fard was going to take Sonia to Beagles hunt at Hatch. However motor [bike] wouldn't start & in running it down the hill

& trying to get on Fard fell down, motor wheel went over his head
& grazed his forehead. He was not much hurt but gave up going.

Feb 20 Desperate telegram from Gerald.

Feb 22 Letter from Oenone & also from Elspeth [Lionel's second
wife][E] inviting F & me to stay at Kent House.

March 6 Wrote to Arnott woman.

March 8 Heard by 2nd post from the Arnott woman. Impudent letter.
Sent my letter to Gerald.

March 9 Heard from Oenone that Harry Allhusen was dead, wrote to
Dorothy – also to Lady Agnes Cooper.

April 3 Had letter in morning from Lady Agnes C, very upsetting,
answered by 2nd post.

April 5 Sent letter to Gerald but did not mention last letter. Beb came
back from Longthorns.

April 10 Beb started work at Hatch House.

April 11 Beb went Hatch, began to learn to drive a tractor.

April 16 Fard tried to take me to church in the m.b. but it stopped
going up the hill so I walked. Honor Oenone & Sonia went & we
all heard Beb read the lessons.

April 20 Honor brought most horrible letter from Koka wanting to be
'freed'.

April 26 Fard & I went in motor bicycle to Berwick & called on Mrs
Henry Farquharson.[F]

April 30 Went to see the Hardys at Max Gate Dorchester, great
pleasure. Hardy looking well.

June 19 Telegram from Gerald saying he had gone to Matajanal
[Lower California][H]

June 23 Letters from Gerald & Fard. Gerald explained why he left
Melbourne.

July 29 Patrick Grove[E] came over from Bovington Camp on his
return from Germany.

Aug 11 Lionel Elsie & Joan came to luncheon in their motor bi & side
car. Heard that Douglas was very bad.

Aug 13 Jack Benett[F] came after tea & told us of St James's club
gossip.

Aug 14 Fard & I went to Pyt House to the tennis tournament.

Aug 22 Heard from Gerald from San Diego.

Sept 8 Met Canon Abott & talked about Beb's temperance.

Sept 9 Fard's birthday 70 today. We gave him presents.

Sept 17 We all Fard OE Beb & I played lawn tennis 13 games.

Sept 20 Telegram to say Douglas had died last night.

Sept 26 Honor heard from Koka that he was going away again 1st
    week in October so she decided to go to Paris tomorrow.

Oct 6 Beb went to Sedgehill to blow organ. Oenone sailed for Egypt.

Oct 8 Lady Stalbridge came to see me about letting this house.

Nov 22 [In London] Up at 7 took Beb & saw him safely on board the
    'Loch Katrina' by which he sailed to San Pedro on Royal Mail
    Steam Packet. Went after to see S.Q. 16 Draycott Place.

Dec 19 Fard fetched Sonia from Warminster. They arrived at 2, F
    exhausted by struggle with motor b.

Dec 25 Christmas Day. Mended pyjamas knitted Fard's stockings &
    read. Damp & dark.

1923

N.J. Powell & Co's Pocket Diary & Almanack. Similar in style and size to
preceding year's but binding in poor condition. Flyleaf and spare pages used
for addresses, shopping lists, jam-making totals & draft of a letter to a neighbour in a dispute over the use of the word 'Manor'.

With Gerald and Beb in California, Oenone in Egypt and Honor in Paris the
diary is much occupied with the writing and receiving of letters, the contents of
which are seldom revealed. In writing to Gerald she can hardly have failed to
mention the death of 'the woman A', Hermione Arnott. During the year Agnes
renewed acquaintance with Hermione's ex-husband, Noel Arnott, whom she
had known as a colleague and friend of Gerald's African years.

The need to retain a family house began to be questioned and Agnes
considered letting Sedgehill Manor again as in 1904-1909. To be alone with
Walter and lacking dependable transport was a deprivation of the intellectual
companionship and fresh interests that, for Agnes, gave life its savour.

The 'motor-bi' was finally abandoned and replaced with a motor-car of
unpromising pedigree.

Jan 9 Long Diary letter from Beb recounting each day on ship &
    meeting with Tom at San Pedro.

March 25 Found I could not write very well. I get frightened.

May 28 Woolley [Salisbury estate agent] came & Fard visited cottages
    & farms with him.

June 7 Left Thorpe arrived [London] Regent Palace Hotel.
    Telephoned Arnott, dined Ritz with Frank [Russell] & Stephen
    McKenna.

June 8 Lunched Tott[enham[Ct Rd, went see Arnott 4, dined Taylor.

June 9 Had luncheon Sibyl Q 16 Drayton Place. Left London.

June 28 A Mrs Mann came to look at the house.

July 3 Heard from Gerald from San Diego where he is doing a job for an American called Llewellyn.

July 5 Mrs Mann came with a friend to see the house again.

July 10 Heard from Mrs Mann that she was not taking the house.

July 26 Buck[ingham] Palace Garden party. Arnott came to see us off at Waterloo.

Sept 21 Heard from & wrote to Gerald who wrote from Ensenada & had seen Beb.

Oct 16 Letter from Gerald from 1443 Iowa Avenue, Hollywood, California.

Oct 19 Letter from Oenone saying doctor said she had TB & must give up her work. Agony not being able to get to her.

Nov 1 Wrote to Oenone. F[ard] heard from W. Shaw Stewart saying that he never disputed his lordship of the Manor [of Sedgehill] which is quite untrue!

Dec 4 Heard from Beb, Warren Hotel, San Diego.

Dec 10 Heard from Beb, OE [in Egypt] & Gerald who sent 2 addresses 6660 Selma Avenue, Hollywood & the old one c/o Marcus Martinez & Co, Customs Brokers, San Diego.

Dec 24 Fard brought his 'Albert' motor car back from Longthorns.

Dec 31 I went to Shaftesbury in the new Albert but it was not a great success.

1924

N.J. Powell & Co's Imperial Diary. Not significantly different from last year's. Binding disintegrating. Miscellaneous notes & calculations on fly-leaves etc. The year's fuel statistics – Coal over 10½ tons, coke 2 tons.

The return of Oenone from Egypt, where she had been working for the YWCA, brought a welcome companionship to Agnes for a while, but the year as a whole was uneventful. A reference to the behaviour of Jack Benett as a magistrate relates to his unconventional affability in court with any defendant who happened to be a friend of his: after a chat about matters of mutual interest he would invite the offender to dinner that evening.

Agnes's handwriting varies greatly, partly because of a blunt pencil at times but also from the physical difficulty which troubled her and produced such badly formed letters as to be illegible.

The installation of a wireless receiver added a touch of novelty but did little to dispel her sense of boredom at the year's end. On December 8 she entered the words 'Went no where. Saw no one', and on each of the next eight days wrote simply 'Ditto'.

The Albert motor car was not a success. It scarcely needs saying that the manufacturers immediately went bankrupt and no spare parts were available. 'A good old Ford would have been the thing to have', Agnes wrote to Oenone on Christmas Day. 'The fact is Fard is <u>not</u> good for machinery. The man said the whole engine was 'worn' for lack of oil. But he <u>saturates</u> it with oil but simply doesn't understand it'.

Jan 4   Letter from W.S.S. to Fard saying he would discard the name 'Manor' [see 1/11/23]

Feb 26   Heard from Gerald & Beb, both from Matajanal.[H]

Feb 27   Telegram from Willy to say Blossie died this afternoon.

March 4   Letter from Oenone saying she was leaving Egypt for good on the 11th.

March 18   Fard went to meeting of magistrates convened in Shaftesbury to keep Jack Benett in order.

April 3   Mr Everingham came in morning & Fard ordered a listening-in apparatus.

April 7   Mr Everingham came to install wireless & stayed to luncheon & tea.

April 9   Mr Everingham brought me headphones & stayed to tea.

April 17   Mr Everingham came to tea, put wireless in good order.

April 21   We started for Wincanton races but a part got loose just as we were getting into Gillingham so we left the motor & came home by train.

June 3   Oenone arrived home, looks very thin but otherwise as beautiful as ever.

June 6   Oenone & Fard went Warminster to fetch Sonia [from school]. Motor broke down on way home.

July 5   Fard & I went to London, met Oenone & went to Buckingham Palace garden party.

July 26   Letter from Tom about Beb. Very unsatisfactory.

Sept 3   Fard Oeno & I went Larmer Tree Motor gymkhana.

Oct 11   Eliot [Grove family solicitor] sent £5/2/8. Bought wireless licence.

Oct 30   Dreadful news of Tory victories all over the country.

Nov 27   Heard from Oenone that she leaves today for Switzerland with Mrs Matthews.

Dec 2 Fard & I went to Gillingham. The motor broke down outside. Returned in Stickland's Ford. Motor towed into Gilliingham.

Dec 22 Fard & I went to Gillingham. Motor no forwarder.

Dec 25 Fine bright day. Heard from Oenone, Atkin & Sibyl Q.

1925

Again the Imperial diary, as last year.

With Oenone on holiday in the Alps, and the Albert motorcar increasingly unreliable, the winter months brought little for Agnes to record in her diary beyond the familiar arrivals and departures of cooks and house-parlourmaids. Sonia was at school in Warminster and her mother, Honor, does not appear. The one exciting event was a letter from Gerald. He was breaking into the film industry, as an actor and an adviser on English manners in the drawing-room romances of the period. It must have seemed an ironically appropriate role for the son of the author of *The Social Fetich*.

March brought the death of Walter's aunt Emma. There had been the tacit assumption in Agnes's mind that the wealth of the older generation would gradually pass as reinforcements to their nephews and nieces. She had been disappointed that her godmother, Aunt Maude, left her only £2000: Emma was the last hope and Agnes expected at least £3000 for Walter. The outcome was £500 which, in a letter to Oenone, Agnes said 'will just about & only just clear our local debts, the butcher & the coal man both owed several hundred. I don't think you have any idea of the nightmare this has been to me, the sense of humiliation & the horror of local debt. I had so hoped that Emma's legacy would have cleared the debt at the bank & released a little more income but that hope is over.'

Jan 7 Heard from Oenone, & Fard from Stickland that more fresh parts are wanted.

Jan 10 Most exciting letter from Gerald & excellent photoes.

Jan 23 Fard fetched Albert in morning.

Jan 24 Fard & I were going to Shaftesbury but motor refused to wind up.

March 4 Fard & I went to Berwick to Aunt Emma's funeral. Saw Kathleen, Husseys, Rosses, Selwyns etc.

March 5 Heard 2nd post from Henrietta H[ussey] that Emma had left Fard £500 & Charlotte £2000, which last I am very glad of.

March 7 Heard from Oenone from Chamonix.

March 13 Fard & I went to Shaftesbury & brought back black puddings & went round by Donhead to Haskell basket man & bought a basket.

March 14 Oenone arrived – looked very well, shingled hair & all.

April 11 G.P.R. [George Pitt-Rivers] brought Mildred Mansel & Mr Balfour over to tea.

April 28 Letter from Beb postmark April 13 Los Angeles.

July 7 Oenone & I went to London. OE took flowers to S.Q. & I went to Swan & Edgar [shop].

July 9 Dined Berkeley [Hotel] Cunningham Graham.

July 10 Oenone went Lords, I had luncheon Sibyl.

July 11 Oenone & I went to see the Epstein in Hyde Park. Hideous.

July 16 Dined Sherborne, met Vachell[F] who talked to me about his book for which he is consulting the Social Fe[tich].

July 24 Fard & I went Salisbury in motor then London to Charing X [hotel] met OE there then all 3 went garden party Buckingham Palace & then to the Tivoli where we saw Gerald in Cinema in 'Man & Maid'. Gerald very good & sympathetic.

July 25 Waterloo & home by 3 [o'clock] train. Motor broke down & Mrs Trotter kindly brought us home.

Aug 22 Oenone & I went to Shaftesbury. Motor broke down & we left it there.

Aug 25 Fard OE & I went to Shaftesbury in Malet to see about the Albert.

Aug 26 A Major Parsons came to look at house, said he knew me. Jane [servant] said it was not to let!

Sept 10 Fard went to Shaftesbury in motor where it broke down.

Oct 27 Heard from Margaret that Henrietta [Hussey] died yesterday.

Nov 11 [Armistice Day] Heard the 'silence' by wireless.

Nov 20 Queen Alexandra died. The wireless stopped so I thought it had happened.

Dec 14 Had my head washed. Fard took Sonia back to Warminster & the motor broke down again!

Dec 26 Telegram from Ruth asking us to go to Rushmore. Also from Gerald merry Xmas.

Dec 28 OE went off to London en route for Switzerland.

July 11. The W.H. Hudson memorial sculpted by Jacob Epstein aroused bitter controversy at the time.

1926

There is no diary for this year. Agnes died on December 7th and was buried at Berwick St. John. Messages of condolence included one from Thomas Hardy, now aged 86, and his second wife. It was presumably addressed to Walter but it was answered by Oenone, who wrote

> My Mother was so wonderful in mind, body & spirit. She was the centre of our world & without her we seem utterly lost.

Looking back on a friendship that extended over nearly thirty years Hardy added a personal comment in his elegiac poem *Concerning Agnes*.

> I am stopped from hoping what I have hoped before -
>   Yes, many a time! -
> To dance with that fair woman yet once more
>   As in the prime
> Of August, when the wide-faced moon looked through
> The boughs at the faery lamps of the Larmer Avenue.
>
> I could not, though I should wish, have over again
>   That old romance,
> And sit apart in the shade as we sat then
>   After the dance
> The while I held her hand, and, to the booms
> Of contrabassos, feet still pulsed from the distant rooms.
>
> I could not. And you do not ask me why.
>   Hence you infer
> That what may chance to the fairest under the sky
>   Has chanced to her.
> Yes. She lies white, straight, features marble-keen,
> Unapproachable, mute, in a nook I have never seen.
>
> There she may rest like some vague goddess, shaped
>   As out of snow;
> Say Aphrodite sleeping; or bedraped
>   Like Kalupso;
> Or Amphitrite stretched on the Mid-sea swell,
> Or one of the Nine grown stiff from thought. I cannot tell!

Select Bibliography

GROVE

Diaries of Harriet Grove 1809, 1810. Ms in Pforzheimer Collection, New York Public Library, USA.

> Edited by Roger Ingpen, London 1932. Twelve copies privately printed.

> Vol. 2 of *Shelley and his Circle*, ed. Kenneth Neill Cameron, annotated F.L. Jones, Harvard Univ. Press 1961.

Diaries of Charlotte Grove (Mrs Downes) 1811-1858 (incomplete series). Ms in Wiltshire Record Office, Trowbridge: WRO 1641/157-191. Unpublished.

Diaries of Sir Thomas Grove 1855-1897 (incomplete series). Ms in Wiltshire Record Office: WRO 1641.197-229. Unpublished.

Diaries of Agnes, Lady Grove 1879-1925 (incomplete series). Ms in Wiltshire Record Office: WRO 1641/235-266. Unpublished.

The Correspondence of Agnes, Lady Grove and her daughter Oenone: privately owned.

Concerning Agnes, biography of Agnes Grove: Desmond Hawkins. Gloucester 1982.

Books by Agnes Grove –
1. *Seventy-one Days Camping in Morocco*. London 1902.
2. *The Social Fetich* (dedicated to Thomas Hardy) London 1907.
3. *The Human Woman* London 1908.
4. *On Fads* London 1910.

Grove family papers. Wiltshire Record Office. WRO 1641

Helyar family papers (for Harriet Grove) Somerset Record Office, Taunton. SRO-DD/WHh 61.

SHELLEY

Diary of Percy Bysshe Shelley, 1810. Ms in Pforzheimer Collection, New York Public Library. Text published in *Shelley's First Love*: Desmond Hawkins. London and New York 1992.

The Letters of Percy Bysshe Shelley: ed. F.L. Jones, 2 vols. Oxford 1964.

Original Poetry of Victor and Cazire: ed. Richard Garnett. London 1898
(Worthing 1810).
Zastrozzi and St. Irvyne (1810): Two novels by Shelley, reissued Oxford 1986.
The Esdaile Notebook: Early poems ed. Kenneth Neill Cameron. New York
and London 1964.
The text of Charles Henry Grove's recollections of Shelley, communicated in
1837 to Hellen Shelley, is published in *The Life of Percy Bysshe Shelley* by
Thomas Jefferson Hogg, 2 vols. London 1858.

THOMAS HARDY
The Life of Thomas Hardy: F.E.Hardy. London 1962
The Life and Work of Thomas Hardy: ed. Michael Millgate,
London 1984.
The Collected Letters of Thomas Hardy: ed. R. L. Purdy & M.
Millgate, 7 vols. Oxford 1978-1988.
Jude the Obscure, London 1895.

GENERAL
Beckford, Peter: *Thoughts on Hunting* 1781.
Bowden, Mark: *Pitt-Rivers*, his Life and Work. Cambridge 1994.
Bowles, Charles: *The Hundred of Chalke*, Shaftesbury 1830.
Chafin, William: *Anecdotes & History of Cranbourn Chase*, 1818/1991.
Dakers, Caroline: *Clouds*. New Haven and London, 1993
Gray, H.St.G: *A Memoir of General Pitt-Rivers*, 1905 Oxford.
Henry-Higginson, A: *The Meynell of the West*, a biography of J. J.
Farquharson. London 1936.
Henry-Higginson, A: *Peter Beckford*, a biography. London 1937.
Hoare, R. Colt: *The History of Modern Wiltshire*, London 1830.
Hunt, Henry: *Memoirs of Henry Hunt*, London 1820.
Hutchins, John: *History and Antiquities of Dorset*, 3rd edition 1861-64,
reprinted 1973.
Mitford, Nancy, ed: *The Ladies of Alderley* (Stanley family correspondence),
London 1938.
Mitford, Nancy, ed: *The Stanleys of Alderley* (Stanley family
correspondence), London 1939-1968.
Pitt-Rivers, Lt-Gen. FRS: *Guide to the Larmer Grounds, Rushmore, Kings
John's House and the Museum at Farnham*, n.d. (c.1900).
Smart, T.W. Wake: *A Chronicle of Cranborne and the Cranborne Chase*,
1841/1943.
Watson, E. W.: *Ashmore* (a village history), Salisbury 1890.

Index

Names are given in the form in which they appear in the diaries.

Aaron (footman), 160
Abbot, Abner, 187
Abercorn, Duke of, 320, 330
Aberdeen, Lord and Lady, 305
Abernethy, Mr, 148
  Adams, Mr and Mrs (of Handley), 89, 92
Adeane, Marie, 215, 297
Aidé, Hamilton, 313-14
Ailesbury, 3rd Marquis (Sir Ernest Bruce P.C.), 215, 232
Ailesbury, Lady, 215, 271
Alexander, George (actor), 314
Alington, Henry Gerard Sturt, 1st baron, 216, 291
Allenby, captain later viscount, 216, 264
Allhusen, Henry, MP, 314, 349,
  Dorothy (née Stanley), 209, 314, 345
Amy [Amey], 157
Annesley family, 55, 56
Arnim, Mary, 209, 339
Arnott, Hermione (née Cooper), 216, 347-50
  Noel, 216, 350-51
Arundell of Wardour, 21, 216
  James Everard 9th baron, 21, 55-56, 79, 87-88, 101, 109
  Lady Mary, his wife, 21, 55-56, 78, 87-89, 101, 109, 117, 122, 133, 139
  Catherine, daughter, 21, 122
  Julia, daughter, 21, 78, 128
  Laura, daughter, 21, 56, 78
  Mr and Mrs Raymond, 21, 61, 87, 89, 106, 122
  Miss W[yndham], 21, 59
  James Everard, 10th baron, 21, 177

Henry Benedict, 11th baron, 21, 177, 179, Lady 182
  John, 12th baron and lady, 216, 252
  Gerald, 15th baron and lady, 216, 348
  Mr (unidentified), 100, 122
  Mr (unidentified), 346
Ashcombe, 29, 56, 61, 78, 86, 88, 105-06, 109, 126-29, 139, 142, 144, 148
Asquith, Herbert Henry, MP, 310, 314, 320
  his wife Margot (née Tennant), 314, 320
  their son Raymond, 332
Astley, Mr (parliamentary candidate), 141
Atkin (servant), 332-34
Auber, Jane (née Grove of Zeals), 19, 129
Austen, Jane, 132
Austin, Alfred (poet laureate 1896), 320
Avebury, Lord: see Lubbock, Sir John
Aylesbury, see Ailesbury

Baiss, Mr (publican), 173, 180
  Mrs and daughter Hannah, 183
Baker, Mr and Mrs, 91
  Sir Edward, 28, 166, 187
Balfour, Arthur James, MP, 304, 334, 345, 354
Bankes (or Banks), George, 216, 132
  Miss, 117
  Mr, 151
  Ralph, 216, 295
Barker, Harley Granville, 313-14
Bastard, Rev J and Mrs, 91
  Mr, 98

Miss, 98, 142
Bayers, Lady, 77.
Bearwood, Dr, 80
Beaufort, Duke of , 234
Beaufoy, Mark, MP, 216, 247, 256, 259, 262
Beaumont, Fred (artist), 223, 304
Beckford, Peter, 21-22, 85
 William (of Fonthill), 22, 108, 152, 161
Beerbohm, Max, 333
Belloc, Hilaire, 330
Benett of Donhead St. Andrew etc, 22
 Catherine, 22, 48, 49, 52, 57, 59, 62, 70-73, 78-79, 85-88, 91, 110-11, 122
 Charles Cowper, 22, 57, 71-72, 87
 his wife Sarah (née Burlton q.v.)
 Frances, 22, 48, 52, 72, 85, 87-88, 91, 101, 110, 113-14, 119, 124
 George, 22, 99, 114
 William, 22, 49, 57, 78, 80
Benett of Pythouse, 22
 John, MP, 22, 43, 56, 69, 78, 87-88, 100, 126, 129, 136-37, 141-44, 162, 173
 his wife Lucy, 22, 43-46, 51, 54-55, 78, 84, 87-88, 99, 117, 119, 126
Benett-Stanford, Col. Vere Fane, 216, 284
 his wife Ellen ('Nelly'), 216, 284, 291-92
 their son Jack, 217, 349, 351-52
Benson, Miss, 89
Bernhardt, Sarah, 253, 320
Berridge, Mr, 239
Berry Court, 29, 46, 115-16, 140-41, 155, 191
Berwick, Lord, 333
Besant, Mrs, 310
Best (family name of the barons Wynford), 209
 Mrs Frances Hinton, 209, 245
 (marriage to Sir Thomas Grove q.v.)
 Capt and Mrs Robert, 210, 247, 249, 321
 Colonel, 250
 Marion, 210, 343
Bingham, Rev Peregrine, 28, 59, 72, 86, 114, 134, 163
 his wife Amy (née Bowles), 23, 28, 86,

138-39, 159, 163, 166
 their son Peregrine, 28, 86
 their son Edward, 28, 114
 their daughter, Miss, 23, 161
Blackett, Nesta (m. Lionel Fox-Pitt q.v.), 320, 336
Blackmore, Rev R.W, 28, 193, 245
Blanche, Jacques-Emile, 217, 336-37
Blandford, James, 194
Blavatski, Mme, 293, 310
Bontine, Mrs, 217, 272
'Boob' or 'Booby', 217, 270, 302
Botta, Mrs, 285
Bowles family, 22
 Charles, 22, 87, 117, 136, 171-72
 Mrs, 104, 111
Boys, Rev P, 28, 52, 56, 63, 111, 119, 131, 134, 168
 his wife, 52, 56, 63, 111, 124
Bradley, widow, 152
Brereton, Col. and Mrs, 46, 51, 59, 77, 172
Brine, John, 98, 142
 Mrs, 193
Brockway, Alice:154
 'Old', 151, 154
 the gardener, 323
Bromley family, 28, 48, 50, 73, 127, 131, 136
Brotherton, Mr, 58
Bruce family of Stenhouse, 210, 295, 343
 Corinna, 210, 261
 Grace, 210, 261, 295
 Lord Henry (later 5th Marquess of Ailesbury), 217, 253
 Sir William C, 210, 232, 261
 Willie, 210, 252, 257, 284, 287, 316
Bryne: see Brine
Bullock, Troyte, 290
Buonaparte (Napoleon), 173, 122, 124, 127
Burden, Alice, 140
Burlton, Mrs, 23, 53, 56, 87, 105, 128, 147, 183, 191, 193, 195
 her son Charles, 23, 116
 her daughter Marianne, 23, 105
 her daughter Sarah, 23, 56, 72, 87-88, 103

her son, Colonel William, 23, 201
Burns, Rt. Hon. John, 310
Burt, James, 168
Bury, Lucy, 28, 82, 85, 92, 102
Butler, Rev William, 28, 117, 119, 133
Butt, Dame Clara, 323

Campbell, Mrs Patrick (actress), 217,
312, 314-15, 317-18, 320, 323, 344
her daughter Stella, later Mrs Beech,
217, 317, 344
Camplin, Miss, 63
Carew, Lady, 306
Carlow, George Dawson Damer,
Viscount, 217, 273, 299-300, 302
Carnegie, Lady Mary: married Walter
Long of Preshaw, q.v.
Cary, Rev Tupper and family, 223, 247
Chafin, Rev William, of Chettle, 23, 63,
113
Challoner, Capt, 255, 301
Mr (bank Manager), 261
Chamberlain, Rt. Hon. Joseph, 252
Chapman family, 217,
Rev Horace and Mrs, 217, 239, 249,
251, 253-54, 259-60, 264, 292, 294, 307
Bruce, 217, 260
Florence, 217, 259, 307
Kyrle, 217, 257
Mabel, 217, 264
'Chev' (Mlle. Chevalier), 279-81
Chitty, Mr (Shaftesbury lawyer), 128,
163, 168
Chowne, John, 185
Clay, Sir George, 238
Cleveland, Mr, of West Lodge, 259
Clowes, Miss, 187
Cluse, Miss (possibly same person as
preceding), 77
Cockburn, Sir Alexander, 217, 232
Cockram (? Cochrane) Mrs, 203
Coit, Dr Stanton, 306
Colley, Mr, 51
Connaught, Duke and Duchess of, 242
Conyers, Sackville George Lane-Fox,
12th baron, 210, 292
Marcia Amelia, 13th baroness, 210,
272, 301

Cook, Rev Mr, 84
Cooke, Mrs, of Donhead Lodge, 23,
48-49, 53-59, 61, 78, 84, 86-90, 100,
111, 113, 115-19, 123-24, 146
Mr, her brother-in-law, 56
her daughter Louisa, 23, 53-54, 57, 61,
85-86, 107, 111, 113, 116-17, 119, 126,
146, 191 (later, Mrs Devonshire q.v.)
Cooper, Lady Agnes, 218, 348-49
Courtney, Mr, 60
Craigie, Mrs Pearl, 218, 320, 330, 332-33
Cratton, Mr, 103-04, 110
Crewe, Marquis of, 218, 307-10, 313-14,
317, 320
Croom, Miss, 52, 56
Crosse family, 210
Avis, née Winn or Wynne, 210,
262-64, 317, 321
Ella, 210, 246, 248-49, 264, 290
Herbert, 210, 245-47, 251-53, 255, 257,
260, 262-64, 284, 296, 303, 317, 321,
327
Mrs (senior), 210, 249, 252
Cull, Elinor, 177-78, 181, 183. See also
Herring
Cwm Elan (Welsh estate), 30, 39, 54, 79,
116-17, 126, 128, 165, 174-75

Daniel (servant), see Lampard
Dansey, Rev William, 28, 98, 155, 171,
176, 186, 191
Davis, Gilbert (m. Charlotte Augusta
Grove q.v. 208), 341
Dawson-Damer, see Carlow
De Hoghton, Aimée, Lady: Grove q.v,
208
Sir James, 239, 247, 310
De Montmorency, Harvey John, 235
his wife Grace née Grove q.v, 207,
235, 241, 244
their daughter Kathleen, 207, 241
their son Tom, 207, 241
Devonshire, Mrs, née Louisa Cooke q.v,
191, 195
her daughter Augusta, 191, 193, 195
Dewy, Mrs John, 151-52
Dibbin, Elizabeth, 191
Dicketts, Mr, 176, 180

Dimmer, Job, 149
  Mary, 28, 56, 58-59, 64, 70-71, 78, 81, 83-84, 90, 92-94
Dippers, Society of, 160
Dixon, Miss (governess), 326
Dobson, Mrs and Miss, 88
Donaldson, Capt, 85, 101, 125, 132
Dotter, Mr and Mrs, 89
Douglas, John Sholto, 9th Marquis of Queensberry, 218, 323
  Sybil his wife, 218, 261, 263, 308, 312-320, 322-23, 327-28, 330, 332, 335-36, 346, 350-51, 353-54
  Francis Archibald, Viscount Drumlanrig, their son, 218, 308
  Percy Sholto, their son, 10th Marquis, and his wife, 218, 333
  Lord Alfred, their son and his wife, 218, 332
  Lord Sholto George, their son and his wife, 218, 332
  Lady Edith, their daughter, 218, 261, 308, 312-13, 319-20, 327, 346
  Muriel (unidentified), 312
  Dorothy (unidentified), 347
Dowding, Ann, 166
Downes, Rev Richard (m. Charlotte Grove, q.v.), 17, 163-68, 172-75, 179-80, 182-87, 190-93, 199, 200, 229
  Henrietta (his sister), 165, 189
  Rev Robert (his brother), 189
Doyle, Gregory, 124
Drumlanrig, Lord: see Douglas, Francis Archibald
Du Boulay family, 23, 171, 176, 200, 245, 253, 305

Earle, Rev Walter, 134
Eason or Easton, Rev Mr, 28, 53, 58, 84, 87, 90, 92, 109-10, 122
  William, his son, 128
Edwards (butler at Ferne); 28, 107, 111, 121, 124, 130, 135, 144, 163, 166
Elcho, Mary Lady, née Wyndham, 223, 305
Elwin, Mr and Mrs, 104-05
Eyre family of Newhouse, 24, 119-20
  Mrs, 24, 119-20

Misses, 24, 119-20
  Charlotte, m. George Grove q.v., 18

'Fard': nickname of Sir Walter Grove, 208, 334
Farquhar, John, 161-62
Farquharson family of Blandford St. Mary, Langton Long and Eastbury, 24, 218-19
  James John, 24, 47, 61, 72, 109, 113, 129, 133, 151, 155, 170, 173, 229, 264
  Mrs (his mother), 24, 113, 117, 133, 146, 184
  Ann his first wife, née Stevens, 24, 47, 59, 61, 64, 85, 91, 109, 117, 131, 133, 155, 173, 177
  their son James John junior, 24, 129, 184
  Robert, 24, 155, 242
  Frederick, 24, 123, 155, 181
  Henry (father of Henry Richard), 24
  J. J. senior's second wife, Mary Anne, 184
  his sister Henrietta Ann (m. Thomas Grove junior q.v. 17)
  Captain and son (unidentified), 101
  Mr (unidentified), 90, 111
  J. J. senior's grandchildren –
  Archibald, 218
  Henry Richard MP, 218, 242
  Constance, Henry Richard's wife and cousin, 218, 349
  Ronald of Tilshead, 219, 296
Farrer, Frederick W, 244, 281-83
Fenwick, Mrs, 243-44
Ferne House: origin 33-35; decay 51, 65; rebuilt 109; enlarged 230; for sale 265, 315; sold 326
Ferrers, Mr and Miss, 60
Ferret, Mr, 176
Fitzgerald, Lady Amicia, 219, 309-10, 313-14
  Mrs, 138
Fitzwilliam, Reginald Wentworth, 306
Fletcher, Rev Nathaniel, 28, 58, 62, 86, 116, 139
  his wife, 62, 64, 86, 116
  a daughter, 64, 86

a son, 86
Rev William, 28, 56
Foot family, 107, 167
Mr, 167, 178, 181-82, 189, 193, 200
Mrs, 174, 178-79, 193
Master, 179
Doctor, 191
Anna, 179
Mr C, 173
Harriet, 179
Samuel, 170-71
Sophia, 200
Ford, Mr, 91
Forster, Rachel: see Pitt-Rivers, George
Fosse, Mr (actor), 314
Foster, Edmund Benson, 210, 236-37,
246, 295, 343
Edith Eleanor, née Grove, 208, 236-37,
246, 265, 292, 295, 304, 343, 345
Florence, their daughter, 336
Eddy, their son: at Matajanal, 230
Captain (of Dorchester), 323
Fox: shortened form of Lane-Fox
Fox, Lane: see Lane-Fox
Fox-Pitt, Agnes Geraldine, 211, 242-43,
245 (m. Walter Grove q.v.); her diaries
268-355
Alex: see Pitt-Rivers
Alice, 211, 242, 268-71, 273-76,
279-80, 282, 284, 292; m. Sir John
Lubbock q.v.
Arthur, 211, 269, 302-03, 305-06, 311
Douglas, 211, 243, 268-69, 274, 276,
293, 304, 306, 337-38, 343, 349
Lionel, 211, 243, 251, 268-72, 284,
287-88, 290, 293, 320, 323, 328, 330,
349
his first wife, Nesta, 336
his second wife, Elspeth, 349
St. George, 211, 247, 254, 277, 280,
290, 296-97, 300, 302, 308, 317, 320,
322, 330, 334-35, 340, 345, 347
Ursula: see Scott
William, 211, 270-71, 274, 293, 295-96,
304, 306, 308, 311, 352
his wife, Blossie, 306, 308, 352
Fraser, Sir William, 24, 50, 121, 132-33,
136

Georgina or Georgiana, his sister, 211,
257
Elizabeth, his wife, née Farquharson,
24, 49, 75, 121
their daughter Jean Helen, 24, 60-61,
71, 124, m. John Grove of Ferne 17 q.v.
their daughter Eleanora, 133
their son William (later baronet), 24,
59-61, 69, 75, 140, 163
their grandson, William (later
baronet), 183
James, their younger son, 85
unnamed daughters: passim (50-121)
Fuchs, Emil, 332

Garnier family, 55
Ghost, The Salisbury, 162
Gillett, Mr, 234
Gipsys School, 256
Gladstone, Henry, MP, 297-98
William Ewart, MP, 234, 236, 251,
254, 297-98, 305, 319
his wife, 297-98
Glove Inn, 31, 52, 78(fire), 87, 112, 114,
119, 123-24, 128, 172
Glyn or Glin family, 24 and 219 see also
Wolverton
Elinor, 310
George, 24, 134
Pascoe Charles, 219, 298
Sir Richard Carr, 24, 134, 144
his wife, 24, 49, 132
Sir Richard George, 219, 247
Sidney Carr, MP, 219, 240, 242
Golejewski, Nikola ('Koka'), 211, 339,
343-46, 348-50
his wife Honor, née Grove q.v, 208,
their daughter Kira, 343
their daughter Sonya, 345-46, 348-50,
352, 354
Goodford, Mr, 137
Gordon family of Wincombe Park, 24
John, 24, 43, 56, 80, 88, 90, 93, 99-100,
107, 109, 111, 127, 158-60
Sybella, his first wife, 24, 51, 56, 80,
84, 88, 90, 99-100, 111
their son John, 24, 56, 109, 111
their son Tom, 24, 134, 162

Marie, John senior's second wife, 159-60
Goslin, Mrs, 49
Gouldings (shop), 179, 181
Graham, Charles Cunninghame, 219, 272
    Robert Bontine Cunninghame, 219, 324, 354
    Edward Fergus, 76-77
Grant, Lady, 330, 336
Green, Mr and Mrs, 50, 75, 77
Greenway, Mrs, née Foot, 166-67
Grey, Mrs, 50, 76
Griffith, Mary Jane, 201
Grisdale, Rev Mr, 188, 192
Grossmith, George (actor), 219, 301, 314
Grosvenor, Mr, 328
    Mrs, 127
GROVE of Ferne, 1st generation , 17
    Thomas, 17, 43, 45, 51-52, 56-59, 62-64, 67, 69-72, 78-85, 87, 89-90, 94, 101, 105-08, 111, 115-120, 122, 124, 126-30, 133-38, 141-45, 148-49, 152, 154, 159, 160, 165, 167, 169, 174-76, 180, 182, 185, 187, 196-99
    Charlotte, his wife, 17, 45, 50, 53, 55-57, 61, 72, 75, 77-78, 82-84, 89, 92, 101, 105, 107, 110, 125, 127-31, 141-42, 146, 149, 152, 156, 158, 160, 162, 164-65
    Philippa, his sister (Aunt Grove), 17, 45, 47-48, 51, 54, 59-60, 69-70, 77, 80-84, 105-07, 115-16, 124, 128, 131, 134, 137, 142, 146, 154-57, 160-61, 168, 170, 183, 188
    Elizabeth, his sister (Aunt Chafin), 17, 47, 69, 86, 99, 102-04, 108, 115, 124, 131, 175-76
Grove of Zeals, 1st generation –
    Elizabeth, née Acland, widow of Dr Charles Grove of Salisbury, 19, 140, 148, 166, 190
Grove of Ferne, 2nd generation –
    Tom, 17, 47, 59, 64, 68-73, 78-79, 86-87, 89-90, 92, 98, 106, 114, 119, 126-28, 135, 137, 141, 146, 149-50, 153-56, 158-60, 162-63, 165, 170, 172-74, 180-81, 184, 187-88, 196, 198

his 1st wife, Henrietta, 17, 46-47, 54, 59, 64, 71, 78, 86-87, 89, 98, 106, 114, 126, 128, 137, 146
his 2nd wife, Elizabeth ('Bessy'), 17, 153-56, 158-59, 162-63, 165, 168, 188, 196, 198, 201, 229, 246
Charlotte (m. Richard Downes q.v.), 17, 45-47, 49, 52, 56, 59-62, 68, 71-75, 78, 83-87, 90-92, (Her diaries 97-204) 229, 231-32
Dr John, 17, 44-48, 53, 56-58, 67-68, 70, 75, 77, 87, 93, 99, 107-10, 112, 118-21, 125, 131-36, 140-41, 146, 155, 157, 172-73, 177, 182, 198-99, 201
his wife Jean or Jane (née Fraser q.v.), 136, 149, 153, 184, 201-02, 231-32
Emma: married John Horsey Waddington q.v,
William, 18, 50, 58-63, 69-71, 74-75, 84-85, 90, 100, 107, 111-14, 121, 125, 127-28, 132-33, 155-57, 160, 166, 168, 178, 187-88, 199, 259
his wife Fanny, née Frances Grove, 18-19, 166, 168, 177, 187-88, 190, 201, 203
Harriet, 18, 14-80 (her diaries), 98-103, 105-111 (marriage, continues as Helyar q.v.)
Marianne, 18, 54
George, 18, 44, 47, 54, 71, 83-93, 98-100, 115-19, 125-26, 130-33, 135-36, 138-42, 146-48, 151-52, 154-55, 160-62, 165, 175-77, 186, 315-36
his wife Charlotte, née Eyre, 24, 176-77, 198, 240, 244
Charles Henry, 18, 43-47, 62-64, 67-71, 73, 75, 77-79, 81-85, 87, 94-95, 99, 107-12, 114, 116-19, 124-25, 128, 130-32, 134-37, 143-44, 148-49, 152, 155, 160, 163, 166, 174-75, 181, 183, 190, 196, 203, 231, 240
his wife Elizabeth, née Hopkins, 143, 148-49, 152, 165-66, 183, 190-91, 194
Louisa, 18, 43-47, 51-54, 57, 64, 67-70, 79-81, 165
Grove of Zeals, 2nd generation –
    Chafin, 18, 124, 180; his wife, 180
    Charles, rector of Odstock and his

wife, 18, 166, 229
William Chafin, 18, 130, 139, 156, 175, 232; his wife, 156, 178, 229
Frances Harriet, m. William Grove of Ferne q.v.
Harry, 19, 148
Jane, m. 1793 Rev John Auber, 19, 129
Maria Caroline, 209, 108
Grove of Ferne, 3rd generation –
Charlotte, daughter of Thomas junior, 17, 163
Mary, daughter of Thomas junior, 17, 158, 165, 167, 171, 174, 183, 196-98, 203
Thomas Fraser, son of John, 17-18, 149, 191, 193, 198, 202, 204, 227-265 (his diaries), 270-71, 276, 280-82, 284, 291, 293-95, 300-01, 303, 305, 316
his 1st wife Kate, 17-18, 203, 228, 230-32, 234, 237-38, 240
his 2nd wife Frances (widow, Mrs Best), 209-10, 245-49, 252-54, 256-57, 259, 261-62, 264-65, 284, 290, 293, 311, 317, 321, 328
John, of Mudeford, son of Dr John, 18, 170, 187, 199-200, 203, 229, 232
his wife Clara, née Burrow, 200, 202
Henrietta, daughter of Dr John, m. James Hussey, 17, 177, 202, 259
Emma, daughter of John; did not marry, 18, 200-02, 229, 353
Helen, daughter of John, m. John Ross, 18, 200-02, 229, 232, 247
Louisa daughter of John, m. Frederick Selwyn, 18, 170, 189, 201
Elizabeth, daughter of Charles Henry, 190
Emily Charlotte, daughter of Charles Henry, m. Charles Townsend, 190, 203
Julia, daughter of Charles Henry, 190
Philippa, daughter of Charles Henry, 190
Agnes, daughter of Charles Henry, m. John Fraser Hussey q.v:
Alice, daughter of Charles Henry, m. Charles William Gordon:
Grove of Zeals 3rd generation –

William Chafin, 209, 232, 234
Julia Elizabeth, 209
Mary Anne, married Mr. St Lo, 19, 166
Grove of Ferne, 4th generation –
children of Thomas Fraser and his brother, John of Mudeford
Grace Kathleen, m. Harvey de Montmorency q.v. and (2) General F. Hamilton, 264
Edith, m. Edmund Benson Foster q.v.
Walter, 208, 231, 234-35, 237, 240-50, 253-56, 261-63, 265, 268-78, 280-84, 287-88, 290-91, 293-306, 310, 315, 319-21, 323-334, 336, 338, 340-54
his wife Agnes Geraldine, née Fox-Pitt q.v, 211, 246-54, 259-60, 263, 267, her diaries 267-354
Charlotte, m. Gilbert Davis, 208, 231, 239, 241-42, 244-45, 250-51, 259, 270, 272, 290, 293-95, 301, 304, 316-17, 321, 330, 341, 346, 353
Emily Kathleen ('Kat'), 208, 239, 241, 244, 249 married Edmund Mansel Pleydell q.v.
Tom, 208, 235, 246-47, 253-57, 262-63, 270, 284, 290, 292, 321, 348, 352
Olivia Frances, 208, 248, 262-63, 317, 321
Aimée Jean, m. Sir James de Hoghton q.v, 208, 234, 238-39, 309
William Henry, 208, 234, 238, 241, 249, 260, 293, 307
Hubert Farquharson, 208, 234, 238, 263
Grove of Ferne, 5th generation –
children of Sir Walter and Agnes
Honor, 208, 246-47, 252, 290-91, 302-03, 316, 322, 324, 329, 338-39, 343-46, 350; her daughters, Kira 343; and Sonia 345-46, 348-50, 352, 354
Gerald, 208, 295, 302, 308, 316, 321-22, 326, 335, 339, 342, 345, 347-54
Oenone, 208, 254, 300, 302, 308, 318-19, 326, 328-29, 334-336, 338, 340-44, 346-47, 349-55
Terence, 208, 307, 318-19, 326, 330
Walter Peel ('Beb'), 208, 329-30, 335,

340, 344, 346-52, 354
(unidentified) Patrick, 349
'Grovina' nickname of Frances, 2nd wife
    Sir Thomas Grove qv
Guest, Henry, 219, 328-29
    Ivor, 219, 293, 302, 322-23
    Lady Theodora, 219-20, 294
Gurd, Lucy, 180

Habbersham, Mrs, 28, 45, 99-100, later
    see Merrick
Haines, Capt, 142, 146, 159
Hakewill, Mr (architect), 223, 203, 231
Halford family, 273, 293, 302
Halyburton, Mr and Mrs, 240-41
Hambro family, 293, 302, 321, 332
Hamilton, Mr (architect), 28, 52, 54, 57,
    61, 65, 73, 80, 83-85, 87, 92, 105
    Mrs and family, 50, 77
    General F, 264
    Rev Joseph, of Ashmore, 186-87, 195
    Mary, daughter of Thomas Grove
    junior q.v., 17
Hansford, Martha, 191
Harcourt, Sir William MP, 249, 255, 298,
    308
Hardy, Thomas, 220, 310-15, 323, 327,
    331, 336-39, 349, 355
    Emma, his 1st wife, 313-14, 323, 327,
    331, 336-37
    Florence, his 2nd wife, 349
Hare, Mark, 191
Harman, Sarah, 187-88
Harris, Mrs, 51
Harvey or Hervey, Mr (at Rushmore),
    159, 165, 168-69, 173, 184-85
    George, 176
Hascal's (shop), 138
Haskell, basket maker, 354
Hawkins, Sir Anthony Hope, 220, 314,
    332
Haynes, Daniel Franco, 140
    his wife Mary née Shelley q.v.
Heathcote, Capt, 77
    Grace, née Hussey, 212, 320
Heathfield, Mr: see Hethfield
Heemstra, Baron Franz van, 211, 329-30
Helyar of Coker Court, Somerset, 25

William (1745-1820), 25, 77, 91, 111,
    114, 118-19, 144
    Elizabeth, his wife, 25, 111, 114, 118
    his brother, Rev John, 25, 59, 61-65, 68,
    70, 78-79, 84, 88-90, 101-02, 105, 108,
    110, 117-18, 121-22, 129, 153
    Maria, John's wife, 25, 59, 62-63,
    68-69, 78, 84-86, 89-90, 102-04, 117, 122
Helyar, 2nd generation – children of
    William and Elizabeth, 25
    William of Sedgehill, 25, 57, 59, 62-64,
    72, 77, 94-95, 101, 104, 108-11, 115-18,
    121, 130, 137, 139, 141, 143-44, 152,
    157, 192
    Harriet, his wife, née Grove q.v,
    113-18, 121-23, 130, 136, 140, 144,
    148, 152-54, 157, 166, 171-72, 180,
    192, 196, 201
    Henry, his brother, 25, 64, 100-01,
    104, 152
    George, his brother, 25, 143, 157
    Hugh, his brother, 25, 101, 117
    Charles John, his brother, 25, 179
    Caroline, his sister, 25, 62-63, 125, 179
    Ellen Maria, unidentified, 172
Helyar, 3rd generation – children of
    William and Harriet
    Agnes Grove, 211, 123, 143, 168, 177,
    196
    Albert, 136-37, 145
    Ambrose Weston, 166, 168
    Ann, 168, 196
    Carey, 121, 158
    Charles, 172
    Edwin, 211, 237
    Ellen Harriet, 211, 95, 130, 177, 194,
    196-97
    Emma Charlotte, 154, 163
    Lucy Elizabeth, 157, 182
    Marian Elizabeth, 144 (Mary? 196)
    William Hawker, 211, 118, 192, 194,
    196
    his son Horace Augustus, m. his
    cousin Violet Wedderburn, 211
Henniker, Florence, 220, 310, 314, 317,
    320
Henstridge (a workman), 172, 178-79
Herbert senior, Sidney, 220, 173, 179,

184, 200-01, 230, 232-34
junior, Sidney, 220, 238, 249, later
14th Earl of Pembroke
Beatie, 220, 306
Capt, 306
Herridge (Grove tenant at Berry Court)
Mrs, 155
Herring, Ann, 149
Lizzy, 149
William, 149, 181, 183
his wife Elinor, formerly Cull, 183
Hervey: see Harvey
Hethfield, Mr, 70
Mrs, 79
Hetley, Mr H, 131, 161-62
Hewitt, Rev Mr, 177, 182, 184
Hill, Elizabeth, 153-56 (m. Thomas
Grove junior, 17 q.v.)
Hinton, Lord, 50
Hinxman, Mr H and Mrs, 115
Hobson family, 81
Hodges family, 92, 131
Parry (artist), 179
Hodgson or Hodson, Rev Mr, 144,
193-94
Holland House, 304, 310
Hope, Anthony: see Hawkins
Hopkins, Elizabeth Harriet, 143 (m.
Charles Henry Grove 18 q.v.)
Horton Tower, 31, 128
Houghton, Lord: see Crewe, marquis of
Hozier, Blanche, 212, 304
'Clemmy', 212, 331
Hughes, Miss and Mr, 73, 85, 88
Hulse, Sir Edward and Lady, 220, 235,
262
Humby, Joseph, 251, 259, 295
Hunt, Henry ('Orator'), 126
Hussey, Henrietta, d. of John Grove q.v,
17
Henrietta junior, 212, 353
Grace, m. Mr Heathcote q.v.
Margaret, 212, 354
Agnes, 212, 255
Hutchins, Miss (Waddingtons'
governess), 141-42
Hyscock, Mr, 106, 125
Harriet, 151, 154

Inchiquin, Lord, 309
Indian Jugglers, 132
Irving, Sir Henry, 296

Jackson, Very Rev Gilbert, 19, 43, 50,
53-54, 58, 97, 124, 131
Bathia, his wife ('Aunt Jackson'), 19,
43, 50, 52, 54, 57-58, 63, 69, 78, 80,
84-85, 88, 104, 120, 124, 146, 148-49,
165, 175, 180, 194-95, 198-99
their children –
Jackson, Arabella, 19, 44, 53, 59, 61,
78, 85, 88, 90, 148 (later see Walsh)
Charles Richard, 19, 56, 83, 101, 138,
140, 147, 158, 160, 182
Fanny, 19, 44, 59, 61, 111, 115, 127,
137, 142, 149, 166, 170, 199
Capt. Frederick, 19, 104, 164, 191,
194, 196, 198
Henry, 163-64, 166, 172, 194
John, 19, 174, 195
Maria Jane, 19, 57-58, 203
Thomas, 19, 149, 195-97
Major William, 19, 140, 177, 182,
194-95
Jagger (miniaturist), 104
James, Mr (bailiff at Ashcombe), 127;
his daughter(?) Mary, 178
James of Hereford, Lord, 324
Jarvis, Mr, 58
Jekyll, Mrs, 103
Jenkins, Mrs, 77
Jessup, Mary, 81, 102-03
Jeune, Sir Francis, 212, 293, 308 later
Lord St. Helier
Lady (Mary), 212, 293, 308-09
Johnson, Lionel (poet), 314
Joy, Thomas Musgrove (artist), 203,
231-32

Kean, Edmund (actor), 150
Kelly, George, 192
Henry, 198
James, 154, 184; his son(?), 169
Mary Ann, 185
Susan, 171
Kelsey, Mr, 236
Kemble, Rev Arthur

John Philip (actor), 110
Kerley, Mr, 116
Kilderbee family, 50
Kimber family, 157
King, Mr, 104, 293
  Mrs, 127, 184, 270
  Robin, 165
  Thomas of Alvediston, 129-30, 161;
  his nephew(?), 179
King John's House or Palace, 31, 62
Kipling, J.L, 315
  Rudyard, 308
Kirbey, Mrs, 91
Kneller, 'Old Mr' [John], 25, 49, 111
  Miss, 100, 120
  Miss Charlotte, 111
  'Jacky', Mr and Mrs, 25, 58, 111, 115,
  117, 126, 132, 138, 143, 146-47
  family, 25, 151
Knightley family, 102
Koka: see Golejewski
Kropotkin, Prince, 343

Lambert, William Charles, 196
Lampard, Daniel, 28, 68, 85, 93, 112,
  125, 165, 168
  Mrs (his wife), 28, 164-65
Landor, Henry Savage, 320
Lane, Miss, 174, 189
  Mrs Thomas, 193
Lane-Fox, Augustus Henry: see
  Pitt-Rivers
  Edith, 212, 306
  Marcia: see Conyers
  Sackville George: see Conyers
  St. George: see Fox-Pitt
Langley, Molly, 304
Larmer Tree (Gardens), 224, 252, 260,
  296, 308, 310-12, 320, 347, 352, 355
Lascelles, Gerald, 308
Lathy, Robert, 128
  Mrs, 169; Mary (? daughter), 187
Lee, Mrs, 75
Leslie, Mr (m. Helen Pilfold 20), 176,
  178
Lipscombe, Rev Mr, 87, 116-17
  the Misses, 86-88, 116-17
Lloyd, Mr, of Cardiganshire, 98

Locke, Mr, 107
Long of Lincoln's Inn and Marwell
  Park, 20
  William, 20, 51, 75-77, 82, 122, 137
  his wife, 20, 49, 51, 75, 110, 147, 149
Long of Rood Ashton, 20, 109
  Richard Godolphin, 20, 58, 76, 107,
  109, 119
  Ann, 20, 109
  Dianntia [Dionysia], 20, 109
  Flora, 20, 58, 76, 107, 109
  Walter, 20, 109
Long of Corhampton (Preshaw House),
  Walter, senior, 19, 106
  Walter, junior, 20, 49, 51, 60, 106, 113,
  116, 147
  his wife, Lady Mary, née Carnegie, 20,
  60, 84, 103, 106, 110, 114, 116, 147
  their daughter Ellen, 20, 116
Long of Salisbury, 20
  Samuel, 20, 54, 81, 106
  Eleanor, his wife, 20, 54, 81, 106, 125,
  155
Longman, Charlotte, 169
  Repentance, 200
Loring, Capt, 183
Lowdon, Mr, 73
Lowndes, William Loftus, 185
Lubbock, Alice, formerly Fox-Pitt q.v,
  211, 295, 302, 314, 316-17, 320, 343-44
  Sir John, her husband, later Lord
  Avebury, 292, 320
  Harold, their son, 212, 320, 344-45
Lush, a numerous local family, not
  identified individually, 138, 152-53,
  171-72, 180, 182, 184, 192, 196, 295

Macdonall, Col and Mrs, née Laura
  Arundell, 21, 144
Mackyllop, Fanny, 197-98
Maidment, John, 159, 162, 182
Mansel, Col, 126
  Mildred, 354
Mansel Pleydell, Edmund, 212, 249, 294,
  304, 322, 324-25
  Kathleen, née Grove q.v, 208, 250-51,
  261, 270-71, 273-74, 290-91, 294-95,
  301, 304, 323, 325, 327, 340, 342, 348

their daughter, Daphne, 212-13, 342, 346
their son, Harry junior, 212-13, 342
their son, Teddy, 212, 340
their daughter, Vivien, 212-13, 340, 342, 348
Harry senior, 212-13, 247, 282-83, 291-92, 294-95
Rev John Clavell, 212-13, 249
Markland, John Duff, RN, 62, 116, 124, 126, 128, 133, 177
his wife Helen, née Tregonwell q.v, 27, 127-28, 133, 177, 193
Mr, his brother, 60
Marryat, Mr, 254
Marsh family, 91
Edward ('Eddie'), 337, 344
Maskelyne and Cooke's Anti-Spiritualists Exhibition, 237
Matcham, George, and his wife née Eyre, 132
Matthews, Lieut 'Billy', RN, 221, 341-43
Mrs, his mother, 221, 340, 343, 347, 353
McAllister, Ward, 288-89
McClagan, Dr, 304, 316-17
McKenna, Stephen, 346, 350
Mead, Rev Mr, 184
Medlycott, Sir W., and son, 238
Mrs, 172
Medwin, Mrs, 20, 189
Tom, 20, 76
Merrick, Mr, 100, 103
Mrs (formerly Mrs Habbersham q.v.), 102-04, 184
Methuen, Paul, MP, 28, 106, 109, 111, 119, 128, 137-38, 141-42
Meux, Sir H, 296, 302
Meynell, Alice (poet), 333
Mildmay, Lady, 60, 84
Sir H, 125
Minchin, Mr, of Botley Grange, 55
Mont, Mrs de: see De Montmorency
Moon the conjuror, 117
Morley, Arnold, 297-98
Morrison, Alfred, of Fonthill, 221, 246, 262, 269, 299
Lady May (his daughter in law), 221,

330, 348
Moustard, Captain, 71
Munro, Lionel, 221, 294

Napier 'boy', 269-70
(or Napper), Rev John Tregonwell, 63, 68, 71, 73, 108
Napoleon Bonaparte: see Buonaparte
Neville, the Misses, 116
Niagara Falls, 286
Nixon, Miss (governess), 223, 302
Noel, Captain, 256-57
Norman, Henry, 314
Northesk, William, 7th earl of, 60, 104
Novello, Clara, 180

Ocden: see Okeden
Ogle, Rev John Savile, 28, 117
Mrs, 59
Okeden, Mr and Mrs, 61
Oliver, Mrs: see Gordon, Marie
Osborne, Mr, 184
Packington, Miss, 60, 75, 90, 171
Paget, Sir Arthur, 85
Parham, Mr and Mrs, 181-82, 185, 293
Parker family, 56
Mr, 128, 141
Mrs, 103-04, 115
Mr R, 85
Sir William George, RN, 25, 58, 105
his wife Elizabeth, née Still, 26-27, 58, 62, 88, 110
Partington, Mr, 168
Partridge, Emma, 28, 84, 163
Patti, Adelina (opera diva), 285
Payne, Blossie, m. William Fox-Pitt q.v.
Peachey, Col. William, 28, 43, 63, 104, 114
Peel, Willie, 221, 320, 323, 328-32, 334-36, 344
Pelly, Lady, 221, 336
Pembroke, Earls of: see also Herbert
George Herbert, 11th earl, 112, 114
George Robert, 13th earl, 221, 249-51, 269
Sidney Herbert, 14th earl: see Herbert, Sidney, junior
Penruddocke family, 25, 102, 105, 107

John Hungerford, 25, 136, 187
his first wife, Maria, 25, 58, 73, 103, 136, 138
his brother Edward, 25, 107
his brother George, 25, 105
Thomas, his nephew, son of Thomas, 25, 170
Miss E, 124
Phelips of Montecute, 221
Mr, 95, 113, 118, 135
Mary, m. J.J. Farquharson junior q.v, 184
Richard, 222, 240
William; m. Ellen Helyar, 222, 198
their son Willie, 222, 261, 263, 284, 287
Pilfold, Bathia, m. Rev Gilbert Jackson q.v.
Charlotte, m. Thomas Grove senior q.v.
Elizabeth, m. Timothy Shelley q.v.
James ('Uncle Jem'), 20, 76-77, 144, 147, 160-61
his daughter Elizabeth, 20, 147
Capt. John, RN, 20, 66, 75-78, 110, 112, 128, 144, 147, 165, 170, 177
Mrs, his wife, 20, 75
Emma, their daughter, 20, 147, 178
Helen, their daughter, 20, 176, 178
Kate, 175
Pinnock, Sally, 142, 145, 147, 151, 179, 188
Pitt: abbreviation of Fox-Pitt
Horace, 6th baron Rivers: see Rivers
Pitt-Rivers, General Augustus, 213, 240-41, 243-45, 247, 249, 256, 269, 271, 274-75, 279-82, 300-02, 304, 307, 311, 322-23
his wife Alice, née Stanley, 214, 241, 244-45, 253, 268-69, 272-75, 277, 279-81, 289, 293, 302, 327, 330, 337
their son Alex, 213, 243, 272-73, 281, 294, 309, 327, 334, 337
his wife Ruth, née Thynne, 213, 309, 334, 336-38, 340-41, 348, 354
their son George ('Jo'), 213, 341, 346, 354
his wife Rachel, née Forster, 213, 341, 346
Pleydell, Colonel, 106
Edmund Morton, 26, 91, 106
Mrs Elizabeth Margaretta, 26, 91, 106
Cornelia, 26, 92
Emma, 26, 92, 122
Louisa, 26, 91, 106, 122, 126
Margaretta, 26, 106
abbreviation of Mansel Pleydell q.v.
Plumtree, Miss, 128
Pole, Chandos, 294, 299-300
Pollen, Sir John, 131
Popham, Mr (of Clarendon Park), 101, 120-21
his sister Laetitia, 26, 44, 46, 48, 88, 101, 113-14, 121, 129, 146-47, 176
Porter, Miss Walsh, 103
Portman family of Bryanston, 26
Edward Berkeley, 26, 43, 61, 151
his first wife Lucy, 26, 64, 67, 91, 106, 108
their son Edward, 1st Baron, later Viscount, 26, 151, 242
his son Edwin Berkeley, MP, 222, 298
William Henry Berkeley, second Viscount, 222, 301
Miss W, 108
Powell, Mr, 58
Practical Suffragists, 316
Prince of Wales, HRH the, later Edward VII, 301
later George IV, 73, 98

Queensberry, Sybil marchioness of ('Sybil Q'), see Douglas

Racquet, Miss, 99
Radnor, Lady, 313
Railstone, George, m. Vivien Mansel Pleydell q.v, 348
Raymond, John Gatehouse, 236, 242, 253, 260, 262
Resuel, Theodora, m. William Hawker Helyar, q.v, 211, 194
Ribblesdale, Lord, 308
Riddon, Mr, 61
Ridout, Rev Mr, 100
Hannah, 182

Rivers, George Pitt, 2nd Baron, 26, 85,
    127, 129, 131, 142, 157, 160, 167
    George Pitt-Rivers, 4th Baron, 213,
    176, 184, 187-88, 193
    his wife Susan, née Leveson Gower,
    184, 188, 193
    Horace Pitt-Rivers, 6th Baron, 213,
    235, 240
    his wife Emmeline, née Bastard, 235,
    237
Roberts, Dr, 255
Robertson, Forbes (actor), 313, 320
Rock and Chinese Steel Band, 199
Rodney, Corin, 328
Rolles, Rev Mr, 188-89, 191-93
    his brother, Rev Edward, 195, 198
Roos, Mr, 103
Rosebery, 4th earl of, 125
    5th earl of, 308
Ross, John, 247
    Helen (d. of John Grove of Ferne), 18,
    247
Rowland, Mr, 180-81
Rudge family, 20
    Aunt, 20, 49, 103, 115
    Mr, 49
    Rev Mr, junior, 122
    Mr E, 114
Rusham, Mrs, 74
Russell, Bertrand, 3rd earl, 214, 267, 280
    Caroline, 98
    Claud, 214, 325, 330-36, 341, 344
    Conrad, 214, 331
    Flora, 331
    Frank, 2nd earl, 214, 319, 342, 346,
    350
    his 3rd wife Mary, formerly Arnim
    q.v, 209
    Gilbert, 214, 331, 335
    Lord John, 214, 267
Russian Horn Band, 171
Rutland, Duchess of, 107
Rutter, Clarence, 249-50

St. Helier: see Jeune
Schuster, Mrs, 320
Scott, Ursula, formerly Fox-Pitt, 211,
    284, 304-05, 310, 314

    William, her husband, 214, 280, 307
Selwyn, Arthur, 264
Sergison, Col. Warden, 26, 48-50, 67, 75,
    78, 107
Sesame Club, 320, 328, 332
Shaftesbury, Anthony, 9th earl of, 301
Shakspear, Mr and Mrs, 116
Sharp, Farmer (tenant of Berry Court),
    178, 191
Shelley, Timothy, MP, 20, 48-50, 55, 65,
    68, 77, 87, 112, 126, 134, 158, 160, 174,
    189, 191, 196
    his wife Elizabeth, née Pilfold, 21,
    43-51, 53, 55, 57, 59, 61-63, 67-68,
    75-76, 82, 88, 127, 130, 134-36, 140,
    174, 183, 189, 198
    Percy Bysshe, 21, 43-50, 52-57, 59,
    65-66, 68, 71, 73, 75-77, 79, 82, 85-86,
    98, 106, 111-12, 137, 139, 149
    Elizabeth, 21, 53, 55-61, 64, 67-73,
    75-77, 82, 86, 113-15, 119, 127, 130,
    134, 140, 172, 174
    Mary, 21, 43-44, 50, 53, 64, 127, 130,
    134, 140, 144, 175, 189
    Hellen, 21, 63, 65, 127, 130, 134, 140,
    174, 189, 201, 242
    Margaret, 21, 130, 134, 140, 174, 189,
    201, 242
    John, 21, 189
    Sir Percy Florence, 214, 191, 236
    Sir Edward, 214, 189, 235, 239
    Sir Charles, 214, 256, 302
    Sir John, 214, 234
Shere, Thomas and family, 29, 67, 84,
    140, 142, 151-53, 155, 172, 185, 192,
    196, 198
Siddons, Mrs (actress), 110
Singleton, Mr, 239
Skiffington, Mr, 73
Skinner, Mr, 68
    Miss, 71
Snooke, Mr, 188-89
Snow, George, 29, 59, 67-68, 91, 99, 117,
    121
Somerset, Duke and Duchess of, 347
    Lord John, 121
South, George, 29, 138, 192
    Mrs, 29, 145

Spettisbury convent, 91
Spurgeon, Rev Mr, 223, 230
Stanford, Mr (headmaster, Rottingdean School), 316
Stanhope, Mr, 74
Stanley of Alderley family, 214-15
  Monsignor Algernon, 215, 330
  Blanche, Countess of Airlie, 215, 267, 344, 346
  Henrietta Maria, 2nd Baroness, 215, 267, 271-72
  Kate, Viscountess Amberley, 215, 267
  Lyulph, 215, 341
  Maude, 215, 247, 267-73, 275-76, 281, 283-84, 290, 308, 310, 314, 316-17, 319, 328, 341
  Oliver, 215, 346
  Rianetta, 215, 275
  Rosalind, Countess of Carlisle, 215, 267, 305-06, 309-10
Stewart, Mr, 98
  brother of Lady Rivers, 188
  [Stuart] Lady, 82
Still family of Clouds, East Knoyle, 26-27
  Elizabeth, m. Sir William Parker q.v:
  Fanny, 27, 123, 156
  James, 26, 105, 118, 156
  his wife Charlotte, 26, 102, 156
  Rev Mr John, 26, 59, 62, 144
  Mr and Mrs Peter, 26, 49, 88, 118
  Robert, 26, 105, 133, 187
Stockwell, Marian, 29, 192, 197, 200-02, 204
Story, William Wetmore, 285
  Mrs, his wife, 286
Stretch, Betty, 143-44
  Fanny her daughter, 144
  John, 194
Strickland, Mr, 123, 199
  Mrs F, 202
Sturt, Humphry, 132 see also Alington
Sullivan, T.D., MP, 255-56
Susan (servant), 29, 44, 69, 85, 99, 101, 121, 127

Talbot, Sir John, 128
Talbot's (shop), 138, 142, 145, 149

Tarbat, Lord, 284-85
Taylor, (artist friend of Douglas Fox-Pitt), 338, 343
Teck, Duke of, 308
Tempest, Lord H, 306
Tennant, Edward Wyndham, 223, 347
  Pamela: see Wyndham, 223
Terry, Ellen (actress), 296
Thompson, M (nut gatherer), 187
Thorneycroft, Sir Hamo, 314
Thurber, Mrs, of New York, 285, 288-89
Thynne, Alex, 215, 322
  Lord Henry, MP, 215, 229-30, 232, 247
Tobin, Agnes, 336
Trafalgar, Lord and Lady, 295
Tregonwell family of Cranborne, 27
  Mr, 27, 62, 81-82, 106, 108
  Mrs, 27, 62, 81-82, 108, 110
  their daughter Helen, 27, 45-47, 55, 61-62, 67, 70-71, 81-82, 84, 98, 100-01, 104-05, 108, 111, 113, 116, 121, 124: subsequently Mrs Markland q.v.
  their son St. Barbe, 27, 61, 84, 106, 108
Mr Trenchard, wine merchant, 195
Treves, Sir Frederick, 315-17
Trevor, Mary, née Shelley q.v.
Troyte-Bullock: see Bullock
Tupper, Sir Charles, 317

Vachell, Horace Annesley, 222, 354
Vashti, Mrs, 29, 161, 171
Vauxhall Gardens, 156-57
Verschoyle family, 306
  Theresa, 314, 332
Victoria, Queen, 190, 324
Village Idiot, 61, 72
von Hügel, Baroness, 269

Waddington family, 21, 46-47, 54-55, 60, 74, 82, 101-02, 111, 121 (move to Clay Hall)
  John Horsey, 21, 45, 49-50, 64, 73, 83, 91, 102, 121, 141, 143-44, 146-148, 150, 156, 161, 174
  Emma, his wife, née Grove, 18, 45, 47, 55, 57, 60, 63, 71, 74, 82-83, 102, 121, 140-41
  Charles, 146-48

Emma junior, 44-45, 54-55, 60, 74,
82-84, 102, 111, 151, 161
Mr George, 44
George Grove, 71, 74, 102, 174
John junior, 44, 55, 74, 82-83, 151
Madeline (? Matty), 74, 83
Tom, 162
Wadley, Mr & Mrs, 145
Wagner, Cosima, 314
Wake, Rev Henry, 29, 43-44, 53, 56-58,
78, 104-05, 110, 118
Camilla, his wife, née Wallop, 126
Waldo, Meade, 326
Wales, Prince of: see Prince of Wales
Walker, Mabel Zoe (later Walker
Munro), 222, 306
Wallinger, Mr, 143
Wallop, Miss Camilla, 118, later see
Wake
Walsh, Mr and Mrs née Arabella
Jackson q.v.)
Ware family (or Warre?), 67
Warre, Mrs, 88
Warren, Mr, 111
Mrs, 100, 106
Waterfall family, 223, 268
Weeks (or Wicks), Sarah, 177, 190, 193
Ann, her daughter (?), 178
Emma, her daughter, 151, 154, 160,
193, 200
Weld, Miss, 252
Wellesley, Long, 137-38, 143
West, Benjamin (artist), 156
Rev John, 223, 256
Westeridge, Mr (of the Glove Inn), 79
Whindham: see Wyndham
White, Mrs (schoolmistress), 153,
159-60
Whitehead, Mr and Mrs, 200-03
Whyte Melville, G.J, 237
Wicks: see Weeks
Wilde, Oscar, 286
Wilkins, Mr (physician), 79-80, 83
Mrs (washerwoman), 145
Wilkinson, Canon, 274, 279, 283
William (the groom), 112
Williams family, 98, 106
Mr (Rushmore), 166

Sir R, 166
Williamson, Miss, 77
Willis's Rooms, London, 226, 232, 252
Wilson, Miss (governess), 185, 188
Wilsonn, Mrs, 29, 46, 55, 57-58, 69, 72,
103
Capt, 102
Emma, 60, 102
Winn or Wynne, Avis: see Crosse
Wolverton, George Carr Glyn, 1st
Baron, 222, 236-37
George Grenfell Glyn, 2nd Baron, 222,
295, 297-99
Frederic Glyn, 4th Baron, 222, 255,
305
Woodbine, Sara, 304
Woodridge, Mr and Mrs (?Westeridge),
119
Wright, Samuel and Ann (emigrants),
183
Wyndham of Norrington, Dinton,
Salisbury, Donhead and East Knoyle,
27 & 222-223
Alex, 27, 174
Charles, 27, 138, 159, 178
Rt. Hon. George, MP, 222, 301, 310,
320, 333
Mrs Henry Penruddock, 27, 51, 82
Mary later Lady Elcho q.v, 223, 305
Pamela, m. David Tennant, 223,
313-14
Percy Scawen, 222, 294, 301, 305, 332
Wadham, MP, 27, 150
William, MP, 27, 111, 125-27, 129-31,
151, 170-71, 182
Mrs, his wife, 27, 88, 111
their eldest son, William, MP, 27, 111,
127, 201, 230
the Misses, 125
Wynford, Lady (Jane, wife of 2nd Baron
Wynford), 215, 245, 262
Lady (Edith Anne, wife of 5th Baron
Wynford), 215, 314, 320, 336, 343
see also Best, 209

Yarborough, Marcia née Lane-Fox) m.
4th earl of: see Conyers
Zastrozzi, (Shelley's first novel), 73

List of Subscribers

The publishers would like to thank all those whose names are listed below, as well as the many subscribers who chose to remain anonymous. Their support and interest helped make this book possible.

Harold and Eileen Anderton
Frances Austin
S.F. Austin

Nicholas Baker M.P.
G. A. Beale
Anne Becher
James Bieri
Gordon Bowker
Jessie & Ronald Bradford
Robert Walter Breach
Richard Burleigh
Eddie Burton
John F. Bushell

Michael V. Carey
Miss Gay Carr
Christabel Cayford
Mr. & Mrs. A. J. Chaffin
D. E. Chaffin
Louise J. Chaffin
Charles Chaffyn-Grove
John & Alison Chandler
Elsa M. Chapman
Desmond S. Chichester
Laurence Clark
Pip Compton
Dr. L. M. Connor
Penny Copland-Griffiths
Anthony Copley

Jaimie Corke
Michael & Ann Craik
Geoffrey Crowe
Cecil N. Cullingford

Ann Dannatt
John Darke
Muriel E. Davis
F. M. Dineley
P. C. Dineley
Mrs. E. Dollery
Teresa Donovan
Dorset County Library
Phyllis Drake
Roma Draper
S. Dunford

Michael Egerton-Clarke
Angela Evans

Charlotte Farquharson
Harriet Farquharson
J. J. Farquharson
Harold Fassnidge
Patricia M. Favier
C. Frankfort
Michael J. French
C. R. Fry
Mariota Fuller

Elizabeth Buckler Gale
Revd. P.W. Gallup
Brendan C. Garnsworthy
J. H. P. Gibb, F.S.A.
James Gibson
The Guildhall Library
Charles P. Gould
Martin T. Green
Thomas A. Green
Mr. & Mrs. G. B. Greenwood
Patrick D. H. Grove-White
Mrs Pamela Gueritz
Mr. A. R. Gurd

G. Hamilton-Sharp
Sir Michael Hanham, Bt
Mr. P. D. G. & Mrs. V. M. Hares
Frank Harwood
Charlotte Hawkins
Mr. T. Hawkins
Mr. & Mrs. T. G. Hazlewood
Trevor Hearl
R. G. F. Heath
John & Shirley Hebbert
Angela Helyar
Simon Heneage
Alison E. Higson (nee Chaffin)
Maurice R. Hill
Steven Hobbs
Sir Bernard de Hoghton Bt.KM.DL
R. C. Hollick
Mrs. J. Rachel Holtam
Ralph Hopton
Horsham Museum, Shelley Library
Horsham Museum, West Sussex
Jane Howells
Katharine Huggett
Ella Humphreys
Mrs. Julia C. Hunt
D. Hunter

Brenda Innes
Jude James
R. S. A. & G. F. Johnson
Mrs. Lucy Judd

University of Kansas Libraries
Michael Kempster
G. W. S. & M. A. Knowles

Tim Laycock
Kim Leslie, West Sussex Record Office
Frank and Edna Lockyer
Dr Gordon Lush

Mrs. Hyacinthe Mackintosh
Morna MacLaren
Mrs Edith Maidment
J. C. Mansel
Marita
R. G. Mathews
Janet McNeill
Mere Historical Society
Alan Merryweather
Penelope Milburn
Michael Millgate
Mrs. Margaret Montgomery
D. M. Morris
Nora Bell Morris
Francis J. Murphy

Joan M. Nash
Rachel E. M. Neame
Christopher Coles Newbury
Walter E. Ninniss
Christine North

Howard and Joanna Page
Susan Palmer
Anne Parnwell
Pompi Parry
Lady Paskin
Denis Paxman
Charles P. C. Pettit
Jean Phelips
Malcolm Pinhorn
Anthony Pitt-Rivers
M.A. Pitt Rivers
Michael Pollard
Tony Pomeroy

Mrs Nicola Powell
Richard Prior

Norman Read
E. M. Ridding
Peter Roberts
Sara Ross
Mrs. Kate Roth
Pauline, Lady Rumbold
Jo & Jan Rutter

The Marquess of Salisbury
Salisbury and South Wiltshire
Museum
Rex Sawyer
S. E. Scammell, Clouds Estate Office,
East Knoyle
Robert and Joanne Schweik
Shaftesbury Historical Society
Mrs. A. E. Shearing
Susan Shearn
Abigail Shepherd
Marie & Geoff Simcox
Donald Simpson
A. K. Sims-Neighbour
Doreen Slatter
Kenneth Smith
M. M. Smith
Mrs. Margaret Snell
Pauline Spender
Hope Stancomb
M. E. J. Stokes
Jacqueline Stone
Miss Pamela Stone
Andrew Swinton

Barbara E. Swinton
David Swinton
Jane Swinton
Jill Swinton-Luesink
Ruth Swinton-Nadeau

Philippa Tapper
Mervyn G. de S. Taunton
Brian and Claire Taylor
Dr. Brian Tippett
Tisbury Local History Society
Gordon Trebilcock-Hindon

Angela Veale
Flavia Vernon

A. & K. Walker
Colin Walls
Kevin Walters
A. St. G. Walton
Dorothy Betty Waterworth
D. S. Whitelegge
T. R. Wightman
Robert G. J. Williams
Wiltshire County Council: Library,
Museum and Art Service
Mr. J. K. Winders
Denys Wingfield
Lieut. Col. G. F. Woolnough, M.C.
Georgia Wordsworth
Mary Wrightson

Michelle & Colin Younger
Mrs. Mary Yoward